Navigating Narratives

HARVARD EAST ASIAN MONOGRAPHS 470

辛とこえれするは乱ぎりんのを
ふむ孔くしてみんよてあくろわ
それのそみ︱はあのけつつあま
わひ︱そのつのねれどよろかつて
あるよ︱あくうんれよろまつく
あるひさあるのをつをけて
れいのときみれしくてけれ
にあてれくちしわそみねま

Navigating Narratives

Tsurayuki's *Tosa Diary* as History and Fiction

Gustav Heldt

Published by the Harvard University Asia Center
Distributed by Harvard University Press
Cambridge (Massachusetts) and London 2024

© 2024 by the President and Fellows of Harvard College
Printed in the United States of America

The Harvard University Asia Center publishes a monograph series and, in coordination with the Fairbank Center for Chinese Studies, the Korea Institute, the Reischauer Institute of Japanese Studies, and other faculties and institutes, administers research projects designed to further scholarly understanding of China, Japan, Vietnam, Korea, and other Asian countries. The Center also sponsors projects addressing multidisciplinary and regional issues in Asia.

Frontispiece: *Tosa nikki*, by Ki no Tsurayuki. First page from a copy made by Fujiwara Tameie in 1236. Ink on paper, ht. 16.8 cm, w. 15.3 cm. National Treasure. Photograph courtesy of the Osaka Aoyama Daigaku Rekishi Bungaku Hakubutsukan.

Library of Congress Cataloging-in-Publication Data

Names: Heldt, Gustav, author. | Ki, Tsurayuki, –945 or 946. Tosa nikki. |
    Ki, Tsurayuki, –945 or 946. Tosa nikki. English (Heldt)
Title: Navigating narratives : Tsurayuki's Tosa Diary as history and fiction / Gustav Heldt.
Other titles: Harvard East Asian monographs ; 470.
Description: Cambridge, Massachusetts : Harvard University Asia Center, 2024. |
    Series: Harvard East Asian Monographs ; 470 | Includes bibliographical references and index. | English; text of Tosa nikki in Japanese and English translation.
Identifiers: LCCN 2023037233 | ISBN 9780674295827 (hardcover)
Subjects: LCSH: Ki, Tsurayuki, –945 or 946. Tosa nikki. | Ki, Tsurayuki, –945 or 946—Criticism and interpretation. | Japanese diaries—Heian period, 794–1185—History and criticism. | Japanese literature—Heian period, 794–1185—History and criticism.
Classification: LCC PL788.3.T63 H45 2024
LC record available at https://lccn.loc.gov/2023037233

Index by Mary Mortensen

∞ Printed on acid-free paper

Last figure below indicates year of this printing
33 32 31 30 29 28 27 26 25 24

For Gillian Smith (1963–2021)

Contents

Acknowledgments   ix
Abbreviations   xiii
Conventions   xv

Introduction   1

PART I
Diaristic Divergences

1. Parody as Prologue   19
2. Bitter Regrets   70

PART II
Between History and Fiction

3. Shipside Songs   117
4. Liquid Landscapes   162

PART III
More Than a Poem

5. Narihira's Poem-Tellings   207
6. Nakamaro's Cosmopolitanisms   254

Epilogue   301

Appendix 1: Tosa nikki *Translation and Text*   309
Appendix 2: Tsurayuki's Chronology   349
Bibliography   353
Index   377

Acknowledgments

Like the voyage recounted in *Tosa nikki*, the process of writing this book took much longer than initially expected. In that span of time, I have been fortunate first of all to receive feedback from anonymous readers who set aside time to give their impartial assessments. In addition to the two reviewers who engaged closely with the entire manuscript, this group includes the individuals who evaluated earlier iterations of different portions published as: "Writing Like a Man: Poetic Literacy, Textual Property and Gender in the *Tosa Diary*," *Journal of Asian Studies* 64:1 (February 2005): 7–34; "Abe no Nakamaro at the End of the Silk Road," in *China and Beyond in the Mediaeval Period*, edited by Dorothy C. Wong, and Gustav Heldt (Amherst, NY: Cambria Press, 2014): 279–89; "Longing for Home: *The Tosa Diary's Funa Uta* and Heian Popular Song," *Japan Forum* 29: 4 (August 2017): 450–69; and "Liquid Landscapes: *The Tosa Diary's* Pioneering Poetic Contribution to Travelogue Prose," *Japan Review* 32 (2019): 1–39. I am also duly grateful to the publishers for giving me permission to build on those materials here.

At the Harvard University Asia Center Publications Program, both Deborah Del Gais and Bob Graham provided expert guidance through the review process. Since then, Kristen Wanner has proven herself to be an ideal editor in every way one could possibly imagine. I am also indebted to Michelle Asakawa for copyediting, Angela Piliouras for assisting with production, and Mary Mortensen for indexing the book. Melissa McCormick sparked the idea of including a frontispiece. The

Osaka Aoyama Daigaku Rekishi Bungaku Hakubutsukan graciously granted permission for me to use the image from the Tameie-bon manuscript of *Tosa nikki* housed in its collection for that purpose.

The process of producing this book has been nurtured in no small part by the intellectual stimulation and material support provided by the community I have been fortunate to be a part of at the University of Virginia. Jack Chen, Anne Kinney, and Ellen Zhang were always quick to answer my questions about premodern Chinese texts. Dorothy Wong has been instrumental in inspiring me to place Heian texts within a broader context, an attitude further fostered through conversations with Adrienne Ghaly, Miyabi Goto, Paul Kershaw, Charles Laughlin, Deborah McGrady, Geeta Patel, Eric Ramirez-Weaver, and Tony Spearing. Tomomi Sato offered invaluable logistical assistance in securing permission to use the image for the frontispiece. Calvin Hsu and Wei Wang at the University of Virginia Library expeditiously procured books through thick and thin. Students in the seminar on Heian women's memoirs that I have been privileged to teach here helped me to refine my translation of *Tosa nikki* in particular and my thoughts about gender and writing more generally. A publication grant from the East Asia Center at the University of Virginia provided support for completing the index. Sabbatical leaves provided by the office of the Dean of the College of Arts and Sciences made it possible for me to devote swathes of time to thinking and writing apart from the demands of teaching and administration.

Colleagues further afield who have generously shared their knowledge and offered encouragement over the years in the context of conferences, correspondences, invited talks, and more informal exchanges include Mikael Adolphson, Sonja Arntzen, John Breen, Roselee Bundy, Jonathan Chaves, Maggie Childs, Anne Commons, Wiebke Denecke, Stephen Dodd, Torquil Duthie, Janet Goodwin, Mack Horton, Mikiko Iwaya, Thomas Keirstead, Robert Khan, Keller Kimbrough, Christina Laffin, David Lurie, Susan Matisoff, Melissa McCormick, Brendan Morley, Gian Piero Persiani, Joan Piggott, Paul Rouzer, Catherine Ryu, Edith Sarra, James Scanlon-Canegata, Haruo Shirane, Joseph Sorensen, Kendra Strand, Marcus Jacobus Teeuwen, Loren Waller, and Takeshi Watanabe.

Friends and family have helped to make this book possible in ways that are less immediate but no less vital. Nathan Asmoucha and Patricia

Mason have provided an anchorage enabling me to map out where I was coming from and where I was headed to ever since we were small. Annie Lorrie Anderson-Lazo, Richard Ferris, Ann Fridlind, Yelena Ginzburg, and Steven Siegal were always ready with advice on how to simultaneously navigate more than one current with conviction. Dianne Farris hosted me countless times in a space where I could see things differently. Barbara Heldt and Gerald Smith have never wavered in emboldening me to pursue my interests wherever they took me. For his contribution to the title of this book and its cover design, among many other things, I remain most deeply indebted to my fellow traveler, David Hopper.

Abbreviations

GR	*Gunsho ruijū.* 29 vols. Tokyo: Zoku Gunsho Ruijū Kansei-kai, 1983–2002.
KST	*Shintei zōho kokushi taikei.* 66 vols. Tokyo: Yoshikawa Kōbunkan, 1929–64.
KT	*Shinpen kokka taikan.* 20 vols. Tokyo: Kadokawa Shoten, 1983–92.
NKT	*Nihon kagaku taikei.* 10 vols. Tokyo: Kazama Shobō, 1956–65.
QTS	*Quan Tangshi.* 12 vols. Beijing: Zhonghua Shuju, 1960.
SKT	*Shinshaku kanbun taikei.* 120 vols. Tokyo: Meiji Shoin, 1960–2018.
SNKBT	*Shin Nihon koten bungaku taikei.* 106 vols. Tokyo: Iwanami Shoten, 1989–2005.
SNKBZ	*Shinpen Nihon koten bungaku zenshū.* 88 vols. Tokyo: Shōgakukan, 1994–2001.
SNKS	*Shinchō Nihon koten shūsei.* 85 vols. Tokyo: Shinchōsha, 1976–89.
TN	*Tosa nikki.* Edited by Kikuchi Yasuhiko, SNKBZ 13. Tokyo: Shōgakukan, 1994.
TNZ	*Tosa nikki zenchūshaku.* Tokyo: Kadokawa Shoten, 1967.
ZGR	*Zoku gunsho ruijū.* 37 vols. and 3 supplementary vols. Tokyo: Zoku Gunsho Ruijū Kansei-kai, 1959–60.
ZZGR	*Zokuzoku gunsho ruijū.* 17 vols. Tokyo: Zoku Gunsho Ruijū Kansei-kai, 1969–78.

Conventions

In the interests of accessibility, the majority of East Asian words have been romanized according to their modern pronunciations in the systems currently used most commonly by scholars: Hepburn for Japanese, Hanyu Pinyin for Chinese, and McCune-Reischauer for Korean. In cases where an individual word is commonly recognized in Chinese and Japanese, both romanized forms are included with the abbreviations "C." and "J." respectively. I have opted for the original Sinographs in their traditional unsimplified forms when citing passages from Literary Sinitic texts. Due to the frequency with which I cite both Hagitani Boku's *Tosa nikki zenchūshaku* (Tokyo: Kadokawa Shoten, 1967) and the *Shinpen Nihon koten bungaku zenshū* edition of *Tosa nikki* throughout, all such references appear in the text with the abbreviations "TNZ" and "TN" respectively. Individual entries in *Tosa nikki* are identified first by month and then day in the traditional lunisolar calendar in order to facilitate readers' ability to place them within the larger narrative. All other traditional dates follow the same order but begin with the era name and year, with intercalary months in the lunisolar calendar also preceded by an asterisk. Translations of government posts and offices follow those provided in William and Helen Craig McCullough, *A Tale of Flowering Fortunes: Annals of Japanese Aristocratic Life in the Heian Period* (Stanford, CA: Stanford University Press, 1980), 789–831. These have occasionally been adapted, however, when I felt another rendering would help clarify their function in the context where they appear.

All translations are my own unless otherwise indicated. With a few exceptions, I have sought to observe standard conventions in them, such as presenting *waka* in five lines in order to make their metrical structures immediately apparent to a lay reader. I have slightly deviated in my lineation of *shi*, which is designed to stress their couplet structures. The rendering of *Tosa nikki* observes a few additional conventions of its own. These are designed in lieu of footnotes to thicken the translation at certain points by incorporating contextual information for words with particularly rich connotations so that nonspecialists can directly apprehend their significance. One way I attempt to do this is by using italics to mark two different socially elevated registers of language: allusions to lines from poems and Sinographs. Sinographs are also capitalized in order to convey something of their exaggerated visual and tonal impact in the original text. Place names have undoubtedly presented the greatest challenge to navigating between history and fiction. Because many of the locales in Shikoku that are first mentioned by Tsurayuki are now commonly recognized as historical and geographical entities, I have preserved their names in Japanese, while also prefacing them with a more descriptive literal rendering to convey their pictorial qualities as fictional and poetic devices. Place names whose discursive nature is highlighted by the diarist are rendered literally and in quotes.

INTRODUCTION

This book addresses several singular contributions to our understanding of Heian Japan provided by a single text. Named after the province where he had served as governor for four years, *Tosa nikki* (The Tosa Diary) was written by the famed poet Ki no Tsurayuki (d. 946) after his return to the capital in 934. Its content describes the fifty-five days spent by an anonymous ex-governor following the same route in a combination of prose and poetry, conveying varying degrees of irony, mockery, sarcasm, anger, joy, disappointment, grief, fear, and frustration that arise during the voyage. *Tosa nikki* is best known for its prologue, which identifies the narrator as a woman attempting to write a diary akin to those she has heard that men keep. Although numerous reasons have been offered for this double mimicry on the male writer's part, the simplest and most certain one is to differentiate author from narrator. Because a reading centered on either one of these figures effectively erases the other, and because the historical narrative that arises in either case appears much later, I have sought instead to apply the frames of reference that the diary's initial readers would have brought to bear in order to place it within its immediate historical context. In the process, we can expand our understanding of *Tosa nikki*'s time and place in new ways while also deepening our appreciation for the subtly complex manner in which it steers between the worlds of historical author and fictional narrator. Indeed, the sophisticated diversity of its form and content merit reevaluating this remarkable work's place within not only Japanese history but also that of world literature.

Amounting to little over forty pages in most modern editions, the brevity of *Tosa nikki* stands in inverse proportion to its immense significance in Japanese cultural history as the first literary diary, the first complete text possessing an identifiably female narrator, and the first vernacular work whose authorship and original form are reasonably certain.[1] This disparity between its modest dimensions and immense significance has meant that scholarly accounts of *Tosa nikki* are more likely to form a portion of any given book rather than to comprise an entire monograph. Only a handful of such studies have been published in the last fifty years, most of which either chart the route it describes or bring together individual essays in one edited volume. Contrasted to this relative dearth of books, on the other hand, is a constantly expanding corpus of journal articles. Even if most scholars find a few pages sufficient for what they have to say about the diary, there seems little chance of exhausting all there remains to be discovered within its text. Indeed, this book makes no claim to being a definitive account of *Tosa nikki*. It is my hope, rather, that it will encourage further engagement with this endlessly fascinating text.

This capacity for generating new readings has much to do with the distinctive manner in which the content of *Tosa nikki* is presented. As one scholar has pointed out, the simplicity of its (mostly) terse sentences entails its own interpretive challenges.[2] Indeed, one of the more recent monographs focused on the diary eloquently attests to its ability to sustain close readings by devoting most of its analysis to dissecting the prologue.[3] Tsurayuki's ability to craft such evocative and ambiguous prose can be ascribed at least in part to the finely honed sensibilities of a *waka* poet capable of creating the maximum amount of meaning possible out of thirty-one syllables. As a result, even seemingly banal observations and

---

1. The diary also features prominently in an environmentally oriented global history, where it is used to represent maritime cultures shaped by monsoon climates (Fernández-Armesto, *Civilizations*, 323–27). The epilogue will place it within a different historical framework that is similar in scale.
2. Shibuya, "Bunshō kara mita *Tosa nikki*," 18.
3. Komatsu, *Koten sainyūmon*.

brief asides exert such an influence on the narrative that they merit the sort of close attention more typically accorded to poems.

These ambiguities are further compounded by the uncertainty every reader faces in determining whether to approach *Tosa nikki* from the perspective of its author or narrator. The diarist herself often leaves us wondering if the views she presents belong to her, to another individual, or to the travelers as a whole. Any reading of *Tosa nikki*, whether engaging with its text in whole or in part, is thus caught to one extent or another between interpretive crosscurrents that pull it toward her perspective or his. These two interpretive currents have also shaped the narratives in which scholars usually situate the diary when assigning it historical significance, often quite literally by placing their discussions within books devoted to either account. In the narrative privileging her, *Tosa nikki* marks the beginning of women's memoirs as a distinct vernacular literary genre. In the other one privileging him, it marks the end of Tsurayuki's eventful literary career, which included overseeing the compilation of the first and most esteemed imperial anthology, *Kokin wakashū* (or *Kokinshū*, Collection of Old and New Poems, ca. 905), and writing a preface to it whose account of *waka*'s historical, stylistic, and pragmatic dimensions would be authoritative for over six hundred years.

Even readers stressing the female narrator's subjectivity, however, have historically struggled against a seemingly inexorable pull toward that of the author, whose modern standing as a creative literary genius is rooted in a centuries-long process of canonization that began shortly after his death. In accounts of *Tosa nikki* that uphold it as a pioneering example of women's diary literature, the force of this authorial undertow can be felt in their tendency to concern themselves with identifying the personal affective or artistic motives of its creator. By contrast, this book seeks to avoid following either narrative current because both *Tosa nikki*'s association with the later genre of memoir literature and with the notion of Tsurayuki as an autonomous literary giant who charted his own artistic course divert us from the immediate historical context in which the diary was produced and the novel aspects of that context that it illuminates. Consequently, the title of this book is intended to reflect not only the waterborne journey the diary covers but also my attempts to maneuver between narratives that focus on either its author or narrator, along with the distinctions between history and fiction they represent.

In order to identify *Tosa nikki*'s connections with the wider world its author and initial readers inhabited, this book draws upon a diverse array of vernacular and Literary Sinitic texts, primarily from the eighth to eleventh centuries, including *monogatari* tales, historical chronicles, testaments, men's diaries, administrative codes, women's memoirs, popular anecdotes, religious texts, poetics treatises, biographies, and prefaces to anthologies. I have cast this wide net in the belief that, as one recent study of medieval European life-writings puts it, "the intensive study of one particular period in an individual life can result in a sense of immersion in a time and place, even when only traces remain in the documentary record."[4] In other words, the depiction of particular periods in particular lives, however fictional or fragmentary, tell us about far more than simply those individuals. *Tosa nikki*'s narrator and author both immerse us in settings that are historically unique in different ways. By limiting herself to the experience of a single shipbound community, the diarist envelops us in a world unlike any other represented in court literature. By writing his own copy of the diary, Tsurayuki allows us to situate its production within a span of time whose specificity is unmatched by any other vernacular prose fiction written in the Heian period (794–1185).

The unusual nature of *Tosa nikki*'s connection to its author can be demonstrated by comparing it with the oldest and most extensive single source of information about his life represented in the eponymous *Tsurayuki shū* (Tsurayuki Anthology, ca. mid- or late tenth century). Like other such anthologies named after individual poets, it probably took shape in response to a growing demand for guides to composition that resulted from *waka*'s increasing importance as a means for social intercourse at court.[5] To this end, *Tsurayuki shū* is divided into nine books devoted to different topics, with the contents of each further arranged along loosely chronological lines.[6] Biographical information is particularly abundant in the final book, whose headnotes allow us to trace Tsurayuki's relationships with patrons and peers through the various details they provide concerning *waka* he produced on commission, wrote in cor-

---

4. Smith and Watson, *Writing the Lives*, 4.
5. Harries, "Personal Poetry Collections," 310.
6. For a concise account of the anthology's structure and textual history, see Tanaka and Tanaka, *Tsurayuki shū zenshaku*, 1–65.

respondences, or composed at banquets and other social occasions. The existence of this chronological substratum suggests that Tsurayuki's biography was considered valuable in some sense from early on. His diary, on the other hand, could not be more different in this regard. Insofar as its author and narrator are neither the same gender nor its main protagonists, *Tosa nikki* flagrantly ignores the "autobiographical pact" defined by Philippe Lejeune as a reader's identification between all three of these textual figures.[7]

By neglecting to include any of *Tosa nikki*'s poems, *Tsurayuki shū* likewise seems to view the diary as a purely imaginative work of fiction with no direct connection to its author's life. Yet the difficulty of distinguishing autobiographical elements from biographical ones in the anthology makes its connection to Tsurayuki oblique in different ways. The survival of five different variants in three textual lines reflects the fact that it, like most *waka* anthologies named after particular poets, was shaped by an unknown number of other people over an unknown period of time. Although these later additions are obvious in the case of headnotes that use the story-telling auxiliary verb *keri*, we have no way of identifying every such alteration in order to arrive at an original version compiled by Tsurayuki himself. The absence of such later interventions within *Tosa nikki*, by contrast, makes its connection to him uniquely unambiguous and unadulterated, resulting in a correspondingly immediate and unmediated connection between the fictional world represented in the text and the historical one experienced by its writer.

The fact that it is the earliest vernacular text by an identifiable historical individual preserved in a version made by that same person thus makes the assertion that *Tosa nikki* was written by Tsurayuki between 934 and 946 much more than an incidental or banal detail. In addition to being able to determine the diary's dimensions to an extent that is not possible for other vernacular works of fiction created in its own time or earlier, moreover, we possess an unusual wealth of information about the author's life. Tsurayuki's posthumous stature has engendered a biography that is remarkably detailed for someone of such a relatively humble background. In addition to his poems in *Tsurayuki shū*, his own writings, and a few brief mentions in contemporaneous accounts, we possess

---

7. Lejeune, *On Autobiography*, 12.

information about his life from Heian and medieval scholarly works such as *Sanjū rokunin kasen den* (Biographies of the Thirty-Six Poetic Immortals, ca. 1094); *Kokin wakashū mokuroku* (*Kokin wakashū* Annotated, ca. 1113) by Fujiwara no Nakazane (1064–1122); and the fourteenth-century *Sonpi bunmyaku* (Lineages of Nobility and Commoners). This material has been thoroughly utilized by modern scholars in numerous book-length biographies of Tsurayuki.[8]

At the same time as I want to avoid overemphasizing the agency of *Tosa nikki*'s author, therefore, I am reluctant to jettison the opportunities his biography offers for illuminating the historical context in which the diary was produced. My approach to identifying the author's historical experience in this regard differs from earlier conventional biographies in its framing. I have not sought to present Tsurayuki's life in a chronologically comprehensive fashion, both in order to avoid subsuming the fictional narrator under him and in order to avoid the impression of stability, coherence, and consistency that narrative imposes on the inherent mutability of lived experience. My primary interest is rather with those aspects of his career that help situate *Tosa nikki* within its immediate historical context. As a result, each chapter only alludes to those stages in Tsurayuki's life illuminating the particular aspects of Heian culture which that chapter focuses on. Those wanting to also navigate a more conventionally linear narrative while reading this book may refer to the appendix I have provided at its end.

The identity of Tsurayuki's patrons is particularly important in this regard because they are also likely to have been the diary's intended readership, making it a reflection of their tastes and interests more than his. Crucially, however, it is the ways in which the diary's attractiveness for these aristocrats resided in its differences from their own experiences and expectations that make it uniquely valuable as a historical resource. Unlike Tsurayuki's posthumous admirers, *Tosa nikki*'s initial readership would have had less interest in the details of his life than in his depiction of a world that was completely unlike the court-centered one portrayed

---

8. These biographies include: Ōoka, *Ki no Tsurayuki*; Mezaki, *Ki no Tsurayuki*; Murase, *Ki no Tsurayuki den no kenkyū* and *Kyūtei kajin Ki no Tsurayuki*; Kikuchi, *Kokinshū igo ni okeru Tsurayuki*; Fujioka, *Ki no Tsurayuki: utakotoba o tsukuru*; and Kanda, *Ki no Tsurayuki: aru ka naki ka no yo ni koso arikere*.

in the historical chronicles and fictional tales they were familiar with. Other aspects of the author's biography are also relevant in this regard, insofar as his sense of what might interest his readers and his ability to describe it are both informed by the notably diverse array of governmental branches he served in, including not only provincial administration but also the palace kitchen, library, secretariat, storehouses, and foreign affairs.[9]

Aside from these aspects of Tsurayuki's career, I have sought to avoid the dominant tendency to drift so far toward reading *Tosa nikki* through his biography that we lose sight of its fictional narrator altogether, replacing her voice with his in the process.[10] If anything, such readings have the unintendedly ironic effect of diminishing the same regard for the author's writerly genius that inspires them. I will confess to harboring such an estimation of Tsurayuki's talents myself, not on account of his prior poetic achievements but precisely because of the versatility demonstrated by such a radically dissimilar text, one whose distinctiveness resides both in its focus on a world external to court society and in that world's refraction through a semi-opaque narrator who is more vividly depicted than any before her, and whose vested interests in shaping readers' perspectives endow the narrative with unprecedented complexity. For this reason, I tend to refer to the voice of "the diarist" when describing or summarizing particular passages in order to foreground the author's investment in establishing her as a convincing and complicated figure who plays a decisive role in shaping *Tosa nikki*'s contents. Rather than subsume her narratorial agency within his authorial one, I believe this approach allows both to support each other.

The diarist's presence is especially essential to establishing *Tosa nikki*'s parodic effects, which result from her uneven and uninformed attempt to write a text of the sort she associates with men. As is true of parody in general, both the author's mimicry of her and her mimicry of other men illuminate the same conventions that they ironically undermine. In this case, the chief target appears to be representational conventions claiming

---

9. For an informative summary of these posts, see Arai, "Ōchō kannin Ki no Tsurayuki."

10. One rare example of this critique is offered in Kanai, "'Omuna' no tame ni," 28–29.

to mimetically reproduce actual events. Diaries at the time were valued first and foremost for their facticity, insofar as the details they recorded offered precedents for their readers to consult when faced with similar situations in their own lives. *Tosa nikki*, by contrast, mobilizes such details in an inconsistent and unreliable manner. Devices used to create a sense of facticity in travelogues by delineating movements across time and space, for example, are manipulated in a way that draws attention to those devices rather than simply allowing them to function as a transparent medium for representing historical experience. *Tosa nikki* even ends up departing from the weaker ontological claims of *monogatari*, whose amorphous amalgams of speculation and rumor were always grounded in settings that bore actual place names, and thus actual histories. These parodic departures from established representational modes also draw our attention to the distinctively metalinguistic position from which the diary observes, reflects upon, and evaluates many other forms of language. Although most scholars' interest in this area has been limited to the script it uses and the poetic ideals it appears to articulate, the historical value of *Tosa nikki* also stems from its uniquely detailed depictions of three discursive practices—popular song, oral story-telling, and translation—for which we can find little or no mention in other sources.

Although the novelty of *Tosa nikki*'s world is initially established through its flamboyantly parodic prologue, the diary's departures from representational conventions are subsequently fostered and sustained by the spatial alterity represented in the voyage encompassing its narrative. *Tosa nikki*'s nautical setting exposes the contingent nature of social relationships by constantly resituating its miniaturized society within the ones it passes through, while also embodying in itself a community that is inherently transient, thereby simultaneously representing both senses of the word "vessel" as conveyance and container. In thinking about the relationship between this nautical community and the novelty of the social world elaborated in *Tosa nikki*, I have found it useful to consider the pithily suggestive observation once made by Michel Foucault (1926–1984) that "the boat is a floating piece of space, a place without a place, that exists by itself, that is enclosed in on itself and at the same time is given over to the infinity of the sea."[11] For Foucault, this spatial configuration

---

11. Foucault, "Of Other Spaces," 27.

constituted a "heterotopia," representing a self-contained universe that mirrors the real one while disrupting its usual relationships. In a similar fashion, *Tosa nikki*'s world displaces that of the court and its structures of authority by transforming the ex-governor who represented them into someone whose mobility and nourishment is now entirely dependent on his former charges. One result of this heterotopic inversion is that the diary devotes much more space to elaborating forms of speech and song associated with commoners than most other Heian vernacular texts.

Its central but largely invisible role in shaping the social contours of *Tosa nikki*'s narrative makes it worthwhile to briefly introduce the vessel's basic physical features here. As our only means for understanding life aboard a ship in tenth-century Japan, the diary's account of this environment is itself one of the ways in which *Tosa nikki* provides us with unique historical insights. In the absence of any corroborating visual or verbal representations of ships from the same period, scholars seeking to reconstruct its dimensions have relied on the depiction of a craft taking Sugawara no Michizane (845–903) into exile provided by the thirteenth-century picture scroll *Kitano Tenjin engi* (Legendary Origins of the Kitano Shrine). On this basis we can envisage a vessel accommodating twenty-five tons, approximately a sixth the displacement of those used by earlier diplomatic missions to the continent. It was divided into a bow where luggage was stored, a main cabin occupying roughly a third of the ship's length, and a smaller cabin in the stern for its steersman. This latter individual would have been accompanied by ten or so crew as well as roughly twenty passengers—at least half of whom would be servants.[12] The different spaces occupied by all three groups within these cramped confines shapes the narrative's soundscape as well: the steersman is often described as shouting, while the diarist's frequent recourse to hearsay suggests a division between those within the cabin and the humbler members of the ex-governor's household outside it. Uncertainty regarding which side of that divide she occupies lends added ambiguity to the diary's fluid narratorial perspective. Taken as a whole, these features create

---

12. This description is taken from Kashima, "Fune no naka no 'mienai' hitobito," 168–72. See also Kimura, *Rekishi kara yomu Tosa nikki*, 64–71. On the picture scroll, see Sumpter, "From the Monstrous to the God-Like."

a social world characterized by shared vulnerability, intimate proximity, and disparate desires.

Complementing this simultaneously claustrophobic and heterogenous space is the ever-shifting and unsympathetic seascape it continuously negotiates. Despite the Heian elite's claims to ruling an archipelago, representations of the sea in *monogatari* suggest they found it to be a profoundly alien and terrifying place. One of the many ways in which *Tosa nikki* is unique is thus the degree to which its prose is immersed within that foreign environment. This maritime setting also requires readers to engage in an equally unusual mode of movement as they traverse the story. It has often been pointed out that travel represents both an early form of narrative and a means for thinking about narrative more generally. Mikhail Bakhtin (1895–1975) famously observed that "On the road the spatial and temporal series defining human fates and lives combine with one another" in many early forms of Western literature.[13] Michel de Certeau (1925–1986) once asserted: "Every story is a travel story—a spatial practice."[14] Perhaps the most eloquent summation of this connection is provided by Mieke Bal, whose germinal account of narratology points to the importance of movement through space in the creation of a contiguous chain of events, such that "a traveler in narrative is in a sense always an allegory of the travel that narrative is."[15]

Unlike movement across the relatively fixed terrestrial pathways described in these accounts, however, the fluid changeability of *Tosa nikki*'s liquid landscape creates a different relationship between space and movement in establishing the consecutive and causal units that connect its narrative. Most forms of navigation prior to the establishment of modern cartographic regimes did not entail traveling along the most efficient route in a straight line between two locations. Instead, they required constant adjustment to the exigencies of currents, weather, reefs, and other obstructions. As the voyage in *Tosa nikki* progresses, its passengers' constantly shifting relationship to the boundary between sea and land along an irregular coastline resembles its readers' ceaseless need to steer through an equally fluid border between history and fiction. Although there is sig-

13. Bakhtin, *The Dialogic Imagination*, 243.
14. De Certeau, *The Practice of Everyday Life*, 115.
15. Bal, *Narratology*, 137.

Introduction

nificantly less at stake for us, making sense of the diary requires an equally strategic and flexible approach to its world from moment to moment. It would be too much to presume this or any study of *Tosa nikki* can plot a straight line through the constantly shifting crosscurrents that carry its narrative along between history and fiction. I can only hope to avoid being entirely swept away by one or the other.

My navigation of *Tosa nikki* proceeds through six chapters that are divided into three sections. The first, "Diaristic Divergences," charts its parodic and satirical departures from contemporaneous diary-keeping practices. Because both modes of representation are comparatively rare in premodern vernacular Japanese literature (as opposed to its early modern successor), each chapter concludes with a consideration of potentially productive parallels offered by formulations of parody and satire in Western literary history. The second part of the book ("Between History and Fiction") illustrates two complementary ways in which *Tosa nikki* maneuvers between these representational modes. In both cases I will be going against predominant interpretive currents, first by arguing for the documentary value of the diary's more eccentric contents, and then by countering assumptions about the historicity of the voyage it represents. The most powerful examples of this brief work's potential for productive close readings occupy the final two chapters making up part 3 ("More Than a Poem"), which explore the metalinguistic commentary on poetic praxis the diary provides in *waka* by its only two named poets, Ariwara no Narihira (825–880) and Abe no Nakamaro (698–770), and the larger histories their poetic biographies were embedded in. Although the former's presence in the diary has been largely ignored, the latter has attracted the most attention among Anglophone scholars outside of the prologue discussed in chapter 1, making it a bookend of sorts to the study as a whole.

Chapter 1 ("Parody as Prologue") focuses on the opening passage introducing *Tosa nikki*'s female narrator in order to provide an overview of its reception history and establish my own approach in subsequent chapters. The sustained interest in establishing Tsurayuki's connection to *Tosa nikki* characterizing that history also presents a unique opportunity to trace varying notions of authorship in vernacular Japanese texts more broadly. As an alternative to readers' persistent interest in Tsurayuki's motives for choosing a female narrator, I argue that the textual activities of his patrons offer a better prism for understanding her presence. Her lack of familiarity with the diaries she seeks to emulate, which reflects her social status more than her gender, is intended to amuse *Tosa nikki*'s readership with its parodic departures from the temporal and perspectival features they valued in their own personal diaries. The establishment of this parodic stance in the prologue also aligns the diary with recent literary theoretical formulations of parody that stress the self-reflexivity and linguistic diversity it enables, both of which characterize the unique aspects of the diary that are addressed in subsequent chapters.

Chapter 2 ("Bitter Regrets") takes up *Tosa nikki*'s satirical depiction of the secular and religious economies informing the circulation of material goods within it, a unique perspective made possible by parodying the attention aristocratic diaries paid to tracking the receipt and disbursement of gifts. Particular attention is given to the circulation of food, which *Tosa nikki* describes in greater detail than any other vernacular Heian text. Its satirical stance also reveals new connections between the diary and other texts such as *Fujiwara no Yasunori den*, *Nihon ryōiki*, and *Taketori monogatari*. All of its sardonic observations cohere in the term "bitter regrets" (*kuchi-oshi*) summarizing *Tosa nikki*'s content in the epilogue by linking consumption to criticism. I then conclude by considering how the limits of this critical commentary reflect an elitist orientation similar to Menippean satire, while also being more radical in its incisive appraisal of the role exchange plays in negotiating social relationships, and of the role power structures play in constraining critique.

Chapter 3 ("Shipside Songs") identifies new opportunities the diary affords for understanding Heian song culture, including the pansexual perspectives afforded by its erotically charged language, its frequently porous boundary with *waka* poetry, the separability of its melodies from lyrics, its use of refrains, and its transcription of an otherwise invisible song genre. This last aspect is particularly significant due to the questions it raises about the supposed preeminence of folk songs in standard histories of Heian vocal music and the place of money in the popular imagination. The chapter concludes by relating the diary's unusually pronounced interest in vocal music to Tsurayuki's mother, and the ways in which his textual appropriations of her musical knowledge, like his attempts to distinguish song from poetry, illustrate the ease with which both forms of verse, along with the diary itself, were open to appropriation by people other than their practitioners through gendered distinctions in authorial attribution.

Chapter 4 ("Liquid Landscapes") treats the diary's preference for representing travel through fictional poetic devices as a profoundly parodic and creative departure from earlier travelogue conventions. Although the landscapes in *Tosa nikki* gesture to earlier narratives surrounding the author's clan at its beginning and end, the intervening space of the open ocean is unmoored from any historical locations, thus enabling an entirely new form of poetic prose capable of depicting landscapes that bore no connection to the seasonal settings favored in court poetry. Poetic devices also endow the narrative with visual and affective dimensions by, for example, creating fictional place names with vivid qualities, or through the sequencing of journal entries in which nothing happens according to anthological strategies for creating narrative progressions. I conclude by suggesting how these stylistic oddities might reflect the diary's origins as an illustrated picture scroll (*emaki*).

Chapter 5 ("Narihira's Poem-Tellings") employs the diary's transcription of an oral anecdote about a poem by Narihira as a key to understanding the practice of *uta-gatari* (poem-tellings) relating the origins of certain *waka*. Narihira's scandalous behavior and ambiguous poetic rhetoric made his *waka* a popular topic for such anecdotes, including those in the tenth-century poem tale *Ise monogatari*. In addition to confirming several features of *uta-gatari* suggested by the small number of instances in which the word appears in other texts, the relationship between *Tosa nikki*'s representation of poem-telling and *Ise* calls into question the assumption that oral poetic anecdotes invariably preceded textual versions. The diary further illustrates how *waka* were adapted to the particular performative contexts of each poem-telling, and the importance of encouraging speculation in an audience who could then contribute their own *waka* to the narrative. The remarkable degree of attention it gives to *uta-gatari* is also reflected in the diary's own attempts to distinguish its parodic hybridity from the genre fluidity characterizing most Heian vernacular narratives.

Chapter 6 ("Nakamaro's Cosmopolitanisms") offers a new reading of the diary's depiction of Japan's most celebrated resident abroad explaining *waka* poetry to a foreign audience by drawing on both traditional notions of cosmopolitanism and the linguistic forms identified by scholars of the premodern world more recently. Nakamaro has often represented Japan's increasing estrangement from the continent as the Tang empire entered a period of political decline. Different forms of rupture and continuity are brought into relief by comparing his *waka* in *Tosa nikki* with the *shi* his historical counterpart produced on a similar occasion. The preference for diplomatically ambiguous spaces and hybrid diction characterizing his poems in both settings are historically connected in the intervening ninth century before being given a new maritime inflection within *Tosa nikki*. By focusing on the hitherto-ignored role of the interpreter in the diary's depiction of Nakamaro, and on the transpolitical and transcultural spaces of its maritime *waka*, this chapter identifies aspects of his image that reflect political, geographical, and cultural changes then taking place within the dramatically shifting multipolar Northeast Asia that had replaced the previous Sinocentric discursive and political order experienced by the historical Nakamaro. In this setting, *Tosa nikki* also articulates a notion of vernacular identity through a sacralized landscape situated within a cosmopolitan poetic seascape, and through a capacious notion of translation encompassing inscription, interpretation, and adaptation.

The epilogue considers how all these insights into *Tosa nikki*'s novel features allow us to place this extraordinary text within two broader interconnected narratives. The first one traces its influence on the subsequent development of prose by Heian court women enabled by its attribution to a female author, something that is hinted at in both their texts and those of medieval readers. The connection to *Genji monogatari* (The Tale of Genji, ca. 1008) that results from this line of enquiry makes it possible to place the diary within a second, broader historical framework in which it represents a similarly significant contribution to world literature as its first novella, a genre it epitomizes not merely on account of its brevity but also its plot devices and other formal features that predate the *Decameron* by several centuries.

Two appendices appear at the end of the book. Appendix 1 provides a complete translation of *Tosa nikki* reflecting the various observations made in this study. The translation is accompanied by a version of the original text based on the Seikeisho'oku-bon manuscript, including its occasional orthographic inconsistencies, in recognition of the diary's unique historical value as the earliest extant example of a complete text in vernacular Japanese from the tenth century. It is my hope that its inclusion will make the original accessible to readers with varying levels of proficiency in Japanese. Appendix 2 provides a brief chronological summary of Tsurayuki's biography. In keeping with scholarly convention, it is limited to those events for which a particular year can be identified.

PART I

Diaristic Divergences

CHAPTER 1

Parody as Prologue

Why does the male author of *The Tosa Diary* assume the voice of a female narrator adopting a male genre in its prologue? It is no exaggeration to say that, in one form or another, the bulk of scholarship on *Tosa nikki* has sought to answer this question. Even in those cases where different topics have been taken up, it remains a convention to begin by citing the diary's opening in which the narrator establishes her reasons for writing it.

> I am attempting this out of curiosity about what it would be like for a woman to try her hand at keeping one of those so-called *Daily Journals* I hear men keep. One year, at around eight in the evening one day past the twentieth of the final month, we set out from the gate of the governor's mansion to prepare for our journey home. I will scrawl down a few jottings regarding that affair on what I have to hand. (TN 15, 12/21)

The remarkable self-reflexivity of this opening declaration is only matched by that of the next diary narrated by a woman, *Kagerō nikki* (Kagerō Diary, ca. 974), which begins with its writer declaring that she will record her recollections of marriage in a novel way that rejects the fabrications supplied by popular romantic fiction. The self-reflexivity of both female narrators has led these texts to be viewed in modern Japanese literary histories as self-conscious attempts to pioneer new forms of autobiography.[1]

---

1. See, for example, Wallace, *Objects of Discourse*, 20.

What makes *Tosa nikki* unique, however, is the complexity arising from the pivotal placement of its narrator between two parodic performances of gender: that of a male author writing as a female diarist, and that of the female diarist writing in an ostensibly male genre.

In this chapter I will investigate both modes of mimicry in the prologue—starting diachronically with the male author and ending synchronically with the female diarist—as a way of orienting my approach to *Tosa nikki* going forward. I will begin by tracing the varying notions of Tsurayuki's relationship to the diary that have dominated accounts of it during the first millennium after his death. In addition to providing a summary of the diary's reception, this history limns a broader one for the concept of authorship in Japanese vernacular fiction due to its status as the first such text for which we have a manuscript written by the historical individual it has been consistently connected with. As a consequence of this history, readers from early modern times onward have often focused on Tsurayuki's motives for assuming a female persona in ways that fail to account for the context in which *Tosa nikki* was written. In the remainder of the chapter I will attempt to reconstruct that context by focusing on the diary's intended readership, consisting of Tsurayuki's patrons after his return from Tosa, all of whom displayed a pronounced interest in developing new forms of diary-keeping. I will then show how these practices are parodied in *Tosa nikki* by the diarist in her attempt to mimic "male diaries" due to the ersatz nature of the material she is forced to use and her own marginal social status. Last, I will consider how accounts of parody in Western literary criticism can help explain why the diary is capable of providing the sort of unique insights into aspects of Heian culture that I will explore in subsequent chapters.

Tsurayuki's Diary and Waka

Tosa nikki's first recorded reader appears soon after its author's death in the headnote to a poem from *Egyō hōshi shū* (The Reverend Egyō Anthology) in which its eponymous poet is portrayed composing a poem after seeing illustrations to "Tsurayuki's *Tosa Diary*" (*Tsurayuki ga Tosa no nikki*).² This otherwise obscure priest may have received this version from Tsurayuki's son, Tokifumi (ca. 922–966), who is portrayed lending his father's poetry collection to the same man in another headnote from the same anthology.³ Perhaps Egyō's interest in *Tosa nikki* was inspired by his own experiments in *kana* prose, which included the preface to a hundred-verse sequence.⁴ His description of the diary poses another puzzle by leaving it unspecified whether Tsurayuki is its subject ("The diary about Tsurayuki's time in Tosa"), its author ("*The Tosa Diary* by Tsurayuki"), or its calligrapher ("the version of *The Tosa Diary* in Tsurayuki's hand").⁵ All three possibilities would be imagined at one time or another within the diary's subsequent reception history.

Tosa nikki's poems provide us with the earliest surviving traces of this reception history due to both Tsurayuki's stature as a *waka* poet and that genre's cultural prestige. Their absence from every extant version of his personal *waka* anthology suggests the diary and its poems were initially viewed as purely fictional creations divorced from the author's biography. A similar view appears to inform the roughly contemporaneous anthology *Kokin waka rokujō* (A Compendium of Old and New Waka in Six Scrolls, tenth century), whose encyclopedic contents include fourteen poems from the diary under Tsurayuki's name. Because many of these are composed by women and children within *Tosa nikki*, this attribution suggests an awareness that they are fictional creations.

Two *waka* from the diary are treated in an unambiguously autobiographical manner, on the other hand, when they resurface in the Travel section of *Gosen wakashū* (or *Gosenshū*, Anthology of Later Selections of Waka, ca. 951), whose compilers included Tokifumi as well as two other acquaintances of Egyō: Kiyohara no Motosuke (908–990) and Ōnakatomi no Yoshinobu (921–991). Both poems appear in the diary as anonymous compositions inspired by earlier *waka* by the famed poets Narihira and Nakamaro. Although the *Gosenshū* typically provides a narrative context

---

2. *Egyō hōshi shū* poem 192, KT 3:1:184.
3. *Egyō hōshi shū* poem 491, KT 3:1:488.
4. For more on this preface, see Bundy, "A Format of Their Own," 17–18.
5. Ikeda, "*Tosa nikki* wa hatashite Tsurayuki no saku ka," 3–6. Titles for poem tales such as "Diary of the Fifth Ariwara Middle Captain" (*Zaigo chūjō no nikki*) are similarly ambiguous.

for its poems by placing them in dialogic exchanges with one another, the anthologizers separated these two and reversed their order of appearance. In addition to the overall absence of poetic dialogue within *Tosa nikki*, this unusual disposition probably reflects the compilers' desire to situate Tsurayuki within a genealogy of travel poets.

This stress on poetic lineage also explains their attribution to the diary's historical author, who is by far the best-represented poet in the anthology. The poems' headnotes go beyond mere authorial attribution, however, by using the diary's own language to represent them as products of Tsurayuki's lived experience.

> Apparently, he composed this while he was looking out at the moon from the ship returning to the capital from Tosa, which seemed to rise from the waves rather than mountain peaks, calling to mind the words of the poem "my gaze sweeps out to see" that Abe no Nakamaro uttered long ago on the continent.[6]
>
> Apparently, he was on his way back to the capital after having completed the term of his posting in Tosa when, gazing at the moon while on the ship, he composed this.[7]

Both headnotes use the auxiliary verb *keri* to frame their accounts as hearsay, reflecting the editors' exclusive concern with poems composed prior to their own time. This narrative distance takes on added significance when we consider the likelihood both were written by the poet's son. Tokifumi would have been around ten during Tsurayuki's tenure in Tosa and was thus likely to have joined his father in the province, as was stipulated for children under the age of twenty-one in the *ritsuryō* state codes.[8] Perhaps his youth at the time explains why these headnotes mark the events they narrate as something Tokifumi had no direct recollection of. It is also possible they reflect his later experience as an adult reading either Tsurayuki's original record of the voyage home or brief notations his father had attached to earlier drafts of his poems.[9] In

---

6. *Gosen wakashū* poem 1355, SNKBT 6:411.
7. *Gosen wakashū* poem 1363, SNKBT 6:414.
8. *Ritsu-ryō* 2:8:21 (Kujiki-ryō), 406.
9. The theory that Tsurayuki created *Tosa nikki* from a journal he kept recording his own voyage back to the capital is first offered in Higuchi, "*Shinsen waka* no seiritsu."

other words, the *Gosenshū*'s treatment of these *waka* might indicate there was an autobiographical precursor to the fictional diary.

Due to the strong impression it left on early readers, the first lament for a dead girl in *Tosa nikki* offers another early indication of Tsurayuki's perceived relationship to the diary. This poem first resurfaces in *Wakatai jisshu* (Ten Styles of Waka, ca. 1000) as the last of five examples illustrating its "direct style" (*jikitai*) of composition. Although this treatise is traditionally ascribed to Tsurayuki's fellow *Kokinshū* editor Mibu no Tadamine (d. 920), with whom he was often paired in *waka* poetics, the anonymous writer of its preface claims *Wakatai jisshu* was finished shortly before the death of "my teacher, the former governor of Tosa" (先師土州 刺史) in 946, over two decades after the historical Tadamine's death. Neither the murky history of this text nor its evaluation of the poem suggests a close connection with Tsurayuki. Insofar as the "direct style" is defined as "sounding fit and true without resorting to figurative indirection" (義實以無曲折爲得耳), the poem was likely singled out for its lack of natural imagery rather than emotional authenticity.[10] The anonymity of all *Wakatai jisshu*'s poems, coupled with its replacement of *omou* (feels) in the original version with *isogu* (hastens), also makes it doubtful that this lament is being attributed to Tsurayuki.

The ease and frequency with which such changes could be made to the wording and attribution of individual poems can perhaps be attributed to the lack of strong proprietary claims to poetic authorship others have identified as characteristic of *waka*.[11] By the same token, however, this fluidity allowed the fictional voice of its anonymous composer in the diary to become the historical one of its author when the same lament (with still other alterations in its wording) subsequently appeared in three *setsuwa* anecdotes from the twelfth century preserved in *Kohon setsuwa shū* (A Collection of Anecdotes from Old Books), *Uji shūi monogatari* (Tales Gleaned from Uji), and *Konjaku monogatari shū* (Collection of Tales of Times Now Past).[12] Among these three texts, all of which claim his grief over losing a child led Tsurayuki to write the *waka* when he was in

---

10. *Wakatai jisshu*, NKT 1:46.
11. See, for example, Watanabe, "Waka ni okeru 'sakusha.'"
12. *Kohon setsuwa shū* story 41, SNKBT 42:447, and *Uji shūi monogatari* story 2:149, SNKBT 42:305–6. A translation of the latter version can be found in Mills, *A Collection of Tales from Uji*, 367–68.

Tosa, the version in *Kohon setsuwa shū* is the briefest, and thus probably oldest. Its intended readership can be inferred from the anecdote's placement within a group of poem-centered vignettes designed to entertain and educate members of the lower-ranking nobility and provincial governor class.[13] The most expansive version in *Konjaku* includes several unique details that make it worth citing in full.

> In a time now past, there was a poet named Ki no Tsurayuki. Upon becoming the governor of Tosa he went there to carry out his term of office. He had a son, then seven or eight years old, who possessed a fragile appeal that made him particularly beloved. But after suffering from an illness for several days, he passed away and was placed in an unmarked grave. Tsurayuki was assailed by boundless sorrow that left him weeping and wailing. The final month of his tenure in Tosa arrived while he brooded over his son's fatal illness, so he had no recourse but to say he would return to the capital. As he was about to do so, he was struck by recollections of the various places in the governor's mansion where the boy had played. Greatly grieved, he then wrote the following poem on a pillar:
>
> | *miyako e to* | Towards the capital city |
> |---|---|
> | *omou kokoro no* | thoughts turn in a heart |
> | *wabishiki wa* | filled with misery |
> | *kaeranu hito no* | for one not returning |
> | *areba narikeri* | with me here and now! |
>
> They say the sorrow in his heart never abated. The poem he had written on the office pillar apparently remained there his whole life. Such is the story that has been handed down.[14]

In addition to making him a boy, this version is the only one to mention the child's hasty burial and unmarked grave, details that also imply he will remain a restless ghost. Tsurayuki's reluctance to leave the body behind under these circumstances also foreshadows the conflict between official duties and private desires, which many readers would later view as his chief motive for writing the diary.

13. Ishihara, "Setsuwa, denpan, imi," 148.
14. *Konjaku monogatari shū* story 24:43, SNKBZ 37:356–57. In *Tosa nikki*, the second and third measures are *omou o mono no* (thoughts turn while haunted) and *kanashiki wa* (this grief) respectively.

The child's age and Tsurayuki's parentage are common to all three *setsuwa*, along with the final scene in which he inscribes his *waka*. Although this last detail is possibly inspired by the eponymous cypress pillar in the *Genji* chapter Makibashira, onto which a daughter with the same sobriquet writes a *waka* bidding farewell to her father's house, it also recalls the poem's distinctive origins in the diary as one of the few that is explicitly described as being written out. This makes it possible for all three *setsuwa* to stay true to the original account by supplying details of its inscription that *Tosa nikki* never specified, and perhaps further implies that slight variations in their wording reflect discontinuities between a fictional account and the author's actual historical circumstances. Although the image of Tsurayuki as a bereaved parent would eventually resurface in early modern accounts of his authorial intentions, it was his role as inscriber in these *setsuwa* that would dominate depictions of *Tosa nikki* in the interim.

Tsurayuki's Hand in Medieval Manuscripts

The human dimension to depictions of Tsurayuki as a grieving father in twelfth-century *setsuwa* set them apart from the reverence Shunzei (1114–1204) and other late Heian poet-scholars held for a figure they considered to be a "poetic sage" (*uta no hijiri*).[15] This worshipful stance toward the chief editor of the *Kokinshū* undoubtedly helped ensure *Tosa nikki*'s survival, making it the only extant complete facsimile of a Heian vernacular text written by a historical individual. By identifying paleographic and interpretive challenges that the tenth-century holograph posed for them, the thirteenth-century copyists who preserved it also generated the first scholarly engagement with *Tosa nikki*. Although their preservation of Tsurayuki's holograph would later enable modern academics to arrive at an authoritative version of the diary, however, the stress these scholar-poets laid on his role as its calligrapher and copyist point to relatively weak notions of authorship in the case of vernacular literature at the time.

---

15. Ishihara, "Setsuwa, denpan, imi," 146–47.

This looser attitude toward authorship is exemplified by Fujiwara no Teika (1162–1241). His colophon from 1235, appended to a copy of *Tosa nikki* that he made over the course of two days, constitutes the next explicit reference to the diary after Egyō. His approach to this endeavor exemplifies Teika's idiosyncratic contribution to the establishment of an authoritative canon of Heian classics. But his description of the diary is also noteworthy for the vividness with which it represents Tsurayuki's tangible presence within the original.

> Though nearly blind in my old age, I unexpectedly came across a text in Master Ki's own hand from the Rengeō-in library on the thirteenth day in the Second Month of Bunreki 2. It is made from plain white paper that has not been beaten to make it glossy, nor does it have lines demarcating the columns of writing. The text consists of twenty-six sheets joined together without a spindle, each roughly thirteen inches tall and eight inches wide. The cover sheet is a plain piece of white paper that is slightly folded back at the end. The text lacks any bamboo inserts, nor is it held together with a cord. It bears a title on the outside: "*The Tosa Diary* (by Tsurayuki's brush)." The manner in which it is written does not provide separate lines for the poems. Tsurayuki leaves an indentation of one space before the beginning of each verse, but none afterwards. I am overwhelmed with joy and excitement at this opportunity to make a personal copy, which I completed over the course of yesterday and today. [. . .] Though three hundred and one years have elapsed since it was written, the paper has not rotted away, and the characters remain crisp and clear. There are several places that are difficult to read, but in any case I have followed the manuscript to the best of my abilities.
>
> 文暦二年乙未五月十三日乙己老病中雖眼如盲不慮之外見紀氏自筆本蓮華王院本。料紙白紙不打無堺。高一尺一寸二分許紙也廿六枚無軸。表紙續白紙一枚端聊折返不立竹無紐。有外題。土左日記貫之筆。其書樣和歌非別行定行二貫之聊有闕字歌下無闕字而書後詞。不堪感興自書寫之昨今二ケ日終功。[. . .] 今年乙未歴三百一年紙不朽損其字又鮮明也。不讀得所々多只任本書也。[16]

Unlike Egyō's anthology, the designation "*The Tosa Diary* (by Tsurayuki's brush)" (土左日記貫之筆) on the opening page of the holograph clearly distinguishes its writer's name from its title. As with most Heian texts,

---

16. As cited (with ellipsis) in Suzuki T., *Tosa nikki*, 18.

this information was likely supplied by a later reader, probably either a librarian in the Rengeō-in or someone connected to its founding patron, Go-Shirakawa (1127–1192, r. 1155–1158). Distinguishing writer from title as separate categories would have helped to locate it within a collection whose extensive holdings also included Tsurayuki's personal *waka* anthology. Teika adds his own historical footnote to this bibliographical one by declaring at the end of the colophon that Tsurayuki completed the holograph in 934, implying he wrote it on his voyage back to the capital or immediately afterward. This surmise about the early date would have been warranted by the stripped-down format of the original manuscript, which suggests it was a draft copy rather than a completed version intended for presentation.[17]

These details in Teika's colophon give us closer access to the original version of a text written by a single historical individual than is possible for any other early work of vernacular Japanese fiction. Yet, lacking as it does the illustrations mentioned in Egyō's anthology, Tsurayuki's holograph was probably neither intended to be authoritative nor read by anyone else. The paradoxical nature of our dependance on a private draft in order to fix its authorial attribution, thereby defining that version as official, is a striking illustration of the inherent challenges we face in applying modern concepts of authorship and authoritative editions to texts produced by a manuscript culture that did not strictly observe distinctions between authorial original and readerly copies.

Teika's own rendering of the holograph illustrates how little importance was assigned to such categories. Despite the high esteem in which he held "Master Ki" (紀氏), the poet-scholar only sought to reproduce a few lines of Tsurayuki's original *kana* at the end of his copy in order to prove its authenticity. The relatively greater weight accorded to readers than authors is also seen in Teika's prioritization of legibility over historical fidelity when he cites his failing eyesight and Tsurayuki's archaic style of calligraphy as reasons for making his own alterations. To this end, he applied the same strategies he used in copying other Heian classics, such as adding Sinographs and replacing earlier phonographs (*jibo*) with their standard thirteenth-century counterparts.[18]

17. Ii, "Tameie-bon *Tosa nikki* ni tsuite," 1–11.
18. Tsumoto, "*Tosa nikki, Sarashina nikki* ni miru Teika," 30. See also Komatsu, *Nihongo shokishi genron*, 133.

Teika's copy also makes a noteworthy change to the diary's content by replacing the phrase "see if a woman can also do" (*omuna mo shite mimu*) in the opening sentence with "try to do in women's letters" (*omuna moji te-kokoromimu*), doubtless because he thought the narrator was using an abbreviated cursive style of calligraphy commonly known as "women's hand" (*onnade*). Although the diarist describes Sinographs as "men's letters" (*otoko moji*) elsewhere in *Tosa nikki*, however, the idiosyncratic nature of Teika's copy has persuaded most scholars to reject this interpretation.[19] In addition to gendering *Tosa nikki*'s brushwork, Teika's alteration indicates the importance that he and others placed on Tsurayuki's reputation as a calligrapher. Eleventh-century prose works by women in particular point to the high esteem in which he was held in this regard. The eponymous picture contest depicted in *Genji*'s Eawase chapter, for example, features his copy of *Taketori monogatari* (Tale of the Bamboo Cutter, ca. late ninth century), while *Eiga monogatari* (Tale of Flowering Fortunes, ca. 1092) mentions the presentation of a version of the *Kokinshū* in his hand.[20]

Growing demand in the thirteenth century for facsimiles (*mosha*) of Heian texts that could serve as calligraphic models likely led Teika's son, Tameie (1198–1275), to make a faithful copy of the same holograph in 1236 that concluded with a colophon asserting, "Not a single character in this copy differs from the original, including a few instances where they are hard to decipher or comprehend" (書寫之一字不違。不讀解事少々在之。).[21] Virtually every modern scholar has taken Tameie at his word after Ikeda Kikan (1896–1956) based his own reconstruction of a putative original on a seventeenth-century copy known as the Seikeisho'oku-bon. Indeed, modern editions continue to be based on Ikeda's reconstruction, even after a version in Tameie's own hand was rediscovered in 1984.[22]

---

19. Kimura, "*Tosa nikki* no kōzō," 68–69 and Komatsu, *Koten sainyūmon*, 108.
20. *Eiga monogatari* chapter 19, SNKBZ 32:340–41; see also McCullough and McCullough, *Tale of Flowering Fortunes*, 586.
21. As cited in Suzuki, *Tosa nikki*, 20.
22. For a recent assessment of the copies made by Teika and Tameie after Ikeda, see Yano, "'*Tosa nikki*' Teika-bon to Tameie-bon to Ki no Tsurayuki no sho ni tsuite."

Although Tameie's transcription provided the modern philological basis for establishing *Tosa nikki*'s authorship, thirteenth-century readers appear to have viewed Tsurayuki as its copyist instead. The strongest such indication appears in the prologue to the *kana* diary *Saga no kayoi* (Trek to Saga, 1269), written by the courtier Asukai Masaari (1241–1301). After describing his receipt of a copy of *Tosa nikki* from Tameie, Masaari proceeds to include the diary among the female-authored memoirs on which he modeled his own journal.

> As I spent my time gazing listlessly, it came to my attention that the Novice Middle Councilor Lord Tameie had been living nearby for some time now. Because our families had been well-acquainted for generations, we had occasion from time to time to exchange words by letter or in person. He sent diaries over to me such as *The Diary of Tosa*, *The Diary of Murasaki*, *The Diary of Sarashina*, and *The Diary of Kagerō*. Because these texts were originally written by women, they are all in *kana*. Men, too, seem to have written their words in *kana* because it was the practice in our land. *The Tales of Ise* also uses the letters of our Dragonfly Isles. Of course, *mana* are preferable when writing about weighty matters involving public affairs. Hence, I have written in that fashion in those instances. But from now onwards I feel it is fitting to write poems in *kana*. I ought to also do this when writing down my recollections of the past.[23]

The characteristics shared by the works on Masaari's list—female authorship, *kana* script, *waka* poetry, and the recollection of private matters—all prefigure the category of "women's diary literature" (*joryū nikki bungaku*) that would be articulated in modern times. In addition to the author and Tameie, the men who treated these works as a distinct genre are likely to have included retired emperor Go-Fukakusa (1243–1304, r. 1246–1260), who Masaari identifies as another avid collector of such texts, and Teika, who made the copy of *Sarashina nikki* (Sarashina Diary, ca. 1060) Tameie lent him. Overall, the stress both Teika and Tameie place on Tsurayuki's role as calligrapher leaves open the possibility they also believed *Tosa nikki* was originally by a woman.[24] Such differences between medieval and modern views of Tsurayuki's relationship to the diary thus

---

23. *Saga no kayoi*, 43–44.
24. Ikeda, "*Tosa nikki* wa hatashite Tsurayuki no saku ka," 13.

ultimately attest to the historically contingent nature of authorial attribution as a means for appraising it.

Tsurayuki's holograph last appears in the fifteenth century, when it was transferred to the official residence of the Muromachi shoguns after being given to Ashikaga Yoshimasa (1436–1490) by the poet-priest Gyōkō Hōin (1391–1455), a grandson of the scholar Ton'a (1289–1372) who authored several poetic travel journals of his own. It was subsequently inherited by Yoshihira's heir, Yoshihisa (1465–1489), after whose death it was entrusted to the latter's widow. Its disappearance from the historical record at this point coincides with the appearance of different textual lines based on copies that proliferated in response to increased interest in Heian literature, doubtless spurred on by a heightened sense of their physical vulnerability after the Ōnin War (1467–1477). The vast majority of *Tosa nikki*'s 120 or so extant manuscripts date from this period, including two textual lineages that are distinct from the ones made by Teika and Tameie. The first of these originated in a copy made by the courtier Matsunoki Munetsuna (1445–1525) in 1490 at the order of Go-Tsuchimikado (1442–1500, r. 1464–1500). The other textual line was inaugurated two years later by the famed scholar Sanjōnishi Sanetaka (1455–1537), who perhaps intended to sell his version to the same warriors for whom he also made multiple handwritten copies of *Genji*.[25]

In an entry from the same year in which he made his copy of *Tosa nikki*, Sanetaka notes his addition of *shōten* (voice markers) indicating the relative pitch of individual syllables and *kuten* (phrase markers) indicating sentence divisions within it.[26] These diacritics were intended for a reading of the diary and accompanying lecture Sanetaka gave at the shogun's behest. Although this version has not survived, the nature of the diacritics *Sanetaka kōki* mentions gives us a sense of the hermeneutical challenges *Tosa nikki* posed for fifteenth-century readers. The accents provided by voice markers distinguished words that were orthographically identical, while phrase markers demarcated dialogue and shifts in subject within the diary's longer stretches of prose. Even with such supplements, however, Sanetaka ruefully noted that "there are many points at which the

---

25. On these copies of *Genji*, see Horton, "Portrait of a Medieval Japanese Marriage," 136–37.

26. *Sanetaka kōki* entry for Meiō 1/10/4, 2:672.

meaning of this diary is difficult to fully comprehend" (件日記更不得覺悟之所々多之).[27] The comment suggests Sanetaka encountered interpretive challenges in reading *Tosa nikki* that went beyond questions related to its legibility. Such concerns would be further defined and debated in subsequent centuries.

An Early Modern Classic

Like his scholarly labor on other Heian classics, Sanetaka's efforts to preserve and annotate the diary would form a bridge between the late medieval and early modern periods. The majority of *Tosa nikki*'s extant manuscripts are secondary or tertiary copies of Muromachi-period texts such as his that were produced in the sixteenth and seventeenth centuries to meet the demand for facsimiles of Heian calligraphy. One such copy of Sanetaka's text made by the scholar Fujiwara Seika (1561–1619) became the earliest known study of the diary, *Tosa nikki fuchū* (An Appended Commentary to *The Tosa Diary*, 1661), when Seika's disciple Hitomi Bokuyū (1599–1670) appended his own notes to it. In keeping with the author's Neo-Confucian orientation, *Tosa nikki fuchū* focused on identifying allusions to earlier Sinitic texts.

Although many of Bokuyū's contemporaries shared his interest in identifying textual precedents, scholars would also increasingly focus on the novelty of the diary's content and Tsurayuki's reasons for writing it at a time when new notions of authorship fostered by print culture were taking shape. The diffusion of *Tosa nikki*'s text and scholarship on it both increased dramatically with the development of commercialized printing in the early modern period. With woodblock editions circulating as early as 1625, the diary soon occupied a prominent position within the newly popularized canon of Heian literature. This prominence in turn would make it a source of inspiration for plays and prose fiction from both the "noble and base" (*gazoku*) ends of the literary spectrum. Early examples include the premier experimenters in poetic prose during the Genroku

---

27. *Sanetaka kōki* entry for Meiō 1/10/15, 2:674–75.

era (1688–1704), Matsuo Bashō (1644–1694) and Ihara Saikaku (1642–1693), who praised and parodied it respectively.

The diary had already attracted scholarly accounts among other practitioners of *haikai* poetry prior to Bashō. The earliest such commentary was *Tosa nikki kenmonshō* (Notes on Impressions of *The Tosa Diary*, 1655) by the poet-scholar Katō Bansai (1625–1674), which recorded lectures on it that his teacher Matsunaga Teitoku (1571–1653) delivered in 1648. In keeping with his role in founding the conservative Teimon school of *haikai* poetry, Teitoku's lectures were chiefly concerned with elucidating the meanings of individual words and identifying earlier sources of inspiration. For example, he saw poetic precedents for the male author's assumption of a female persona in such texts as "The Song of Everlasting Sorrow" (C. *Changhenge*, J. *Chōgonka*) by Bai Juyi (772–846) and *Ise* episode 107. Perhaps because the adoption of female voices by male poets was such an established tradition, early commentators tended not to dwell extensively on Tsurayuki's choice of narrator.

Teitoku's overall approach to the diary further influenced the two-volume *Tosa nikki shō* (Notes on *The Tosa Diary*, 1661), written by his student Kitamura Kigin (1625–1705).[28] As was the case with his commentaries on *The Pillow Book*, *Genji*, and *Kokinshū*, Kigin's study of *Tosa nikki* would become a touchstone for later scholars. Although he largely followed Teitoku's example by explicating particular words and identifying allusions, Kigin's efforts extended to producing the first "base text" (*teihon*) for the diary by collating different manuscripts. He was also the first scholar to argue that Tsurayuki sought to conceal his identity by adopting a female voice, thereby laying the groundwork for further exploration of this line of reasoning in the nineteenth century.

Tosa nikki also appears in this period within a short story from Saikaku's *Nanshoku ōkagami* (Great Mirror of Male Love, 1687). The precision with which Saikaku parodies the original is a revealing indication in its own right of the degree to which he assumes readers were already familiar with its contents. For example, the title of this story, "Onnagata mo su naru Tosa nikki" (A *Tosa Diary* Such as Female Impersonators Are Said to Do), closely mimics the diary's opening sentence. The chief

---

28. An accessible version of Kigin's study is listed as the entry for *Tosa nikki shō* in the bibliography.

reference to it comes in the form of a journal kept by the boy protagonist's last lover during his voyage home to Tosa. Tsurayuki's text is parodied so closely in this truncated travelogue that it even includes entries in which nothing happens. While mimicking the original, Saikaku's parody simultaneously inverts its social and spatial contexts, turning the government official who is returning to the capital region into a merchant going back home to Tosa. Its plot also shifts the locus of loss from parental love to sexual desire by replacing the death of a daughter with that of the merchant who kills himself when he can no longer afford the boy actor he longs for.[29]

Soon after the publication of Saikaku's story, a dramatic reimagining of *Tosa nikki* appeared in a six-act *jōruri* play bearing the same name that debuted in 1702. After rescuing his historical contemporary Lady Ise (Ise no Go) from an evil suitor while he is enroute to Tosa, Tsurayuki escorts her back to the capital in the play's fourth act. Although this voyage would have presented an ideal opportunity to showcase the virtuoso performance of a *michiyuki* travel passage listing places that appeared in *Tosa nikki*, the play instead portrays a dance performance at the Sumiyoshi shrine.[30] Another departure from *Tosa nikki*'s narrative framework occurs in a scene from the penultimate act, in which Tsurayuki is portrayed writing the diary in response to not only the hardships he encountered on his return voyage but also those he experienced while governing Tosa. Like its title, these references to *Tosa nikki* and Tsurayuki appear to have been additions made by the Tosa *Jōruri* troupe of puppeteers to an earlier play by the reciter Uji Kaga no Jō (1635–1711), named *Ise monogatari*, which had focused exclusively on Lady Ise.[31]

In the eighteenth century, *Tosa nikki* was compared favorably with *Ise* and *Genji* as an early example of vernacular Japanese prose (*wabun*) by such luminaries of *kokugaku* nativism as Keichū (1640–1701), Kamo no Mabuchi (1697–1769), and Motoori Norinaga (1730–1801). In his *Niimanabi* (An Introduction to Learning, ca. 1765), for example, Mabuchi

---

29. *Nanshoku ōkagami* story 7:2, SNKBZ 67:530–37. For a complete English translation, see Schalow, *Great Mirror of Male Love*, 254–60.
30. The historical event this dance is based on is taken up in chapter 6.
31. A more extended account of this play is offered in Torii, "Tosa jōruri no kyakushoku-hō."

claimed the diary surpassed Tsurayuki's earlier *kana* preface to the *Kokinshū* because it was "written about things just as they occurred" (*aru koto o jika ni kakishi*), without recourse to such poetic devices as parallelism or epithets.[32] Perhaps because Mabuchi held the diary in such high esteem, his disciple Katō Umaki (1721–1777) subsequently devoted an entire text to it, *Tosa nikki kai* (A Commentary on *The Tosa Diary*). After laboring over a decade on Umaki's text, Ueda Akinari (1734–1809) finished revising his instructor's commentary in 1801. Although he relied heavily on Kigin's observations, Akinari was also the first to argue that Tsurayuki sought to express his grief at losing a daughter through the female narrator while also speaking with his own voice in its more humorous moments.[33]

Akinari's scholarly labors also informed his short story "Kaizoku" (Pirates) in *Harusame monogatari* (Tales of Spring Rain, 1808).[34] Coming as it did toward the end of his life, "Kaizoku" represented the culmination of its author's attempts to incorporate nativist scholarship in literary depictions of Japan's past.[35] His story's parodic treatment of the diary and scholarship on its author is as complex as *Tosa nikki*'s own relationship to fact and fiction. Greater specificity is lent to the original, for example, by placing the "certain year" at its opening within the Jōwa era (834–848). In setting the events it relates prior to Tsurayuki's birth, however, this detail ultimately ends up undermining the diary's relationship to history. Akinari's departure from the original becomes most apparent when Tsurayuki encounters pirates who only appear as rumors in the diary. Instead of subjecting his captives to physical harm, the pirate captain forces them to endure a sustained assault on Tsurayuki's literary reputation so lengthy that it is only completed later in a letter sent to the ex-governor. Among other things, this wide-ranging critique of Tsurayuki questions the morality of the love poems he included in the *Kokinshū*, his application of foreign poetic terminology to *waka* in its *kana* preface, and his purportedly shaky grasp of Literary Sinitic. The increasingly pedantic tone of this

---

32. *Niimanabi*, NKT 7:228.
33. Ichinoe, "Akinari to *Tosa nikki*," 44–46.
34. The original story can be found in SNKBZ 78:446–57. For an English translation, see Jackman, *Tales of the Spring Rain*, 49–65.
35. Ichinoe, *Ueda Akinari no jidai*, 125–27.

screed eventually becomes self-parody when Tsurayuki is accused of mispronouncing his own name. Perhaps to forestall criticism for this irreverent treatment of such a revered literary figure, Akinari concludes by defending his "stabbing someone with a brush" (*fude hito o sasu*) as a bloodless act.[36]

Akinari's interest in Tsurayuki's motives for writing *Tosa nikki* was shared by other nativist scholars who published book-length studies of the diary shortly afterward. The most frequently cited of these, *Tosa nikki sōken* (Personal Observations on *The Tosa Diary*, 1823) by Kagawa Kageki (1768–1843), generally affirms the opinions of Akinari and Kigin. Like Kigin, Kageki's training in classical poetry led him to focus on the diary's *waka*. Unlike his seventeenth-century predecessor, however, Kageki was chiefly interested in identifying new expressions that Tsurayuki coined. In keeping with the priority his Keien school placed on *waka* that expressed the poet's emotions, Kageki additionally singled out the poem lamenting a dead child that had reappeared in *setsuwa* as an encapsulation of its author's motives. Because he had previously recorded his wintertime journey to Kyoto shortly after the death of his own daughter in a journal titled *Nakazora no nikki* (Empty Sky Diary, 1818), this reading was also a deeply personal one for Kageki. Along with this melancholic substratum, he saw piracy as another major concern in the diary, leading him to claim its humor represented an attempt to ameliorate the feelings of grief and fear that permeate the voyage. Although his view of the author's motives was essentially identical to that of Akinari and Kigin, Kageki differed in stressing the role played by Tsurayuki's social identity as a Confucian scholar-official (*jusha*) in his decision to employ a female narrator who could more easily express personal emotions.

This same social identity led the *kokugaku* scholar Fujitani Mitsue (1768–1823) to view Tsurayuki's authorial motives very differently from Kageki in his *Tosa nikki tomoshibi* (A Lantern Illuminating *The Tosa Diary*, 1817). After addressing various philological and etymological issues in the "exterior" (*omote*) portion forming the first half of his study, Mitsue devoted the second "interior" (*ura*) portion to arguing that Tsurayuki adopted a fictional persona in order to express his disappointment at being assigned the governorship of Tosa rather than that of a larger, wealthier

---

36. *Harusame monogatari*, SNKBZ 78:457.

province. Overall, Mitsue's preference for reading literature through a Confucian lens that chiefly valued it as a means for evaluating the efficacy of governmental policy led him to view *Tosa nikki* as a critique of the decline in meritocratic advancement and effective provincial government during Tsurayuki's time.[37] His focus on social criticism also made Mitsue the first of many scholars who would read the diary's final sentence declaring the writer's intention to discard it as a direct expression of the author's personal frustration over the hardships he encountered away from home.

Another motive for writing *Tosa nikki* was offered by the nativist scholar Kishimoto Yuzuru (1788–1846) in his *Tosa nikki kōshō* (A Philological Analysis of *The Tosa Diary*, 1818). According to Yuzuru, Tsurayuki was forced to adopt a female persona because writing *kana* prose was considered a "feminine undertaking" (*memeshiki waza*) at the time. This view would go on to exert considerable influence due to the stature of *Tosa nikki kōshō*, which remains one of the most frequently cited studies of the diary from the nineteenth century due to its detailed explanations of individual words and wealth of sources. Comparison of Yuzuru's commentary with that of Kigin also offers a striking illustration of the changes in scholarly praxis that transpired during the early modern period. Unlike the sprawling structure of Kigin's study, Yuzuru adopted an extremely organized format, complete with a preface, a summary of its chief arguments, brief individual essays, and a biography of Tsurayuki.[38]

Other nineteenth-century texts reveal the increasingly broad range of geographic, social, and cultural spaces *Tosa nikki* occupied at the end of the Edo period (1603–1867). *Tosa nikki fune no tadaji* (A Direct Route to *The Tosa Diary*, 1842) by Tachibana no Moribe (1781–1849) aimed to make the diary accessible to a wide audience through extensive annotations, including ones that specified the subject in each of its sentences.[39] Moribe's study also drew on local histories to identify the route taken by the diary's travelers. Several of these observations were subsequently revised by the Tosa native Kamochi Masazumi (1791–1858) in his *Tosa nikki*

---

37. Burns, *Before the Nation*, 143–44.
38. Torizuka, "Edo jidai ni okeru *Tosa nikki*," 48–49.
39. For detailed examples of Moribe's approach, see Suzuki, "*Tosa nikki fune no tadaji.*"

chiri ben (Geographical Observations on *The Tosa Diary*, 1857). The spread of scholarship on *Tosa nikki* beyond major urban centers that Masazumi's commentary attests to is exemplified by the eight-volume *Tosa nikki kai* (A Commentary on *The Tosa Diary*, 1832), written by Tanaka Ōhide (1777–1847).[40] Despite spending most of his life in Hida province, Ōhide drew extensively on both scholarly predecessors and contemporaries, while also formulating his own opinions about such matters as the proper pronunciation of the Sinographs used in the title. Widespread familiarity with scholarship on *Tosa nikki* also inspired sophisticated forms of verbal and visual play in deluxe woodblock prints known as *surimono* that provide us with its earliest surviving pictorializations.[41]

Over the course of the Edo period, *Tosa nikki* can therefore be said to have become an early modern classic in several senses. First, it was a classical text that was widely read and studied at the time. Second, this status encouraged parodies of it through which writers could highlight their own modernity. Third, it anticipated early modern sensibilities to an unusual extent for a vernacular narrative from the Heian court. Unlike *Genji* or *Ise*, for example, the diary's prose brims with humorous wordplay, colloquial speech, and physical appetites. Fourth, the motives of its creator became integral to its meaning in tandem with the gradual establishment of authorship as a commercial and legal concept.[42] This final characteristic would also occupy a prominent place in subsequent accounts.

Modern Fictions of Women's Memoirs

So considerable were the achievements of early modern scholarship on *Tosa nikki* that a translation into modern Japanese made by Sasaki Nobutsuna (1872–1963) in 1894 was the only significant contribution to its

---

40. The commentaries of Yuzuru, Kageki, Ōhide, and Masazumi are available together in Takano, *Tosa nikki kochūshaku taisei*.
41. Kok, "Visualizing the Classics," 182–202. For examples of *surimono* referring to *Tosa nikki*, see Carpenter, *Reading Surimono*, 33, 151, and 391.
42. On the history of authorship in this period, see Kornicki, *The Book in Japan*, 225–39.

understanding in the Meiji period (1868–1912). Edo-period commentators also influenced its earliest translations into English. The first, made by the wife of a Methodist missionary named Florence Best Harris (1850–1909), was issued by the US publisher Flood and Vincent in 1891 after initially appearing in *The Japan Mail*. Although the only assistance Harris acknowledges is from a professor at Aoyama Gakuin, the influence of early modern scholars can be detected in her assertion that the diary's gender switch offers a humorous justification for writing in the vernacular.[43] The introduction William N. Porter wrote to his subsequent translation, issued by the London publisher Henry Frowde in 1912, likewise names individuals who assisted him (in this case a "Mr. Chochi Fujino" and "Major H. Haraguchi") but also explicitly cites Kageki to assert that a male author would have been ashamed to express grief at losing a child or fear at the prospect of encountering pirates.[44]

Modern scholarship on *Tosa nikki* would begin in earnest with the creation of a collotype edition of Teika's text in 1928, followed in 1941 by Ikeda's reconstruction of a putative original from Tameie's copy. Between them, these achievements enabled the production of new translations into modern Japanese, as well as annotated editions and forays into interpretation in the twentieth century.[45] Explanations for the presence of a female narrator also proliferated to the point where twenty-one separate theories were listed in an essay from 1954.[46] As a whole, they can be divided into three groups—sometimes combined with one or more of the other two—which ascribe her presence to the goals of developing *kana* prose, expressing personal emotions, or teaching *waka* composition.

These beliefs originated in the 1920s, when script, gender, and affect were combined to create "women's diary literature" as a distinct genre that *Tosa nikki* was now credited with beginning. Inclusion of the neologism "literature" (*bungaku*) in its name reflected the role these texts played in providing a historical precursor to the modern Japanese genre of first-

---

43. Harris, *Log of a Japanese Journey*, i–ii.
44. Porter, *The Tosa Diary*, 8–11.
45. Helpful overviews of scholarship up to the 1970s and 1980s can be found in Miyazaki, "*Tosa nikki* no genzai," and Kikuchi, "Ki no Tsurayuki kenkyūshi" respectively.
46. Nanba, "*Tosa nikki* no honshitsu."

person prose fiction known as the "I-novel" (*shishōsetsu* or *watakushi shōsetsu*).[47] During the same period in which Ikeda was fashioning an authoritative version of *Tosa nikki*, he and other scholars grouped together female-authored texts bearing the term "diaries" (*nikki*) in their titles. According to these men, all such diaries were autobiographical memoirs that directly expressed their female authors' "self-reflections" (*jishō*) on personal memories of the past.[48] In a formulation that soon acquired the status of a critical commonplace, Ikeda distinguished this "subjective" orientation from the ostensibly more "objective" approach men adopted in *kanbun* journals.[49] Another similar definition that became influential was provided by Tamai Kōsuke (1882–1969), who, after arriving at a broad definition of *nikki* as records of actual historical events, went on to distinguish diary literature as a sub-grouping that primarily sought to elicit readerly sympathy by depicting their authors' emotional responses to events in their lives.[50] Another influential formulation was proposed in the second half of the twentieth century by Akiyama Ken (1924–2015), who viewed women's diary literature as a means for liberating their female authors from the frustrations and anxieties of their lived experiences through the creation of an autonomous fictional world that resisted and critiqued the social constraints they lived under.[51]

From the 1950s onward *Tosa nikki* was increasingly viewed through this paradigm of diary literature, even as scholarship expanded to include such topics as its internal stylistic and structural characteristics and its connections to other vernacular narratives. The diary invariably headed volumes devoted to Heian women's memoirs in annotated series of classical Japanese literature, such as those published by Iwanami Shoten in 1965 and 1989 and by Shōgakukan in 1970 and 1994. One noteworthy exception was the version published by Shinchōsha in 1988, which paired it with Tsurayuki's personal *waka* anthology in a single volume devoted to his oeuvre.

47. Suzuki, "Gender and Genre," 71.
48. Kimura, "Nikki bungaku no honshitsu," 100–8.
49. Ikeda, "Nikki bungaku to kikō bungaku," 1.
50. Tamai, *Nikki bungaku no kenkyū*, 5–6.
51. Akiyama, "Kodai ni okeru nikki bungaku." The same view is espoused in Mezaki, *Ki no Tsurayuki*, 156–57.

Attempts to categorize the diary as an early example of women's memoirs were all confronted by the obvious challenge its male authorship posed to arguments for the genre's emotional authenticity. Ikeda, in fact, thought it fell short as an example of diary literature for this reason. Most scholars sought to resolve the issue by treating *Tosa nikki* as an indirect expression of its author's emotional responses to events in his life, in the process often reproducing Edo views of the supposed role that his gender and social position played in preventing Tsurayuki from speaking in his own voice. Some shared Akinari's belief that *Tosa nikki* was inspired by the grief he felt over the loss of an actual child. Others followed Hasegawa Masaharu in taking the diary's allusions to poems by Fujiwara no Kanesuke (877–933) as an indication the author was using the figure of a dead girl to lament the passing of his former patron. Still others shared Mitsue's belief that the diary reflects Tsurayuki's discontent with his posting to a distant province, or claimed it resulted from his dissatisfaction with the more mannered poetic style he had promulgated in the *Kokinshū*.[52]

The two historical narratives in which standard annotated editions placed the diary as either a pioneering example of Heian women's memoirs or the culmination of Tsurayuki's literary career would be reproduced in modified form when a pair of English-language translations were subsequently published within larger academic volumes devoted to the evolution of diary literature and Tsurayuki's artistic output respectively. The first of these, by Earl Miner (1927–2004), placed *Tosa nikki* at the beginning of a selection of poetic diaries that culminated with the journal *Botan kuroku* (Peony Verse Record, 1899) kept by Tsurayuki's harshest critic, Masaoka Shiki (1867–1902). As Miner himself acknowledged, this rendering of the diary went further than any Japanese scholar in treating it as a first-person account.[53] Many *waka* attributed to anonymous individuals and the bereaved mother in the original, for example, are represented as the diarist's in his translation. Helen McCullough's more faithful rendering in 1985, on the other hand, employed a biographical account of Tsurayuki's aesthetic evolution that

---

52. This last view appears in Konishi, *A History of Japanese Literature*, 239.
53. Miner, *Japanese Poetic Diaries*, 24–25. Miner relied largely on Konishi's *Tosa nikki hyōkai*.

included his *Shinsen waka* anthology, leading her to characterize *Tosa nikki* as a demonstration of his "mature poetic practice."[54]

The chief alternative to these quasi-autobiographical rubrics stressing the author's personal emotions and aesthetic ideals was provided by scholars who saw *Tosa nikki* as a work of dramatic fiction designed to impart lessons in composing *waka*. This notion can be traced back at least as far as 1943, when Higuchi Hiroshi argued that the distribution of poems among multiple characters allowed Tsurayuki to sketch out their social contexts more vividly and dramatically than was possible with the headnotes used in anthologies.[55] This view of the diary as an engaging work of fiction also manifested in its dramatization by NHK Radio in 1947, making it one of the few vernacular classics popularized during the occupation (1945–1951). Higuchi's view became firmly established in 1967 by Hagitani Boku (1917–2009) within his magisterial commentary *Tosa nikki zenchūshaku*, in which he argued that the diary was intended to serve as a poetic primer for aristocratic children, thus leading Tsurayuki to choose a woman narrator in order to convey its lessons on *waka* composition in simple but appealing terms. His emphasis on the diary's vivid dramatic qualities also led Hagitani to treat its representations of speech as instances of dialogue among multiple characters, and to view the diarist as a character with her own complex motivations. The thoroughness with which it approached *Tosa nikki* made this monumental six-hundred-page tome a touchstone for all subsequent studies of its text.

The emphasis Hagitani placed on its narrator was shared by the Anglophone scholars who began to give *Tosa nikki* sustained attention after Miner and McCullough. Perhaps in part due to their adoption of theoretical approaches that deemphasized authorial agency, these accounts made no mention of diary literature at all. The first article-length treatment of *Tosa nikki*, by Meera Viswanathan, explored the similarities between its portrayal of poetic conduct and the modes of spectacle and codified competition characterizing courtly culture in medieval Europe.[56]

---

54. McCullough, *Kokin Wakashū*, v. Accessible versions of *Shinsen waka* in Japanese and English respectively can be found in Kikuchi, *Kokinshū igo ni okeru Tsurayuki*, 188–217, and McCullough, *Kokin Wakashū*, 294–361.
55. Higuchi, "*Tosa nikki* ni okeru Tsurayuki no tachiba," 45–46.
56. Viswanathan, "Poetry, Play, and the Court in the Tosa Nikki."

In a wide-ranging engagement with Japanese scholarship on the diary from Edo times through to the 1980s, Lynne Miyake employed Judith Butler's conceptualization of gender as performative and contingent to argue that masculine and feminine perspectives coexisted on a constantly shifting continuum within it.[57] The feminization of *kana* writing was subsequently interrogated in other accounts. Noting extensive references to women's familiarity with Literary Sinitic in Heian vernacular texts, Joshua Mostow suggested her ignorance of these activities indicates that *Tosa nikki*'s narrator is significantly lower-ranking than most of the court women whose writings have survived.[58] Tomiko Yoda went on to critique earlier readings of *Tosa nikki* in which Tsurayuki appropriated women's supposed monolingualism to construct a national identity based on a spoken language, arguing instead that the choice of a female narrator possessing limited familiarity with Chinese is intended to create a narrative context in which *waka* is the only written form of poetry.[59] Later accounts by Atsuko Sakaki and David Lurie focused on the ways in which the diary relates Japanese language and culture to its Sinitic counterparts.[60] Peter Kornicki also adopted a different approach by detailing *Tosa nikki*'s contribution to Ikeda Kikan's philological methodology.[61]

Overtly or not, all these Anglophone accounts indicate the limited utility offered by the concept of women's diary literature in coming to grips with *Tosa nikki*. There is, in fact, no evidence to suggest Tsurayuki produced it at a time when writers faced any purely gender-based restrictions on the content, script, or style they could employ. Despite assertions from the Edo period onward that men could not express emotional attachments to their children, for example, the single most famed Heian *waka* on this topic is by a man.[62] Insofar as its composer was a former

---

57. Miyake, "The *Tosa Diary*," 42.
58. Mostow, "Mother Tongue and Father Script." Additional evidence that calls into question previous assumptions about women's literacy is provided in Shimura, "Heian jidai josei no mana."
59. Yoda, *Gender and National Literature*, 81–110.
60. Sakaki, *Obsessions with the Sino-Japanese Polarity*, 22–25; Lurie, *Realms of Literacy*, 327–28.
61. Kornicki, "Ikeda Kikan and the Textual Tradition of the *Tosa Nikki*."
62. *Gosen wakashū* poem 1102, SNKBT 6:327: "Though the heart of / someone's parent / might not always be / cloaked in gloom, / mine has gone astray / in thinking of

patron of the author whose poetry is cited elsewhere in *Tosa nikki*, moreover, this *waka* may in fact have inspired the diary's recurring mention of a dead girl.[63] Conversely, women can be seen relating events without reference to their own emotions in such *kana* records as an account of the 913 Teiji'in poetry match. As we will see later in this chapter, one high-ranking woman was the subject of a similarly "objective" *kana* diary that predates *Tosa nikki*. Even instances of supposedly masculine language in the diary, such as its frequent employment of *kundoku* syntax and diction derived from the practice of reading Literary Sinitic texts aloud, are viewed by the foremost authority on their usage as a common feature of tenth-century *kana* prose in general.[64]

At the same time as these examples call into question many of the assumptions surrounding *Tosa nikki*, they also help us begin to understand its initial reception. Because the narrator's simplistic views about what men and women wrote are presented to an elite readership of both genders who knew better from their own collective experience, *Tosa nikki* was clearly intended to be read ironically. Other aspects of the diary produce the same effect. When its numerous *kundoku*-derived expressions are related to the diarist's social status rather than her gender, for example, they create the humorous impression of a clumsily exaggerated attempt at mimicking her social betters. Her overly liberal use of such formal expressions takes on an added ironic edge when she mocks the steersman for doing the same thing in the prayer he offers up on 1/26.[65] As a result, both the diarist and those she critiques provide a source of amusement for more sophisticated readers. Like the narrator's mimicry of her superiors' *kundoku*-inflected language, her attempt to reproduce a type of diary she has never seen would have been perceived as inadvertently comical. With that in mind, I will in the remainder of this chapter take a closer look at the composition of *Tosa nikki*'s initial readership and the ways in which it parodies the diary culture they promulgated.

---

this child" (*hito no oya no / kokoro wa yami ni / aranedomo / ko o omou michi ni / madoinuru kana*).

63. Watanabe, "Ko o nakushita oya,'" 54.
64. Tsukishima, "*Tosa nikki* to kanbun kundoku."
65. Her mockery of the steersman here is noted in Yasuda, "*Tosa nikki* no kajitori zō," 44–45.

Tsurayuki After Tosa

The courtly context in which *Tosa nikki* was produced bears little relation to either the concept of diary literature as an intensely personal confessional genre or that of the author's autonomous development as an artist. Because he remained dependent on the patronage of powerful figures at court throughout his life, Tsurayuki's most obvious motive for writing the diary would have been to please those people. The record of his posts and poems documented by the author and others in the final ten years of his life makes it possible to identify these initial readers with some precision. Examining his biography after he had returned from Tosa in this light can thus offer insights into how and why *Tosa nikki* took shape without assuming this process was driven by the author's own aesthetic tastes or emotional concerns.

Tsurayuki's loss of his chief poetic patrons during his time away from the capital made the search for support at court a particularly pressing concern when he returned from Tosa in 934. Daigo (885–930, r. 897–930), under whom he had overseen compilation of the *Kokinshū*, died in the same year that Tsurayuki set off for his governorship. The following year saw the death of Daigo's predecessor Uda (867–931, r. 887–897), who had also sponsored poetic venues in which Tsurayuki had appeared. The following two years saw the deaths of his Fujiwara patron Sadakata (873–932) and then Sadakata's junior kinsman Kanesuke in 933. The resulting sense of abandonment Tsurayuki felt toward the end of his life as he recalled the situation he found himself in shortly after returning to the capital is eloquently conveyed in the preface he wrote for the *Shinsen waka* anthology nearly a decade after he had left Tosa.

> I, Tsurayuki intended to present this anthology to His Majesty when I returned to the capital. But grieving clouds had gathered to cast their shadows over the venerable pines on the slopes of Mount Qiao; and the wind's wailing cries had faded from the autumnal bamboo lining the Xiang River. The Counselor who had transmitted His Majesty's command to me had also passed away. With a feeling of futility, I entrust these fine words to the inside of a chest. Left alone with scraps of paper, tears splash down onto my collar.

貫之秩罷歸日。將以上獻之。橘山晚松愁雲之影已結。湘濱秋竹悲風之聲忽幽。傳敕納言亦已薨逝。空貯妙辭於箱中。獨屑落淚于襟上。⁶⁶

A version of this text preserved in *Chōya gunsai* (Records of Court and Country, ca. 1116) adds the question "to whom will I now present this collection?" (向何方而上獻).⁶⁷ This plaintive query poignantly conveys the uncertainty Tsurayuki faced without a royal patron after Tosa. During the final decade of his life, the court was headed by a sovereign with little interest in sponsoring *waka*. Suzaku (923–952, r. 930–946), who was a child when he ascended the throne shortly after Tsurayuki left the capital, retired in the same year that *Tosa nikki*'s author died. Due to his youth and the deaths of his predecessors, Suzaku lacked the extensive network of consorts and relatives during his reign who had assisted his father and grandfather in their own poetic projects. The absence of such support led to a drastic reduction in the number of formal gatherings that took place at the palace.⁶⁸ Perhaps most notably of all, not a single poetry match was held despite their evident popularity before and after his reign.

In the absence of royal patronage, sponsorship of poetic activities at court shifted to a new locus of political power centered around Fujiwara no Tadahira (880–949), who became regent after a long period in which the post had remained vacant under Uda and Daigo. Tadahira's eldest son, Saneyori (900–970), would initially inherit the regency from his father, after which the center of political gravity shifted to the family of Saneyori's younger brother, Morosuke (908–960). With regard to *waka*, both Saneyori and Morosuke appear to have chiefly been interested in preserving their own poetic correspondences in anthologies that could be passed on to other family members. As we will see, this desire to establish a textual patrimony also informed their interest in diaries.

66. Kikuchi, *Kokinshū igo ni okeru Tsurayuki*, 188–89; see also McCullough, *Kokin Wakashū*, 294–95. The title Tsurayuki identifies himself by in this preface indicates it was completed between 943 and 944. Daigo is represented by Mount Qiao, where the legendary Emperor Huangdi was said to be buried. The Xiang River possibly refers to Daigo and Uda alike.
67. *Chōya gunsai*, KST 29:9.
68. Yamaguchi, *Ōchō kadan no kenkyū*, 509–13. One exception was screen *waka*, which Tsurayuki continued to supply for the palace throughout Suzaku's reign.

The absence of imperially sponsored anthologies and poetry matches under Suzaku meant that the chief opportunity for lower-ranking courtiers to compose poetry on commission involved writing screen *waka* (*byōbu uta*) for the birthday celebrations of Tadahira and his immediate relatives. Tsurayuki appears to have been particularly sought-after in this regard. Although he had been producing poems for Tadahira's family since at least the 920s, the number of *waka* they commissioned from him increased significantly after he returned from Tosa. One of the earliest poems by Tsurayuki from this period for which we have a date was composed at Tadahira's Shirakawa-dono mansion in 935.[69] At the end of that same year, he also wrote screen *waka* for a grand coming-of-age celebration that Saneyori held for three of his children.[70]

Tsurayuki also began to address poetic plaints for promotion to members of Tadahira's family in this same period. In 936, for example, he included two *waka* requesting an official post at the end of a preface that Tadahira commissioned for a compilation of poems composed at a banquet the regent had held to celebrate the first Day of the Rat in the new year.[71] Despite these poetic pleas, Tsurayuki did not receive a position when new appointments were determined in the Third Month that same year. Nothing is known of his activities in 937 and 938, other than one correspondence with Masatada (d. 961), who was the son of his former patron Kanesuke. In his preface to *Shinsen waka*, Tsurayuki refers to himself as having been "a minister hidden among the grasses" (草莽臣) at the time who lacked any official post, leading many scholars to think he wrote *Tosa nikki* during this period of unemployment, either in an attempt to garner the interest of potential patrons or for personal reasons of his own.

Tsurayuki's situation had improved significantly by 940, when Tadahira can be seen taking a direct interest in his circumstances. An entry from that year in the regent's diary, in which he addresses the poet with a noteworthy degree of intimacy and respect as "Lord Tsurayuki" (貫之朝臣), mentions Tadahira's intention to renew his position as steward

---

69. *Tsurayuki shū* poem 694, SNKS 80:240–41.
70. *Tsurayuki shū* poem 697, SNKS 80:242. The identities of these children are unknown.
71. *Tsurayuki shū* poems 872–73, SNKS 80:300.

(*bettō*) of the Suzaku'in villa.[72] A spacious old residence named after its location on the southwestern side of the Suzaku Avenue bisecting the capital, this villa was supported by income from a substantial number of properties. No doubt it was the significant administrative responsibilities entailed by managing such wealth that led Tadahira to divide these duties between Tsurayuki and Minamoto no Kintada (899–948), another individual from whom the regent was commissioning *waka* at that time. Although it remains unclear when Tsurayuki was first appointed to this position, his oversight in 939 of a poetry match in Suō province could have been connected to business there involving estates held by the villa. Both the location of this "Tsurayuki Household Poetry Match" (*Tsurayuki ie no uta-awase*) and the anonymity of its surviving poems suggest the other participants were provincial gentry of the sort who appear as erstwhile poets in *Tosa nikki*.[73]

Although the income he received as steward of the Suzaku'in villa was doubtless substantial, this position lay outside the official administrative system that provided courtiers with the opportunity to increase their permanent stipends by advancing in rank. Tsurayuki must therefore have been relieved by his promotion earlier that year to the post of *genba no kami* (head of the department of Buddhist and foreign affairs) when official government appointments finally resumed after a hiatus caused by provincial military disturbances. His new post made Tsurayuki responsible for keeping a census of the realm's temples and clergy, as well as for entertaining foreign dignitaries. As we will see in chapter 6, this latter activity may have also informed the diary's depiction of Nakamaro.

Despite these indications that Tsurayuki was being supported, his attempts to secure future employment continued unabated. Three years into his tenure as *genba no kami*, he composed a *waka* requesting a new position from Saneyori.[74] In response to this appeal, Tsurayuki was raised to the upper grade of the Junior Fifth Rank in the New Year's Day promotions of 943, after having spent twenty-six years at the lower grade.

72. *Teishin kōki* entry for Tengyō 3/5/14, ZZGR 5:199.
73. Hagitani provides a partial reconstruction of this poetry match in *Heianchō uta-awase taisei* 1:287–94.
74. *Tsurayuki shū* poem 879, SNKS 80:303.

This, his final rank, is the one he identifies himself by, along with the post of *genba no kami*, in the *Shinsen waka* preface. Although his promotion placed Tsurayuki among the select group of courtiers who could attend the emperor in person, there is no indication he ever served Suzaku in that capacity. Regardless, the significant increase in his stipend that came with his new rank must have been welcome. Circumstantial evidence suggests it was Saneyori's younger brother Morosuke who was most directly responsible for this promotion.[75] The two men's extensive dealings with one another at the time can be seen in an unusually lengthy headnote from *Tsurayuki shū* that cites the contents of a letter from Morosuke requesting a poem with which to express gratitude to his father, Tadahira, for having previously lent his son a belt ornament of the sort worn on formal court occasions.[76]

Information about Tsurayuki's life after this point comes from much later sources. According to *Sanjū rokunin kasen den*, he was appointed in 945 to the post of *mokugon no kami* (acting head of the carpenters office), charged with procuring lumber and other construction materials for repairs to the palace. This post, which would have entailed more work and a higher salary than that of *genba no kami*, is the last one Tsurayuki is known to have occupied, and it is used to identify him posthumously in the title of the Nishi-Honganji-bon version of his personal *waka* anthology, *Ki no shōsaku kashū* (The Ki Head Carpenter's Anthology of Verse). The last poems by Tsurayuki that can be firmly dated are also from 945. Both *Sanjū rokunin kasen den* and the roughly contemporaneous *Kokin wakashū mokuroku* claim he died the subsequent year. His final *waka* in the *Ki no shōsaku kashū* has traditionally been identified as Tsurayuki's death poem.[77] According to its headnote, he sent it to the same Kintada with whom he had previously served as steward of the Suzaku'in villa, suggesting this colleague was involved in shaping an early version of Tsurayuki's personal *waka* anthology.

---

75. Murase, *Kyūtei kajin Ki no Tsurayuki*, 247–48.
76. *Tsurayuki shū* poem 699, SNKS 80:242–3.
77. *Tsurayuki shū* poem 878, SNKS 80:302: "Cupped hands holding / water that lodges / flickering moonlight / now here, now gone / as our time in this world!" (*te ni musubu / mizu ni yadoreru / tsukikage no / aru ka naki ka no / yo ni koso arikere*).

Two general aspects of Tsurayuki's biography in this period are particularly germane to understanding the context in which *Tosa nikki* took shape. This first of these is that we have no clear indication of a particular point in time at which he completed a definitive version of *Tosa nikki*. Rather than being written soon after his return to the capital, as many scholars have assumed, the holograph he left behind could have been made at any point between then and his death. The diary's brevity would have made it a relatively simple matter to create multiple iterations ranging from the plain draft Teika describes to the illustrated version Egyō mentions. The existence of these two dramatically different texts also makes it easy to imagine *Tosa nikki* was popular enough to merit numerous versions over a period of years. His unceasing quest for support later in life suggests Tsurayuki would have had every incentive to do so.

The second point is that Tadahira's family was likely to have been the initial readership for whom *Tosa nikki* was written. In addition to commissioning *waka* from its author for their own purposes, members of this group demonstrated interest in his other writings. Tadahira's kin likely commissioned the smallest version of Tsurayuki's own anthology, the Kasenkeshū-bon, whose ninety-one *waka* are largely composed for relatives of the regent.[78] Hagitani believed the diary was originally intended for Saneyori's two oldest sons, Atsutoshi (918–947) and Yoritada (924–989), both of whom would have been in their early teens when Tsurayuki returned from Tosa (TNZ 470). Others think it was written for an adult male, such as Morosuke or Saneyori, who then presented it to a female member of the family, such as Morosuke's wife Princess Kinshi (904–938).[79] Morosuke's aunt Onshi (885–954) would also have likely been intrigued by *Tosa nikki*, given her own involvement with a similar *kana* diary. This range of possibilities points to an intended readership whose members, like the diary's characters, varied in gender and age. As we will see next, a connection between Tadahira's family and the genesis of *Tosa nikki* is further suggested by their germinal role in developing new modes of diary-keeping at court.

---

78. Tanaka, *Kōtei Tsurayuki shū*, 69.
79. Murase, *Ki no Tsurayuki den*, 417.

The Political Rise of Personal Diaries

Over the course of the Heian period, texts referred to as *nikki* (diary) or *ki* (record) came to encompass a plethora of genres: multi-entry records kept by secretaries tasked with recording ceremonies in the inner and outer portions of the palace (*naiki no nikki* and *geki no nikki*); ones by hall courtiers covering daily activities in the royal residence (*tenjō nikki*); personal diaries kept by sovereigns (*gyoki*) and aristocrats (*shiki* or *watakushi no nikki*); records of criminal investigations (*kanmon no nikki*); and Buddhist priests' accounts of pilgrimages to the continent (*jun'yūki*). Other diaries limited themselves to particular events, such as poetry matches (*uta-awase no nikki*), palace banquets (*sechie no nikki*), Shinto rites (*saiji no nikki*), and memorial services (*kuyō no ki*). Their sheer diversity led Tamai Kōsuke to conclude an exhaustive study of the several hundred instances in which the word *nikki* appears by stating all such texts shared a common interest in recording actual happenings, even if they were limited to a single day's event, neglected to mention dates, or were semi-fictional.[80]

Beginning with Ikeda, modern scholars have viewed the "men's diaries" that *Tosa nikki*'s narrator claims to be emulating in nearly as broad a manner by using the umbrella term *kanbun nikki* to describe any journal in Literary Sinitic employing a daily entry format. Such diaries typically began as annual almanacs (*guchūreki*), which were widely available in both the capital and provinces from the eighth century onward.[81] After an initial draft made by the Onmyō-ryō (Bureau of Divination) was presented to the sovereign on the first of the Eleventh Month, copies known as "distributed calendars" (*hanreki*) of these almanacs were disseminated to every branch of government. The higher-grade versions reserved for aristocrats and governors included several blank lines (*ma-aki*) for recording brief observations made by their owners.[82] This format would have enabled Tsurayuki to collect the raw materials for *Tosa nikki* by providing

---

80. Tamai, *Nikki bungaku gaisetsu*, 255–57.
81. The earliest extant almanac was kept by an anonymous sutra copier at the Nara court in 746. See Hayashi, "Shōsōin komonjo-chū no guchūreki."
82. Yamashita, *Heian kizoku shakai to guchūreki*, 61.

space for him to make notes about his voyage home. His aristocratic readers, on the other hand, began utilizing this format to develop new diary forms that appropriated palace precedents around the same time.

The earliest surviving reference to *nikki* comes from a government document written in 821, preserved in the *Ruijū fusenshō* (Government Proclamations by Topic, 1121), that mentions *geki no nikki* (outer palace diaries) kept by clerks (*sakan*) in the Office of the Council of State (Dajōkan).[83] A few citations from these records describing large-scale court rituals can be found in the last official history, *Nihon sandai jitsuroku* (or *Sandai jitsuroku*, True Record of Three Reigns, 901), as well as the later informal chronicles *Nihon kiryaku* (Abbreviated Chronicles of Japan, eleventh century) and *Honchō seiki* (Record of Our Court's Reigns, twelfth century). Complementing the *geki no nikki*'s focus on the larger body of officialdom were daily accounts of the sovereign's actions known as *naiki no nikki* (inner palace diaries), kept by officials in the Naiki (Inner Palace Secretariat) within the Central Affairs Ministry (Nakatsukasashō). Although the earliest references to *naiki no nikki* date from slightly later, the *Yōrō ritsuryō* (Legal Codes of the Yōrō Era, 718) establishing administrative procedures for the *ritsuryō* state mentions the need to keep such records.[84] Continental precedents for this practice date back to Han-dynasty accounts of emperors' words and actions, known as *qijuzhu* (records from rising to repose), and include one from the Jin dynasty (266–420) cited in *Nihon shoki*.[85] In the tenth century, these records began to be supplemented by *tenjō nikki* (hall courtier's diaries), kept by chamberlains (*kurōdo*) who recorded the emperor's meals and other daily observances taking place in his living quarters.[86]

The early tenth century also witnessed the sudden appearance of lengthier autobiographical forms of daily record-keeping among the uppermost echelons of court society. Known as *shiki* (personal records) or *watakushi nikki* (personal diaries), these multi-year journals compiled from the almanacs of individual aristocrats were "personal" both in the sense that they focused on the activities and impressions of a single individual,

83. Horiuchi, "Nikki kara nikki bungaku e," 6–7.
84. *Ryō no gige* (Shokuin-ryō), KST 22:33.
85. Sakamoto, *The Six National Histories of Japan*, 49.
86. Morita, "Tenjō nikki," 305–15.

and in the sense that they became the property of that individual's household. The earliest one we know of, *Motoyasu shinnō nikki*, was written by Prince Motoyasu (d. 901), the fifth son of Emperor Ninmyō (810–850, r. 833–850).[87] It was followed soon after by Uda's *Kanpyō gyoki* (Diary of the Kanpyō Sovereign, 887–897) and the *Engi gyoki* (Diary of the Engi Sovereign, 897–930) of his successor Daigo. Both sovereigns' daily records of their reigns were housed in their living quarters, where they could also be consulted by later rulers.[88] *Kanpyō gyoki* offers a particularly striking example of a man's diary whose content includes the sort of "emotional" subjects that scholars usually associate with women's memoirs, including Uda's affection for a favorite cat and his despondency over the physical tolls (including impotence) he suffered at moments of heightened political tension.[89]

All of Tsurayuki's patrons within the Fujiwara regental household had also adopted this imperial autobiographical privilege soon after Uda had embraced the practice, beginning with the earliest personal diary for which we still possess significant portions, Tadahira's *Teishin kōki* (ca. 907–948).[90] Lacking as it did any precedent in the regencies of his father, Mototsune (836–891), or his grandfather Yoshifusa (804–872), it was likely modeled after that of Prince Motoyasu, who could have provided Tadahira with the sort of information about court rituals he would have received from his father if he had not died during the Fujiwara nobleman's childhood. Tadahira was also likely to have been interested in emulating the diaries kept by Uda and Daigo due to his role as a substitute for the sovereign during formal court events, including the annual round of court promotions the regent presided over within his living quarters at the palace. This regental role is suggested at various points where *Teishin kōki*

---

87. Because the titles posthumously assigned to personal diaries referred to their authors' residences or official posts, many possess multiple designations (themselves often with multiple pronunciations). For convenience, I have chosen only one common designation in each case. Accompanying dates indicate the years covered by their surviving contents.

88. Yoneda, "Rekidai tennō no hongi to itsubun," 77–90. Daigo's own son, Prince Shigeakira (906–954), also kept a personal diary, known as the *Rihō ōki* (ca. 920–953).

89. *Kanpyō gyoki* entries for Kanpyō 1/2/6 and 1/8/10, ZZGR 5:7 and 8.

90. An English-language translation of the portion covering the year 939 is provided in Piggott and Yoshida, *Teishinkōki*.

can be seen replicating the division between the sovereign's body and that of officialdom in court records. For example, Tadahira concludes an account of the investiture of the Ise Shrine priestess in 938 by stating, "matters extraneous to my person were recorded by the outer palace scribes" (自餘事外史記之).[91]

Tadahira's diary also resembled those of Uda and Daigo in being compiled with the intention of assisting his heirs. This was also true of the diaries kept by his two senior sons: the no-longer extant *Seishin kōki* by Saneyori and the *Kyūreki* (ca. 930–960) by Morosuke. Their utility was further facilitated by rewriting the two men's journals as "separate records" (*bekki*) organized by topic. Indeed, *Teishin kōki* itself appears to have been edited at some point by Tadahira's heir Saneyori with this purpose in mind.[92] One entry within Tadahira's journal also describes him commanding Morosuke to convert it into a condensed version.[93] Like the personal diaries they were extracted from, the *bekki* emulated earlier textual genres at court, in this case, ritual formularies known as *gishiki-sho*, which shared a similarly condensed format.

The personal diaries of Uda and Daigo may have also inspired a daily record of activities in the household of Tadahira's younger sister Onshi. Its connection with their journals is suggested by the title, *Taikō gyoki* (Diary of the Queen Mother), which marks Onshi's royal status as the mother of Suzaku and Murakami (926–967, r. 946–967). Insofar as this record was kept by an anonymous scribe, however, it bears a closer resemblance to *naiki no nikki*. There are intriguing hints in historical documents that female-authored versions of such records were in fact being kept in Literary Sinitic at the time. According to the portion of *Ryō no shūge* (Collected Commentaries to the Administrative Code, ca. 868) detailing the administration of the palace quarters inhabited by high-ranking consorts, the Naishi no Tsukasa (Palace Handmaids Office) was required to "record the palace officials' daily accomplishments and shortcomings" (記宮人之上日功過) and "make note of daily observances" (註上日行事).[94]

91. *Teishin kōki* entry for Tengyō 1/9/15, ZZGR 5:184.
92. Yamanaka, "Kojin no nikki," 11. See also Murai, "Watakushi nikki no tōjō," 73–74.
93. *Teishin kōki* entry for Tengyō 8/4/16, ZZGR 5:202–3.
94. Ishihara, *Heian nikki bungaku no kenkyū*, 5.

It is thus possible that Onshi's use of a female diarist was, at least in part, inspired by such practices.

The honorific language directed toward Onshi and her kin in *Taikō gyoki* further suggests the writer was one of her attendants. Its use of *kana* to convey such expressions makes her diary significant in its own right as the earliest extant example of a Japanese vernacular text written by a woman. Only portions from six entries dating between 907 to 934 have survived in the fourteenth-century commentary *Kakaishō*, which cites them in order to elucidate aspects of formal occasions depicted in *Genji*. These entries describe: (1) gifts handed out for the men's *tōka* dance performance on the fourteenth day of the New Year; (2) Tadahira's role in the coming-of-age ceremony for Onshi's daughter Yasuko (920–957); (3) robes handed out by Tadahira for Onshi's fiftieth birthday; (4) two folding screens presented at Tadahira's fiftieth birthday celebration hosted by Saneyori; (5) other gifts from Onshi for the same celebration, including a copy of the *Man'yōshū* in Daigo's hand; and (6) gifts to a messenger who had presented Onshi with bamboo shoots sent by Uda. Additional entries detailing ceremonies surrounding the births of two princes appearing in the *Seikyūki* diary of Minamoto no Takaakira (914–982) were likely rewritten from the original *kana*.

Despite their fragmentary nature, these citations exhibit several intriguing similarities with contemporaneous diaries kept by other men and women, including *Tosa nikki*. Like the autobiographical accounts kept by her male relatives, *Taikō gyoki* functions both as a personal diary focused on Onshi and as the private property of her household. This latter characteristic is evident in the treatment it was accorded in later diaries kept by her male kin. In addition to Takaakira's journal, for example, *Taikō gyoki* is mentioned in passing by Sanesuke (957–1046) within his *Shōyūki* diary, suggesting both men treated Onshi's diary in the same manner as those by their male forebears. Conversely, the honorific-laden prose and third-person narration in *Taikō gyoki* more closely resembles the later records by Murasaki Shikibu and Sei Shōnagon chronicling the lives of their own mistresses than it does male autobiographical diaries.[95] Their shared interest in gift-giving makes the relationship between Onshi's di-

---

95. Miyazaki, *Nyōbō nikki no ronri to kōzō*, 105–30.

ary and *Murasaki Shikibu nikki* particularly close in this regard.[96] Most important for our purposes, the existence of *Taikō gyoki* makes clear that Tsurayuki's patrons would not have viewed a woman attendant's vernacular diary as the novel phenomenon *Tosa nikki*'s narrator assumes it to be. Rather, they would have been amused by the ways in which her diary parodically diverged from their own.

Parodying Diaristic Time

The means by which *Tosa nikki* structures its narrative clearly parodied the conventions its aristocratic readers would have expected from a diary. Scholars who describe *Tosa nikki* as a parody often take earlier vernacular literature to be its target. Hasegawa Masaharu has claimed, for example, that it humorously inverts literary norms by focusing on parental love instead of romance.[97] Others view *waka* by Narihira and Nakamaro as the diary's primary target.[98] Less has been said about how *Tosa nikki* might be parodying the male diaries its narrator claims to mimic. One important exception is provided by Watanabe Hideo, who has argued that *Tosa nikki* deliberately inverts the characteristics of daily bureaucratic records by replacing their public content with private concerns, official duties with their cessation, and adult male subjects with women and children.[99]

Tsurayuki's career at court would have exposed him to a variety of different diary forms that could have inspired *Tosa nikki* in this regard, especially during his time serving as *gosho-dokoro no azukari* (palace library custodian) while he was overseeing compilation of the *Kokinshū*. In addition to the almanacs used by him and other officials, moreover, the author's employment from 910 to 917 in the Inner Palace Secretariat would have familiarized him with its *naiki no nikki*. The travelogues whose

---

96. *Murasaki Shikibu nikki* mentions gifts on two separate occasions (SNKS 35:33 and 61).
97. Hasegawa, "'Bungakushi' o enshutsu shita otoko," 20–22.
98. Satō, "*Tosa nikki* ni okeru 'parodi,'" 22–30; and Higashihara, *Tosa nikki kyokō ron*, 57–90.
99. Watanabe, *Heianchō bungaku to kanbun sekai*, 263–65.

conventions he works with are numerous enough to merit their own discussion in chapter 4. My focus here will be on *Tosa nikki*'s parodic divergence from the personal diaries of its aristocratic readers for two reasons. The first is that they were more familiar to Tsurayuki's patrons than the records kept by low-ranking officials. The second is that their relative novelty led his superiors to describe the aims of personal diaries, and the methods employed to achieve them, with a level of detail that makes their comparison with *Tosa nikki* particularly fruitful.

Personal diaries were still such a recent phenomenon in the tenth century that Morosuke felt it necessary to stress the importance of keeping them in his admonitions to his heirs. His methodical approach to the subject in *Kujōdono goyuikai* (Testament of the Ninth Avenue Lord, ca. 947–960) has made the following passage one of the most frequently cited in modern accounts of Heian aristocratic life.

> When you rise in the morning first intone the name of the year's star seven times, then observe any changes in your appearance in a mirror. Next, look at your almanac to ascertain whether or not it is an auspicious day. Append abbreviated accounts of annual observances to the entry. Each day, look at the entry for the following day to familiarize yourself with it and prepare accordingly. Furthermore, the public affairs of the previous day and those personal matters that you are unable to put to rest in your mind should be briefly noted under that entry to avoid forgetting them soon afterward. Those concerning important public affairs or one's lord and father should be noted down separately to serve as a mirror for later generations.
>
> 夙興照鏡先窺形體變。次見暦書可知日之吉凶。年中行事畧附件暦。毎日視日之次。先知其事。兼以用意。又昨日公事若私不得心事等。爲備忘忘、又聊可註附件暦。但其中要樞公事及君父所在事等。別以記之。可備後鑑。[100]

Morosuke begins by noting the important purpose diaries served in preparing one for the subsequent day, a function that is then replicated at the end of the passage when he urges his sons to save their own diaries so that their descendants can prepare for similar occasions in the future.

---

100. *Kujōdono goyuikai*, GR 27:137.

Although the primary aim is to record ritual and public events, Morosuke also encourages the diarist to include "personal matters that you are unable to put to rest in your mind" (私不得心事) if any space remains. Perhaps the stipulation that they be written in the morning was designed to ensure the journals only concerned themselves with past events that were important enough to still be remembered.

Notably, *Tosa nikki* ignores each of the above injunctions. It lacks calendrical information worth consulting, is filled with random observations and marginalia instead of ritual practices, and is available to anyone other than its writer instead of becoming the exclusive patrimony of that person's family. Among these elements, it is the particular temporal relationship between text and writer stressed by Morosuke that occasions Tsurayuki's initial and most fundamental divergence from his patron's injunctions. Lacking access to an actual almanac, the diarist's ability to predict and manage time is constrained by the material circumstances that force her to "scrawl down a few jottings regarding that affair on what I have to hand" (*sono yoshi, isasaka ni mono ni kaki-tsuku*). Although the simplicity of a daily entry format allows her to mimic the basic temporal divisions of *guchūreki* without ever seeing one, the ersatz nature of her version prevents the narrator from drawing on the wealth of additional calendrical information that made them useful.

The sheer profusion of calendrical information Heian almanacs provided set them apart from their predecessors in both Japan and China. Within the individual scrolls allocated for each month, the upper portion of the entry for each day (*hizuke*) included a zodiac animal (*eto*), one of the five elements determining an individual's fate (*nachin*), and one of twelve signs (*jūnichoku*) indicating auspiciousness. The middle portions indicated the corresponding third of the month, one of twenty-four solar terms (*sekki*), and one of seventy-two climates (*kō*). The bottom section might mention the position of Jupiter (*daisai*), days of ill fortune (*kuenichi*), auspicious events (*kichiji*), gods overseeing directional taboos (*nichiyūshin*), predicted eclipses (*shokubun*), and the hours of sunrise and sunset. Such information was particularly useful for identifying calendrical taboos. Because these were contingent on additional factors such as an individual's age, however, the challenges inherent to identifying such prohibitions led the ever-acerbic Sei Shōnagon to include them in her list of "Things People Have No Idea About" (*Koto ni hito ni shirarenu mono*).[101] No doubt the elaborate requirements entailed by such calculations are one reason why Morosuke recommends his male descendants consult the entry for the following day in advance.

By contrast, *Tosa nikki* gives scant attention to such matters due to its twofold divergence from diaristic norms: its lack of the detailed calendrical information provided by almanacs, and its lack of the biographical focus on an individual organizing a personal diary, both of which were required in order to identify calendrical taboos. *Tosa nikki* also ignores other calendrical practices the Fujiwara aristocrat's testament enjoins his heirs to observe. Although *Kujōdono goyuikai* lists particular days of the month recommended for cutting nails, for example, a comment by the diarist on 2/9 suggests she is only aware of the need to avoid doing so on the first Day of the Rat (*ne no hi*) in the new year.[102] Ill-omened days are treated in an equally eccentric manner. Although the narrator's declaration on 1/15 that "the day boded ill" (*hi no ashi*) accords with a common belief that the midmost day of any month was inauspicious, she makes no such comment on 2/15. Nor is there any attempt to inform us about the specific nature of the obstacles that force her vessel to remain at anchor on 1/8 and 2/10, rendering these comments superfluous for readers who, in theory at least, might have found such details offered valuable precedents in the event they were ever at sea.

Other means of marking time in *Tosa nikki* also diverge from the practices its initial readership observed in their own diaries. For example, the prologue mentions the precise hour at which the traveling party departs from the governor's mansion while neglecting to mention the year this happened. Although this initial specificity is attributable to the presence of a water clock in the governor's mansion, moreover, hours of the day are also given on 1/21 and 1/30 when no such means of calculating time are available at sea. These inconsistencies must have seemed odd to Tsurayuki's patrons, whose own journals frequently noted the times of day at which their events took place. *Tosa nikki* also ignores the temporal conventions for writing diaries that Morosuke prescribes by failing to con-

101. *Makura no sōshi* section 243, SNKBZ 18:375; see also McKinney, *The Pillow Book*, 205.
102. *Kujōdono goyuikai*, GR 27:136.

sistently record the events of any given day on the following morning. Because most of the diary's sentences lack any tense, they can be read as indicating past or present. The few occasions where time is specified, however, use expressions such as "today" or "now" to indicate the diarist is recording events soon after they take place. Proleptical comments such as "this sort of thing happened at other times as well" (*kakaru koto nao arinu*) on 1/14, on the other hand, suggest that an unknown number of other details have been added to entries much later. These divergences create a dual temporal structure combining the reader's experience of a plot that unfolds day by day with the diarist's retrospective appraisal of the entire voyage.[103] Because the unprecedented complexity of such a narrative structure is predicated on its writer's ignorance of the temporal conventions governing diaries, this innovation is the direct result of a parodic stance. For its readers, *Tosa nikki*'s eccentric approach to representing time thus ultimately marks it as a fictional work intended to entertain rather than inform.

Parodying Diaristic Perspective

Diary conventions are also creatively parodied through the perspective her social position requires the narrator to adopt. Opinions differ as to how and where her point of view appears in the text. Even Masaari's belief that she is the historical author occasionally resurfaces in modern accounts. One scholar, for example, has argued that the "hindrances" (*sawaru koto*) preventing travel on two occasions involve menstrual taboos that would have held little interest for a male author.[104] At the other extreme are those who maintain that she only appears in the first sentence in order to justify the diary's use of *kana*.[105] Most think the gendered perspectives of *Tosa nikki*'s narrator and author can both be detected at different points in its text. The resulting complexity has led one scholar to claim the diary produces an aggregate form of subjectivity through the

103. Horikawa, "*Tosa nikki* no bōtō no ichibun," 10–15.
104. Nakajima, "*Tosa nikki* no chosha wa josei de aru," 9.
105. Morita, "*Tosa nikki* ron," 31. See also Miyake, "*The Tosa Diary*," 47 and 68.

accumulation of the contradictions engendered by these different perspectives.[106] Another describes the diary's narrative as a cyclical movement in which the perspectives of author, narrator, and character continually replace one another.[107]

The lack of any strictures concerning what women could write in fact makes it impossible for all intents and purposes to determine where the author's voice ends and that of the narrator begins. Given this situation, choosing to foreground the diarist's presence is attractive for a number of reasons. In addition to avoiding overly general assumptions about gendered language at the time *Tosa nikki* was written, attributing its entire contents to her enables us to better appreciate its sophistication. That is to say, if Murasaki Shikibu could represent the inner and outer lives of male characters in *Genji* with such penetrating acumen that they were as plausible for her readers then as they continue to be for us now, why should we assume Tsurayuki's portrayal of the diarist is incapable of achieving a similar degree of verisimilitude? It is difficult to see how the author's attempt at representing a woman writing like a man would have otherwise engaged his readership, all the more so because they were well aware of both the author's gender and the existence of women involved in similar forms of diary writing. Treating the diarist as a vivid fictional character possessing her own motives for adopting different representational strategies, moreover, also creates varying degrees of distance from her perspective that parodically undermine the facticity that enabled diaries to claim practical value.

Aside from her gender, *Tosa nikki* offers few indications of the diarist's identity. Traditional readings that assume Tsurayuki is represented by the bereaved father typically identify her as the dead girl's mother.[108] However, the diarist's use of honorific language toward the parents indicates she is subordinate to them. Nor is she wife to the ex-governor, a position most likely occupied by the "dame of Awaji" (Awaji no tōme), who appears alongside him near the end of the journey. Because the inclusion of Awaji in her title indicates a male relative was once posted to that prov-

---

106. Kimura, "Nikki bungaku no honshitsu to sōsaku shinri," 114. See also Hirasawa, "*Tosa nikki* ni okeru kundokugo," 43–44.
107. Kristeva, "Ichininshō no bungaku keishiki," 30.
108. Imai, *Heianchō nikki no kenkyū*, 146.

ince, the similarity in their social standing suggests this woman is his primary wife; and because her chronic complaints indicate a similar age in the seventh decade of life, the dead girl is clearly not her child. The bereaved mother is therefore more likely to be a daughter-in-law or other junior relative of the ex-governor, thus further implying the diarist's subordinate position makes her the dead girl's former wet-nurse, a close relative of her bereaved mother, or an attendant to her, the ex-governor, or his wife.[109] Any one of these possibilities makes the narrator's social background significantly humbler than that of the provincial governors' daughters who waited on the diary's aristocratic readers (as the dead girl would have done had she lived to adulthood). If the diarist is an attendant to the recently bereaved daughter-in-law of the ex-governor, her continued employment is contingent on her mistress' equally precarious reliance on the ability to produce children for a family headed by a middle-ranking official who is himself facing the bleak prospect of unemployment back in the capital. Placing the diarist in such a multiply marginalized position would invest the entire text with black humor of the most ironic sort.

Many scholars have argued convincingly for the potential to produce a particularly complex narrative structure enabled by employing a diarist who occupies the position of an attendant. As a peripheral observer, she would be ideally placed to modulate her psychological distance from the people she portrays.[110] Her low status also makes it possible for the narrator to empathize with those characters who are the most marginalized on account of their age, gender, or status.[111] Yet the ambiguous stance she adopts in evaluating people throughout the diary makes it equally possible to see her harshly criticizing those same individuals. Ultimately, the tendency for her sentences to omit subjects allows readers to attribute the opinions they contain to either the diarist or others.[112] These ambiguities represent a significant innovation in their own right, enabling an unprecedently subtle shading of narrative perspective that quite likely inspired the writers of later *monogatari* and *nikki* to employ similarly

109. Takei, "*Tosa nikki* no katarite," 178–79.
110. Hijikata, *Nikki no seiiki*, 137.
111. Imazeki, "*Tosa nikki* kō," 347.
112. Yamashita, "*Tosa nikki* no ninshō kōzō," 125–27.

distinctive narrators.[113] Such innovations were made possible by a choosing a figure whose peripheral social position sensitizes her to the potentially adverse social and material consequences of such evaluations.

The diarist's strategically ambiguous stance also leads her to blur distinctions between experience and hearsay, thereby undermining the basis for claims to facticity in personal diaries. The opening declaration that she has "only heard about diary-keeping" (*su naru nikki*) but will "set out to do one" (*suru nari*) offers a textbook example of the grammatical distinction between these epistemological registers resulting from the different conjugations that could precede *nari* to indicate an inference based on hearsay (with the *shūshikei*) or certainty through a declarative copula (with the *rentaikei*). As Hagitani notes, these two registers are often morphologically indistinguishable within *Tosa nikki* (TNZ 52). As a result, it is unclear in such cases whether she is asserting something with the certainty of direct experience or conveying her impression of someone else's speech. The latter option would imply that another person bears responsibility for the comment or, if such an attribution creates its own difficulties, makes it possible for the diarist to claim she has simply misheard what that other person said. A similar uncertainty obtains in the diary's use of the auxiliary verb *keri*, which can mark the narrator's sudden realization of something that is ongoing or indicate that the person has no direct experience of what is being related. Such grammatical indeterminacies make it possible for the diarist to avoid responsibility for the content of her narration by refusing to specify whether she is making a statement based on personal observation or simply relaying the (possibly unreliable) account of someone else.

This strategic obfuscation of the narrator's perspective also parodies its consistency in noblemen's personal diaries. Except for the royal "We" (*chin*) Uda repeatedly uses in *Kanpyō gyoki*, first-person pronouns were superfluous in such texts precisely because they were, by definition, concerned solely with their authors.[114] By contrast, it is often unclear if it is an "I" or a "we" who is the subject in *Tosa nikki*, even when the diarist describes feelings of sorrow or joy. The sentiments expressed in the poems she records are likewise potentially shared with her fellow travelers,

---

113. Ishizaka, *Heianki nikki bungei no kenkyū*, 37.
114. Ishihara, "Nikki bungaku no hassō," 40–42.

making them very different from the *waka* appearing in such tenth-century tales as *Ise*, *Taketori*, and *Yamato monogatari* (Tales of Yamato), in which they instead convey the sentiments of individuals addressing others.[115] *Tosa nikki* is closer in this regard to the poetic means for marking grammatical person in the eighth-century *Man'yōshū*, which annexed the individual to a larger social whole in what Torquil Duthie has termed a "politics of the first person."[116] By replacing panegyric verse intended to praise royalty with prose shaped by a low-ranking attendant's need to be discreet, *Tosa nikki* produces a parodically mundane diminution of the political effects this subordination to the collective was originally designed to produce.

Like its grammatical distinctions between certainty and inference, those delineating individual subjects in the prologue also swiftly dissolve in a manner that parodically undermines the facticity and detail personal diaries aimed for. As a general rule, aristocrats' journals took care to specify the identities of participants at the events they described, presumably because such information would be relevant to later readers seeking precedents for carrying out the same observances in similar company. Aside from the inconsequential provincial gentry she names, by contrast, the diarist shows no interest in identifying individuals beyond the most minimal terms required by the contexts in which they appear or the poems they recite.[117] This approach is foregrounded in the prologue by introducing a series of anonymous subjects who are formed in distinction from one another as the diarist moves from initially identifying herself as "a woman" (*omuna*) writing like "men" (*otoko*), to describing "someone" (*aru hito*) who "people" (*hitobito*) are seeing off. Even this contingent means of delineating subjects is undermined, however, when "someone" subsequently expands to include anyone other than the diarist. The result of this simultaneously ambiguous and prolific means for designating individuals in the diary is to parodically exaggerate its lack of utility.

Prolifically ambiguous detail also characterizes *Tosa nikki*'s treatment of its most socially prominent figure, who, after initially appearing as

---

115. Watase, "*Tosa nikki* no 'aru hito,'" 83–85.
116. Duthie, Man'yōshū *and the Imperial Imagination*, 224. I follow Duthie in using "grammatical person" in a contextual sense rather than a morphological one.
117. Takeuchi, "*Tosa nikki* no tensu, asupekuto," 66–67.

"someone" in the prologue, is subsequently designated with nouns more frequently and inconsistently than any other character. On the one hand, this frequency reflects the narrator's position as an attendant who is expected to represent her employers rather than herself. On the other hand, their variety reflects her awareness of the marginal social position the master of her household now occupies in an alien and transitional setting located outside officialdom. This tension between the expectation that she exalt the ex-governor and her own sardonic appraisal of his shrunken status is reflected in the diarist's tendency to elevate him in terms that simultaneously mark his abjection ironically through the contexts in which they are employed. Thus, he appears as "the elderly man" (*okina*) when his physical frailty is foregrounded, as "the former governor" (*saki no kami*) when he is still in the province he no longer oversees, and as "the lord on board" (*funagimi*) when he is subjected to the whims of the steersman.

Tosa nikki's sporadic employment of honorifics also parodically undermines their pragmatic purpose as a means for identifying individuals within vernacular texts. In total, they are used four times for the ex-governor, twice for locals who feed the travelers, and once for the bereaved mother. With the exception of one of the locals, who appears only once, none of these individuals are accorded honorifics consistently. For example, the diarist initially addresses a senior provincial Buddhist prelate in a respectful manner when he travels over to their harborage on 12/24 to fete them, but then subsequently omits such language when he sends food and saké from even further away on 1/2. This inconsistency is all the more striking given the consistency with which both entries employ the Sinographs 講師 in order to represent his title of "lector" (*kōji*), thereby stressing the weightiness of his position overseeing the province's monks and nuns from its provincial head temple (*kokubunji*). Perhaps the diarist increasingly suspects his gifts are motivated by an expectation of future reciprocation in kind. Perhaps she is bitter that the second set of gifts come a day after the New Year's Day celebrations when they would have been most useful. Perhaps their first appearance is only intended to highlight their absence from her description of the new governor the following day in a pointed indication of how poorly he comes across by comparison. Whereas the lector went out of his way to travel in person to the party, the new governor uses a messenger to summon them back to his mansion. What is more, replying to this summons extends the delay in returning to the capital that his late arrival has already occasioned, a situation that is further exacerbated when the farewell banquet ends up continuing until daybreak. Like a detective novel (to use Hagitani's analogy), her motives gradually and subtly gain definition through the accumulation of such clues over successive entries (TNZ 123).

The inconsistent manner in which the diarist acknowledges the lector's gifts is yet another example of *Tosa nikki*'s parodic relationship to the personal diaries of Tadahira's family. Such records took particular pains to note the nature and amount of goods exchanged at various events in order to establish precedents that could be consulted on similar occasions. *Tosa nikki* would appear to be specifically mimicking *Taikō gyoki* in this regard, insofar as Onshi's diary was also written by an attendant in *kana*, and also tracks the disbursement and receipt of gifts. But whereas the anonymous writer of *Taikō gyoki* consistently uses honorifics for her mistress' male kin in order to draw attention to them rather than herself, their inconsistent use in *Tosa nikki* foregrounds its diarist's subjectivity by hinting at her own evaluations of these exchanges. Coupled with the care she also takes to avoid sole responsibility for such opinions, these evaluations form one of the diary's many satirical aspects that will be addressed in the next chapter.

Conclusion

From the earliest readers who mention it through to the present day, *Tosa nikki*'s relationship to Tsurayuki has occupied a central place in its reception history, reflecting both his fame and the distinctive mode of authorship it represents as the earliest surviving piece of vernacular fiction attributable in its entirety to a single individual. Although modern philological studies have affirmed the seemingly stable nature of this connection between text and writer, however, it was in fact the relatively late product of a lengthy history dominated by more amorphous forms of attribution shaped by the cultures of *waka* poetry and calligraphy, modes of cultural production whose prestige and authority were only gradually supplanted by a stronger concept of authorship as the critical locus of creative agency fostered by print culture. As a consequence of our modern tendency to fixate on the author, most accounts of *Tosa nikki* continue to uncritically reproduce the starkly gendered language of its prologue in order to identify supposedly feminine forms of language Tsurayuki is purportedly attempting to access. In fact, the intimate familiarity with diaries that his initial readers possessed as a result of their personal and political investments in such texts would have led them to view the significance its diarist attributes to her own actions as an indication of profound ignorance, thereby ironically undermining her reliability as a narrator from the start. The primary purpose of its prologue is therefore to signal the parodic nature of *Tosa nikki* as a would-be diary whose haphazard observation of the conventions for marking time, perspective, and person undercut the claims to facticity by which such texts sought to assert their value as future reference sources.

Tosa nikki's parodic orientation merits greater attention on account of its being as distinctive in a historical sense as it is critical to the diary's aims. Apart from the corporeal and comic dimensions of *Man'yōshū* poetry and medieval *renga* verse, there is still little Anglophone scholarship on humor in premodern Japanese literature.[118] Significantly more attention has been directed toward parody in Saikaku's works, as well as its central place within early modern Japanese culture overall, in which the classical past was self-consciously and ostentatiously juxtaposed with a modern present through such figures as *mitate* (visual allusion) in word and image.[119] In discussing these phenomena, Joshua Mostow has argued for the value of applying critical accounts of parody derived from Western literature, in part because terms intrinsic to an Edo-period context are typically refracted through translation.[120] An approach to parody in *Tosa nikki* that draws on Western literary criticism would seem to be particularly warranted in light of the fact that, unlike in the Edo period,

---

118. Palmer, "A Poem to Carp About?"; Keene, "The Comic Tradition in Renga." The most wide-ranging Anglophone account of Japanese humor begins with the sixteenth century (Hibbett, *The Chrysanthemum and the Fish*).

119. Anglophone studies of parody in Saikaku's works include Gundry, *Parody, Irony and Ideology in the Fiction of Ihara Saikaku*; Hibbett, "Saikaku and Burlesque Fiction"; and Johnson, "Saikaku and the Narrative Turnabout."

120. Mostow, "*The Tale of Light Snow*," 365.

there appears to be no widely recognized terminology for describing such representational modes in the diary's own time.

In fact, many of *Tosa nikki*'s most distinctive characteristics resemble those ascribed to parody in Western critical theory. The concept is as old in that context as the tradition of literary criticism itself, with roots that can be traced back to the term *parodia* Aristotle used in his *Poetics* (ca. 355 BCE) to describe humorous narrative poems that borrowed the meter and vocabulary of Homeric epics. Over the course of its lengthy history in the West, the purpose of parody has been either to create comical effects or to provide metafictional commentary on the structure, production, or reception of the texts it imitates.[121] The two most prominent modern critics to assign the greatest cultural and political significance to parody have emphasized this metafictional dimension. Because Anglophone scholarship on Edo-period fiction has engaged with both figures, a consideration of their relevance to *Tosa nikki* can extend current conversations about the place of parody in Japanese cultural history back to a much earlier time.

The first of these critics, Bakhtin, located the origins of the European novel in medieval forms of parody that mingled multiple social languages in order to challenge elite claims to cultural authority represented by the aristocratic genre of lyric poetry.[122] As will become apparent over the course of this book, similarly heterogenous forms of language can be seen in *Tosa nikki*'s representation of class-specific sociolects, its transcriptions of popular song, and its adoption of a narrative stance that combines diary conventions with those of fictional prose narratives. If anything, the remarkably dense diversity of these languages within its spare prose makes the diary more "novelistic" in a Bakhtinian sense than *Genji* or indeed any other vernacular text produced at the Heian court.

The second critic, Linda Hutcheon, describes parody as "a form of repetition with ironic critical distance, marking difference rather than similarity."[123] The primary premodern example she draws on to illustrate this formulation happens to be particularly germane to *Tosa nikki*. For Hutcheon, the ironic inversions that characterize parody are exemplified

---

121. Rose, *Parody*, 277–78.
122. Bakhtin, "Discourse in the Novel," in *The Dialogic Imagination*, 272–73.
123. Hutcheon, *A Theory of Parody*, 6.

by the Greek tragedy *Medea* (531 BCE), which turns the traditional male aristocratic protagonist into a queen who is socially marginal on account of both her gender and foreign background, while also replacing the standard dramatic chorus of elite men with city women who join her in subverting the domestic patriarchal order. *Tosa nikki* also inverts the structures of class and gender typically associated with its genre in a twofold manner, by replacing the aristocratic male subject of diary writing with a low-ranking woman, and by transforming the community represented by these noblemen into one whose most prominent figures are socially marginal women, male commoners, and children of both genders. On a metafictional level, Hutcheon's formulation can also be applied to *Tosa nikki*'s flagrant falsehoods, which constitute a parodic "repetition" of diaries' historicity with a "critical distance" on their claims to veracity that ends up favoring amusement over utility.

In light of these similarities, it is also important to note that *Tosa nikki*'s relative lack of emphasis on the anti-poetic and political qualities both critics ascribe to premodern parody also highlights the limitations that historical and cultural contingencies place on their accounts. Although Hutcheon views the affirmation of tradition in the *honka-dori* allusive techniques used in *waka* poetry as fundamentally anti-parodic, Anglophone studies of Japanese humor and Japanese scholarship taking up parody in *Tosa nikki* both note that poetry was one of the earliest mediums for its expression.[124] Although some of the more deliberately clumsy *waka* in *Tosa nikki* can be viewed in this light, the diffuse nature of poetic intertextuality in Tsurayuki's day identified by David Bialock poses a fundamental challenge to locating specific *waka* as targets for parody.[125] In other words, the practice of altering poems was too pervasive at the time to support the firm distinctions between original and copy that parody relies on.[126] The political charge parody possesses in the diary is even more questionable, insofar as the failings of its semi-educated nar-

---

124. Hutcheon's description of *honka-dori* draws on Brower and Miner, *Japanese Court Poetry*, 14–15. On *haikai*'s divergence from Bakhtin's prose-driven model, see Shirane, *Traces of Dreams*, 52–53.

125. Bialock, "Voice, Text, and the Question of Poetic Borrowing," 192–97.

126. Even works by the most revered Tang poets were frequently altered, as Christopher Nugent has pointed out in *Manifest in Words, Written on Paper*.

rator end up reinforcing social hierarchies rather than subverting them. As we will see in the next chapter, this is also true of *Tosa nikki*'s satirical observations.

These caveats aside, our capacity to appreciate the literary appeal and historical value of *Tosa nikki* are both enhanced by viewing it as a parody. Regardless of whether one sees it as humorous, metafictional, or both, parody by its very nature implies the existence of knowledgeable readers who can recognize what is being imitated and the ways in which its ironic repetition diverges from the original. Treating the diary as a parody thus enhances our appreciation of its audience's sophistication, its author's gift for mimicry, and the multiple forms of irony that inhabit the text, all while furthering our understanding of the cultural and social conventions it puts into relief. Because parody is self-reflexive, moreover, the diary's prologue is only the first of several sites within its text where the processes undergirding different modes of oral and textual representation become visible. All these aspects of *Tosa nikki* will be addressed in subsequent chapters.

CHAPTER 2

Bitter Regrets

As Edo-period scholars often noted, humor permeates *Tosa nikki*. One recent attempt to categorize its many examples identifies three categories: wordplay, satirical ridicule, and comical absurdity.[1] The social concerns that occupy the middle of these three makes it a particularly rich resource for historically contextualizing the diary. One of the chief ways in which *Tosa nikki* parodied aristocratic diaries was by transforming their neutral accounts of the disbursement and receipt of material objects into critical observations regarding their social effects. The sheer number of words devoted to such matters within the diary's otherwise austere discursive economy led Hagitani to view satire (*fūshi*) as its second-most prominent concern after poetics.

Tosa nikki's overall tendency toward social observations, particularly ones involving transactions among commoners, also distinguishes it from other vernacular Heian texts. Unlike earlier representations of travel, for example, it spends more time describing social settings than landscapes. Its difference from Tsurayuki's earlier *kana* prose is particularly stark in this regard. Whereas his preface to the *Kokinshū* uses the word *kokoro* to describe a universal poetic response to the natural world shared by all humans, *Tosa nikki* applies it to the self-aggrandizing motivations of a socially diverse cast of characters that includes provincial gentry, sailors,

---

1. Kimu, *Heian jidai no warai*, 46–73.

and city dwellers.² And whereas "things" (*mono*) in the *kana* preface originate in a cosmology extrinsic to the humans who collectively experience its sensory phenomena, those in the diary are typically products of human labor that appear in social contexts intrinsic to the identities of people who experience them differently according to the particular positions they occupy in those contexts.

Material matters make their first appearance when the final sentence of the prologue mentions the ex-governor's receipt of the "official discharge" (*geyu*) that allows his household to embark for home. As the "custodian" (*zuryō*) of a province, his term ended with the receipt of this document from his successor after the latter had (at least nominally) consulted financial documents in order to certify that there were no missing revenues, unpaid reimbursements, or neglected duties such as repairs to office buildings. Because pressures of time mitigated against a thorough audit, both men would typically sign a document explaining "the non-deliverance of the discharge letter" (*fuyo geyujō*) and establishing any outstanding expenses. Even after being granted this provisional discharge, however, the ex-governor was expected to submit documents from his tenure to auditors back in the capital.³

The importance of such audits reflected the tenth-century court's growing reliance on governors for the collection of provincial wealth that resulted from an increasing need to accommodate more localized forms of ownership and authority.⁴ Concern over this shift was reflected in the repeated attention paid to government policies at the time by such scholar-officials as Miyoshi no Kiyoyuki (847–918), whose "Twelve Opinions Submitted to the Throne" (*Iken jūnikajō*, 914) offered various proposals based on his experience administering Bicchū province. As far back as Mitsue's time, *Tosa nikki* was viewed through this historical lens as an implicit critique of the supposed corruption that resulted from the central government's loosening grip on the provinces.

The heightened scrutiny governors were subject to in this period is also reflected in its literary output. One prime example is provided by Kiyoyuki's political rival, Michizane, a third of whose extant poems are

2. Takano, "*Tosa nikki* o yomu," 21–22.
3. Hérail, "The Position and Role of Provincial Governors."
4. Kiley, "Provincial Administration and Land Tenure," 315–16.

devoted to documenting his intermittent oversight of Sanuki province by describing tours of inspection, complaints about local corruption, exchanges with subordinates, dialogue with local elders, and the suffering of his charges. The most celebrated of these are a set of ten *shi* poems named after their opening line, "For whom does the cold come early?" (何人寒氣早), each depicting the hardships suffered by a different type of provincial resident.[5] Perhaps in part to absolve himself of any responsibility for their suffering, Michizane also criticizes his predecessor in Sanuki. No doubt such poetically polished accounts held greater appeal for his superiors than the dry financial documents he was expected to submit.

Similar motivations have been ascribed to the diary's recurring mentions of privation, whose intent may have been to demonstrate its author's probity as a provincial governor to readers who might grant him another such post. Tadahira was particularly interested in provincial administration throughout his career. Entries from his diary during Tsurayuki's first year as governor of Tosa, for example, reveal the Fujiwara regent immersing himself in such matters as repairs to provincial facilities, missing silk levies, piracy, and food supplies for the palace kitchen.[6] Perhaps not coincidentally, the last two of these concerns appear in the diary. If *Tosa nikki* was intended to promote its author's rectitude as a governor, however, his lack of any subsequent provincial posting would suggest it failed to achieve this goal. If anything, its overt fictionality makes it more likely that the diarist's descriptions of deprivation were intended to amuse readers rather than elicit respect or sympathy for the author.

In this chapter I will argue that *Tosa nikki* aims to entertain its readership by ironically commenting on the various ways in which all of its characters are implicated in the circulation of material things, including the narrator herself. Along with the more obvious spatio-temporal movements shaping the diary as a travelogue, the milieus in which objects circulate provide it with another narrative structure that progresses from farewell banquets to new year's rites, followed by transactions with human and supernatural entities. Even the girl whose death occasions the purest expressions of sentiment in the diary is implicated in the logics under-

---

5. Borgen, *Sugawara no Michizane*, 147–96. *Tosa nikki* in fact shares many words with these ten poems, as detailed in Satō, "Ki no Tsurayuki *Tosa nikki* to Sugawara no Michizane."
6. Piggott, "Court and Provinces Under Regent Fujiwara no Tadahira," 43.

lying these material forms of exchange. The series of misfortunes that arise in all of these settings share a common focus on the mouth's role in mediating the movement of objects and language, often through economies in which the latter replaces the former. I will then conclude with a consideration of the parallels that obtain between *Tosa nikki*'s portrayal of such matters and modern Western accounts of both satire and the creation of social ties through exchange.

Parting Gifts

The majority of *Tosa nikki* is set in a liminal space located physically between the governor's provincial headquarters and the capital, as well as ritually between the occasions at which food, gifts, and poems are exchanged in those settings.[7] The first thirteen days of travel alone are devoted to gatherings at which the ex-governor's entourage are fed and entertained by well-wishers. A staple feature of tenth-century vernacular tales, such banquets and the poems composed at them are depicted most extensively in *Utsuho monogatari*, which, as Brian Steininger notes, devotes considerable attention to tracing the bonds established between members of the provincial governor class and court elites through the movements of gifts in such settings.[8] By contrast, *Tosa nikki*'s banquets situate the ex-governors' relationships with provincial gentry in settings that are plagued by linguistic, social, and ritual failures. The sardonic observations these failures occasion also set the stage for later dramatic ironies in the narrative.

A foreshadowing of future difficulties is already apparent on the first day of travel, which is marked in *Tosa nikki*'s second entry by a banquet whose inauspiciousness undermines its ostensible purpose, as does its description in prose filled with puns evoking the same dangers the travelers seek to shield themselves from.

> On *The Twenty-Second* we raised *Prayers* in level tones for smooth seas at least as far as Izumi province. Though the path before us lies on the sea,

---

7. Fukazawa, "*Tosa nikki* jikūron," 65–66.
8. Steininger, *Chinese Literary Forms in Heian Japan*, 41–43.

Fujiwara no Tokizane bade farewell to our steeds at the traditional banquet seeing us off. High, middling, and low all had more than their share of saké. It made for a bizarre spectacle to see their riotously rotten behavior here by the brine of the sea. (TN 15–16, 12/22)

By incorporating the date into its first sentence, this entry draws attention to the inauspicious nature of the twenty-second, which was considered a day of ill fortune (*kuenichi*) for travel (TNZ 66). This unfortunate timing undercuts the calm voices with which prayers for a smooth passage are uttered, just as the vertical manner in which they rise foreshadows the towering waves that will later obstruct forward progress. Its maritime setting is also ill-suited to the rite's etymological origins as a "steed nose-turning" (*muma no hanamuke*) designed to ensure a safe journey over land by pointing travelers' horses in the direction of their destination. Even the feast's social efficacy is undermined in the final pun on "rotten" and "riotous" in *azare*, which combines the sea brine's failure to preserve food with the occasion's failure to maintain decorum. Judging from Sei Shōnagon's description of inebriated banquet attendees in her list of "Hateful Things" (*Nikuki mono*)—where grimaces, shouting, and touching the mouth and beard are singled out as especially egregious acts—this banquet's disorderliness likely includes similar behavior.[9] As we will see, many of the misfortunes that occur during the journey involve this same orifice.

The following day introduces an additional element of irony when the diarist inadvertently discloses her underlying motivations in portraying such gatherings. As other scholars have noted, the passage represents a particularly rich layering of affect as she moves from joy at their host's generosity, to pride in her master, to criticism of people in general, and finally to guilt over her own greed.[10] In the process, the passage plays a critical role in revealing her own biases.

A person named Yagi no Yasunori was here. He is not someone who serves in the governor's office, I gather, and yet he has given us such an impres-

---

9. *Makura no sōshi* section 26, SNKBZ 18:66; see also McKinney, *The Pillow Book*, 27. Like this entry, "Hateful Things" often castigates the dissolution of class boundaries (Angles, "Watching Commoners, Performing Class," 45–46).

10. Watanabe, "*Tosa nikki* no kaigyaku hyōgen," 58–60.

sive farewell banquet! Could this be a result of the governor's qualities? I am told that it is typical for people in the provinces to say, "Well, this is it," and then vanish from sight, yet here was someone with a heart coming over to us without concern for what others might think! My praise is not in any way based on the things we were given. (TN 16, 12/23)

As noted in the previous chapter, *Tosa nikki*'s frequent naming of gift-givers who are both fictional and inconsequential parodies the value placed on such details in aristocratic diaries. Here, it also parodies the hagiography of an earlier historical individual, Fujiwara no Yasunori (825–895), provided by Kiyoyuki in his *Fujiwara no Yasunori den* (Biography of Fujiwara no Yasunori, 907). When his biography praises Yasunori's tenure as governor of Bizen province from 871 to 875, it spends as much time describing his leave-taking as it does his actual term of office. So unrelenting is the stream of saké and side-dishes with which his former charges fete Yasunori that he is forced to depart secretly without provisioning his ship. When inclement weather forces him into a harbor, Yasunori reluctantly (but gratefully) receives two hundred bushels of rice at the insistence of the provincial officials who catch up with him there. He is eventually able to leave the harbor after the province's lector comes to calm its waters with sutra recitations.

The sheer number of contrasting parallels between the characters and situations described here and in *Tosa nikki* indicate a deliberate parody.[11] Its fictive Yasunori differs from his historical namesake by becoming the donor rather than the recipient of provincial largess, and by representing individual sentiments rather than collective ones. The two texts' depictions of their governors' interactions with their charges also suggest a shared awareness of the concerns those relationships could give rise to at court. On the one hand, a governor's ability to execute his duties depended on good relations with provincial gentry.[12] On the other hand, these relations could lead to personal ties that exceeded official interests. Kiyoyuki's biography seeks to paper over such contradictions when it

---

11. Perhaps not coincidentally, Tsurayuki also composed screen *waka* for Yasunori's fourth son (see appendix 2).
12. On the growing power of local gentry, see Kiley, "Provincial Administration and Land Tenure," 237–43.

describes the rice Yasunori receives from the elders of Bizen as a parting gift that is both extralegal and a testament to his impartial benevolence as a public official. The elders are pleased he accepts the rice, despite expecting him not to do so, because he was a good governor. For his part, Yasunori realizes he should not accept the rice as a good governor, but he is also aware that not doing so puts him in danger of disrespecting the elders who offer it, thereby disregarding the Confucian hierarchies an upright official ought to respect.[13] Inadvertently or not, Kiyoyuki's portrayal of this conundrum points to the potential difficulties posed by the different interests both parties brought to their relationship.

Similar conflicts of interest between legal and extralegal relationships inform *Tosa nikki*'s portrayal of the historical Yasunori's fictional counterpart. As a singular example of altruism, his character offers a pointed commentary on the connections local gentry cultivated with governors. Given their illicit nature, it would not have been in the interests of these figures to publicly acknowledge their former superior, particularly given the pressing need to establish ties with his replacement (TNZ 70–74). Thus, the high regard in which this fictional Yasunori holds the ex-governor overcomes any potential shame he might feel at appearing naïve before his peers. At the same time, readers might also interpret his exceptional behavior as a sign that the ex-governor has shown favoritism to him in the past. Such potentially problematic implications are perhaps why the diarist abruptly makes the assertion that her evaluation is not influenced by the quality of his gifts. In fact, however, the sudden, definitive, and labored nature of this disavowal encourages readers to evaluate all of the diarist's subsequent depictions of gift-giving in precisely the opposite manner from the one she intends.

Readerly suspicion that the narrator is in fact evaluating the relative lavishness of these parting banquets is confirmed the next day, when honorifics are suddenly bestowed on the lector, who provides them with an even more sumptuous feast complete with musical entertainments. So great is this generosity, moreover, that the diarist neglects to criticize the ensuing drunkenness this time, even though it now includes youthful members of the ex-governor's entourage and entertainers alike. Further confirmation of this prejudice is suggested soon afterward when the sta-

---

13. *Fujiwara no Yasunori den*, 63–64. For a complete translation, see Hérail, "The Position and Role of Provincial Governors," appendix 1.

tus of another host and the quality of his hosting both take the opposite form. Despite being superior in rank to the lector, no honorifics are extended to the new governor after he invites the party back to his mansion on 12/25. The occasion also suffers by comparison when it is sarcastically described as "what passed for entertainment" (*asobu yō nite*) (TN 16, 12/25).

As the banquet drags on into the next day, gifts are also subjected to critical scrutiny in prose that repeatedly stresses the social positions of the former governor and his successor. References to the host as the mansion's "master" (*aruji*) emphasize his largesse, which is bestowed with such excessive generosity that even the ex-governor's men-at-arms are beneficiaries. The attention paid to these younger sons of middle-ranking officials is in fact so remarkable that the Sinographs indicating their position are the earliest surviving mention of *rōdō* (men-at-arms) in the historical record. This unusual degree of interest could reflect their involvement with the storage and distribution of provincial goods in the capital region, as memorably detailed in the eleventh-century *Shin sarugaku ki* (Record of New Monkey Music). By singling out the new governor's generosity toward these retainers, in other words, the diarist might be suggesting that his gifts are a down payment for their future assistance in facilitating the transfer of provincial wealth to his personal holdings.

It is in this fraught setting that the first poems in the diary appear. Like similar scenes in *monogatari* depicting the recitation of *shi* and *waka* at such gatherings, only a few of the latter are transcribed. In this case, the pair selected by *Tosa nikki*'s narrator portray an awkward exchange between the new governor and his predecessor that begins with a verbose poem by the former.

miyako idete	Leaving the capital city
kimi ni awamu to	to be with you, milord,
koshi mono o	I came here, and yet
koshi kai mo naku	I came here to no avail
wakarenuru kana	as we now part ways!
(TN 17, 12/26)	

The repetition of *koshi* (I came here) in the host's *waka* matches his excessive gifting with excessive wording. This discursive redundancy likely indicates a sense of guilt on his part over his tardy arrival in Tosa, which has prevented the ex-governor from returning to the capital in time to receive a new position.

By comparison with his host's stumbling efforts, the ex-governor's poem is masterful in its sarcastic manipulation of descriptive detail and semantic ambiguity. Even its use of an "I" (*ware*) to match the earlier poem's "you" (*kimi*) implicitly dismisses the previous *waka* by echoing it in the most minimal manner possible.

shirotae no	White as bleached hemp
nami-ji o tōku	is the waveborne path
yuki-kaite	we cross in the distance.
ware ni nibeki wa	In resemblance to me
tare naranaku ni	who else might there be?
(TN 17, 12/26)	

By employing the archaic epithet *shirotae no* (white as bleached hemp) to describe waves rather than cloth, the ex-governor's *waka* depicts the physical setting in a novel manner. In doing so, however, he also rebukes the equally novel generosity extended to his men-at-arms by drawing on the epithet's traditional association with textiles in order to evoke the bolts of cloth typically gifted to subordinates. Words are put to even more work in the final query, which leaves both the basis for comparison with the new governor and its answer unspecified. Readers have variously treated these last two measures as: (1) an expression of sympathy for his successor who is about to endure the hardships of a distant provincial posting; (2) a prayer that his successor's tenure be without incident; (3) a neutral assertion of their shared circumstances; and (4) gloating anticipation of the future difficulties his successor will encounter (TNZ 85). In keeping with the theory that *Tosa nikki* functions as a *waka* primer, the ex-governor's reply can be viewed as an exemplary instance of poetic banquet etiquette.[14] Even so, it ends up sounding halfway between a blessing and a malediction.

Latent tension also lurks in the words exchanged between host and guest at the banquet's conclusion: "After saying this and that, I am told that both the previous governor and the current one descended to the

---

14. Hasegawa, "*Tosa nikki* no zōtōka," 94–95.

courtyard, whose current master clasped hands with its former one and exchanged niceties in slurred speech before the one set out and the other went inside" (TN 17, 12/26). Beginning with Ōhide, this sentence has often been praised for its intricate parallelisms. Words weave the two men into a chiasm in which the initial mutuality of shared action gives way to their divergent trajectories. Insofar as this shift pivots around slurred niceties exchanged between host and guest that would have included felicitous expressions of well-wishing and good fortune, however, the sentence's formal beauty belies the tensions underlying its content. Like the inebriated conduct at the first banquet, this drunken failure to properly articulate appropriate language thus holds ritually ominous implications.

Further criticism of the new governor is implied the next day when a lavish farewell party given by his maternal brothers leads the diarist to observe, "We couldn't help but whisper among ourselves that, out of all the people from the governor's mansion, it is those who had come here to put in a brief appearance who seem to truly have a heart" (TN 18, 12/27). Even as she cites the conduct of these new hosts to criticize the motives of their predecessor, the diarist implicitly casts doubt on their intentions by stating that they *seem* to be solicitous. Her skepticism is confirmed the next day when she briefly notes that provincial notables descended from earlier governors have traveled even farther to make their final farewells. In addition to indicating that the new governor's brothers have gone to less trouble, these new visitors offer a pointed reminder that the former well-wishers will follow in the footsteps of their predecessors by using their positions as members of the new governor's staff to forge marriage alliances with local gentry.

As well as being the last farewell banquet with provincial notables recounted at any length in the diary, the one held on 12/27 is framed by the debut of two central characters—a dead girl and the ship's steersman—who respectively represent a concern for sentiments and food that exceed the feast's ritual requirements. Whereas grief over the girl is subordinated to this occasion's social demands, the steersman subordinates others' sentiments to his wishes when he abruptly ends the proceedings: "While all this was being said, the steersman had been guzzling down saké, oblivious to the poignancy of the moment. Suddenly desiring a speedy departure, he bellowed, 'The tide is already in. The wind will soon blow.' So we proceeded to get back on board" (TN 19, 12/27). Like *rōdō*, the phrase *mono no aware* (poignancy of the moment) used here to describe poetic expressions of pathos at parting makes its first documented appearance in *Tosa nikki*.[15] Here, the same delicate sensibility later linked to *Genji* is entirely lacking in the steersman, whose mouth is occupied with guzzling liquor rather than reciting poems.[16] The volume of alcohol entering his mouth is matched by the volume of the commands issuing from it in speech that parodically replicates poetic parallelisms. This inverse relationship between poetry and consumption subsequently intensifies in the new year, along with the linguistic failures and fraught social conditions introduced in the parting banquets.

Frugal Rites

Aside from *wakame* seaweed and the young herbs (*wakana*) consumed on the seventh day of the new year, *waka* poetry barely refers to food.[17] It was only slightly less infrequently mentioned in Heian vernacular prose, perhaps due, as Takeshi Watanabe suggests, both to its generally unappetizing nature at the time and to Buddhist prohibitions against its pleasures.[18] This scarcity makes the frequency and detail with which it is described in a text as frugal with words as *Tosa nikki* all the more remarkable. Alimentary matters play a central role in delineating *Tosa nikki* as a whole: whereas the initial parting banquets describe food generically as simply "things" (*mono*) or "fine things" (*yoki mono*), mention of particular foodstuffs proliferate with the advent of the new year and its rituals of consumption.

This level of detail can in part be attributed to the author's prior experience overseeing the sovereign's meals as a palace kitchen chef (*naizenshi no tenzen*), and then subsequently as head of the Inner Palace Secretariat whose *naiki no nikki* were still recording royal consumption

---

15. Yamamoto, *Chiisa na shōzōga*, 105.
16. This uncouth behavior is further accentuated by using a vulgar verb to describe his consumption (Endō, "Tsurayuki no 'buntai to hyōgen ishiki,'" 107).
17. Shirane, "Shiika, shokubunka, sakana," 30.
18. Watanabe, "Gifting Melons to the Shining Prince."

before *tenjō nikki* usurped this function.[19] Both posts reflected the important role played by the sovereign's ritualized ingestion of the realm in establishing his claims to its bounty, a practice that was inaugurated at his enthronement and subsequently enacted through the use of specific ingredients from particular provinces in his daily meals.[20] By repeatedly referring to the absence of appropriate new year's fare, *Tosa nikki*'s discursive economy parodically inverts the correspondence between words and things such rites of royal consumption were intended to affirm.

This litany of lack begins with the *tōso* tonic customarily imbibed on New Year's Day to ensure good health in the coming year. Both the number of different substances involved and the precision with which they were blended represent a significant accumulation of specialized materials and skilled labor whose value is further compounded when the diarist tells us that the provincial head doctor (*kusushi*) has gone out of his way to bring it over to the party, along with another medicinal compound and saké to dissolve both in. That the third most important provincial official after the governor and lector would take time from his duties to personally provide the tonic even leads the diarist to grudgingly note that "it's as though he holds good will towards us" (TN 20, 12/29).

The tale of its journey thus adds to the tonic's generic value in a manner reminiscent of the attention paid by *Utsuho monogatari* and other fictional narratives to the routes by which musical instruments and other aristocratic heirlooms changed owners. In a bitterly ironic twist, however, the same portability that enables this accumulation of value also causes the tonic to be blown overboard, in the process revealing a host of other miscalculations.

> Because the person who was in charge of the *Medicines* apparently propped them up against the cabin overnight, they blew out to sea when a howling wind whipped up, so we ended up not taking them. We are even without dried taro stems or rough-skinned kelp, nothing of that sort for the day's teeth-firming rite. Our present land lacks all such things. No one even thought to find them ahead of time. We simply sucked on the mouths of dried sweetfish pressed flat to our lips. (TN 20, 1/1)

19. Kitayama, "*Tosa nikki* no shōgatsu gyōji," 12.
20. Heldt, *The Pursuit of Harmony*, 143–44.

Poor planning is evident in the failure to stow the tonic safely inside the cabin (or under the prow with the other luggage) and to stock appropriate foodstuffs for the annual rite of "teeth-firming" (*hagatame*) held on the third day of the new year. The party lacks not only the sort of fibrous vegetables and sinewy meat—such as daikon, gourds, venison, and boar—that were usually intended for this purpose, but even such barely acceptable substitutes as dried taro stems or the sort of rough-skinned kelp making up the lowest grade of edible seaweed.[21] The only other option available to the travelers, cured sweetfish, were so abundant in Tosa that they supplied the palace kitchen. As a result, the travelers find themselves in a situation in which the "land" (*kuni*) that provided the court with provincial bounty has shrunk to a poorly provisioned vessel.

Scant supplies also constrain the travelers' ability to meet other ritual obligations. As they struggle to respond to an offering of food with something of equivalent value three days later, even the implicit principle of reciprocity governing gift-giving is explicitly called into question.

> Masatsura offered up saké and various delicacies to the former governor. We could hardly stand by and do nothing in response to such generosity, and so we returned the kindness with some trifle. We have nothing of worth for that purpose. Everything seemed fine on the surface, but it feels somehow as though we have lost face. (TN 21, 1/4)

Masatsura is the only provincial figure in *Tosa nikki* identified solely by his personal name, an intimate form of address suggesting this low-ranking man had previously served on the ex-governor's staff. The man's humble status is further underscored by the humilific language used to describe his offering, which serves to ironically draw attention to his betters' inability to fulfill their own social obligations toward him.

Even token gestures of reciprocity disappear on 1/7, when two provincial figures provide food to the travelers as they lament their absence from the annual Presentation of White Steeds (*aomuma no sechie*) taking place at court that day in conjunction with the conferral of promotions. The first of these figures is a local woman who supplies the seven greens traditionally used to make a broth that was imbibed on the seventh day

---

21. Satō and Ikezoe, "Heianchō no shokubunka kō," 39.

of the new year.[22] In addition to providing the customary poem mentioning these "young herbs" (*wakana*), she responds to the travelers' underlying hunger with a generosity inspiring an equally lavish sentence: "During this time, one long chest after another was sent from the home of a person living in a place named 'Pond' which, though lacking in handsome ornamental carp, include the crucian variety, as well as all manner of other things from rivers and sea" (TN 22, 1/7). The presentation of these provisions in long chests (*nagabitsu*), typically reserved for large amounts of prepared food at banquets, highlights their quality as well as their quantity.[23] Even the absent ornamental carp at the beginning of this sentence are put to use as metaphors for men who complement the women represented by their crucian counterparts.[24] The diarist proceeds to further unpack this piscatory figure by informing us that their benefactor is now stranded in the provinces after the man whom she originally accompanied from the capital had died. This detail casts her as a familiar figure from *monogatari*, as does her doubly unique standing in the diary as its only named female character and the only local who writes *waka* for the travelers.

The widow's gifts and actions are further defined later that same day through their contrast with those of a boorish male.[25] Instead of the luxurious chests she sent her food in, he brings his in plain cypress-wood boxes (*warigo*). Whereas the diarist lavishes words on both the widow and her gifts, she now makes no mention of particular foodstuffs and, in a marked departure from her usual practice of identifying donors, claims to have forgotten his name. Whereas the widow avoided imposing herself on the party by sending a written poem, moreover, the boor forces himself and his *waka* on them in a mendacious show of spontaneity: "At any rate, his heart seems to have been set on reciting a verse. After speaking about this and that, he sorrowfully declared 'How the waves rise!'" (TN 22, 1/7). By taking advantage of a pause in the conversation to insert a comment that allows him to recite a *waka* he had prepared in

---

22. Satō and Ikezoe, "Heianchō no shokubunka kō," 41. Both the color green and the number seven were associated with *yang* energy.
23. *Engi shiki* section 39, KST 26:868.
24. On these gendered metaphors, see Palmer, "A Poem to Carp About?," 429–30.
25. The boor's gender is implied through its contrast with that of the widow.

advance, the boor's actions also parody orthodox accounts of poetic genesis as a spontaneous emotional response to one's surroundings.

Despite plotting his poem in advance, the boor's efforts manage to sound both ominous and egotistical.[26] His *waka* is implicitly condemned by the silence that greets it, as the travelers studiously occupy their mouths with the food he has provided in order to avoid employing them in reciprocating poetically:

> How could we compare this verse with the things he brought? Everyone made a show of being moved, but not a single person offered a verse in reply. Even though there are some among us who are certainly capable of doing so, we did nothing but praise his poem and go on eating until night fell. Finally, the poem's owner said: "Another time, then" and got up to leave. (TN 23, 1/7)

Their decision to choose consumption over composition makes the travelers guilty of the same behavior for which the steersman had been criticized on 12/27. Unlike him, however, they at least pretend to be moved by the boor's poem in an exaggerated display that mockingly imitates his feigned show of spontaneity. When the awkward silence draws on so long that it becomes uncomfortable even for him, the boor compounds his poetic errors by excusing himself in language that confuses different formal expressions. Scholars have long noted that his final sentence can be taken to mean either that he will not return or the opposite (TNZ 139–42). Taking advantage of this ambiguity, the travelers choose to believe they still have time to make a reply after he has left.

Ogawa Kōzō has pointed out that this encounter violates rules of decorum laid out in the *Liji* (Book of Rites, ca. early first century BCE), a Confucian classic familiar to Tsurayuki's readership. The boor's abrupt announcement of his poem contravenes its admonition that speaking first without waiting for others is impolite. Its stipulation that children not speak unless spoken to is similarly ignored by the child who subsequently announces they have composed a reply to the boor's *waka*.[27] For all its

---

26. Both his poem and that of the widow are addressed at greater length in chapter 4.
27. Ogawa, "*Tosa nikki* no bunshō zōkei," 100–103. For the passages in question, see *Liji*, SKT 27:55 and 18.

potential social didacticism, however, the correlation this entry establishes between words and food gives the impression that the different treatment accorded to the widow and boor by the diarist is ultimately informed by their relative generosity.

In general, the *Liji* tends to stress the danger of rituals failing due either to individual incompetence or to external circumstances.[28] Although the boor is clearly an example of the former, the same can also be said of the poor planning that causes the travelers' own ritual failures. Rather than reflecting a commendable sense of probity, as Mitsue and others have argued, the deprivations his charges suffer in fact expose the administrative incompetence of an ex-governor who fails to properly provision them. This failure to plan ahead concludes on 1/15 with a return to the sardonic humor and etymological play typifying the first banquet. Food is again described by its absence when we are told that "there was no azuki bean porridge simmering today, to our mouths' bitter regret" (TN 30, 1/15).[29] As with the first day of banqueting, the absence of ritual norms is marked through puns in prose: embedded within the "bitter regret" (*kuchi-oshi*) felt by the party are the empty "mouths" (*kuchi*) that cause it. This return to wordplay also suggests that the previously pervasive anxiety over a lack of provisions has now receded. In the process, as we will see next, optional rituals of consumption replace necessary ones, and food changes from being an object that is gifted to one that functions as a medium of exchange.

Food Worth Taking

Overall, *Tosa nikki*'s stance toward wealth is informed by the realities of its time. Despite moralistic accusations of their cupidity, the court actively encouraged governors to personally accumulate largesse as a way of

---

28. Ing, *The Dysfunction of Ritual*, 9.
29. The ritual consumption of this porridge to ward off evil influences in a rite known as the "lesser New Year's Day" (*koshōgatsu*) was a fairly recent practice established under Uda (Satō and Ikezoe, "Heianchō no shokubunka kō," 43).

funding its activities.³⁰ In addition to covering such provincial expenses as staff salaries, governors were expected to support their household dependents and supply gifts to the powerful families upon whose goodwill future postings depended. Given the very real prospect that a new promotion might not arrive, the need to get through lean times would have been another concern. The communal consequences entailed by a middle-ranking courtier's failure to gain employment are vividly illustrated in *The Pillow Book*'s list of "Disenchanting Things" (*Susamajiki mono*) when a man's dependents are disappointed to learn he has not received a new appointment, forcing them to refer to him as "a former provincial official" (*nani no zenji*) before their peers.³¹ Similar references to his former position made by the diarist underscore the uncertain situation which the ex-governor and his household face back in the capital.

Confirmation of the need to bring back as much wealth as possible can be seen on 1/12, when the diarist notes several stragglers who have caught up with her ship. The mention of two names suggests two vessels, while their comparatively slow advance suggests they are weighed down with goods and supplies. Like the diarist's previous disavowal of concern over the relative quality of gifts, this single sentence inflects the subsequent narrative to an inordinate degree. Her next reference to food on the following day indulges in the luxury of metaphorical play by referring to women's genitalia as shellfish. Although the specter of starvation disappears with the arrival of these ships, new challenges arise in the form of rapacious transactions in which food changes from a source of sustenance into a medium of exchange.

This new economy is first described on two separate days in which fish are purchased with rice during a vegetarian fast (*sechimi*). By noting in both cases that similar transactions occurred at other times, the diarist makes a notable departure from her usual practice of limiting the contents of her entries to the events of a single day, thereby further suggesting just how significant these transactions are. In itself, the decision to observe such fasts is informed by optional desires rather than ritual necessities. Although Buddhist practitioners were enjoined to abstain from meat and

---

30. Steininger, *Chinese Literary Forms in Heian Japan*, 38–39.
31. *Makura no sōshi* section 23, SNKBZ 18:60–61; see also McKinney, *The Pillow Book*, 24–25.

fish five times a month, observance of this rule was so casual that it heads Sei Shōnagon's list of "Things One Can Neglect" (*Tayamaru mono*).[32] The ex-governor exhibits a similarly lax attitude when his desultory attempt at fasting ends soon after it begins.

> The lord on board observed a vegetarian fast. Since we lack appropriate food, his lordship desisted in the afternoon after bestowing rice and saké on the steersman, since we have no coins, in exchange for some sea bream caught yesterday. This sort of thing happens more than once. The steersman brings over more sea breams. We give out rice and saké other times. The steersman does not seem displeased with this arrangement. (TN 29–30, 1/14)

Despite calling him "the lord on board" for the first time, the diarist deploys honorific language ironically to criticize the ex-governor's actions. We are told that he "desisted" (*ochirarenu*) from his fast at noon because there is no suitable vegetarian fare (thus further implying he is unwilling to actually forgo food for any significant period of time). His purchase of the fish is described in equally sardonic terms as "bestowing" (*torikake*) payment, using a word typically indicating an award being conferred upon a subordinate, even though it is the steersman who dictates the terms of exchange by demanding payment in rice and saké. The latter's satisfied expression, expertly mimicked in the diarist's coyly understated remark that he "does not seem displeased" (*keshiki ashikarazu*), makes it clear he believes he has the upper hand in the situation.

Both the steersman's untrustworthiness as a trading partner and the ex-governor's inability to negotiate effectively are implied by their exclusion from the next such transaction on 2/8. Instead, it is the buyers who now believe they have profited from the exchange.

> We were still struggling upstream at a sickly pace when we stopped in the vicinity of a place supporting cormorant fishermen that is called "Royal Birdkeepers' Pasturage." Tonight the lord on board has been suffering greatly from a recurrence of his chronic ailment. Someone brought over a fresh catch. We exchanged rice for it. The men seemed to be muttering under their breath. I think I heard someone say: "That's what you'd call,

---

32. *Makura no sōshi* section 24, SNKBZ 18:63; see also McKinney, *The Pillow Book*, 26.

'hooking a big globefish with a few grains of parched rice,' I suppose." The same thing happened in other places. We were observing a vegetarian fast today, rendering the fish *Of No Use*. (TN 49–50, 2/8)

The analogy with fishing employed to describe this piscatory purchase is probably a precursor to the modern aphorism "catching bream with shrimp" (*ebi de tai o tsuru*), used to refer to something gained at little cost (TNZ 354–55). As Yuzuru first noted, this expression also references the history of the locale, something *Tosa nikki* subtly stresses by making it the first place name to appear in two days. The same cormorant fishermen after whom Torikai no Mimaki (Royal Birdkeepers' Pasturage) was named are doubtless the ones selling the fish.[33] The parched rice mentioned by the men also references this locale by echoing the name of a landholder there, one Ihibo, who is described in *Nihon shoki* as having lived during the reign of Ankan (466–536, r. 531–535). In gratitude to Ihibo for having willingly donated land, Ankan grants him the punitive payments levied on another local proprietor who sought to avoid taxation by lying about the quality of his holdings.[34] In other words, the story represents one person's loss as another's gain, thereby transforming *torikai* into an etymological pun on "birdkeepers" as something "worth taking."

In noting that a vegetarian fast has rendered the fish useless, the diarist appears to implicitly question how this exchange can be considered a bargain, all the more so because there is no compelling reason to abstain from food. An answer is suggested the next day after the travelers have "practiced almsgiving when begged for such things as rice and fish" (TN 50, 2/9). The protruding sandbar at a shallow crossing where the food is donated would have been an ideal site for begging monks to accost a slow-moving vessel, making it likely that the party has saved the fish purchased on the previous day with this eventuality in mind.[35] The calculus at work in this passage is further elucidated when we turn to anecdotes

---

33. Income from this pasturage was intended to support the cormorant fishermen (*Engi shiki* section 48, KST 26:975).
34. *Nihon shoki* entry for Ankan 1/*12/4, SNKBZ 3:338–41; see also Aston, *Nihongi* (2), 29–30.
35. For a detailed account of this setting and its shifting geography, see Uchida, "*Tosa nikki* 'Wada no tomari no akare no tokoro.'"

from *Nihon ryōiki* (Record of Miraculous Events in Japan, ca. 822), whose vivid illustrations of karmic consequences continued to circulate centuries later in *Konjaku* and other *setsuwa* collections. Four of its stories (1:15, 1:29, 3:15, and 3:33) detail the retribution visited on laypeople for violently rejecting begging monks. The incantation (*jubaku*) cast in self-defense by the mendicant in story 1:15 additionally reveals the potential threat such curses could pose to less egregiously aggressive refusals of charity.[36]

Other anecdotes from the same text illustrate the karmic costs of catching or consuming fish, while also encouraging its acquisition for religious purposes. A novice ascetic's purchase of mullets from a fisherman at the request of his ailing master in story 3:6 is justified by the merit the latter has accrued through years of austerity. Despite being informed of the good karma that arises from releasing living beings, the fisherman in story 2:16 is only persuaded to give up ten live oysters when he is paid two and a half bushels of rice by the servant of a wealthy man. This purchase subsequently benefits his master when the oysters, now in the guise of ten men, warn him that he will suffer the fate of a hungry ghost unless he devotes himself to charity. The fisherman protagonist in story 1:11, on the other hand, must repent for taking life with donations after an ascetic's incantations deliver him from punishment for engaging in a profession that takes lives.

These didactic anecdotes suggest the transaction at Torikai no Mimaki ultimately benefits the purchaser because its financial cost is more than compensated for when the karmic cost incurred by the seller in acquiring them becomes merit accrued through almsgiving, or at least a means to avoid retribution for refusing such charity. By analogy with the property Ihibo gains in *Nihon shoki* at the expense of his peer, in other words, the karmic merit accrued by the purchaser of fish implies an equivalent loss on the seller's part. Profit arises when the latent value of food that cannot be ingested by its possessor, either because it is currency (as rice) or taboo (as fish), is realized by converting it into something that others can use. Even the pun on "birdkeepers" and "worth taking" that *tori-kai* signifies in this passage economically conveys the unequal terms of exchange that transform local labor into the karmic profit of mobile trading

---

36. *Nihon ryōiki* story 1:15, SNKBZ 10:66–67; see also Nakamura, *Miraculous Stories*, 126–27. The anecdote is retold in *Konjaku* story 10:25.

partners. Consequently, this anecdote points to what Fabio Rambelli has characterized as a uniquely Buddhist perspective on materiality in which "relations between an object and its users, producers and actual processes involved tend to be emphasized, displayed, and sacralized."[37] Rather than simply celebrate material processes, however, *Tosa nikki* highlights the uneven transactional relationships that subtend them in a wry comment on the connections between religious and material economies.

Transactions also occupy the final days of the journey in two banquets where the implicit principle of reciprocation that was deferable in the parting feasts is now explicit and mandatory. This difference is partially conveyed through the different settings in which these exchanges occur. Whereas the sea's depths were likened to the profound solicitude of banquet hosts for their guests, the Yodo-gawa's shallowness resembles the superficial hospitality its local residents display toward "guests" they view as customers. Both scene and sentiment thus impede further progress: the surroundings require towing the vessel upstream at a crawling pace, while the desires of others lead to a delay of several days at Yamazaki. An oblique reference to "there being some matters to settle" (*tokaku sadamuru koto ari*) (TN 52, 2/11) on the first day spent at that port suggests this delay results from protracted negotiations with the steersman and local residents over the transportation costs entailed respectively by the voyage and the final overland journey to the capital by carriage.

An awkward end to their negotiations with the steersman probably accounts for the difficulties on board that lead the travelers to disembark on the penultimate day. In an ironic twist, however, this move incurs additional costs when greedy locals offer room and board in the guise of hospitality. The diarist's negative reaction to their seeming solicitude is conveyed as much through the scene's resonance with earlier exchanges as through overt commentary: "The people in this house seemed pleased to be acting as hosts. Seeing these hosts being such fine hosts felt overwhelming. We returned the kindness in various ways. The people in this house were leaving and entering without giving offense. All was as it should have been" (TN 53, 2/15). The description of this hospitality as "overwhelming" (*utate*) combines all three uses of the word to denote something unexpected, unpleasant, or excessive. The last of these three

---

37. Rambelli, "Buddhist Sacred Commodities," 273.

meanings is also sarcastically mimicked by using *aruji* three times to mark the action of hosting as a verb, then the hosts as a noun subject, and finally the quality of their hospitality as an adjective. Other parallels with preceding entries further flesh out this picture. Like the new governor's banquet at which his role as host was repeatedly stressed, repetitive wording implies excessive behavior. Like the steersman's triumphant expression after selling his fish, the pleased countenances of these hosts suggest they too are benefiting from the situation. Like her prior praise of Yasunori, superfluous speech ultimately exposes the diarist's own materialism once again when her repeated observation of their hosts' immaculate conduct in the last two sentences suggests she is searching for faults that could justify being less generous in return.

One last banquet on the final day reveals the increasing strain of responding to such hospitality: "On our way to *The Capital*, a person hosted us at Shimasaka. This was a most unexpected deed on their part. People have been doing much more for us on our return than they ever did when we departed. Here yet again we returned the kindness" (TN 54, 2/16). This banquet's superfluity—conveyed by the diarist's exasperated description of the need to reciprocate with gifts "here yet again" (*kore ni mo*)—is made worse for being twofold: in addition to the lack of solicitude their hosts displayed when they had departed for Tosa, the banquet takes place just outside the capital. This final delay probably reflects the necessity of waiting until sundown before entering the city, as appears to have been customary practice among ex-governors.[38] Doubtless this timing was intended to conceal one's wealth in order to avoid appearing either greedy (due to it being excessive) or ineffectual (due to it being scant). In either case, a nighttime arrival would avoid having one's possessions gauged by an equally rapacious but vastly more numerous populace than that encountered on the capital's outskirts. The diarist's frustration with this final banquet at Shimasaka thus suggests that, as with the earlier decision to stay in Yamazaki, such cost-saving strategies entailed their own expenses. Like the previous purchases of fish, in other words, the diary's final banquets enfold individual exchanges within an overarching economy.

38. *Sarashina nikki*, SNKBT 24:382; see also Arntzen and Moriyuki, *The Sarashina Diary*, 106–7.

Divining Desires

In addition to inaugurating a transactional economy, the steersman's avarice reveals a materialistic relationship with gods. On the few occasions when travelers invoke supernatural forces, their primary aim is to ward off dangers, such as the prayers for a safe journey uttered on 12/27, or the fingers that are snapped in a vain attempt to scatter the evil influences behind bad weather on 1/27. Religious specialists, on the other hand, are notably absent from *Tosa nikki*, other than the lector who, in another possible parody of Yasunori's biography, offers the travelers entertainment rather than incantations. For her part, the diarist adopts a skeptical view of humans' ability to harness supernatural forces when she notes that "Our *Prayers* appear to have worked" (TN 35, 1/21), or that good weather is "as if we had received the blessings of gods and buddhas" (TN 41, 1/30). This skepticism becomes overt cynicism on two separate occasions when the steersman claims to comprehend supernatural intentions.

A steersman's duties included such ritual practices as divination based on the color of water, winds, or currents, as well as the performance of prayers designed to influence the shape they took.[39] As was the case with other premodern cultures that did not depend on compasses, coastal navigation required constant alert responsiveness to fluid exigencies that inevitably demanded adjustments to even the most familiar route.[40] Such performative aspects of maritime travel are portrayed in a notably cynical light when they are depicted in detail on 1/26.

> Can it be true? Word has it that pirates are pursuing us, and so we set out around the middle of the night, rowing to a place where placatory offerings for safe passage are made. We had the steersman do his thing with the prayer slips, which scattered to the east, after which he entreated thusly: "If it please you o gods, grant this fair ship leave to proceed with all haste in the direction towards which these prayer slips may scatter." Thus did he pray. Hearing his words, a girl child composed this:

---

39. Horton, *Traversing the Frontier*, 149.
40. Mack, *The Sea*, 105–35.

watatsumi no	May the wind chasing prayers
chiburi no kami ni	scattered in offering
tamuke suru	to gods granting safe passage
nusa no oikaze	over the sacred sea
yamazu fukanamu	blow without ceasing!

That's what she recited! During this time we caught a good wind, causing the steersman to swell with pride as he joyfully issued commands to raise the sail and such (TN 37–38, 1/26)

Doubts over the steersman's judgment begin with the opening expression of skepticism over whether rumors of pirates justify his decision to sail at night along a coastline so dangerous it merited a designated place for entreating safe passage from local gods. The prayer slips (*nusa*) of cloth he offers up at that location are akin to the textiles, rice, and coins mentioned elsewhere in the diary in functioning as a medium of exchange, in this case as part of a transaction with local deities.[41] Both their materiality and sacrality are portrayed cynically in this instance. The content of the steersman's incantation—which is the only one *Tosa nikki* quotes in full—suggests he deliberately manipulates the slips' motility to impress his passengers rather than sway the gods. Ultimately, his performance simply confirms the direction in which he knows the wind will take his vessel. If anything, the poetic prayer recited by a little girl beseeching this wind to continue blowing is more efficacious. Like the smug expression he assumes after selling his fish, the steersman's self-satisfied demeanor in this episode suggests he believes that he has duped his passengers once again.

The steersman's actual incompetence is subsequently exposed the day before his second attempt to mediate between a deity and the travelers, when his mistaken reading of the wind and clouds on 2/4 leads the diarist to call him "a blockhead who has no idea how to gauge the weather" (TN 44, 2/4). Fair weather on the following day turns the entry for 2/5 into one of the longest in the diary, as the ship makes a stately progress to various locales where poems are composed. The peaceful atmosphere is abruptly shattered, however, when a storm suddenly rises at

---

41. Unlike the food and metal implements that were also offered up in court rituals, *nusa* had no practical value (Bock, *Engi Shiki*, 1:42 and 2:10).

Sumiyoshi. As dramatic tension builds through rhythmic sentences conveying the growing precarity of the situation, the steersman's words intrude once again.

> The steersman said: "*The Deity* of Sumiyoshi is your typical god. There must be something desirable in your lordship's possession." How very in keeping with the times this is! Then he said: "Please, your lordship, make an offering of prayer slips." Following his words, an offering of prayer slips was made. But though we did this, the gale didn't let up in the slightest. Winds gusted ever stronger and threatening waves towered ever higher, leading the steersman to speak again: "The prayer slips do not seem to have satisfied the god. Your lordship's vessel will not advance. Please, your lordship, offer up something that will bring happiness to the god's heart." Once again we follow his words, thinking there is nothing else we can do. The decision was made to offer up a single mirror, more precious than either eye, much to our bitter regret. (TN 47, 2/5)

The steersman's assumption that any relationship with the Sumiyoshi god would be transactional is subtly amplified by using the Sinographs 明神 (*myōjin*) denoting a divine benefactor. According to *Engi shiki*, the deity's shrine complex included a Funadama Jinja (Ship Soul Shrine), which likely received offerings in exchange for safeguarding trading vessels, a protective function later replicated by wooden objects with the same name that were stowed aboard individual ships.[42] For her part, the diarist tartly observes that the god's attitude is in keeping with the times, suggesting the deity's traditional role in protecting ships is here more akin to the avariciousness of pirates threatening commerce in this period.[43]

Despite the diarist's indignation, long-standing associations with continental trade made this deity a transactional god par excellence. In the *Sumiyoshi taisha jindaiki* (Account of the Divine Origins of the Grand Shrine of Sumiyoshi, ca. eighth–tenth centuries), for example, he nego-

---

42. On the history of medieval *funadama*, see Rambelli, "Sea Theologies," 194–99.
43. Yato, "Heianchō no Sumiyoshi shinkō," 111. A similarly rapacious desire for luxury items is suggested earlier on 1/13 when we are told the passengers have not worn red silk robes to avoid attracting the sea god's attention (Kawanaka, "Waga kuni no kodai bungaku," 119).

tiates with Jingū (169–269, r. 201–269) when she seeks assistance in invading the Korean peninsula.[44] Such associations make it unsurprising that prayer strips now prove of little worth. The much costlier mirror that is subsequently offered up at the steersman's urging was an entirely appropriate choice not only for its value but also because such offerings were commonly believed to calm waters, as can be seen in a similar scene found in the earlier travelogue *Nittō guhō junrai kōki* (Account of a Pilgrimage Overseas in Search of the Holy Law, ca. 838–847). Its accompaniment by a *waka* at Sumiyoshi is equally conventional, albeit notably wry in its description of the mirror's twofold ability to reflect the world's external appearance and the deity's internal motives.[45]

Given this context, the diarist's dismay upon discovering that the deity is more interested in precious objects than poetic epithets, along with the "bitter regret" (*kuchi-oshi*) she feels at having to sacrifice the mirror, ultimately points to her own ignorance and cupidity. Such shortcomings on her part perhaps lead Tsurayuki to attribute her with the tart observation that "The heart of the steersman is in fact the mighty heart of a god" (TN 47–48, 2/5), which is typically read as a criticism of the ship captain for projecting his own materialist mindset onto the Sumiyoshi deity. It might also be a form of wordplay in which *kajitori* is transformed from "steersman" into "removing the letter *ka*" (*ka ji tori*) in order to convert "mirror" (*kagami*) into "god" (*kami*) (TNZ 335).[46] Whether such humor avoids the otherwise baldly blasphemous implications of her statement, the equation between religious praxis and mundane transactions in this passage resembles the similar associations enabled by the pun on *tori-kai*.

Like the other instances in which the steersman's cupidity is portrayed, this last and longest depiction of him on 2/5 could have been informed by the extensive dealings Tsurayuki would have had with such individuals in Tosa.[47] The diary's aristocratic readership, on the other

---

44. Simpson, "An Empress at Sea," 66–69.
45. "Fierce and mighty / the god whose heart / we glimpse / upon casting a mirror / into the rough sea!" (*chihayaburu / kami no kokoro o / aruru umi ni / kagami o irete / katsu mitsuru kana*) (TN 47, 2/5).
46. In fact, different *kana* are used to write *ji* in these words.
47. Takano, "*Tosa nikki* ni okeru kajitori no zōkei," 32.

hand, were more likely to have been familiar with such men through *monogatari*. Perhaps not coincidentally, the depiction of the steersman's actions at Sumiyoshi are strikingly reminiscent of a similar scene in *Taketori monogatari* depicting the suitor Ōtomo no Miyuki seeking guidance from his own steersman when a storm arises at sea during his quest to obtain a jewel from the neck of a dragon.[48] Like the ship in *Tosa nikki*, the one in *Taketori* is a heterotopic space inverting normal power relations: despite coming from the martial Ōtomo clan, the suitor loses heart when he see the steersman do the same. Like the travelers in *Tosa nikki*, moreover, he follows the advice of his social inferior without question when he is enjoined to pray for aid. Unlike his counterpart in the diary, however, the steersman in *Taketori* does not attribute materialistic motives to supernatural forces. He is immediately able to identify the dragon's wrath as the cause of the storm and thus does not need to engage in the process of trial and error that eventually leads his counterpart in *Tosa nikki* to divine the Sumiyoshi god's desires. Such contrasts suggest the diary is responding to the tale with a more jaundiced view of human exchanges with supernatural powers.

Scholarship on *Tosa nikki* has yet to comment on its similarities with the earliest *monogatari*, despite *Genji*'s mention of a copy made by Tsurayuki, and despite the two texts' shared interest in commoners' speech, economic exchange, and puns. Both also share a proclivity for turning history into fictional parody. Like the fictional character of Yasunori in the diary, *Taketori*'s five suitors are named after historical figures. The conclusions to these suitors' failed quests also parody history by replacing eighth-century onomastic myths explaining the origin of place names with fictive etymologies for proverbial expressions.[49] These etymologies can be considered both parodic and satirical, insofar as they replace the mighty actions of gods that are celebrated in myth with aristocratic failings that are censured by commoners.

As it happens, another link with *Tosa nikki* is indicated by the etymology associating food with frustration concluding Ōtomo no Miyuki's tale: "People spoke amongst themselves. 'Did his lordship the Ōtomo

---

48. *Taketori monogatari*, SNKBZ 12:46–47; see also Keene, "The Tale of the Bamboo Cutter," 289–90.
49. Okada, *Figures of Resistance*, 54–82.

Grand Counselor get the jewel from a dragon's neck?' 'No, that didn't happen. The only orbs his lordship got were the plum-shaped ones on both his eyes.' Whereupon someone said, 'that must be hard to swallow,' and thus ever since we speak of something foolish as being 'hard to endure.'"[50] The orthographic similitude between eating (たべ) and enduring (たへ) that turns this pseudo-etymology into a proverbial expression for foolish behavior being something "hard to swallow" recalls the diarist's punning use of *kuchi-oshi* (bitter regret) to link consumption with negative emotion when she described the ship's lack of provisions and the sacrifice of a mirror at Sumiyoshi. But there is an additional aspect to the social critique contained in *Taketori*'s pun that also obtains in *Tosa nikki*'s depiction of supernatural forces. It is both foolish to think eyes can be "eaten" as plums, and difficult for the steersman to silently "endure" the suitor's foolhardy attempt to challenge a dragon. As we will see next, equally careless dealings with the dead occasion similar frustrations in the diary.

Spectral Exchanges

At first glance, *Tosa nikki*'s cynical treatment of material things (*mono*) appears diametrically opposed to the earnest emotions occasioned by the dead girl representing their spectral counterpart. As we saw in chapter 1, readers seeking authorial intent have often viewed the supposed authenticity of the grief over her loss as the diary's animating heart. Even Hagitani, who generally treats *Tosa nikki* as a dramatic piece of fiction, and who relegates the dead girl to its third-most important topic, believes she was an actual daughter of Tsurayuki, going so far as to speculate that she died from food poisoning the previous autumn despite the provincial head doctor's ministrations (TNZ 110–11). Others believe Tsurayuki wrote the diary to placate her ghost and comfort her mother.[51] Even readings that treat the girl as a purely fictional construct

---

50. *Taketori monogatari*, SNKBZ 12:49–50.
51. Murase, *Kyūtei kajin Ki no Tsurayuki*, 220.

regard her as an expression of the author's personal grief over losing his chief patrons while he was in Tosa.

Whatever their origin, the feelings of grief and longing she occasions are also tinged with terror of a sort that must have resonated with *Tosa nikki*'s intended readership. Events back in the capital during and after Tsurayuki's tenure in Tosa would have made Tadahira and his family keenly aware of the havoc unhappy ghosts could visit on the living. After Michizane's death in exile, his specter was blamed for a series of disasters over this period of time—including Daigo's demise in 930, a drought that same year, and the rebellion of Taira no Masakado (d. 940) in 939. Similar resentments shape the diary's narrative by making the girl responsible for the bad weather that ends up doubling the normal amount of time taken to journey from Tosa to the capital.[52] Her frustrations are also implicitly linked with those of the party by embedding all six mentions of her within entries that explore homesickness or the hardships of travel.[53] As we will see, these other emotions tempering grief over her loss are as unevenly distributed within the diary as the desires driving its circulation of material goods.

Arguments for the emotional authenticity Tsurayuki supposedly brings to his depiction of this girl often point to the powerful and complex depictions of psychological conflict in the poems describing her. All of these *waka* use direct language that prioritizes sentiment over imagery and repetition over figuration.[54] They also create complex cross-currents of space, time, and emotion that eddy around the girl, conveying conflicting impulses to forget and memorialize her, as well as temporal contrasts between her present absence and past presence.[55] Many convey "longing" (*koi*), a form of desire that originates in a charismatic external force that the speaker is subjected to. Longings for her also generate powerful desires whose appropriateness is questioned by third parties representing the ship as a whole.[56] Such critical comments make it possible to

---

52. Yamaguchi, "*Tosa nikki* no bungei kōzō," 151.
53. Kimura, "*Tosa nikki* no shudai," 99.
54. Ōsugi, "*Tosa nikki* ni okeru eikai" 14–15.
55. Suzuki H., "*Tosa nikki*," 29.
56. Satō, *Heian waka bungaku hyōgen ron*, 90–97.

view the diary's treatment of the girl in terms that are as satirical as they are lyrical.

Many of the above-mentioned characteristics can be seen in the first two *waka* about her, which appear without warning early on 12/27. The abrupt manner in which she is introduced mirrors the sudden shock of separation brought on by the moment of embarkation, as the travelers finally leave behind the site of their last living memories of her. The intensity of this grief and longing is not evenly distributed among the members of the party, however, requiring both a written poem conveying their collective complexity and another describing the feelings of those closest to her.

> There was a girl born in *The Capital* who had suddenly died in this province. Not a single word was spoken about her amid the bustle of our hasty preparations for departure. Now that we are on our way back to *The Capital*, her loss leaves only grief and longing. It is beyond what some people can endure. During this time someone wrote out this poem:
>
> | | |
> |---|---|
> | *miyako e to* | Towards the capital city |
> | *omou o mono no* | thoughts turn while |
> | *kanashiki wa* | haunted by this grief |
> | *kaeranu hito no* | for one not returning |
> | *areba narikeri* | with us here and now! |
>
> And then at another time there was this:
>
> | | |
> |---|---|
> | *aru mono to* | We think her with us |
> | *wasuretsutsu nao* | as we carry on forgetting |
> | *naki hito o* | that person is no more, |
> | *izura to tou zo* | until asking where she is |
> | *kanashikarikeru* | brings on this fresh grief! |
>
> (TN 18, 12/27)

As it moves from a shared longing for home to the grief of a smaller group leaving her behind, the first poem expertly conveys the entire spectrum of emotions and temporalities experienced by the travelers over the course of a voyage that enfolds them within an ever-changing present suspended between their past departure and future destination. This skillful interweaving of different places, times, and emotions is doubtless one reason why, as we saw in chapter 1, the *waka* subsequently attracted notice in

Wakatai jisshu and later *setsuwa*. By contrast, the second poem has garnered more praise in modern times on account of its compelling portrayal of internal psychological conflict engendered by the struggle to fully acknowledge a loved one's death. Tsurayuki's contemporaries would have been more likely to appreciate the links with past elegies created by its use of *izura* (where).[57] Ultimately, both *waka* play an important role in the narrative by establishing a relationship between the desire to look toward the past and to the future, both of which increasingly come into conflict over the course of the journey.

The travelers' differing emotional investments in the girl acquire a ritual dimension when she next appears on 1/11 in a moment of collective remembrance spurred on by another child's poem at a place named Hane (Wings). Divisions within the party come to fore when her mother's grief gives rise to dangers that cause someone else to intone a propitiatory *waka*.

> The child's query about the place named "Wings" brings back memories of the one who once was. Is she ever forgotten? Still, these words bring fresh grief to the mourning mother as she observes the rites required of her on this particular day. Being short one person from the number that originally came out to the provinces, those words from the old song that go *a smaller number now appear homeward bound* came to mind, inspiring someone to compose this:
>
> | *yo no naka ni* | In our thoughts we may imagine |
> | *omoi yaredomo* | all the relationships in this world, |
> | *ko o kouru* | but there are no thoughts |
> | *omoi ni masaru* | that surpass the thoughts |
> | *omoi naki kana* | of one longing for a child! |
>
> That's what they uttered over and over again. (TN 28, 1/11)

The mother's act of grieving is cast in honorific language that suggests the day is a special anniversary (*imibi*) requiring mourning rites and abstentions to ward off spiritual pollution. The unspoken need for her parents to conclude these observances after returning home lends an additional sense of urgency to the travelers' desires for a swift voyage. Because

---

57. Fukuda, "*Tosa nikki* kanken," 1–3. One of the earliest two elegies using this word was composed by Ōtomo no Tabito (665–731) on another voyage back to the capital (*Man'yōshū* poem 3:448, SNKBZ 6:248).

the reclusion observed by mourners in texts such as *Genji* is physically impossible within the cramped confines of a ship, however, everyone on board is exposed to the pollution such rituals sought to contain and the physical threat posed by the girl's restless ghost. This shared vulnerability entails a collective interest in calming her spirit, leading to the incantatory repetitions of the ensuing *waka*, whose threefold invocation of *omoi* (thoughts) are further augmented by repeated recitations designed to reassure the ghost that her mother continues to keep her in mind.

Communal concerns over the mother's grief come to a head during the last two days at sea when she frantically seeks respite from her longings in *waka* that invoke the powers of oblivion promised by poetic flora and fauna on 2/4 and 2/5.[58] Although the reference to *wasure-gai* (forgetting-shells) in her first poem invokes a common belief that longings could be alleviated by grasping the discarded half of a bivalve, the context in which she voices this communally sanctioned belief clashes with the collective desire of her fellow passengers to avoid angering the ghost. This conflict between convention and context deepens when the appropriateness of an alternate trope proposed by a fellow passenger is subsequently questioned by the diarist.

The shore by our anchorage is filled with all sorts of lovely shells and pebbles. And so someone on board who has been doing nothing but longing for the one who once was composed this:

yosuru nami	Approaching waves,
uchi mo yosenamu	may we approach still closer!
waga kouru	In my longing for
hito wasure-gai	that one forgetting-shells
orite hirowamu	would I disembark to gather.

These words led someone who was unable to endure the situation any longer to compose this in order to put the hearts of everyone on board at ease:

wasure-gai	Forgetting-shells
hiroi shimo seji	will we never gather,
shira-tama o	but the gleaming pearl alone

58. Although the speaker is only identified as a parent in this case, the consistent marking of the mother as a poet elsewhere makes it plausible to assume she is the one being referred to.

>   *kouru o dani mo*   will we long for rather
>   *katami to omowamu*   as a keepsake in our thoughts!
>
> That's what they said! The girl has caused the parent to become childish. Some might have reason to claim she was no such poetic pearl in real life. Then again, you often seem to hear people say they remember the features of a dead child being fair. (TN 44, 2/4)

Fear of her restless spirit leads the second poet to praise the girl's memory by replacing her mother's forgetting-shells with something more valuable. The gleaming pearls she is now likened to were an orthodox epithet for deceased children, including the son who the famed poet Yamanoue no Okura (ca. 660–733) laments in a lengthy *Man'yōshū* elegy.[59] The purely conventional nature of this imagery, however, leads the diarist to question whether it accords with the girl's actual appearance. Her concluding observation that "you often seem to hear people say they remember the features of a dead child being fair" sardonically implies the girl was no more attractive than any other child, thereby further suggesting such praise is purely motivated by fear over offending her ghost.

Despite the perils her behavior poses for everyone on the ship, the mother's drive to forget her longing is so strong that she continues in the same vein the next day. This time, however, the powerful nature of this compulsion leads the diarist to rationalize her behavior.

> Now the mother of that past person, who has not once forgotten her for a single day, composed this:
>
>   *Suminoe ni*   To Suminoe's clear cove
>   *fune sashi-yoseyo*   set course in our ship!
>   *wasure-gusa*   Forgetting-herbs
>   *shirushi ari ya to*   they say hold powers surely worth
>   *tsumite yuku beku*   plucking before going onwards.
>
> Although it is certainly not the case that she intends to completely forget her child, a brief respite from her pangs of longing should help her pour strength into them again. (TN 46, 2/5)

---

59. *Man'yōshū* poem 5:904, SNKBZ 7:92.

The diarist's observation that the mother only seeks to forget her longings momentarily so that she can revive their intensity has often been praised as a realistic portrayal of psychological conflict.[60] This rationalization is informed by self-interest as much as empathy, however, insofar as the mother's death from complete psychic depletion would only compound her fellow passengers' problems by creating yet another unhappy ghost to contend with.

The inability of both poetic tropes to provide succor further deepens this conflict between convention and context. Despite the need to rally her energies, the mother turns to objects that cannot nourish her. Just as the missing half of a bivalve represented by the forgetting-shells marks the discarded remains of a past food source, so too are the medicinal and alimentary virtues of the *wasure-gusa* (forgetting-herbs) absent in the wintry landscape at Suminoe.[61] Both tropes are used in an unconventional manner that Kageki and many later readers have praised for being innovative. Up until this point, forgetting-shells had been exclusively linked with Suminoe.[62] Conversely, Tsurayuki may have been the first poet to associate forgetting-herbs with the same place, although the diarist later mentions it as one of several epithets for that locale.[63] Regardless, neither association is portrayed in a positive light: the first is explicitly rejected by other members of the party, while the second is out of season. Whether it is the Sumiyoshi deity's anger at these poems' unorthodox treatment of his domain or that of the ghost at their insistent pleas to forget her, the mother's *waka* not only fail in their purpose but also cause additional problems when a storm ensues immediately after she recites the second one.

When the girl next appears after the day during which the party purchased fish at Torikai no Mimaki, fear of her gives way amid the Yodo-gawa's calm waters to a more balanced perspective in the mother's *waka*, which is the first such to acknowledge the presence of people

---

60. Watanabe, "Ko o nakushita oya no 'kokoro,'" 59.
61. Known in traditional medicine as *kanzō*, the tender shoots and reddish-orange flowers of this rock-dwelling lily were consumed pickled or steamed (Satō and Ikezoe, "Heianchō no shokubunka kō," 44).
62. Busujima, "*Tosa nikki* no hyōgen," 67–68.
63. Komachiya, "Hyōgen ron no oku," 84.

other than herself. Like the piscatory purchase preceding it, a similar calculus of gain and loss is conveyed here in her final poem.

> Among those now returning to *The Capital* are some who had no *Children* when they departed, but gave birth to *Children* after arriving in the provinces. All of them now carry their children in their arms as they disembark from the ship to walk about before coming back on board again. Seeing this, the mother whose child died is unable to contain her grief.
>
> | *nakarishi mo* | Recalling them without |
> |---|---|
> | *aritsutsu kaeru* | those they now return with, |
> | *hito no ko o* | other people's children, |
> | *arishi mo nakute* | without the one I recall, |
> | *kuru ga kanashisa* | comes with such grief! |
>
> That's what she said while she wept! How must the father feel to hear this? Such words and poems are surely not the product of idle whim. It is said both overseas and here that they are undertaken when thoughts are beyond enduring. (TN 51–52, 2/9)

The diarist's concluding assertion that poetry is the product of a universal human need to voice strong emotions is often regarded as a literary manifesto rejecting the elaborate figuration and wordplay associated with Tsurayuki's earlier *waka* in favor of unmediated expressions of affect.[64] However, the statement also gains a satirical edge when we recall that the poetic products of irrepressible maternal grief generated further poems when they give rise to equally powerful feelings of fear and anger in her fellow travelers. By situating *waka* for the dead girl within the heterotopic space of a ship whose frail confines force the griever's captive audience to contend with the dangerous consequences of poetic catharsis, *Tosa nikki* draws attention to the social problems that arise when the powerful emotions generating poetry come into conflict with the communal context in which they circulate.

---

64. For example, Konishi, "Tsurayuki bannen no kafū"; Hirasawa, *Ōchō bungaku no shihatsu*, 303.

Abrupt Endings

Both material and spectral *mono* converge at the end of the diary, as the narrative pace picks up speed before ending with an abruptness reminiscent of the rapid climax (*kyū*) characterizing later dramatic arts. In its movement from Shimasaka to a moonlit Katsura-gawa, then an indistinct capital, and finally back into moonlight at the ex-governor's mansion, the final entry rapidly shifts from scene to scene in a segmented visual flow that Hagitani likened to the separate settings connected by mist in screen paintings (TNZ 413). This visual sequence also provides emotional color: in her eagerness to return, the diarist decries the excessive number of *waka* composed at Katsura-gawa and ignores her urban environs. Yet her growing excitement ends in disappointment when the same moonlight previously celebrated in poetry now mercilessly exposes the parlous state of the ex-governor's home in prose.

It has been suggested that the visual isolation of the ex-governor's mansion in this final nighttime setting conveys the sense of a psychic space which, like the modern home, connotes security and intimacy.[65] If anything, however, the presence of a neighbor whose actions have disfigured that space underscores its vulnerability to external indifference.

> The place is hopelessly dilapidated and in far worse shape than we had heard. Clearly, the heart of the person to whom we had entrusted it has likewise deteriorated! "Since we had always viewed the fence between us as no barrier to seeing our two houses as one, they had actually volunteered to look after it." "That's right! And we never failed finding an opportunity to send them things." "And now to see it like this tonight!" But we can't very well allow ourselves to say such things in raised voices. Despite this glaring evidence of disregard, we will make an earnest show of gratitude with something. At any rate, the garden now has a water-filled depression resembling a pond. I recall there being many pines in that area. Only half now remain, as though the past five or six years had been *A Thousand* years instead! New ones now grow among those remaining. The general state of

---

65. Kikuta, "*Tosa nikki* no jikan-teki kōzō," 6. On this view of the modern home, see Bachelard, *The Poetics of Space*, 72.

utter deterioration inspired people to say how poignant everything is. (TN 55, 2/16)

The curbs on criticism that abruptly stifle an initial outpouring of shocked outrage in this passage arise from the neighbor's physical proximity, conveyed through the fence's double-edged representation of a relationship that is simultaneously intimate and detached. The same constraints are also reflected in the diarist's strategic framing of these criticisms within a long passage that avoids specifying their source.[66]

Both the neighbor's neglect and the need to nonetheless offer some token of gratitude bring the mechanics of exchange depicted over the course of the voyage to a decidedly bitter end. The neighbor's blatant disregard for the ex-governor's household reveals that even the requirements of reciprocity driving the transactional forms of gifting that the party were forced to engage in at Yamazaki and Shimasaka have now ceased to obtain in any meaningful manner. The discovery of a new pond where none was originally intended gives physical shape to this unbalanced relationship. Although the replacement of half the pines that had once grown there with new seedlings echoes the balance between gain and loss expressed in the bereaved mother's previous *waka*, it only serves here to underscore the neighbor's venality: rather than simply neglect the property, that person has in fact actively exploited it by removing the older trees for lumber. This detail endows the "poignancy" of the scene with one last ironic reversal of earlier values: whereas the steersman's lack of *mono no aware* confirmed its dissociation from materialism, those same qualities in the neighbor are now the direct cause of such sentiments.

Poetic conventions are also reversed in the final mention of the dead girl in this setting. *Waka* typically divided domestic space into the house (*ie*) whose communal space travelers yearned to rejoin, and its grounds (*yado*) onto which the individual subject could project their interiority.[67] Here, however, the house becomes the site where community fragments, as the diarist's fellow passengers now become "others from the ship" (*funabito*) whose bustling activity contrasts with her melancholic stasis.

---

66. My translation follows Hagitani in extending the quoted speech beyond "And now to see it like this tonight!" to include the previous three sentences.
67. Wakayama, *Bungaku no naka no toshi to kenchiku*, 56–59.

This sense of alienation is also conveyed by the final two *waka*, which struggle to express the emotions of people other than their composer(s) rather than simply project the feelings of their speakers onto the scene.

> Among those pangs of longing that come ceaselessly to mind, how great the grief at returning unaccompanied by the girl born in this house! Others from the ship gather their children to them and bustle about. A person understanding the unendurable grief this brings whispered a verse:
>
> | | |
> |---|---|
> | *umareshi mo* | Remembering the birth |
> | *kaeranu mono o* | of one not returning, |
> | *waga yado ni* | great is the grief at seeing |
> | *komatsu no aru wo* | pine saplings growing |
> | *miru ga kanashisa* | here on our grounds! |
>
> Those are the words they uttered. It must not have sufficed, for there was also this:
>
> | | |
> |---|---|
> | *mishi hito no* | If I could still see and |
> | *matsu no chitose ni* | pine for a thousand years |
> | *mimashikaba* | over the one I once saw, |
> | *tōku kanashiki* | would we have parted |
> | *wakare semashi ya* | grieving into the distance? |
>
> There are many other bitterly regretful matters that are hard to forget, but I cannot cover them all. In any case, I will soon rip this up. (TN 55–56, 2/16)

Although much ink has been spilled attempting to identify the poet(s) in this passage, its primary interest appears to lie rather in the general challenges posed by poetic attempts to represent the thoughts of others in either an individual or communal sense.[68] The second *waka* is undoubtedly more successful in capturing a range of perspectives. Whereas the first one simply recapitulates the feelings previously described in prose, its successor configures time and space with a complexity approaching that of the first elegy for the girl by using the expression "grieving into the distance" (*tōku kanashiki*) to first cross back to the remote location

---

68. For summaries of the theories regarding the source of these two *waka*, see TNZ 424–25 and Miyake, "*The Tosa Diary*," 69.

where the final parting with her took place before turning forward to face grief that will continue into the distant future.

The act of seeing in both *waka* draws on a poetic tradition known to modern scholars as *kōro shinin no uta* (travel verse for the dead), in which a speaker who is returning home gazes on the exposed corpse of someone who has died far away from their own. In consoling the corpse's restless spirit, this poetic display of empathy is intended to ensure the speaker's safe return. Poems of this sort combined four characteristics shared by both elegiac and viatic poetry in *Tosa nikki*: a longing to return home, sorrow at separation from family, placatory praise of gods or ghosts, and movement across boundaries in space and time.[69] By replacing a threatening setting abroad with the purportedly safer one of home, the diary is perhaps parodically inverting these conventions.[70] Similarly the saplings, which are usually associated in poetry with the birth or coming-of-age rites for children, now represent their loss.[71]

Such associations with earlier poetry could further suggest that the pines in these two *waka* represent the spot where the girl's remains will be interred. Prior to the universal establishment of patrilocal practices at the end of the tenth century, methods of disposal could range from temporary burial for months or years at a matriarchal or uxorilocal site, to simply scattering the bones in public spaces after cremation.[72] Geographical and religious parallels with the diary suggest *Nihon ryōiki*'s account of Prince Nagaya (684–729) offers the most germane example in this instance. When the prince's bones are exiled to Tosa after he is falsely accused of treason, his ghost becomes so angry at being posthumously banished to such a remote location that it causes an outbreak of disease in the province, which is only quelled after the bones are moved closer to the capital.[73] Read in this light, both the diary's title and the recurring mention of distance in its poetic eulogies suggest a need to assuage her ghost by ensuring the girl's own remains avoid a similar fate. The ex-

---

69. On this characterization of *kōro shinin no uta*, see Commons, *Hitomaro*, 31–33.
70. Satō, "*Tosa nikki* ni okeru shin-janru sōzō," 120.
71. Andō, "*Tsurayuki shū* ni okeru Saneyori zōtōka," 20–21.
72. Glassman, "Chinese Buddhist Death Ritual," 384–88.
73. *Nihon ryōiki* story 2:1, SNKBZ 10:119–21; see also Nakamura, *Miraculous Stories*, 159.

governor's household is therefore only assured some measure of security once she is interred at home. Like the neighbor who the pine trees also represent, however, the girl's ghost will likely continue being an intimately problematic presence far into the future.

Both final poems' melding of material "things" (*mono*) with spectral ones resurfaces one last time in the diary's concluding two sentences, which end *Tosa nikki* in a self-reflexive manner that symmetrically mirrors its beginning. Whereas the prologue stated the reason for writing the diary and the content its writer intends to cover, the epilogue begins by summarizing the limits of that content in order to justify ending it. Although the prologue is clearly cast in a female voice, however, many readers, beginning with Mitsue, believe it is the author who bursts into view here. Perhaps he is expressing his shame over having displayed private emotions that are unsuited to his station and lack the practical value expected from a diary.[74] Alternately, he could be conveying a sense of shocked betrayal brought on by the realization that *kana* script's promised ability to reproduce the past in the present cannot overcome the immovable biological fact of death.[75] By charting a narrative progression from fictional pose to authorial confession within its text, such readings also endow *Tosa nikki* with greater historical significance as a teleological prefiguration of the emotional authenticity ascribed to later women's memoirs.

Like the diary's poetic elegies for a dead girl, however, the emotional power of its epilogue does not require an autobiographical reading. If anything, the fact that the diary was never discarded makes its ending as flagrantly fictional as its opening. The force of these final words resides rather in the way they resonate backward in ever-widening frames of reference that expand from referring most immediately to grief over the girl, to include shock at the neighbor's cold-heartedness toward her family, and from there back to the various fraught exchanges and frustrations the travelers have endured over the course of their voyage. The lighthearted sarcasm on display in the diarist's depiction of the parting banquets at the beginning of her account is now overwhelmed by a sense of

---

74. Hasegawa, "'Toku yaritemu' no shisō," 91. See also Mori, "*Tosa nikki* no jishōsei," 56–57.

75. Fukazawa, *Jiko genkyū tekisuto no keifugaku*, 68.

remorse that is as difficult to endure as it is to forget. *Tosa nikki* succinctly captures this entire spectrum of emotions in its final reference to "bitterly regretful matters" (*kuchi-oshiki koto*), drawing as it does on all the preceding misfortunes of the mouth that linked language with consumption in a textual economy whose frugality makes repetitions all the more excessive and minor details all the more significant.

Conclusion

Although the same word used in modern scholarship to describe *Tosa nikki* as "satirical" has its *locus classicus* in the Great Preface to the *Shijing* (Classic of Poetry, ca. 600 BCE), neither ridicule nor humor are integral to the poetic mode of social criticism represented by the term *fengci* in that text. If anything, such appeals persuaded superiors to reform their conduct through tactfully indirect analogies that respected social hierarchies rather than challenge them.[76] Early Sinitic texts in general did not recognize satire as a specific genre, although humorous social or historical commentary can be found in *yuefu* ballads, songs of foretelling (*tongyao*), and the riddling wit of the jesters (*huaji*) who entertained aristocrats.[77] As with parody, works possessing a recognizably satirical focus tend rather to be associated with early modern times.[78] The same was true for Edo-period writers such as Akinari, who we saw in the previous chapter critiquing scholarship on Tsurayuki in his own retelling of *Tosa nikki*.

In light of what we have seen in this chapter, such overly broad historical generalizations clearly need revising.[79] In addition to prose texts such as *Tosa nikki* and *Taketori*, satire is also evident in the *Kokinshū*'s *haikaika* (absurd verse). Like its Sinitic cognate *feixie*, the term *haikai* could convey ridicule, along with puns, personification, vulgar language

---

76. *Shijing*, SKT 110:5.
77. Knechtges, "Wit, Humor, and Satire."
78. Examples include Wu, *Ameliorative Satire and the Seventeenth-Century Chinese Novel*; and Leggieri, "Magistrates, Doctors, and Monks."
79. For one noteworthy exception, see Denecke, *Classical World Literatures*, 234–64. *Tosa nikki*'s focus on the more mundane sphere of economic relations distinguishes it from the scholarly discourses she discusses.

using corporeal terms, and nonstandard words.[80] As we will see in the next chapter, the last two of these characteristics are also shared with song. Whereas the target of ridicule in *haikaika* at most extended to particular character-types, however, *Tosa nikki* widened its scope to scrutinize social conventions such as divination and gift-giving. In fact, as Hagitani noted, the systemic scale of its criticism leads the diary to treat greed as a universal quality (TNZ 397). These materialistic underpinnings to its world also gain metalinguistic dimensions through puns that reduce social and linguistic conventions to physical objects such as horses, mouths, or rotting flesh. As one scholar has pointed out, these humorous juxtapositions often employ the literal meanings implied by their etymologies to undermine the conventional meanings of such words.[81] Hutcheon's formulation of parody is perhaps particularly apposite for understanding these puns, insofar as the critical ironic differences they produce result from repetitions in sound that are also repetitions in prose of the figural strategy used in poetry to double meaning through *kakekotoba* (pivot-words).

Because the diary's sardonicism is so remarkably pronounced in comparison to other texts within its immediate historical context, a comparison with Western examples of satire is potentially revealing. Unlike their peers in early modern East Asia, satirists in the West could draw on numerous classical models in Roman literature that made humorously critical observations about historical figures or character types. The most influential of these models was "Menippean satire," a form of prose that combines two or more different genres, languages, or historical periods to undermine conventional views. One particularly striking area of overlap with *Tosa nikki* can be seen in the narrative frame employed by Menippean satire's most emulated classical writer, Lucian (ca. 125–180), within his *Vera Historia* (A True Story), a text whose account of a fantastical voyage would later inspire *Gulliver's Travels* (1726).[82] By beginning with its narrator asserting the only truthful thing he will say is that every

---

80. Takeoka, *Kokin wakashū zenhyōshaku* 2:2045–50; and McCullough, *Brocade by Night*, 481–88. A concise history of the term *haikaika* is provided in Watanabe, *Heianchō bungaku to kanbun sekai*, 216–34.
81. Ogawa, "'Hito' no kaze nami / 'nami' no hito," 6.
82. Like *Tosa nikki*, Lucian's works are often serio-comic (Branham, *Unruly Eloquence*, 38–46).

subsequent sentence is a lie, *Vera Historia* marks its own fictionality in as flagrant, paradoxical, and strategic a fashion as the prologue to Tsurayuki's diary. Although it is not as overtly outlandish as Lucian's account—which includes a trip to the moon—the cramped confines of shipboard life in *Tosa nikki* represented a world that was similarly remote to its aristocratic readers. As will be discussed in chapter 4, moreover, its landscapes are often equally imaginative.

Rather than attempt to critique social conditions in a manner that is systematic or wide-ranging, Menippean satire is characterized by a preference for highly intellectualized forms of humor involving wordplay, intertextuality, and an ironic stance, all of which encourage the reader to share feelings of amusement and moral superiority toward its characters, often through mockery of popular superstitions.[83] This intellectual orientation also tends to prefer inquiry and provocation to moral instruction and punishment.[84] As the examples I have taken up in this chapter demonstrate, *Tosa nikki* shares all of these same characteristics. Its text blends the multiple sociolects of daily speech, Literary Sinitic, *waka* poetry, popular song, incantations, and diary prose. It parodically reproduces the format of aristocratic diaries and their concerns, as well as idealized accounts of provincial governors, while undermining those genres' truth claims. Its portrayals of karma, divination, prayer, and sacrifice highlight the material calculations through which humans create religious meaning. As already noted, the diary is also a prolific source of puns. By inviting readerly ridicule of more humble characters, *Tosa nikki* shares the conservative elitism evident in Menippean satire's tendentious form of humor. Like the diary's use of a fictional narrator and exotic locale, in other words, the low status of its characters forecloses any possibility of subjecting its aristocratic readers to similar treatment.

Despite these political and social limitations, there remain two aspects of *Tosa nikki*'s satirical stance that possess implications that are both radical and sophisticated. The first of these concerns its representation of various forms of exchange, which foreshadow later anthropological descriptions of the intersection between economics, power relations, and social forces of obligation that were first identified in the 1924 book *The*

---

83. Gilmore, *Satire*, 95.
84. Dustin, *Satire: A Critical Reintroduction*, 35–70.

Gift by Marcel Mauss (1872–1950). By engendering ties of mutual obligation between donor and donee, Mauss argued, the acts of giving, receiving, and returning gifts constituted the primary means for creating premodern communities. As with any foundational attempt to articulate universal cultural principles, this view has been subject to revision. Lévi-Strauss claimed Mauss overemphasized the discrete acts of gifting, receiving, and returning—all of which can be perceived and experienced individually—rather than focusing on the intangible but overarching structure of exchange in which they are accompanied by later responses involving different gifts.[85] This critique led Derrida to argue in turn that Mauss's notion of the gift is an impossibility, insofar as any supposedly altruistic act of giving presupposes receiving something in return.[86] Doubts have also been cast on the assertion that the obligation to return obtains in all cultures and historical periods.[87] All of these critiques are also present in *Tosa nikki*, where the failure to reciprocate, the unspoken expectations that gifts must necessitate further gifts, as well as the spectral and religious dimensions of such material exchanges, are all constantly being negotiated by the traveling party, more often than not to their disadvantage. The sheer scope and sophistication with which gifting is depicted in *Tosa nikki* also offers an opportunity to investigate its history in Japan prior to its comparatively extensive documentation in medieval times.[88]

Ultimately, it is the insistently metalinguistic manner in which *Tosa nikki* draws attention to the constraints on its own critique that presents the most radical criticism of the social forces it satirizes. Like the exchanges that are its target, the diary's sardonic commentary on them revolves around the mouth, which conveys its observations through muffled movements in whispers or silent but telling smiles. Yet another pointed reminder of the need to be politic is apparent when the utterances of one mouth blur into those of another within the diary's longer sentences. In distancing the author from responsibility for his sardonic observations by

---

85. Lévi-Strauss, *Introduction to the Work of Marcell Mauss*, 45–47.
86. Derrida, *Given Time*, 34–70.
87. Testart, "Uncertainties of the 'Obligation to Reciprocate.'"
88. On the early history of gift-giving in Japan, see Chaiklin, *Mediated by Gifts*, 5 and 8.

attributing them to a fictive female narrator, one who herself deploys the same distancing strategy to put criticisms in the mouths of others, *Tosa nikki* thus repeatedly draws attention to the social constraints placed on criticism, thereby implying (as its final sentence suggests) that its critique might be extended still further to other unspecified targets, were it not for the possibility that these might include aristocratic readers.

PART II

Between History and Fiction

CHAPTER 3

Shipside Songs

One of *Tosa nikki*'s distinctive characteristics is the attention it pays to vocal music. In addition to describing its relationship to speech and writing, the diary is our only source for the lyrics to an otherwise unknown song genre. Its only peer in this regard is *Makura no sōshi* (The Pillow Book, ca. 1000), a text whose capacious and eccentric content in itself indicates how remarkable it is to find such features in the diary. The marginal place of song within the Heian literary canon as a whole has led to its being largely overlooked in Anglophone scholarship, aside from a handful of studies devoted to the better-known examples preserved and performed at court, such as *imayō* (current tunes), *saibara* (drover's music), *fuzoku uta* (songs of regional airs), and *kagura uta* (songs to entertain gods).[1] Although these genres have received significant attention in Japanese-language scholarship, the same is not true for the ones *Tosa nikki* mentions.

My approach to song in this chapter reflects the diary's inversion of such norms by progressing from those aspects that are mentioned the most elsewhere to the unique ones on which it lavishes the most attention. I begin with a single word from a popular *saibara* that affords broader insights into Heian representations of sexuality. Another aspect of song

1. Brannen, "Ancient Japanese Songs from the *Kinkafu* Collection"; Harich-Schneider, *Roei*; Markham, *Saibara*; Kim, *Songs to Make the Dust Dance*; Lazarus, "Folk Performance as Transgression."

mentioned elsewhere, albeit to a lesser extent, concerns its connections to writing, speaking, and prosody. The depiction of these relationships in *Tosa nikki* indicates a lack of clear distinctions between vocal music and *waka* at the time, something also evident in the *kai uta* (Kai songs) it gives passing mention to. The only genre for which *Tosa nikki* provides lyrics, *funa uta* (ship songs), appears nowhere else. These transcriptions are equally unique in the challenges they present to conventional accounts of Heian musical history, economics, and popular culture. Last, I consider why Tsurayuki displays such a pronounced interest in song, and how that interest speaks to broader questions of attribution that are germane to *Tosa nikki* itself. The conclusion identifies connections between these different topics and the pronounced discursive mobility characterizing Heian song culture overall.

Pansexual Perspectives in Song

It is a mark of how alien *Tosa nikki*'s world is to its elite audience that the most popular genre of song at court has the smallest presence within it. A single word shared with *saibara* appears on 1/3 in the diarist's description of bathing women who reveal "the sort of abalones and mussels whose inner flesh makes a tasty coupling with pickled sea squirts" (TN 29, 1/13). As noted in chapter 2, this is the only instance in the diary where food appears in a purely figural capacity. The passage is omitted by every translator except McCullough, who mentions in a footnote the possibility these mollusks represent female genitalia.[2] By contrast, nineteenth-century commentators such as Kageki, Ōhide, and Moribe were quick to associate the abalone and sea squirts it mentions with the female and male genitalia they respectively represented in Edo-period poetry.[3] This heteroerotic valence is further underscored through a play on *tsuma* as

---

2. McCullough, *Kokin Wakashū*, 274.
3. Examples of early modern poems treating sea squirts and abalone in this fashion can be found in Gill, *Rise, Ye Sea Slugs!*, 176–77.

spousal coupling and culinary pairing.⁴ One scholar has suggested that the mussels and abalone in *Tosa nikki* indicate younger and more mature women respectively.⁵ Abalone are also included among the shellfish offered up to a prospective son-in-law in the *saibara* "My Household" (*Wa-ie*):

wa-ie wa	My household
tobari chō mo	has curtains and partitions
taretaru o	hanging in place.
ōkimi kimase	Come here my lord!
muko ni semu	I'll make you my son-in-law!
misakana ni	Among the side-dishes
nani yokemu	what would be good?
awabi sadao ka	Abalone and turban-shell?
kase yokemu	Or would sea-urchin be good?
awabi sadao ka	Abalone and turban-shell?
kase yokemu	Or would sea-urchin be good?⁶

This song appears to have circulated widely, judging from the existence of a related version in the *Ryōjin hishō* (Secret Notes to Singing Dust Off the Rafters) and the appearance of its lyrics on three separate occasions in *Genji*. In the Hahakigi chapter, Genji quotes it to suggest his host, the Kii governor, should provide him with women. In Tokonatsu, he and Tamakazura both allude to it in a conversation about his son's marriage prospects. In Wakana-jō, it refers to marriages in which the man visits his wife. Taken as a whole, these references suggest this song was performed at wedding banquets.

The diary's use of such imagery to describe bathing women is often treated as a moment in which the author reveals himself in a purely masculine form of voyeurism. As the example from Tokonatsu indicates, however, such language could be used by either gender. This appears to have

---

4. The culinary pairing alluded to in this passage is also evident in the tendency to combine sea squirts with other mollusks as a tribute item in *Engi shiki* (Satō and Ikezoe, *Heianchō no shokubunka kō*, 42).
5. Suzuki T., *Tosa nikki*, 68–69.
6. *Saibara* song 47, SNKBZ 42:153–54.

been true of *saibara* in general, judging from the first extant reference to them in the obituary of Princess Hiroi (d. 859):

> From her youth she had cultivated steadfast virtue and a proper demeanor. She stood out on account of her singing abilities, being particularly skilled at *saibara*. Lords and youths with a liking for such things flocked to her for instruction. Her death was mourned by many.
>
> 廣井少修德操。舉動有禮。以能歌見稱。特善催馬樂歌。諸大夫及少年及好事者。多就而習之焉。至于殂沒。時人悼之。[7]

Like other such obituaries in the official court histories, *Sandai jitsuroku* opens with a laudatory summary of its subject's character. In this case, it is perhaps implied that Hiroi is all the more praiseworthy for possessing propriety *despite* pursuing *saibara*. Their lewdness is further suggested by the potential for equally lewd behavior between herself and the many male students she attracted, as was often true when aristocratic men sought instruction in such songs from professional female performers at court.

References to the body in *saibara* are shared with earlier *gishōka* (jesting songs), whose humorous portrayals of corporeality even include scatological puns.[8] Most *gishōka* were exchanged between men and women, possibly reflecting the back-and-forth repartee of earlier song-fence contests. Perhaps because humorous *haikai* poems in the Heian period were not dialogic, they tended instead to represent the human body obliquely through flora and fauna.[9] Such metaphors could nonetheless be quite straightforward in their implications. For example, Gen no Naishi signals her sexual interest in Genji by displaying a fan that bears the phrase "grasses beneath the grove have grown so old" (*mori no shita kusa oinureba*), taken from an anonymous *Kokinshū* poem whose speaker laments their current neglect by once-hungry horses.

Ōaraki no	At Ōaraki
mori no shita kusa	grasses beneath the grove

---

7. *Nihon sandai jitsuroku* entry for Jōgan 1/10/23, KST 4:39.
8. Palmer, "A Poem to Carp About?," 16–17.
9. Kubukihara, "Haikaika," 110. Orikuchi Shinobu distinguishes *gishōka* from *haikaika* on this basis in his influential essay "Haikaika no kenkyū," 281–83.

oinureba	have grown so old
koma mo susamezu	that no steed savors them
karu hito mo nashi	nor person reaps them.¹⁰

Given her amorous aims, the grass that Gen no Naishi's fan alludes to can be read as a reference to her own pubic region.¹¹ When Genji neglects to respond, she subsequently resorts to more direct language taken from the *saibara* "Eastland Cottage" (*Azuma-ya*), in which a woman invites a male lover to her open door. Gen no Naishi's use of both sources for the same purpose is probably not coincidental. Lyrics to *saibara* appear as anonymous *waka* within the *Man'yōshū*, *Kokinshū*, and *Kokin waka rokujō* anthologies, making it likely many other anonymous poems, including the Ōaraki one, were also sung. Because these *waka* typically employ natural objects as *jokotoba* (prefatory words) to metaphorically introduce their subjects, it is likely that a much more extensive repertoire of erotic imagery originally existed than is currently ascribed to Heian court poetry.

Erotic language in songs could also include either gender as the subject or object of desire. This pansexual perspective can be seen, for example, in the following lyrics sung by a beggar nun in *The Pillow Book*:

yoru wa tare to ka nemu	Who should I sleep with tonight?
Hitachi no Suke to nemu	I'll sleep with that Aide of Hitachi.
netaru hada yoshi	Asleep with that fine silken skin.¹²

Neither the speaker in this song nor the object of their desire is unambiguously gendered. It is revealing in this regard that commentators who assume its lyrics represent the desire of a man for a woman do not go on to explain why the singer is female.¹³ Although the soft skin of the person who is being desired could belong to a woman, "Aide of Hitachi" was a title used by both genders. The presence of anonymous poems in the *Kokinshū* that appear to be overtly homoerotic further suggests the

---

10. *Kokin wakashū* poem 892, SNKBZ 11:338.
11. Kobayashi, "Seisa to shutai o hakai suru mono," 83–87.
12. *Makura no sōshi* section 83, SNKBZ 18:152; see also McKinney, *The Pillow Book*, 77.
13. Tanaka, *Makura no sōshi zenchūshaku*, 2:158.

beggar nun's ditty, like other songs, could accommodate every possible permutation of sexual desire.[14]

A similar pansexual eroticism can be seen in the subsequent set of erotic lyrics this beggar nun sings. Even though the body they describe is unambiguously gendered, it remains unclear whether the genitalia colorfully represented by Otoko-yama (Mount Man) belong to the speaker or someone else:

> *Otoko-yama no mine no momijiba*　　Mount Man's crimson peak.
> *sazo na wa tatsu ya*　　Giving rise to notoriety!
> *sazo na wa tatsu ya*　　Giving rise to notoriety![15]

The phallic connotations of Otoko-yama's name are echoed in an anonymous poem from the Miscellaneous section of the *Kokinshū* lamenting its speaker's impotence.[16] That same *waka* is also used in the *kana* preface to represent poems recited at banquets by male aristocrats and female entertainers alike, as was probably also the case with the Ōaraki poem and others from the same section of the anthology. Because the beggar nun belongs to neither group, however, and because the above lyrics do not belong to any known song genre, it is possible they possess more common origins. This would make *The Pillow Book* our only source for popular song from the Heian period, other than the *funa uta* in *Tosa nikki* we will subsequently turn to. Regardless of their provenance, the scenarios portrayed by the beggar nun, the diary's reference to mollusks, and the *funa uta* lyrics it transcribes share a pansexual perspective that does not align in a fixed or obvious way with either the affirmation or contestation of gendered distinctions.

---

14. For this reading of anonymous *Kokinshū* poems, see Heldt, "Between Followers and Friends," 7–8.

15. *Makura no sōshi* section 83, SNKBZ 18:152; see also McKinney, *The Pillow Book*, 77.

16. *Kokin wakashū* poem 889, SNKBZ 11:338: "Though now I am like this, / in the past I once was / as Mount Man / whose slopes rose in potency for a time / before coming to this current pass!" (*ima koso are / ware mo mukashi wa / Otoko-yama / sakayuku toki mo / ari koshi mono o*).

Ironic Inversions

The modern tendency to associate sexual expression with social subversion has often held a seductive appeal for those analyzing premodern representations of eroticism. Such connections are central to Bakhtin's account of medieval parody, for example, which identifies the beginnings of proto-novelistic discourse with the depiction of bodily desires that humorously exceed social hierarchies and conventions in the writings of the early modern French writer Rabelais (1483–1553).[17] In a similar vein, the scholar Furuhashi Nobuyoshi has argued that *Tosa nikki*'s depiction of genitalia undermines class distinctions by humorously asserting a common physicality.[18] However, it is perhaps more accurate to say that in most cases it was the social context that determined how erotic language was received. Gen no Naishi's words are shocking due to her age vis-à-vis Genji rather than her social status or gender. Similarly, as Jeffrey Angles points out, it is not the lyrics of the beggar nun's song in *Makura no sōshi* that elicit disgust, but rather their mismatch with her pretensions to a higher social standing.[19]

Given that the depiction of genitalia was not inherently taboo or shocking in a Heian context, their significance in *Tosa nikki* is shaped by the larger narrative they appear in. Reading them contextually suggests they represent an ironic situation in which the desires of subjects turn them into objects. This irony, which unfolds over the course of the entry, is also signaled structurally through the parodic transformation of poetic discourse celebrating the moon's pearlescent glow into song-inflected prose describing bodies exposed to its light.

> At daybreak on *The Thirteenth* rain fell for a bit. After a while it ceased. Thinking to bathe in the river, several of the women descended from the ship and headed off to a spot that would do for that purpose. Gazing out over the sea:

---

17. Bakhtin, *Rabelais and His World*, 303–68. On the links between banquets and bodies, see also 278–304.
18. Furuhashi, "Warai no bungaku," 116.
19. Angles, "Watching Commoners, Performing Class," 44.

kumo mo mina	The clouds all
nami to zo miyuru	look like waves!
ama mogana	Oh, for a diver-woman!
izure ka umi to	I would know from asking her
toite shiru beku	which one is the sea.

That's the poem I composed. Now that the tenth has passed, the moon in the dawn sky makes for an enthralling sight. Since the ship first set out, no woman has once worn fine robes of dark red silk for fear of attracting the sea god. Saying this, some took refuge in the scanty excuse of a few reeds and hitched their skirts up to their knees, seemingly untroubled by the thought that they were displaying the sort of abalones and mussels whose inner flesh makes a tasty coupling with pickled sea squirts! (TN 29, 1/13)

Like the poem, the women aspire to a certain decorousness by seeking to wash themselves on the thirteenth, which was considered a propitious day for this activity. But their desire to do so also results from frustration at having spent the last two weeks at sea without such an opportunity.[20] The eagerness revealed by their decision to disembark as soon as the weather clears also proves to be their undoing, however, when it leads these women to hastily choose an exposed location. The desire for propriety that impels their actions thus ends up putting them in a compromising situation.[21] The diarist sardonically underscores this ironic state of affairs by conflating their reasoning with the evidence that contradicts it through a pun playing on the dual meaning of *nani no ashikage* as "not much harm in it" and "not much cover in the reeds."

This transformation of women from agents into objects occurs when they hitch their robes up to their knees. As it happens, the exact same phrase represents a similar dramatic irony in the following *Kokinshū* poem:

Composed on the sixth day of the Seventh Month on the feelings of the Tanabata lovers. By Lord Fujiwara no Kanesuke:

---

20. *Kujōdono goyuikai* enjoins Morosuke's heirs to bathe every five days (GR 27:136).
21. One scholar argues they deliberately expose themselves to ward off the sea god (Matsumoto, "*Tosa nikki* no kaigyaku," 83–84).

itsu shi ka to	When will it be?
mataku kokoro o	With fretful yearning
hagi ni agete	bare to the knees,
Ama no kawara o	will it be forded today,
kyō ya wataramu	the Riverbed of Heaven?[22]

This poem is placed in the *haikai* section of the *Kokinshū* due to its unorthodox depiction of the Herdboy attempting to meet the Weavermaid a day before these celestial lovers' annual reunion.[23] *Tosa nikki* perhaps adds an additional humorous twist by transferring the act of exposure from poetry expressing male impatience into prose depicting female recklessness. Regardless, the essential irony in both cases is that the desires driving their subjects turn them into objects subjected to the reader's gaze.

A similar confusion between subject and object involving sexual content and edible aquatic life occurs on New Year's Day when the travelers are depicted sucking on the heads of dried sweetfish. Although the quasi-obscene representation of this oral activity is unusual in its own right, the passage is also noteworthy for the confusion its slippery syntax engenders between the thoughts of consumer and consumed.

> We simply sucked on the mouths of dried sweetfish pressed flat to our lips. "What feelings does it stir up in them to have people's lips sucking on theirs?" "I imagine they must be saying to one another such things as, 'I find all my thoughts turning toward the capital city today,' or, 'I wonder how it is for the heads of those dear mullet fellows stuck on *Sprigs* of holly tied to the festive straw ropes festooning the gates of tiny city tenements?'" (TN 20–21, 1/1)

A translation of this passage into either English or modern Japanese faces fundamental choices that arise from its failure to specify where the quotation begins, if it is voiced, and how many subjects produce it. As noted in chapter 1, such questions have taxed scholars since Sanetaka's time. The result in this case is that it is unclear if the diarist is representing banter exchanged among the passengers seeking to lift their spirits

---

22. *Kokin wakashū* poem 1014, SNKBZ 11:389.
23. Watanabe, *Heianchō bungaku to kanbun sekai*, 221. The same verse appears as poem 36 in Kanesuke's personal *waka* anthology.

by imagining what the fish are saying; or if she is imagining what the people would be saying if they were thinking about what the fish would be saying. The comment about missing the capital is particularly open to multiple attributions. Are the fish saying it to one another? Is it said by a traveler, leading them or someone else to imagine what the fish would be saying? Is the diarist saying it to herself, before imagining what the fish would be saying to one another? In keeping with his preference for ironic scenarios, Hagitani treats this passage as a depiction of the diarist imagining the sweetfish longing for intimate contact with their mullet companions after becoming orally aroused by the travelers' lips (TNZ 120–22). However one resolves these issues, the reader is still left wondering who is representing who. These sudden shifts in subject within a single sentence also occur when the "old song" that is cited on 1/11 blends together the perspectives of mother, narrator, and poet.[24] Such phenomena suggest song lyrics were especially amenable to accommodating multiple subjects.

The association of consumption with confusion in the above passage further resonates with the dissolution of social identities grounded in status and age at the farewell banquets preceding it. Tōkai Ryōzō has even suggested that the presence of these settings in *Tosa nikki* reflects its origins as a libretto that was reworked over the course of numerous recitations at such events. In associating the diary's often raucous and earthy humor with such recitations, Tōkai connects it to a tradition of jesters (*okobito*) mentioned in *Sandai jitsuroku*, whose performers he envisages playing a role akin to that of their medieval European counterparts in providing sanctioned transgressions against the social order.[25] It is certainly easy to imagine the diary's humor would have been appreciated by banquet participants engaged in drunken banter, entertaining anecdotes, and song.

For all its casualness, however, the relaxation of social etiquette displayed in *Tosa nikki*'s feasts is contained in comparison to the more comprehensive and programmatic chaos enacted during the medieval European carnivals that Bakhtin associated with Rabelais's portrayal of bodily appetites. This is partly because the body and sexuality did not

24. Soda, "*Tosa nikki* no hyōgen ishiki," 66–67.
25. Tōkai, "Oko no hōhō," 10–13. Tōkai draws on the characterization of medieval European jesters in Takahashi, *Dōke no bungaku*, 12–14.

carry the same social or religious significance in Heian Japan, partly because the diary's banquets take place in a transient marginal space, and partly because its readers are not being invited to identify with that space. Tsurayuki's keen awareness of his distance from his readers never wavers, as can be seen, for example, in the laborious manner with which his narrator often explains puns.[26] Like the satirical observations discussed in the previous chapter, in other words, *Tosa nikki* eschews systemic forms of subversion in its portrayal of bodily desires. Rather, its mollusks and sweetfish embody a wryly detached form of amusement at the ironic transformation of subjects into objects—one that also appears in the song lyrics I will take up later in this chapter. As we will see next, song blurred social distinctions among genres as well as bodies.

Waka *Prosody and Literacy*

Tosa nikki offers a remarkably wide-ranging picture of verse for such a brief text. Its fifty-nine *waka* include all three categories modern scholars apply to Heian poetic composition: cathartic monologues (*dokuei*), exchanges with others (*zōtō*), and choral arrangements (*shōwa*). The people engaged in these activities encompass an equally broad range of ages, genders, and social classes. Its portrayal of poetic composition even includes such singular terms as "hauling" (*ninai*) and "spinning" (*hineri*) in addition to the more common ones indicating singing, writing, speaking, and composing. Although many of these terms overlap, others are mutually exclusive in ways suggesting the diary makes a concerted effort to differentiate *waka* from song and speech.

Tosa nikki's efforts to distinguish song from poetry attest to the frequency with which they were confused at the time. *The Pillow Book*, for example, describes *waka* with the same word used to group a list of such vocalic genres as *fuzoku uta*, *kagura uta*, and *imayō* under the heading "Songs" (*Uta wa*).[27] This ambiguity in *uta*'s meaning has led modern scholars to devise the neologism *kayō* in order to describe vocal music.

26. Watanabe, "*Tosa nikki* no kaigyaku hyōgen," 54–55.
27. *Makura no sōshi* section 262, SNKBZ 18:418; see also McKinney, *The Pillow Book*, 230.

Rather than employing nouns representing reified categories, however, Heian texts made provisional distinctions between genres through verbs emphasizing their performative features in any given context. Thus, songs and poems were typically accompanied by *utau* (to sing) and *yomu* (to compose) respectively. As *waka* became increasingly tied to prose fiction, *iu* (to speak) and *kaku* (to write) eventually became the predominant means for describing poetic production by the eleventh century.[28]

The simultaneous presence of all four verbs within *Tosa nikki* thus makes it particularly significant from a historical perspective. Three of them appear together, for example, either directly or indirectly when the drunken dissolution of normative social and linguistic divisions at the second farewell banquet results in an ironic contrast between the thoughtfulness displayed by the lector in providing musical entertainment for his guests and the ignorance displayed by his illiterate dancers, who remain unaware of the written signs inadvertently produced by their movements: "Everyone attending, high and low alike, right down to the young ones, became silly with drink. Even performers who don't know how to make the single stroke in *The Letter 'One'* stamped out *The Letter 'Ten'* in crisscross patterns with their feet as they swayed to the music" (TN 16, 12/24).

Although the specialist skills of these performers—who frequently provided dramatic masked dances (*gigaku*) at memorial rites and sermons—made them valued members of a provincial lector's entourage, such expertise only serves here to underscore their ignorance of the comparatively commonplace ability to write. Indeed, this ignorance is so profound, we are told, that they cannot even produce the single horizontal stroke used to represent the number "one." This appears to have been a common expression, judging from Murasaki Shikibu's use of a similar phrase when she attempts to conceal her familiarity with Literary Sinitic by "not even writing the character for 'one.'"[29] Like the forms of wordplay discussed in chapter 2, this proverbial expression is wryly literalized in *Tosa nikki* by using the Sinographs 一 and 十 to underscore the simplicity of the knowledge the dancers lack.

---

28. Kamitani, "Yomu' uta kara 'iu' uta." These three verbs are only the most common ones used to describe poetic composition in *monogatari* such as *Genji*, which includes sixteen others.

29. *Murasaki Shikibu nikki*, SNKS 35:97.

The association between dancing feet and writing in this scene also implicitly invokes speech and song by echoing a passage from the Great Preface to the *Shijing* in which various acts of signification are arranged in an ascending scale of spontaneous physical responses to increasingly strong emotional stimuli.

> Poetry is where one's preoccupations go. While in the heart, it exists as preoccupations. Put forth as words, it exists as poetry. Feelings stir within and take shape in speech. When speech falls short, we sigh them. When sighing falls short, we sing them. When singing falls short, we find ourselves gesturing with our hands and stamping our feet.
>
> 詩者志之所之也。在心爲志。發言爲詩。情動於中而形於言。言之不足、故嗟嘆之。嗟嘆之不足、故永歌之。永歌之足、不知手之舞之足之蹈之也。[30]

The reappearance of this passage's first three sentences defining poetry in the *mana* preface to the *Kokinshū* testifies to the Great Preface's status as the single most authoritative account of poetics in Tsurayuki's day. *Tosa nikki* in fact assigns a similar preeminent status to speech. In the Great Preface, it precedes all the other expressive modes that follow it. In the diary, it subtends both singing and poetic composition by frequently accompanying both the verbs *yomu* and *utau* with *iu*.[31] In such cases, as we will see, the first two verbs appear to describe the mode of articulation, while the third stresses the content being articulated.

Speech is twice associated with poetry in the diary's portrayal of the steersman, who, like its dancers, demonstrates a universal human propensity for cultural production that stops short of being either textual or poetic. As with the dancers, song also hovers in the background of the first such instance, which appears just after the first *funa uta* is sung.

> While listening to this, our ship came to a place where birds called "black birds" were huddled together atop some rocks. Waves crashed whitely against the base of the rocks. The steersman said something to the effect of "by black birds approach white waves." Though nothing special in itself,

---

30. Original text as cited in Owen, *Readings in Chinese Literary Thought*, 40–41.
31. Forty of the forty-nine *waka* in the diary are composed, among which fourteen are also spoken.

his manner of saying things catches the ear. "Since such words are a poor fit with a person of his standing, they feel at fault somehow," someone said as we went onwards. (TN 35–36, 1/21)

The steersman's utterance "by black birds approach white waves" (*kurotori no moto ni, shiroki nami o yosu*) constitutes a quasi-poetic "manner of saying things" because its syntactic division into two phrases of eight and seven syllables respectively resembles the paired measures ending *waka*, and also because the color contrast they produce is semantically complementary. Moreover, the formal demands of parallelism seem to generate its black birds, which, because they are unfamiliar to the diarist and absent from the *waka* lexicon, function as a generic descriptive tag inspired by the contrasting white of wave crests rather than as the name of a particular species.

These parallelisms originate in a spontaneous and unmediated response to patterns in the world that are universally apprehensible, regardless of individual talent or social background, because they manifest the complementary yin-yang pairings structuring the entire cosmos. Perhaps the steersman's utterance is also offered up as a model for generating vernacular prose that combines Literary Sinitic parallelisms with *waka* prosody.[32] Even so, the simple contrastive structure he uses pales beside the visual simile deployed in the entry's opening sentence, which offers a more strikingly colorful contrast between red and blue that also evokes the two primary poetic seasons when the diarist likens ships leaving the harbor to autumnal leaves scattered over a vernal sea.[33]

By the time the entry abruptly ends with the challenge to "Say something, steersman!" (*Kajitori, ie*), his accidental production of poetic speech has been further distinguished from the conscious crafting of poetry by highlighting the importance of erudition in creating the latter. Just before the diarist issues her challenge, one of her fellow travelers composes a *waka* whose final measure "o distant island sentinel" (*okitsu shima-mori*) only appears in a single *Man'yōshū* poem.[34] Although some

---

32. Sasanuma, "*Tosa nikki* no waka kan," 17.
33. This simile previously appeared in a poem Tsurayuki composed about the Ōigawa in 907 (Ogawa, "'Ima' ni hitoku sareta 'mukashi,'" 10).
34. *Man'yōshū* poem 4:596, SNKBZ 6:317: "Even hundreds of days spent / counting grains of shore sands / would with my longing / surely never compare, / o distant

scholars think the diarist is asking the steersman to convey the ex-governor's complaints to this island sentinel, or that she is muttering it to herself, most believe she is calling on him to respond with a *waka* of his own (TNZ 247–48). The silence that follows her demand therefore implies he is unable to produce a poem worthy of writing down for posterity because he fails to recognize an unusually recondite allusion.

The other instance in which the steersman unwittingly produces poetic speech illustrates another aspect of literacy's role in ensuring proper *waka* composition. In this instance *yomu* plays a prominent role in confirming the prosodic structure of his commands by drawing on the verb's earlier association with the act of counting.

> The lord on board urged the steersman onward, saying, "Hasten the ship while we have good weather!" The steersman then spoke to his crew, saying: "His lordship has spoken. Pull on the sail-ropes of this fair ship so it may go, before the morning northerly begins to blow!" The poetic quality possessed by these words lies precisely in their spontaneity on our steersman's part. It's not that the steersman had any intention of speaking in verse or anything of that sort. One person who was listening said: "How strange! What he said sounded like a poem!" and wrote it out to reveal that it does in fact come to thirty-one syllables! (TN 45, 2/5)

Aside from *ōsetabu* (his lordship has spoken), the diction used by the steersman in his command is shared with *waka*. Moreover, the syntax he uses precisely mirrors that of *waka* prosody by placing the coordinating particles at points that divide the content of his speech into the same sequence of syllabic units as those forming a poem's five measures (*mifune yori / ōsetabu nari / asagita no / idekonu saki ni / tsunade haya hike*). This prosodic structure is only recognized, however, when it can be quantified through its inscription.

The steersman's recurring failure to employ his quasi-poetic utterances as *waka* is symptomatic of his overall lack of facility at converting sensory impressions into useful knowledge.[35] The most common manifestation of this shortcoming is his repeated failure to transform empirical

---

island sentinel!" (*yaoka yuku / hama no manago mo / aga koi ni / ani masaraji ka / okitsu shima-mori*).

35. Takano, "*Tosa nikki* ni okeru kajitori no zōkei ni tsuite," 35.

observations about the weather into accurate forecasts, including the storm that arises shortly after his quasi-poetic command here.[36] By portraying his poetic shortcomings, *Tosa nikki* highlights literacy's role in ensuring *waka* composition remains a socially exclusive practice, unlike song or speech. It is telling in this regard that the verb *yomu* is never associated with the steersman. His speech thus helps define the notoriously polyvalent significance of this verb, whose semantic range straddled distinctions between production and reception—as well as between orality and literacy—by being used more broadly to describe not only the composition of metrically regular poems but also the acts of counting, prognostication, reading aloud, and chanting in metronome.[37] In other words, the negative example provided by the steersman aligns *yomu* and *waka* with elite modes of cultural production.

This connection between *yomu* and literacy is also evident in the differences that scholars have identified between *waka* that are composed in the diary and those that are spoken. Poems lamenting the dead girl use the archaic term *koi* (longing) when they are composed and the more common expression *kanashi* (grief) when they are uttered.[38] Poems that are composed also often allude to *shi* and earlier *waka*, or employ visual similes favored in poems produced for folding screens and poetry matches.[39] Whereas *waka* addressing a collective audience in the diary are composed, ones intended for interpersonal dialogue are spoken.[40] The latter two characteristics bear an especially close connection to literacy. The older poetry, *shi*, screen *waka*, and submissions to poetry matches used as sources for *waka* that are "composed," for example, are all written texts. Displaying such erudition in a group setting would, moreover, help ensure others found them worthy of writing down for future recitation. Thus, for example, it is only *waka* recorded by the diarist that she describes as having been "composed" at the new governor's farewell ban-

36. Kanda, "*Tosa nikki* ron no tame no nōto," 114.
37. Heldt, *The Pursuit of Harmony*, 121–27. Insofar as "composing" can be applied to a broad range of aesthetic media, it perhaps best conveys the polyvalency of *yomu*.
38. Ōsugi, "*Tosa nikki* ni okeru eikai," 1.
39. Watanabe, *Heianchō bungaku to kanbun sekai*, 291.
40. Ogawa, "Zōtō o kyohi suru uta," 17.

quet on 12/26, in contrast to the many others from the event that are simply portrayed as having been declaimed in raised voices.

Literacy is especially prominent on 1/18, when *yomu* is used three times to describe the composition of three *waka*, and then another three to describe the failed attempt at poetic composition by a fourth individual. As with the steersman's commands on 2/5, writing here once again functions as the ultimate guarantor of prosodic conventions.

> Listening intently to what people say about these poems, someone else composed one. The syllables composed for that verse came to thirty-seven letters. Everyone looked like they were barely able to keep from laughing. The poem's owner seemed very put out and grumbled. Though they emulated others, they weren't able to truly absorb anything. Even if the poem were written out, it would be very hard to manage a properly arranged composition. Today alone it is embarrassing. One can only imagine what it will be like later! (TN 33, 1/18)

This passage joins prosody to writing by interweaving two meanings of *moji* with four of *yomu*. Phonetic "letters" (*moji*) make it possible to divide up the sonic stream into discrete quantifiable units of sound as "syllables" (*moji*) that can be "counted" (*yomu*) to "compose" (*yomu*) a poem worthy of being "recited" (*yomu*) aloud in a group setting and subsequently "read" (*yomu*) after being written down. Writing (in theory at least) also allows poets to reshape an initial version into a "properly arranged composition" (*yomisue*). This last term, which appears nowhere else in the written record, perhaps suggests that inscribing *waka* in *kana* allowed one to subsequently rearrange, remove, or add syllables in order to meet prosodic requirements.

The implication that *waka* prosody was neither obvious nor universally acknowledged can be seen in other texts as well. The same concern with enforcing metrical regularity, for example, is also evident in Michizane's record of Uda's journey to Miyataki.[41] Likewise, when Sei Shōnagon asserts that she is skilled at composing *waka* because she is not "ignorant of their number of syllables" (*moji no kazu shirazu*), the implication is

---

41. Horiuchi, "Nikki kara nikki bungaku e," 9. The Miyataki excursion is discussed further in chapter 4.

that many others lacked such knowledge.⁴² *Tosa nikki*'s stress on literacy as an essential element of *waka* composition might even offer one reason for its choice of genre, insofar as the narrator's frequent descriptions of such poetic practices and evaluations of their products indicate a critical consciousness shared with aristocratic diaries.

The failed attempt at reproducing *waka* meter on 1/18 suggests its porous boundaries with song in other ways as well. Because the deficient composition is just one syllable short of the thirty-eight used in *sedōka*, it has been suggested that a misguided effort to replicate this poetic form accounts for the would-be poet's error. There is, in fact, evidence to suggest Tsurayuki took a particular interest in this poetic genre.⁴³ In terms of rhythm, however, the use of six measures in *sedōka* makes it difficult to imagine such a poem would have been confused with the five prosodic units making up *waka*. Another possibility is that the three earlier *waka* overhead by the erstwhile poet had expanded their own structures from thirty-one syllables to thirty-eight by repeating their final measures, as was also done when such poems were turned into *saibara* songs. In other words, the erstwhile poet's failure is due to a confused understanding of the difference between recitational modes and actual prosody. The ease with which one could stray from metrical norms thus indicates that *waka* could be auditorily indistinguishable from song in performance. As we will see next, the two forms of verse frequently overlapped on this basis.

Continental and Kai Songs

The ability to travel beyond its original performative context accounts for both the popularity of vocal music and its porous boundary with poetry. Unlike *waka* composition, whose only aural aspect was prosody, song involved multiple sonic elements, such as melody and rhythm, which were also often accompanied by instrumental music and dance. Due to their

---

42. *Makura no sōshi* section 95, SNKBZ 18:192; see also McKinney, *The Pillow Book*, 102.

43. Tsurayuki's *sedōka* is the only one with an author among the four included in the imperial anthology (*Kokin wakashū* poem 1010, SNKBZ 11:387).

nonverbal nature, such aspects of song are not conveyed in the diary, making them fundamentally different from the other forms of language it represents. Although its relative scarcity in *Tosa nikki* seems to confirm the common assumption that vocal music was supplanted by poetry during the Heian period, the brief references it makes to particular song forms indicate this same nonverbal musicality facilitated their generic and geographical mobility.

The verb *utau* first appears in the diary when members of the traveling party perform two separate song genres at sea soon after making their final farewells to provincial well-wishers. The context-dependent nature of this performance is highlighted by the diarist's evaluation of its suitability, as well as by the way in which she distinguishes lyrics from music through the addition of the verb for speaking with that for singing: "Meanwhile, people took every available opportunity to utter verses from the continent they deemed suitable to the occasion. Despite being in a western province, one person uttered a song from the eastern province of Kai. I actually heard someone say, 'with such singing, dust is sure to scatter from the cabin roof and clouds waver in the sky!'" (TN 19, 12/27).

The term used for the first of these two song genres, *kara uta* (continental verses), only appears in *Tosa nikki*, which portrays them as an exclusively male genre chanted collectively as a means of either celebration or consolation. The word *kara* indicates their origins in Tang poetry, making it likely these songs rendered *shi* couplets in a distinctive vocal mode akin to the *rōei* style of chanting. Because chanting in Sinitic was in decline during this period, the lyrics were probably vernacularized renditions of the original *shi*.[44]

Although too scarce to attract scholarly interest, a few references in other Heian texts to the *kai uta* (Kai songs) accompanying these continental songs offer at least some sense of their characteristics.[45] This scarcity belies the ubiquity of Kai songs in Tsurayuki's day, which was made possible by the ability of their lyrics and melodies to connect with other genres and geographies both together and separately. Their geographical

---

44. On this historical shift in the vocalization of Literary Sinitic, see Steininger, *Chinese Literary Forms in Heian Japan*, 148.

45. The most sustained treatment of this genre is a philological investigation of their lyrics in Shida, "Kai uta zakkō."

mobility is indicated by the diarist when she contrasts the eastern origins of Kai songs with the western provinces in which the traveling party sings them. Although her comment may be intended as criticism, the acceptability of performing songs outside their region of origin is in fact noted in *Genji* when it describes "The Sea at Ise" (*Ise no umi*) being performed on the shores of Akashi "even though this was not the Ise Sea."[46]

The popularity of *kai uta* was also enhanced by the practice of singing *waka* to their tunes. In one episode from the tenth-century *Heichū monogatari* (Tales of Heichū), its eponymous antihero takes a poem composed by women he has just encountered and proceeds to "sing it as a Kai song while going along" down Suzaku Avenue.[47] A reference in *Utsuho monogatari* to *waka* that adopt the melodies of the *saibara* songs "My Household" and "The Sea at Ise" suggests a wide range of tunes from other such genres could also be utilized in this way.[48] In *Heichū monogatari* this practice also occasions anxieties that reappear in *Tosa nikki*. The ease with which *waka* can become song, for example, appears to undermine proprietary claims to their words when Heichū is accused of "stealing the poem" (*uta o nusumite*) by its female creators. The literal mobility of Heichū's performance as he strolls down one of the largest thoroughfares in the capital also provides ample space and time in which to expose these women's association with the antihero, leading a friend of theirs to rebuke him for singing it aloud. As it happens, similar concerns over their volume of delivery appear to be at work in the diarist's description of Kai songs.

Kai uta tunes also seem to be applied to *waka* in the headnote to poem 565 in *Goyō wakashū* (Waka Anthology of Later Leaves, 1156–57), which describes it as being "on feeling the loss of a lover, as a Kai song" (*Kai uta ni, aite awanu kokoro o*):

Kai ga ne no	The peaks of Kai
kai mo naku mata	leave no hope ever again
ai mo mizu	that we will see each other!

46. *Genji monogatari* (Akashi), SNKBZ 21:243; see also Tyler, *The Tale of Genji*, 264.
47. *Heichū monogatari* episode 25, SNKBZ 12:498; see also Videen, *Tales of Heichū*, 61–66.
48. *Utsuho monogatari* (Matsuri no tsukai), SNKBZ 14:471.

Saya no Naka-yama	Mount Midst Short Nights
saya wa omoishi	makes that all too clear.[49]

Traces of this poem's origins in song lyrics remain in the sound repetitions creating alliterative structures that link toponyms to the speaker's state of mind, as it moves from the name of Kai province to the phrase *kai mo naku* (leave no hope), and then from the name of Saya no Naka-yama (Mount Midst Short Nights) to *saya* (clear). Geography becomes destiny in both cases: the province's rugged terrain increases the speaker's sense of hopelessness at reuniting with their lover, while the brief span of time contained in the name of the mountain indicates there is little likelihood of meeting before dawn.

An even closer connection to song is suggested when this same mountain appears in a pair of "airs of Kai" (*kai fuzoku*) within the Shōtoku-bon edition of the *Koyōshū* (Collection of Old Songs, 1099). Although metrically identical to *waka*, the arrangement of this pair in a choral progression from a *moto-kata* (left-hand chorus) to a *sue-kata* (right-hand chorus) hints at their possession of a distinctive dramatic structure in performance:

Kaibito no	That person of Kai
yome ni wa naraji	will not become my wife.
koto tsurashi	Such a hard thing to bear!
Kai no misaka o	Over Kai's mighty slopes
yoru ya koyu ramu	is she crossing at night?
Kai ga ne no	Of the peaks of Kai
sayo mo mishiyo	I want a clear sight!
kokoro naku	How heartless of you
yokohori seru	to rush right between us,
Saya no Naka-yama	Mount Midst Short Nights!

The sequencing of these verses creates a narrative progression from despair over the distance that hinders a man from meeting his spouse to an appeal directed at the mountain blocking their way. Perhaps the lyrics

---

49. Other than those appearing in the *Kokinshū*, all the *kai uta* lyrics I cite here are taken from Ikeda, "*Tosa nikki* no tabi," 57–58.

describe the feelings of both lovers in turn, or perhaps they chart an internal progression in the man alone. It is also possible they could be adapted to suit either narrative depending on the particular context in which they were performed.

Further insights into the connections between song and *waka* are enabled by a variant of the second *kai fuzoku* verse included in the *Kokinshū* among the *azuma uta* (Eastland songs) performed at court rituals.

> *Kai ga ne o*   Of the peaks of Kai
> *saya ni mo mishiga*   I want a clear sight!
> *kekere naku*   How heartless of you
> *yokohori fuseru*   to lie down between us,
> *Saya no Naka-yama*   Mount Midst Short Nights!
>
> *Kai ga ne o*   Over the peaks of Kai,
> *ne koshi yama koshi* past its peaks, past its mountains!
> *fuku kaze o*   If only those gusts of wind
> *hito ni mo ga mo ya* would send a message telling
> *kotozute yaramu*   my love that I miss them so![50]

Their hint of a love story and traditions associated with the name of a particular place could suggest this pair of Kai songs were originally part of a longer narrative.[51] Perhaps the first *kai fuzoku* song was also part of the same sequence. Differences between the second choral verse and the first *kai uta* in this *Kokinshū* pair also indicate some of the ways in which song lyrics could be altered. Subtle (but potentially significant) changes in meaning occur when the mountain that rushed between lovers in the choral song now lies down sedately between them in the *Kokinshū*, and when *kokoro naku* (heartless) in the *Koyōshū* version is replaced by *kekere naku* in the imperial anthology.[52] The association of these different versions with different companion verses suggests song could also become poetry when anthological sequencing replaces choral progressions, either in an attempt to mimetically reproduce such sung progressions or in or-

---

50. *Kokin wakashū* poems 1097–98, SNKBZ 11:415–16.
51. Ikeda, "*Tosa nikki* no tabi," 59.
52. The words *shiyo* and *shiga* indicating desire in the two different versions probably reflect a similar distinction based on dialect.

der to create a new textual narrative. Such changes in sequencing were aided by the tendency for song to adopt a modular structure enabling the attachment, removal, or rearrangement of individual sets of lyrics.

The lyrics of the *Kokinshū* Kai songs in particular gain added significance through their contrasts and congruences with *Tosa nikki*'s narrative context. Although the sea is entirely absent from both songs in the anthology (in keeping with the landlocked location of Kai province), their common focus on longings for a distant partner must have resonated with the diary's travelers.[53] The performance of the second song might also have raised the prospect of summoning the winds it mentions, as occurs during another song performance at sea described in *The Pillow Book*'s list of "Things One Should Not Risk" (*Uchitoku majiki mono*):

> Boat crossings. The sun is shining gently, and the surface of the sea is very calm, as though wrapped in pale blue silk, and there is nothing even slightly ominous about the scene of a young woman wearing a gown and skirted trousers in the company of a youthful retainer who is singing with gusto as he pushes one of those things called "oars." How very charming, and how nice it would be to show the scene to someone exalted! But then the wind begins to blow fiercely, and the surface of the sea worsens as he rows in single-minded pursuit of harborage amid the crash of waves, making it hard to believe that it had presented such a genial sight only moments earlier.[54]

As the last act prior to the storm's sudden onset, the retainer's singing is implied to be its cause. This link is given an ironic edge through the adverb "with gusto" (*imijiu*), which pivots from positive implications to negative ones when the powerful vocal delivery of the rower leads the weather to respond with equal vigor.

The volume of singing is also linked ironically to weather conditions in the diary's portrayal of these continental and Kai verses. In alluding to the skills of the legendary singers Yu Gong and Qing Qing, the description of their recitation by an anonymous passenger as being powerful enough to shake dust off of the cabin roof and cause clouds to waver would appear

---

53. Watanabe, *Heianchō bungaku to kanbun sekai*, 273.
54. *Makura no sōshi* section 286, SNKBZ 18:439–40; see also McKinney, *The Pillow Book*, 242.

at first sight to be intended as praise. This result, however, would also interfere with the ship's forward movement.[55] Moreover, a delivery that was powerful enough to shake dust off the cabin roof could have unfortunate consequences if it also drew gales of equal force to those described in *The Pillow Book*. The separate dangers posed by their lyrics and delivery in this regard are highlighted by using the verbs for speaking and singing respectively. A similar separation between music and meaning is perhaps also at work in the depiction of Heichū's performance, which appears to be criticized for loudly announcing the contents of a poem whose origins in writing suggest it was intended to be discreet. Insofar as songs consisted of both words and music, the potential for creating problems by performing them was thus twofold in nature.

Reappraising Refrains

The refrains in *Tosa nikki*'s ship songs provide another example of the fluid boundaries between vocal music and poetry. Song was often distinguished from *waka* by repeating a poem's final measure or adding nonsensical rhythmic phrases known as *hayashi kotoba*, as happens to several anonymous *Kokinshū* poems when they reappear in the late-Heian Nabeshima-bon and the Tenji-bon song anthologies. Conversely, the removal of such refrains and repetitions turned songs into poems. In the case of *funa uta*, *hayashi kotoba* combine music and meaning to create a modular structure that allows an indefinite number of lyrics to be attached to one another. Both this function and the diverse scenes that result also challenge several assumptions informing conventional histories of Heian song.

Because the same *hayashi kotoba* appears in both *funa uta*, it seems to have defined the genre. The complete absence of any maritime content in their lyrics would make such a taxonomic function particularly crucial in this case. Hagitani views their presence as an indication that *funa uta* were "work songs" (*rōdōka*) in which the refrain coordinated the movements of a ship's oars (TNZ 170). This definition makes ship songs a maritime subset of the *min'yō* (folk songs) viewed by many scholars as

---

55. Ogawa, "'Funa-yakata no chiri," 20–21.

the source of all early Japanese vocal music. First coined in the Meiji period, *min'yō* was a translation of the term "Volkslied" used by the German thinker Johann Gottfried Herder (1744–1803) to describe popular songs that reflected the thoughts and feelings of an entire nation's "people" (*Volk*). The most influential articulation of this concept in a Japanese context was provided by the folklorist Yanagita Kunio (1875–1962), who believed such "work songs" originated in the communal agrarian activities of village life, making them the purest examples of both *min'yō* and an eternally authentic Japanese ethos.[56]

Modern Japanese literary histories have typically followed Yanagita in viewing folk songs as the oldest source of Japanese vocal music. In accounts of the *Man'yōshū*, for example, communal songs performed by illiterate rural commoners are often regarded as the initial stage in an evolutionary progression ending in individualized poems produced by urban literate aristocrats.[57] A similar spatio-temporal progression from countryside to court informs standard histories of Heian vocal music, which begin with folk songs that were collected and set to continental forms of instrumental music by the Ōuta-dokoro (Bureau of Song) when it was established in the early ninth century in order to oversee performances of indigenous dances and songs, including *kai uta*, on formal occasions.[58]

In fact, this association of the oldest vernacular songs with rural commoners predates the modern category of *min'yō*. Similar origins are attributed to Kai songs, for example, by Ichijō Kanera (1402–1481) in his *Kokinshū dōmōshō* (A *Kokinshū* Primer, 1476).[59] This belief also informed the establishment of the Ōuta-dokoro and its eighth-century predecessors, the Gagakuryō (Bureau of Court Music) and Naikyōbō (Female Performers Office), all of which were inspired by the Han-dynasty Bureau of Music (Yuefu) charged with collecting songs that were circulating among commoners in order to gauge whether they were content with

---

56. Hughes, *Traditional Folk Song in Modern Japan*, 8–18.
57. Duthie, *Man'yōshū and the Imperial Imagination*, 67–68. Song also precedes written poems in recent histories of classical Greek literature (Lardinois, "New Philology and the Classics").
58. Konishi, *A History of Japanese Literature*, 66–88.
59. Takeoka, *Kokin wakashū zenhyōshaku*, 2:2212.

government policies. In combination with indigenous beliefs about the numinous quality inhering in regional place names, this political function also played a role in enthronement ceremonies, where the performance of Kai songs (along with other genres appearing in the final book of the *Kokinshū*) was intended to represent the realm at large. The ubiquitous appearance of toponyms in these songs—including those from the capital region appearing in *saibara*—reflects the symbolic work they performed in this regard.

In order for such songs to legitimate and ritually affirm rulership, it was therefore ideologically imperative to assert the authenticity of their popular origins. In fact, however, similar examples from other places and times suggests such songs were also closely tied to elite culture. The assumption that the oral and anonymous character of *yuefu* indicate folk origins, for example, has been questioned in light of more recent views of medieval European balladry stressing the complex ways in which influence flowed in either direction between literate elites and illiterate commoners.[60] The differences in wording, pronunciation, and narrative progression evident in *kai uta* all suggest similarly complicated connections. Rather than indicating the authentic characteristics of different regional dialects, for example, it is possible to imagine that the stress laid on nonstandard pronunciations in the lyrics of Kai songs and other *azuma uta* preserved in the *Kokinshū* and *Man'yōshū* constituted a purely textual means for representing the realm's eastern borders as a cultural Other vis-à-vis the court at its center.

It is telling in this regard that the only authentic Heian-period example of a communal agricultural song appears in the eccentric text of *Makura no sōshi*, where Sei Shōnagon ruefully observes its inferiority to poetry after her initial delight in seeing the singers turns to dismay when their words become audible.

> While heading to the Kamo Shrine on pilgrimage, we come across women planting paddies. Wearing hats that resemble new serving trays, they stand and sing songs in a large group. It looks like they are bent over and doing something with their hands as they walk backwards. Wondering what they

---

60. Egan, "Were *Yüeh-fu* Ever Folk Songs?"

are up to, you find yourself beguiled by the sight of them, until you can make out lyrics that speak to the *hototogisu* bird in a very rude way.

hototogisu	Hototogisu,
ore kayatsu yo	you there, you fellow!
ore nakite koso	You there, it's your cries
ware wa ta ure	to which we plant paddies.

Hearing them sing makes one wonder what sort of person said *do not cry so loud*.[61]

Like the beggar nun's ditties mentioned previously, their dissimilarity with any song form currently known to us suggests these lyrics possessed popular origins. Modern scholars in fact view this verse as a precursor to the *ta-ue uta* (paddy planting songs), which Yanagita regarded as the single most paradigmatic example of Japanese folk song. The song's association between *hototogisu* and rice-planting is also shared with *waka* found in the *Kokinshū* and *Eiga monogatari*, suggesting perhaps a common tropological origin.[62] In questioning who originally came up with the poetic turn of phrase "do not cry so loud" (*itaku na naki so*) when the planting song encourages the *hototogisu* to do precisely that, Sei Shōnagon also appears to suggest poetry originated with such songs. At the same time, she clearly views the former as an improvement. The insultingly familiar pronoun *ore* (you there) used to address the bird that she takes issue with would only have been made more egregious by song's characteristic use of repetition.

The literal connection between singing groups and communal labor in this rice-planting song becomes metaphorical in *Tosa nikki* when the diarist likens a *waka* that is chanted by provincial well-wishers to the coordinated efforts of fisher folk pulling nets: "those people all lined up their mouths and strained together to haul out a song on the seashore" (TN 19, 12/27). The expression *kuchi-ami* (literally "mouth nets") that is used to describe this choral presentation is unique to the diary, suggesting perhaps that it is a rhetorical conceit rather than the name of a

---

61. *Makura no sōshi* section 210, SNKBZ 18:348; see also McKinney, *The Pillow Book*, 191.
62. Tanaka, *Makura no sōshi zenchūshaku*, 4:297.

particular performance tradition originating among fishermen. The association between song and communal labor that Hagitani ascribes to the diary's *funa uta* is in fact even more tenuous. This is particularly evident in the close resemblance with *waka* displayed by the first ship song's lyrics, metrical structure, and mode of performance.

> Meanwhile, a youth who has come with us intending to find employment in the capital sang this ship song:
>
> | | |
> |---|---|
> | nao koso | All the more |
> | kuni no kata wa | back towards land |
> | mi-yararure | is my gaze drawn, |
> | waga chichi haha | my father and mother |
> | ari to shi omoeba | being there in my thoughts. |
> | | |
> | kaeraya | Oh, to be home! |
>
> (TN 35, 1/21)

Similar expressions of longing for parents can be found in roughly half of the eighty-four poems in the *Man'yōshū* anthology attributed to the border guards (*sakimori*) who were drafted from eastern provinces to defend the western coastline facing Silla.[63] Like those verses, which were reshaped at some point in order to conform with *waka* prosody, the boundary between poetry and song is porous in this case. Although the *funa uta*'s metrical structure deviates from that of *waka* to a significant degree, the sequencing of shorter measures with longer ones in the syllabic pattern 4/6/5/6/7 within the portion of the song preceding its final refrain nonetheless bears a rough resemblance to standard poetic prosody.

In addition to its use of a refrain and the absence of any recognizable dialect, moreover, the agency of the singer differs in significant ways. Whereas the *sakimori* were pressed into service on pain of execution, the youth who is going to the capital "intending to find employment" (*tsukawaremu tote*) has left home by choice. Most significantly of all, the solo nature of his performance makes it impossible to regard this song as a

---

63. These border guard verses are discussed at length in Horton, *Traversing the Frontier*, 245–66.

rowing chant. The youth's social identity as a migrant laborer who forsakes life in the countryside in order to become an urban dweller makes it possible to think of the *funa uta* as a "popular song" that was familiar to a broad cross-section of people who moved between regions and occupations. They thus offer an important reminder that songs recited by ordinary people—as opposed to professional female performers or amateur aristocratic aficionados—must have circulated widely despite being largely absent from the written record. Their status as popular songs, moreover, amplifies the potential historical value of such lyrics insofar as they represent the views of a much larger group of people than is typical for Heian texts.

The *funa uta*'s popular nature is also signaled by the semantic content of its refrain. As Hagitani notes, *kaeraya* could be an abbreviation of *kaeramu ya* (oh, to be home!) rather than a nonsensical rhythm marker (TNZ 243). A similar sort of homesickness is evident in one other possible surviving example of ship song lyrics from *Genji*, in which sailors are depicted singing "How great our sorrow at having come so far!" (*urakanashiku mo tōku kinikeru ka na*) as they take Tamakazura up to the capital from Kyushu at the beginning of her eponymous chapter.[64] In a similar manner, the refrain *kaeraya* provides a means for people aboard ships to express their transient state in isolation from any familiar community. Because both the passengers and crew who sing *funa uta* were equally liable to experience homesickness, this emotional tenor was well-suited to a popular song genre performed by people from disparate backgrounds. This is not to say that the same refrain necessarily always functioned the same way. Studies of medieval European song manuscripts have revealed, for example, that they could be associated with a wide range of different genres, melodies, and meanings.[65] At least in the case of *funa uta*, however, their refrains appear to have played a critical role in defining an otherwise amorphous genre by turning a collection of unrelated scenes into a modular sequence oriented around subjects who moved from one setting to another while remaining firmly fixed on home in their minds.

64. *Genji monogatari* (Tamakazura), SNKBZ 22:90; see also Tyler, *The Tale of Genji*, 408.
65. Butterfield, *Poetry and Music in Medieval France*, 75–102.

Uncertain Exchanges

The versatility of their refrains enabled ship songs to engage with a far wider range of social milieus than simply the agrarian communities associated with folk song. One indication of the broad social world in which they circulated is the distinctively diverse content they possess. This is particularly true of the remarkably varied vocabulary and social contexts portrayed in the more extended *funa uta* sequence sung by the steersman and his crew on 1/9. This sequence has generated the majority of scholarly commentary on *funa uta*, much of which has questioned the role played by their signature refrain in connecting the seemingly disparate agrarian and mercantile worlds it delineates. More broadly, these lyrics also raise questions about the degree of access they potentially afford to a popular imaginary and actual historical conditions in the tenth century.

Whereas most modern scholars believe that the refrain of *kaeraya* separates two different songs on 1/9, earlier commentators tended to think it appears in the middle of one single verse.[66] The first possibility would further imply that the diarist chooses to omit a second concluding refrain, something suggested by the abrupt way in which she ends her transcription by declaring that she has only jotted down a portion of what was sung. On the other hand, continuities between the two sets of lyrics, such as the identical phrasing capping their final two lines (*ramu . . . ramu* and *kozu . . . kozu*), suggest they constitute one song, perhaps also reflecting the common predilection for repetition in Heian vocal music. In fact, the sense of alienation shared by their speakers allows us to accommodate both views if we attribute the lyrics to one individual encountering two different scenarios over the course of a single voyage. In other words, it is possible that the refrain *kaeraya* punctuates the travel sequence as the ship moves from harbor to harbor, distinguishing one locale from another while simultaneously connecting them through a recurring longing for home.

In addition to a sense of alienation, the dramatic irony structuring both scenarios, in which the desires of their speakers make them subject to manipulation by others, suggests the two sets of lyrics are linked. In

---

66. Hashimoto, "*Tosa nikki* 'funa uta' chūshaku," 2.

the opening set, this structure revolves around speculation over the motives of both its speaker and the person they see weeping while they forage for greens, with the man's perspective anchored in his difference and distance from the object of his desire.[67]

haru no no nite zo	In springtime fields
ne oba naku	is the sound of weeping.
waga susuki ni	By blades of pampas grass
te kiru kiru	are hands sliced and slashed
tsundaru na o	plucking greens that will go
oya ya mahoru ramu	to some hungry parent eager to feed,
shūtome ya kū ramu	or a mother-in-law's gobbling greed?
kaeraya	Oh, to be home!
(TN 26, 1/9)	

Because the auxiliary verb *ramu* typically refers to speculation about the cause of a phenomenon that is being directly witnessed, the speaker appears to be an unrelated observer wondering if it is the demands of parents or in-laws that are responsible for the painful labor causing the forager to weep. The association of excessive greed with in-laws and immediate need with parents contained in his question carries additional implications about the forager's identity. Making this person a woman would entail an especially moving predicament. Since virilocal marriage was not practiced at the time, feeding in-laws would have entailed departing from the normal route home in order to make a longer trek to more distant kin whose tenuous relations with her would make their demands for food seem all the more unreasonable.[68]

The springtime setting in which the scene unfolds suggests that the speaker's question is motivated by erotic desires rather than detached curiosity or altruistic sympathy. In the richly dramatic and ironic reading provided by Hagitani, this person decides to help the forager carry out her task in the hope that she will reciprocate by sleeping with him.

---

67. Because the singers are sailors, I have provisionally identified the speaker in both sets of lyrics as male.

68. On marriage practices in the period, see Yoshie, "Gender in Early Classical Japan," 442–45.

However, the assumption about her marital status entailed by the concluding question indicates he ends up realizing that his efforts have only benefited her (TNZ 171). The final ironic twist, in which his desires cause the man to suffer the same wounds as the woman who is their object, takes a syntactically supple form that makes it possible to identify the weeping person here as both the forager and the speaker.

Along with the other song-infused depictions of eroticism discussed at the beginning of this chapter, the ironic transformation of a subject into an object in these lyrics is shared with the ones that follow it. Now, however, the pivotal moment of realization is accompanied by the speaker's added chagrin at realizing he has been swindled by a "little one" (*unai*) of indeterminate gender.[69]

yonbe no	Where is that little one
unai mogana	who spent last night with me?
zeni kowamu	Could I get those coins?
soragoto o shite	Their tall tale I heeded,
oginori-waza o shite	to pay later what was needed.
zeni mo mote kozu	But no coins are they bringing,
onore dani kozu	Nor are they themselves coming.
(TN 26, 1/9)	

Once again, erotic motives lead the speaker to offer his services, in this case by lending the child money in hopes of continuing a sexual relationship that had begun the previous night. Once again, however, expectations of reciprocity end in disappointment.

Most scholars believe the speaker here is a merchant, a detail that would lend further irony to the situation by having a mere child hoodwink someone who is supposedly skilled at gauging others' motives. But if the use of money was so common that even children were acquainted with the concepts of coinage and credit, there is no need to assume the lender is someone who specializes in commercial transactions. Such potential familiarity with financial matters makes the *funa uta* particularly significant from a historical perspective, insofar as it suggests widespread

---

69. Although most modern scholars assume the singers are referring to a girl, the earliest English-language translation of the diary makes them a boy (Harris, *Log of a Japanese Journey*, 19).

acceptance of both money and the sophisticated promissory arrangements it enabled. Actual economic circumstances in Heian times remain subject to debate, particularly given the chronic scarcity of metal in Japan, and the rarity with which coins are mentioned in texts from the eleventh and twelfth centuries.[70] Since they were still being minted up until 938, however, the diary could be an accurate reflection of its immediate historical context, making the *funa uta* all the more noteworthy precisely because that context was so unique within the wider span of Heian history. Far from evoking a timeless agrarian way of life, then, this detail would make the song very much the product of its own particular historical moment. Such temporal distinctions perhaps offer another basis for distinguishing popular song from folk song.

The second set of lyrics also offer insights into the cultural associations that coinage carried. As Jack Chen has noted in the case of premodern China, money always carries symbolic weight beyond its abstract denotation of exchange value.[71] Whereas it primarily appeared there in elite literati discourse that cast coinage as an expression of the ruler's parental concern for his people, the view provided by this *funa uta* is both more representative and less benign. That is to say, the manner in which money circulates in the song suggests a profound ambivalence within the popular cultural imagination toward its physical mobility and the tenuous nature of the relationships it shaped. Because coins are a common unit of exchange that circulate widely, their value is understood by child and adult alike. Insofar as the possessor can abscond with them easily, however, their mobility also makes the promissory relations they enable profoundly unstable. This volatility is conveyed in part through the ambiguous nature of the line *zeni kowamu* (Could I get those coins?), whose subject could either be the adult who wants his coins back or the child who asked him for them. The circulation of money and the syntax of song thus concretize the mobility characterizing both subjects' relationship to the coins as well as the contingent relationships to one another those same coins create.

---

70. Segal, *Coins, Trade, and the State*, 37–39. Heian coins would ultimately be debased to a tenth of their original value due to the scarcity of metal (McCullough, "The Capital and Its Society," 164).

71. Chen, "Sovereignty, Coinage, and Kinship in Early China."

Ultimately, the ease with which the desiring subject becomes an object who is manipulated by others in both sets of lyrics results from their speakers' shared vulnerability to the machinations of people who, unlike them, possess the advantages of local knowledges and social networks. In other words, it is the experience of travel that informs the fraught nature of both exchanges in this *funa uta* by making the gap in knowledge between local and visitor the reason why things end badly for the latter. Although scholars have tended to assume their speakers are entirely unrelated due to the difference between the agrarian and mercantile scenarios they describe, this shared vulnerability makes it equally plausible to view both speakers as a single maritime traveler who encounters these different settings at the same harbor or two separate ones. Whereas a fellow agriculturalist from the area would be likely to either know the forager's marital status or be able to discover it by asking other locals, a visitor to the region would not have been likely to avail themselves of either option. And whereas a merchant who possessed relations with local commercial partners might have been able to ask those people to help them track down the missing money, a transient shipboard passenger would lack such a network.

The epistemological gap between traveler and local in these lyrics might also explain why they fail to mention any place names. Their complete absence is noteworthy in its own right, insofar as it distinguishes these songs from travel poems, which typically invoke toponyms in order to praise the tutelary deities of those locales, thereby ensuring safe passage. By contrast, the lack of any such place names in the *funa uta* signals the speaker's lack of knowledge about his environs, and thus his dissociation from their inhabitants. In other words, this shipborne speaker is defined by an extreme form of physical mobility that places him outside any geographical, cultural, or social setting that is either familiar or even stable.

Both sets of lyrics also serve an important function within the diary by preparing the way for further ironic contrasts in the prose that follows them within the entry and within the narrative arc of *Tosa nikki* as a whole. Right after the *funa uta* are sung, the diarist describes their calming effect on the passengers, who forget their own troubles by laughing at those of the characters in the lyrics: "Hearing people laugh, hearts calmed a bit despite the rough sea. And so we spent the whole day rowing onwards to reach anchorage. Feeling queasy, the elderly man and dame ended up going to sleep without touching a bite of food" (TN 27, 1/9). After describing the comic relief these lyrics offer, the diarist shifts focus from the passengers' inner psychological peace to the outer physical turmoil experienced by the seasick ex-governor and his wife. The pendulum movement in this passage from rough waters to calm hearts expertly evokes the heaving motion of waves that end up having a similar effect on stomachs in the final sentence. In a final ironic gesture back to the *funa uta*, the same food that will be eagerly consumed by the forager's senior family members in song is now in danger of being vomited up by the elderly passengers in prose.

The uncertain nature of the exchanges being depicted in the *funa uta* also plays a significant role within the diary's overall structure by foreshadowing the transactions that occur with increasing frequency as the party approaches the capital. In its environs, the same fate that the *funa uta*'s itinerant speakers suffered at the hands of locals is now experienced by the passengers who had laughed at their expense. Perhaps Tsurayuki included the song lyrics because their ironic inversions complemented these later transactions, or perhaps because they are intended to echo the confusions between subject and object structuring his earlier depictions of edible aquatic life. An aristocratic readership may have also enjoyed the unexpected twist their lyrics provide when they shift from standard poetic diction in the opening two lines (a voice weeping in spring fields and longing for someone seen the previous night) to decidedly inelegant and unpoetic language (gobbling in-laws and money).[72] This play with readerly expectations is reminiscent of the way Sei Shōnagon portrayed the planting song's invocation of the *hototogisu*, suggesting that the differences between popular song and poetry would have provided a source of wry humor. No doubt the exotic nature of their origins and settings would have also intrigued Tsurayuki's patrons.

Read in this way, the diary's transcription of *funa uta* provides several significant insights into Heian song and popular culture. First, *hayashi kotoba* were capable of not only distinguishing song from poetry but also defining genres through their meaning as much as their musicality. Second, these refrains could provide a modular structure enabling discrete

---

72. Hashimoto, "*Tosa nikki* 'funa uta' chūshaku," 12–13.

sets of lyrics that varied dramatically in length and subject matter to be attached, removed, or rearranged at will. Third, *funa uta* indicate the existence of a much larger repertoire of popular songs performed by a broad cross-section of Heian commoners—a repertoire that lacked the regional language, connections to communal labor, and depictions of a timeless agrarian society characterizing the folk songs whose appropriation by the court continues to shape histories of Heian music to this day. Last, they reveal money and maritime travel's association with feelings of alienation and vulnerability in the popular imagination. In different ways, all of these aspects of *funa uta* also indicate the profound mobility of song as a cultural medium whose lyrics, like their performers, could travel from one context to another.

Questions of Attribution

In addition to their content, *funa uta* are unique in the interpretive challenges their fictional context adds to the considerable number of hermeneutic hurdles possessed by Heian song more generally. The early tenth century is particularly significant for the history of Japanese music because it provides us with the oldest surviving examples of musical scores and lyrics. Detailed records of indoor concerts involving *saibara* that were held at the palace, known as *gyoyū* (royal entertainments), appear in its first decades.[73] Song lyrics were also first written down by Fujiwara no Tadafusa (d. 929) in 919. The instrumental notations included in the since-lost *Shinsen ōjōfu* (New Selections of Flute Scores), completed by Prince Sadayasu (870–924) one year later, makes it the earliest such text known to have been produced in Japan.[74] Despite this notable degree of interest, however, Heian song remains defined as much by what is omitted as by what is recorded, insofar as its lyrics do not provide a complete picture of the choreographed gestures, musical accompaniments, and vocal modes of delivery that would have contributed to their meaning in performance.

---

73. Nelson, "Court and Religious Music," 42.
74. On these instrumental scores, see Markham, *Saibara*, 1–27. The earliest extant vocal notations, which were limited to Buddhist liturgies, date from a century later.

This partial picture is further restricted by the diarist's declaration that she has decided to only write down some of the lyrics she heard. This terse statement serves as a particularly stark reminder that, even prior to its partial preservation through historical happenstance, the written corpus of Heian song would have represented a curated selection of a much larger repertoire. The diarist's editorial aside also reflects the critical role played by women attendants such as herself and Sei Shōnagon in preserving these performances. Tsurayuki himself is invoked as an exemplar of this approach by *Genji*'s narrator, who cites him in order to buttress her assertion that a writer should avoid recording inferior verses.[75] Although this opinion has not survived in his extant writings, the drunken banquet in Sakaki that occasions this narratorial comment recalls the diarist's decision to only record two *waka* from the many poems that are declaimed when the new governor hosts a similar event. Even if *Tosa nikki* was not the direct source of inspiration for *Genji*'s editorial stance, therefore, it certainly exemplifies it.

The fictional nature of the diary also raises questions regarding the reliability of these songs as sources of historical information. At one extreme, it could be argued that they appear nowhere else in the written record because they are fabrications. Even if we assume they existed, the possibility remains that the author's attribution of their lyrics to commoners is as imaginary as his attribution of their narrative context to his fictive diarist. To the extent that Heian fiction's appeal for readers lay in its plausibility, however, it is more reasonable to avoid fantastical options. We know that Tsurayuki returned to the capital from Tosa in 934, making it likely that he drew on his own experiences of that journey to one degree or another, rather than create scenes out of whole cloth. Perhaps, like his female narrator, Tsurayuki chose to only write down a smattering of the lyrics he overheard; perhaps he selected an even smaller number from those he originally transcribed in order to suit the diary's narrative aims; or perhaps he even altered individual words within them with this purpose in mind. In and of themselves, none of these possibilities requires us to discount the potential historical value of these songs out of hand.

The shared role that the diarist and Sei Shōnagon play in creating textual versions of popular song entails broader questions of authenticity,

---

75. *Genji monogatari*, SNKBZ 21:142; see also Tyler, *The Tale of Genji*, 217.

attribution, and gender that also have a bearing on Tsurayuki's engagement with vocal music more generally. What little we know about his early biography in fact helps account for the unusual degree of attention *Tosa nikki* pays to recording songs, and thus the likelihood its *funa uta* are authentic. There is admittedly very little to go on in this regard due to his humble background. Although the *Sanjū rokunin kasen den* and *Kokin wakashū mokuroku* note that he died in 946, neither source mentions his age at the time, making it impossible to even determine when he was born. His father, Mochiyuki, is only briefly mentioned in the latter text, which identifies him as a middle-ranking official who drafted documents as a *kanshi* (office scribe). The survival of a single poem by him in the *Kokinshū* probably reflects an attempt on Tsurayuki's part to honor his memory, implying that he died when his son was still quite young.[76]

Although Tsurayuki would rise much higher in rank than his father, his extensive activities composing and anthologizing written poetry for his aristocratic patrons was not dissimilar from the scribal role Mochiyuki played in copying out government documents for his superiors. Another sign of their shared role in producing texts is suggested by the name that may have been his one other paternal legacy. Its allusion to Confucius's famous statement in the *Analects* that "a single thread runs through my Way" (吾道一以貫之) indicates the value placed on education as a means of advancement by members of the Ki clan in general and Tsurayuki's own patriline in particular.[77] Similar allusions to the Confucian classics also inform the names of his great-grandfather Okimichi (d. 834), his grandfather Motomichi (fl. mid-ninth century), and his cousin Tomonori (ca. 850–904). The skill in Literary Sinitic evident in his preface to *Shinsen waka* makes it likely that Tsurayuki fulfilled his paternal family's expectations by studying history and letters (*kidendō*) at the capital university. During this period he would have come to know the three sons of his distant kinsman Ki no Haseo (845–912), who was similarly invested in the education of his children.

---

76. Murase, *Kyūtei kajin Ki no Tsurayuki*, 20. Another *Kokinshū* verse by Tsurayuki in Lamentations (poem 842) might have been composed for his mother or father (Hasegawa, *Ki no Tsurayuki ron*, 54).

77. *Lunyu* 4:15, SKT 1:96.

Prior to embarking on this path, customary child-rearing practices of the time make it likely that Tsurayuki was raised in his mother's home. This period may have been even longer than normal due to the early death of his father. According to a Ki clan genealogy and the twelfth-century scholar Fujiwara no Kiyosuke (1104–1177), she was either a professional dancer (*gijo*) or singer (*shōjo*) affiliated with the Naikyōbō office, whose members were tasked with performing "women's entertainment" (*jogaku*) at court banquets.[78] Her anonymity suggests she occupied a relatively modest position within this group, other of whose members are mentioned by name and court rank in historical sources.[79] Consequently, it is doubtful she became Mochiyuki's chief wife.[80] Like many other men at court who associated with these female performers, he may have initially approached her for instruction in music and singing.

A childhood spent in the Palace Office of Female Performers would have exposed Tsurayuki to an extensive repertoire of songs, something that is further suggested by the one surviving reference he makes to his mother in a *waka* preserved within the Miscellaneous section of the *Gosenshū*. In addition to suggesting that she fostered Tsurayuki's interest in vocal music, the poem is noteworthy for marking multiple textual mediations that highlight the porous boundary between *waka* and song, as well as the contingent nature of attribution obtaining in both cases.

Apparently, this was written at the end of a booklet the Minister of the Left had him copy out.

Hahaso-yama	Mount Mother Oak
mine no arashi no	has been assailed by the gales
kaze o itami	of a storm on its peak,
furu koto no ha o	and so I have swept together
kaki zo atsumuru	these long-fallen leaves of words![81]

78. Mezaki, *Ki no Tsurayuki*, 18–20.

79. For example, *Ruijū kokushi* (A History of the Realm by Topic, ca. 892) mentions a member of the Naikyōbō named Ishikawa no Asomi Iroko who held the lower grade of Junior Fifth Rank (KST 5:338).

80. The primary wife of Tsurayuki's father is likely to have been the mother of two half-siblings, Munesada and Fumisada, who are mentioned in the nineteenth-century *Kishi keizu* (Ki Clan Genealogies).

81. *Gosen wakashū* poem 1289, SNKBT 6:390.

Tsurayuki's placement of this poem at the end of a booklet he compiled at the behest of Saneyori indicates it is describing that text's origins. In lieu of the name that would normally identify the compiler of an anthology, this poetic colophon uses allegorical language to mark the process by which more than one individual contributed to its formation. The mountain, which is unique to this one *waka*, introduces Tsurayuki's mother through the species of "mother oak" (*hahaso*) it is named after. By embedding her identity within this arboreal toponym, Tsurayuki turns the act of sweeping up leaves into a representation of his role in compiling the anthology from verses originating with her. Consequently, the "long-fallen leaves of words" (*furu koto no ha*) representing the booklet's contents mark their origin as "old words" (*furu koto*) from earlier song traditions that were subsequently preserved as "leaves of words" (*koto no ha*) in writing. In other words, the poem marks Tsurayuki's role as the compiler of *waka* originating in songs his mother transmitted to him. The pronounced interest held by many aristocrats in receiving instruction from women performers like her makes it easy to imagine the attraction such an anthology would have possessed for Saneyori.

Although Tsurayuki is unambiguously identified as the booklet's writer, it remains unclear whether it was he or his mother who selected the original songs from a much larger repertoire and transformed them into metrically regular *waka* by writing them down without the original refrains. This uncertainty leads to further questions regarding both the different roles played by mother and son in producing these anonymous poems and concerning the relative weight we should give to each individual in assigning attribution. Which of them is responsible for the poems and at what stage? Do the actions of selection or transcription matter most in assigning credit? Analogous questions can be applied to the anonymous *waka* that make up half of the *Kokinshū*'s contents, many of which could have been selected by Tsurayuki from songs, possibly in collaboration with his mother. No doubt it is these same ambiguities that cause the poem to depict authorship as a collective process rather than an individual achievement.

In specifying that the booklet was commissioned by Saneyori, the *Gosenshū* headnote adds another link to this chain of attributions by making the anonymous poems his personal possession, thereby putting the paternal legacy represented by Tsurayuki's scribal literacy to use in harvesting the maternal legacy represented by his knowledge of vocal music. The resulting distance this collection has traveled from an original corpus of sung pieces is subtly stressed by framing the headnote's account with the auxiliary verb *keri*, thereby suggesting the *Gosenshū* compiler has only heard about the poem's provenance. This detail hints at yet another stage in the development of the poetry collection. Because his role as one of the anthology's compilers makes it likely that Tsurayuki's son is the author of this headnote, it is easy to imagine that Tokifumi took the *waka* from an earlier collection that his father had compiled with another purpose in mind and subsequently added the connection to Saneyori when he learned about it later.

According to one hypothesis, the booklet began as a filial attempt on Tsurayuki's part to preserve his mother's memory and console her spirit, much in the same manner as Buddhist scripture was copied with the intention of transferring the merit gained thereby to deceased relatives in order to benefit them in the afterlife.[82] As it happens, *Tosa nikki* refers to this same religious logic overtly in a sardonic observation about poetic attribution it makes on 1/7, when the child's precocious reply to their boorish benefactor's clumsy *waka* leads someone to suggest an older relative "should sign it with a hand print" (*te oshitsu beshi*) and send it back to the man. This form of signature echoes the Buddhist practice of affixing an individual's palm print (*shuin*) to scriptures that had been copied out by others in order to ensure that person was the sole beneficiary of the karmic merit accrued through such scribal labor. A particularly famous example of this proprietary textual practice can be seen in a *ganmon* (prayer dedication) written by Tachibana no Hayanari (d. 842) on behalf of a daughter of Kanmu (737–806, r. 781–806) named Princess Ito (d. 861). By adding several palm prints made with scarlet ink, she is able to appropriate the karmic merit produced by the famed calligrapher's labors and transfer it to her deceased mother.

The association *Tosa nikki* makes between this mode of attribution in religious prayers and that used for proxy poems also implies a further similarity in the social relations both texts produced. Bryan Lowe has described eighth-century *ganmon* as vehicles for producing a "patron function" in which the text's actual producer was erased in order to represent

---

82. Watanabe, "Ki no Tsurayuki," 258–60.

the sponsor as its ostensible speaker and the agent who initiated its address to someone else.[83] The relationships this "patron function" produced among priestly scribes, their commissioning patrons, and the intended recipients of karmic merit are structurally and functionally homologous with those obtaining among lower-ranking poet-scribes such as Tsurayuki, their commissioning patrons, and the intended recipients whom those patrons addressed through the resulting *waka*. Like the moral economy subtending the purchase of fish at Torikai no Mimaki, karmic logic is used here to recast the "poetic patron function" in a humorous but pointed manner that foregrounds the social contingencies and power relations supporting it.

It is precisely because *waka* constituted such a fluid field of attributions that Tsurayuki resorts to Buddhist practices in order to articulate the specific relationships enabled by the materiality of written poems. The need for such a stratagem, like the need to employ figural expressions in the poetic colophon Tsurayuki attached to the collection of his mother's verses, recalls Foucault's definition of authorship as the product of particular cultural and historical contingencies when he stated: "It is not defined by the spontaneous attribution of a text to its creator, but through a series of precise and complex procedures."[84] The connection to women and children in Tsurayuki's portrayal of poetic authorship suggests that hierarchies of age and gender provided him with the most apposite means for articulating the social forces shaping such procedures in his own day. Both his collection of his mother's songs and his use of a female diarist highlight the ways in which femininity inflected the logics of attribution that transformed texts originating with one person into the property of another. Although the diary's transcriptions of *funa uta* can be attributed to the narrator on account of her scribal and editorial interventions, the resulting text ultimately belongs to the ex-governor's family, just as the songs Tsurayuki recorded in his booklet became the property of his patrons.

The alienation of both fictional narrator and historical author from the products of their labor recalls the contrast Carole Cavanaugh has identified between women's prominent role in producing poems and textiles,

83. Lowe, *Ritualized Writing*, 60.
84. Foucault, "What Is an Author?," 130.

and their limited rights to possessing them.[85] Such gendered divisions also structure the booklet and diary, both of which represent female forms of knowledge that were reproduced in writing for the benefit of powerful males. This state of affairs even makes it possible to imagine that Tsurayuki's authorship of *Tosa nikki* resulted from his appropriation of a diary created by a female attendant in his own household, as Masaari may have thought when he attributed the text to an actual woman. Even so, Tsurayuki's own situation vis-à-vis the patrons he wrote for was ultimately little different in this regard from such women as his fictional narrator, his actual mother, and Sei Shōnagon, all of whom, like him, have played a critical role in conveying Heian song to later readers.

Conclusion

For such a brief text, *Tosa nikki* has a remarkable amount to tell us about song. The many facets of vocal music it touches on give a fuller picture of its place in Heian culture than that presented in conventional histories of the period, which have focused rather on the *waka* that supposedly supplanted it. In fact, song possessed a peculiarly powerful form of mobility that significantly complicates attempts to distinguish it from poetry and determine the range of its influence. In other words, the ability of its lyrics and melodies to circulate apart from one another made it relatively easy for vocal music to move between different genres, media, and spaces. Likewise, the slippery syntax song used to simultaneously mark individuals as subjects and objects enhanced its appeal as a means for producing eroticism and irony.

One example of song's mobility can be seen in *Tosa nikki*'s use of language taken from *saibara* to portray genitalia. Unlike the subversive nature of such language in early European forms of parody, the pansexual panoply of subjects and objects encompassed by Heian song made its eroticism a relatively mundane means for creating scenarios in the diary

---

85. Cavanaugh, "Text and Textile." On this principle of bifurcation, see also Kiley, "Estate and Property in the Late Heian Period"; and Nickerson, "The Meaning of Matrilocality."

whose humor stemmed from desire's ability to transform subjects into objects. These transformations reflect another sort of mobility, one common to both song lyrics and the expressions of erotic and gustatory desire the diary articulated in prose, which enabled various subjects to occupy and affix themselves to multiple perspectives. Perhaps this fluidity was informed in part by the relaxing of social hierarchies typical of the banquet settings where they were sung.

Because the boundaries of song were performative and fluid, rather than reified and static, verbs afforded a more precise means for defining it than the nouns favored in modern classificatory schemes. One sign that clear distinctions between song and other cultural forms were neither self-evident nor universally acknowledged in Tsurayuki's day is apparent in the diary's concerted attempts to distinguish the performance of vocal music from the metrical composition of poetry. This liminality is also exemplified by the diary's *kai uta*, whose lyrics traveled far from the eastern region where they originated and whose melodies were often applied to unrelated *waka* in new contexts. The same mobility could also pose potential problems, however, when the volume at which they were performed elicited equally powerful responses.

Such forms of mobility are most densely concentrated in *Tosa nikki*'s ship songs, whose confusions between subject and object are further accentuated by the inherently fluid relations between people engendered through the transitory exchanges they depicted. By also revealing the existence of popular genres shared among commoners who were not professional performers, aristocratic amateurs, or members of the static agrarian communities celebrated in folk song, *funa uta* are perhaps the most powerful illustration of Heian song's mobility, insofar as their widespread circulation allows us to move beyond the categories that subtend conventional histories of early Japanese vocal music. The lyrics that moved among these groups depict a world in which the mobility possessed by song merged with that of maritime travel and money to create a nostalgic longing for home shared by travelers from all regions and social groups.

Because it remains impossible to determine the precise degree to which the depiction of *funa uta* in *Tosa nikki* is imagined rather than documented, it remains far easier to separate them from a self-contained literary history focused on the evolution of canonical court-sponsored literary forms than it is to treat their lyrics as a historical resource possessing unique insights into Heian culture. Yet pursuing the more conventional and convenient option in this case forecloses an all-too-rare opportunity for us to produce a broader picture of Heian Japan in which illiterate commoners commented on their world with as much sophistication as the elite. Such opportunities are all the more valuable in light of what one historian has characterized as the continuing lack of attention paid to popular culture in this period.[86] Given that our sources are ultimately produced by an elite, it is perhaps safest to identify aspects of popular culture in these songs as "such elements of their [the writers'] thought as were not defined by their education and privileged status," in the words of one prominent European medievalist.[87] However mediated, however brief, and however incomplete their lyrics might be, the few fragments of *funa uta* that have survived are too unique in this regard to discount as fabrications that only speak to the solipsistic concerns of a literate elite.

The unusual degree of interest in song exhibited by *Tosa nikki* can be at least partially attributed to the expertise and sensibilities of the author's mother. His attempts to preserve her knowledge in anthological form also reveal an irony inherent to the process by which oral songs were transformed into written texts. The very same literacy that Tsurayuki upheld as essential to distinguishing an individual's skill in poetic composition from common forms of vocal music also allowed that person's *waka*, like song, to be claimed by others. This paradox also possessed a gendered dimension, insofar as Tsurayuki played a scribal role akin to that of his father in order to transform his mother's expertise with vocal music into written poems possessed by his male patrons. In addition to providing yet another example of song's discursive mobility, the shifting forms of attribution entailed by such maneuvers reflected larger gendered divisions between feminine producers and masculine owners that informed the author's choice of a lower-ranking female narrator as a means of making *Tosa nikki* available to any reader.

---

86. Shigeta, *Shomintachi no Heiankyō*, 22.
87. Gurevich, *Medieval Popular Culture*, xiii.

CHAPTER 4

Liquid Landscapes

Compared to the first sentence in the prologue declaring the narrator's intent to write a diary, much less attention has been accorded the succeeding two describing its content as "that affair" (*sono yoshi*) consisting of the return voyage. Yet it is that journey that has arguably played a more long-standing role in *Tosa nikki*'s reception, particularly during the Edo period when it was chiefly valued as a vernacular travelogue. With both literature and life increasingly taking place along a burgeoning transportation network, many writers in early modern times turned to Heian accounts of travel in *kana* as models for their own autobiographical travelogues.[1] As the earliest example of such a text, *Tosa nikki* constituted a paradigmatic example of *kikōbun* (travel writing).[2]

Perhaps its most esteemed reader in this period was Bashō, who included it in his *Oi no kobumi* (Knapsack Notebook, 1688), along with the writings of Kamo no Chōmei (1155–1216) and *Izayoi nikki* (Diary of the Sixteenth Night, 1283) by Abutsu (ca. 1222–1283), as an exemplary "road journal" (*michi no nikki*) relating travelers' emotions.[3] No doubt its combination of prose with poetry and blending of fact with fiction offered inspiration for the *haikai* master's own travel accounts. In the nineteenth century this status would be officially recognized by the scholar Hanawa

---

1. Nenzi, *Excursions in Identity*, 93–95.
2. Ikeda, "Nikki bungaku to kikō bungaku," 4–5.
3. *Oi no kobumi*, SNKBZ 71:47.

Hokiichi (1746–1821), who placed it at the head of the travel section (*kikō-bu*) of *kana* writings that follows a diary section (*nikki-bu*) devoted to memoirs of life at court in his authoritative compendium of earlier Japanese texts known as *Gunsho ruijū* (Writings by Topic, 1819).

Tosa nikki's generic significance can also be inferred by the history Hanawa constructs for it, in which the diary is followed by another one similar enough in many regards to suggest Tsurayuki's text influenced it. *Io nushi* (Hut Master, ca. 987–1048) is an account of three pilgrimages from the capital to sacred sites and places renowned for their earlier poetic associations made by an otherwise unknown priest named Zōki (ca. 925–957). The preponderance of poetry among its brief prose passages suggests *Io nushi* began as a *waka* anthology, while its frequent use of *keri* might indicate the influence of *monogatari*. Its opening portion, however, seems quite clearly to have been inspired by the diary.

> When was it? Wishing to be free of the world and its constraints, there was a person who set out to visit all the famous places he had heard of, as well as those with some special charm, in order to clear away his cares; and to worship at exalted sites in order to dispel his sins. He was named Hut Master. Around the tenth of the Tenth Month he set out on a pilgrimage to Kumano. Several people spoke of their desire to stay by his side, but since none of them shared his purpose, he slipped away with only a single youthful attendant.[4]

Like *Tosa nikki*, the opening portion of *Io nushi* is divided between a prologue introducing its content and a description of the first stages of the journey on a date that is at once calendrically specific and historically vague. The ensuing structure also bears a resemblance to that of its predecessor: like Tsurayuki's diarist, the priestly protagonist simultaneously moves in two opposing vectors as he progresses forward in space while regressing backward in time through recollections of those who he has left behind him.

The earliest mention of *Tosa nikki* in English, made by William Aston (1841–1911) nearly two decades before Harris's translation, shares the early modern Japanese estimation of its significance as a travelogue, albeit

---

4. *Io nushi*, 348.

somewhat less enthusiastically, when he stated: "It contains no exciting adventures or romantic situations; there are in it no wise maxims or novel information; its only merit is that it describes in simple yet elegant language the ordinary life of a traveler in Japan at the time when it was written."[5] The one scholar to discuss *Tosa nikki* as an instance of travel writing in English, in comparison, found it lacking in descriptive detail, particularly by the standards of the same Edo poet who esteemed it so highly: "It is hard to imagine a Japanese diarist passing the whirlpool at Naruto in the Awa Strait without alluding to it. Even if it had been too dark to see anything, Bashō would surely have been able to imagine what the whirlpool was like, and might even have lied to the extent of saying that the starlight was so bright he could see the swirling waters."[6] This negative evaluation of the diary's landscapes is also a critical commonplace among modern Japanese scholars, who often note the repetitive and restricted nature of their depiction.

In this chapter I will argue that *Tosa nikki* was in fact worthy of esteem by a writer such as Bashō, not simply because of its relative antiquity or the renown of its author, but also on account of the singular contribution it made to Japanese travelogue writing through its innovative application of *waka* poetics to prose. After taking up the predecessors, both literary and historical, that its author might have had at hand as a model for travel writing, I will proceed to identify three ways in which the diary's prose differs. First, although it draws on connections between Ki clan history and the locales it mentions in its title and final portions of the journey, *Tosa nikki* also deploys place names for literary effect rather than geographical veracity to an unprecedented extent. Second, despite scholars' tendency toward negative evaluations of its natural settings, and despite its own sensitivity to the gap between poetic language oriented around the capital and the wider world it sought to represent, the diary presents its surroundings in vivid sentences that embrace *waka*'s rhetorical and structural asymmetries to create new ways of depicting landscapes in travelogue prose. Finally, the large number of uneventful days in the narrative, which have been essentially ignored by critics, appear carefully sequenced for dramatic effect. The first and third of these aspects can also

5. Aston, "An Ancient Japanese Classic," 117.
6. Keene, *Travelers of a Hundred Ages*, 23.

be considered parodic insofar as they fictionalize the very same details through which travelogues signaled their documentary status as actual historical accounts. By way of conclusion, I will argue that these unique aspects of its prose were enabled by the radical distance of its wintry liquid landscape from the usual settings of vernacular court literature and because they were designed with illustrations in mind.

Earlier Travel Narratives

Scholars from Edo times onward have compared *Tosa nikki* with many earlier travel accounts. Yuzuru, for example, noted its similarities to the Tang-dynasty travelogue *Lainan lu* (A Record of Coming South, 809).[7] This journal, which chronicles a six-month journey from the capital at Loyang to a posting in Guangzhou by the literatus Li Ao (774–836), resembles *Tosa nikki* in its daily entry format and content. Both open with a concise description of the journey's destination and purpose, both record the names of well-wishers at banquets, and both mention daughters (in *Lainan lu*'s case, one who is born).[8] At the same time, Li Ao appears to be more concerned than Tsurayuki with offering readers the sort of verifiable and quantifiable details expected from a travelogue recording an actual journey, such as the distance covered in a day. Nor, as one scholar has pointed out, does it contain poetry.[9] Other than occasional citations from older poems, subsequent travel writers in the better-documented Song dynasty (960–1279) also kept their prose accounts separate from their poetic production.[10]

Another Literary Sinitic text *Tosa nikki* has been compared to is the Japanese travelogue *Nittō guhō junrai kōki* by the priest Ennin (794–864),

---

7. A partial translation in English is provided in Schafer, *The Vermilion Bird*, 22–24.
8. Mori, "*Rainanroku*," 31.
9. Kawaguchi, *Heianchō Nihon kanbungaku shi* 1:215–16.
10. On Song representations of travel, see Zhang, *Transformative Journeys*. As we will see in chapter 6, *Tosa nikki* also draws extensively on an exilic tradition in Tang poetry.

recording his nearly decade-long sojourn on the continent.[11] In addition to such details as the custom of tossing mirrors into stormy waters, the two share a tendency to follow the description of a scene with a personal observation or feeling informed by an awareness of their distance from life at court.[12] This or other accounts in Literary Sinitic of voyages to the continent, such as *Gyōrekishō* (Notes from a Pilgrimage, ca. 851–858) by Enchin (814–891) and *Zaitō nikki* (Diary of a Sojourn Overseas, ca. 717–18) by Kibi no Makibi (695–775), could have also inspired Tsurayuki's interest in the potential a maritime setting offered for innovative forms of writing.[13]

Although we cannot say with certainty if Tsurayuki read any of the above travelogues, there are other such accounts he is likely to have known about before becoming governor of Tosa. In his role as *goshodokoro no azukari*, Tsurayuki had access to some version of *Nihon shoki* in the palace library, whose current text includes the earliest surviving fragments of travelogue prose in Japan. One is *Iki no Hakatoko no fumi* (Chronicle of Iki no Hakatoko), describing the fourth embassy to Tang China from 659 to 661. Four citations from it in the historical chronicle include brief mentions of such details as the route, the weather, and the party's reception by Tang authorities.[14] Overlapping with this account is a brief citation from another text, *Naniwa no Kishi Obito no fumi* (Record of the Naniwa Noble Scholar), kept by an immigrant from Koguryŏ.[15] Like the aforementioned records of pilgrimages, however, these journals are exclusively concerned with travel to foreign lands. Although perhaps also being written at the time, domestic travel diaries did not merit inclusion in either the earliest historical chronicle or its five successors.

For domestic travel, Tsurayuki may have turned to the records of the sovereign's movements produced during his time in the Naiki office. The few fragmentary portions of *naiki no nikki* that have survived often refer

---

11. For an English translation of this text, see Reischauer, *Ennin's Diary*.
12. Mekada, "Kyūseiki totōzō nikki kō."
13. Honma, "*Tosa nikki* to *Nittō guhō junrai kōki*," 55–57.
14. *Nihon shoki* entries for Kōtoku 5/2, Saimei 5/7, 6/7, and 7/5, SNKBZ 4:197, 223, 233, and 243. See also Aston, *Nihongi* (2), 246, 260, 266–67, and 271–72.
15. *Nihon shoki* entry for Saimei 5/7, SNKBZ 4:227; Aston, *Nihongi* (2), 263.

to royal excursions. The earliest such example, which recounts a royal procession to the Seri-kawa in 886 made by Kōkō (830–887, r. 884–887), lists its participants and their attire, while the latest mentions a similar journey to the banks of the Ōi-gawa in 1076 by Shirakawa (1053–1129, r. 1073–1087) at which *waka* were composed.[16] Although no such records survive from Uda's reign, we can infer some of their characteristics from similar accounts of a trip he made to Miyataki shortly after abdicating in 898. The three-week affair included a hunt at Katano, in emulation of the capital's founder, Kanmu, and a pilgrimage to the Sumiyoshi shrine.[17] Two records of his journey have survived in fragmentary form: *Teiji'in no Miyataki gokō ki* (Account of His Majesty Uda's Excursion to Miyataki) by Michizane, and *Kisoigariki* (Account of a Hunt for Wild Herbs) by his colleague Haseo.

Kisoigariki appears in *Kike shū* (Ki House Collection), an anthology of Haseo's writings that has survived in a partial copy made by the literatus Ōe no Asatsuna (886–958) in 919. At the beginning of this account, Haseo identifies himself as a "court historian" (史臣), perhaps suggesting he imagines himself in a role similar to that of a *naiki no nikki* scribe, but with a different goal in mind. Accordingly, he states that his record seeks to present Uda's tour as a more suitable mirror for posterity than those of his predecessor Yōzei (869–949, r. 876–884), whose hunting trips allegedly burdened the lives of commoners by requisitioning horses and other possessions.[18] *Kisoigariki*'s detailed description of the expedition's procession from the capital and the ensuing hunt lists the numbers of participants, their clothes and accoutrements, game captured, and the round of drinks at the celebratory banquet afterward before the record is cut short when a riding accident forces Haseo to return to the capital. Its depictions of female entertainers being groped and kissed are particularly reminiscent of the bawdy banquet settings discussed in chapter 3.

16. Tamai, *Nikki bungaku gaisetsu*, 306–7.
17. A more detailed description of these excursions is provided in Borgen, *Sugawara no Michizane*, 260–68.
18. Kawajiri, "'Kike shū' to kokushi hensan," 3. An excellent quality printed version can be found in *Heian Kamakura mikan shishū*, 38–43.

Michizane's more extensive account of the same excursion boasts versions in *kana* and Literary Sinitic. The former text was preserved in *Fukuro-zōshi* (Pocket Book, ca. 1156–59) and *Gosenshū seigi* (Correct Meaning of the *Gosenshū*, ca. 1304); the latter one in *Fusō ryakki* (Abbreviated Chronicles of Japan, ca. 1094).[19] Both share the same names of places and people but are otherwise different in intriguing ways. Whereas the Literary Sinitic version appears to follow the conventions of *naiki no nikki*, the *kana* text takes the form of brief, memo-style jottings.[20] And while the former offers such quantifiable details as times of day, the amount and type of various gifts, and the number of participants at particular events, its *kana* counterpart instead includes an encounter with an elderly woman who is questioned about the waterfall at Miyataki. Both versions mention poems composed for the event: the *kana* text includes one *waka* by Uda, while the Literary Sinitic version features a *shi* couplet by Michizane and makes several brief references (often critical) to *waka*.

As it happens, Tsurayuki's earliest known foray into *kana* prose also involves royal processions. Nine years after Uda's excursion to Miyataki, he composed the *Ōi-gawa gyōkō waka no jo* (Preface to Waka for the Royal Procession to the Ōi River) commemorating visits to the river made by the same sovereign and his successor.[21] This achievement on Tsurayuki's part may have contributed to his own subsequent appointment as a *shōnaiki* (junior inner palace secretary) in 910 before becoming *tainaiki* (senior inner palace secretary) in 913. Like Michizane's *kana* account of the Miyataki excursion, Tsurayuki's preface is accompanied by one in Literary Sinitic. Unlike the former text, however, Tsurayuki's *kana* prose draws on the parallel constructions and epithets employed in earlier Japanese poetry. As we will see, he turned to other forms of *waka* rhetoric in developing *Tosa nikki*'s prose.

---

19. All three records of the journey to Miyataki appear together in Ishihara, *Heian nikki bungaku no kenkyū*, 119–21.

20. Ishihara, *Heian nikki bungaku no kenkyū*, 124. Lingering doubts about Michizane's authorship of the *kana* journal led Ishihara to argue that it was authored by a female attendant in his household, although it is difficult to see what role such a woman would have played in a royal excursion.

21. A study and translation of this preface is provided in Ceadel, "Ōi River Poems and Preface."

Another model for representing domestic travel available to Tsurayuki were *Man'yōshū* poems, including the *kōro shinin no uta* lamenting travelers' corpses, mentioned in chapter 2. An even closer resemblance to *Tosa nikki* within the anthology can be found in travel sequences whose poems are connected by brief prose descriptions of their locations, authors, and topics. Akinari and Mitsue first pointed out the diary's resemblance to the longest and most complex such sequence describing the domestic portions of an embassy's departure to and return from Silla, which likewise includes both seaside poems of parting and elegies for those who died before returning home.[22] If anything, however, an even closer model from the anthology is provided by a sequence attributed to retainers of Ōtomo no Tabito (665–731) describing their return to the capital from Dazaifu.[23] Both its exclusive focus on the travails of a voyage from countryside to capital and its preference for poems by members of a former official's household—many of whom are so low in status that they (like the majority of *Tosa nikki*'s poets) remain anonymous—make this sequence strikingly similar to Tsurayuki's diary.

The most obvious source of inspiration for *Tosa nikki* is the *Kokinshū*'s equally unprecedented Travel section (*kiryo-bu*). Like the diary, place names can be found in either its *waka* themselves or the prose accompanying them.[24] The most detailed study of its tightly organized structure divides Travel into five contexts for composing travel poems: at a journey's beginning, mid-journey, returning to the capital, during a provincial posting, and while on royal processions.[25] All of these situations are evoked to one degree or another in *Tosa nikki*. Furthermore, the diary's only named poets also feature prominently in Travel: Nakamaro inaugurates the section, while Narihira is its best-represented poet. As we saw in chapter 1, *Tosa nikki*'s connections to this anthological category would carry over into *Gosenshū*, whose own Travel section attributes two anonymous poems from the diary to Tsurayuki.

22. Nihei, "*Tosa nikki* zenshi," 30.
23. *Man'yōshū* poems 17:3890–99, SNKBZ 9:149–51. For an English translation of the sequence, see Horton, *Traversing the Frontier*, 360–70.
24. Hasegawa, "*Tosa nikki* no hōhō," 16. The most extensive treatment of this connection to the *Kokinshū*'s Travel section is in Kikuchi, "*Tosa nikki* ron."
25. Matsuda, *Kokinshū no kōzō*, 376–91.

References to Narihira's *Kokinshū* poems in Travel are especially frequent in the diary. One of the most extended examples occurs when the party arrives at Hane:

> Just now we have arrived at a place called "Wings." After being told the name of the place, a child who is still quite immature said: "I wonder if this place called 'Wings' actually resembles bird wings." People laughed at these childishly naïve words. Then a girl who is apparently with us here recited this verse:

makoto nite	If it is truly the case
na ni kiku tokoro	that there are wings
hane naraba	in this place whose name I hear,
tobu ga gotoku ni	then let us fly like birds
miyako e mogana	back towards the capital city!
(TN 27–28, 1/11)	

In its use of a hypothetical construct to invoke the connotations of an avian name while longing for the capital aboard a vessel, the girl's *waka* closely resembles the famous poem addressing "capital birds" (*miyako-dori*) Narihira composes while being ferried across the Sumida-gawa.[26] The prose prefacing this travel poem is perhaps also echoed on 12/27, when the steersman's curt command ordering the party to hurry aboard recalls the ferryman's equally brusque treatment of Narihira.[27]

It is theoretically possible that the diary could be alluding here to the Sumida-gawa episode in *Ise*, some version of which is likely to have been in circulation at the time. As we will see in the next chapter, other portions of *Tosa nikki* hint at a close connection to the poem tale. However, the prose following the Hane poem suggests rather that the *Kokinshū* is its source. When the child's naïve question brings back memories of the ex-governor's deceased daughter, the diarist recalls the final two measures from an anonymous "old song" (*furu uta*) that appears immediately after

---

26. *Kokin wakashū* poem 411, SNKBZ 11:175: "If you bear that name, / let me ask something of you, / capital birds. / Is the one I think of / alive or no?" (*na ni shi owaba / iza koto towamu / miyako-dori / waga omou hito wa / ari ya nashi ya to*).

27. Hasegawa, "Hyōgen, sono senryaku-teki na *Tosa nikki*," 135.

Narihira's Sumida-gawa poem in the anthology.[28] Although both poems also appear in the Travel section of the *Shinsen waka*, moreover, they are not adjacent to one another in that text.[29] Additional hints that *Tosa nikki* is specifically referencing the *Kokinshū* can be found in the commentary that follows this anonymous old song in the anthology, which attributes it to a woman returning to the capital after the man she had originally set out with had passed away while they were in the provinces. This narrative context makes the anonymous song doubly relevant to *Tosa nikki* as both the first poem in Travel depicting a person returning to the capital from a provincial posting, and the first *waka* in that section of the anthology mentioning a loved one who dies before making the same journey.

One close reading of the diary by Ogawa Kōzō suggests that sequencing techniques are also used to organize its poems into four movements dividing the journey into distinct stages. The first consists of exchanges with well-wishers, highlighting human relations through the pronouns *kimi* (you), *hito* (you/that one), and *ware* (myself). Poems in the second movement mark the passage of time through terrain, flora, and fauna. Upon reaching the home provinces, the third movement reenters the human world with *waka* that mention weaving and, perhaps by implication, the wealth (and greed) of the capital region as well. Trees predominate in all the poems belonging to the riparian final movement up the Yodo-gawa to the city. Individual *waka* are further connected to one another across and within these movements, forming pairs and triads through homonyms, homophones, and antonyms.[30]

The evident attention paid to poetic sequencing in the diary may even indicate it originated as an anthology to which prose was added at a later stage.[31] In this sense, *Tosa nikki* could be considered akin to the aforementioned *Man'yōshū* travel poem sequences. As we shall see, however, the sophisticated use of poetic devices in its prose distinguishes the diary

28. *Kokin wakashū* poem 412, SNKBZ 11:176: "Northward fly / the wild geese I hear cry. / Of those that filed here, / a smaller number now / appear homeward bound!" (*kita e yuku / kari zo naku naru / tsurete koshi / kazu wa tarade zo / kaeru bera naru*).

29. The Sumida-gawa and anonymous *waka* appear as poems 194 and 200 respectively in *Shinsen waka*.

30. Ogawa, "*Tosa nikki* ni okeru waka no seishō," 244–45.

31. Seto, "Hōhō toshite no nikki," 12–14.

from both *waka* anthologies and poem tales alike. Whereas the prose of such texts as the *Man'yōshū*, *Kokinshū*, and *Ise* typically lack figural language—perhaps in order to draw attention to these features in their poems—*Tosa nikki* can be seen drawing on *waka*'s rhetorical techniques even in entries that consist entirely of prose.

Ki Clanscapes

Tosa nikki also gestures to earlier texts through references to the history of Tsurayuki's clan that are embedded in its place names. Its most illustrious member, Funamori (731–792), had previously governed Tosa, and Tsurayuki's own cousin Tomonori also served as a secretary (*jō*) in its administration. These historical connections also include Tosa's lengthy association with exile, which many scholars believe Tsurayuki draws on in order to mark his own distance from the centers of power at court as the latter-day scion of a once-powerful clan now living in reduced circumstances.[32] But whereas the long line of men who had been banished to Tosa in disgrace lost rank, office, and wealth, the same province presented Tsurayuki with a chance for advancement that he was probably happy to take, in spite of his advanced age at the time. In reality, men belonging to his echelon of court society competed for such lucrative positions and rejoiced when they got them. The diary's allusions to exile are therefore more likely to be exaggerated fictions designed to flatter his patrons rather than autobiographical truths.

Other than a few references to *waka* his patrons in the capital commissioned from him, the only confident assertion we can make about Tsurayuki's time in Tosa province is when it took place. *Kokin wakashū mokuroku* and the headnote to poem 714 in the *Tsurayuki shū* both confirm he was its governor from 930 to 934. Prior to that point, he had held three subsidiary posts in provincial administration: as the assistant lesser secretary (*gon-shōjō*) of Echizen in 906, as deputy governor (*suke*) of Kaga in 917, and as deputy governor of Mino the subsequent year. These positions were all probably sinecures that allowed Tsurayuki to

---

32. Hasegawa, *Ki no Tsurayuki ron*, 91.

remain in the capital while also providing him with a higher salary than that of equivalent posts in the central administration. Deputy governorships were especially common among officials who occupied the lower grade of the Junior Fifth Rank, as Tsurayuki had done since 917. The lengthy headnote to one poem in *Tsurayuki shū* in fact indicates he actively lobbied for the Mino assignment.[33] Since Mino was the largest province after Michinoku and Musashi, the salaries of its officials would have been especially generous. Mino was also much closer to the capital than its larger counterparts, making it easier for Tsurayuki to return there if he was dispatched to the province for some reason. Regardless, most scholars believe he never actually spent any significant amount of time outside the capital prior to Tosa.[34]

Although the position of governor offered greater prospects for personal enrichment than those of *gon-shōjō* or *suke*, Tosa was in some regards a less appealing assignment than either Kaga or Mino. In addition to being relatively poor, it was the smallest of the four provinces on Shikoku, causing it to be ranked one grade below the others. At the same time, we should remember that the majority of Tosa's governors in the Heian period shared the same background and career trajectory as Tsurayuki. For these men, such a post would have been a privilege that only became available upon attaining the much-coveted Fifth Rank after years of hard work. Coming as it did during a period when floods and disease were ravaging the capital, moreover, Tsurayuki's receipt of this post soon after being appointed assistant magistrate for the western half of the city (*ukyō no suke*) might even indicate his patrons were motivated by concern for his well-being.[35] Shortly after his departure, such concerns would in fact be confirmed in the most unsettling manner imaginable when lightning struck a pillar in Daigo's living quarters. After three of the uppermost nobility in attendance were killed and two others severely burned, the sovereign fell mortally ill.

33. *Tsurayuki shū* poem 778, SNKS 80:269–70.
34. Murase, *Kyūtei kajin Ki no Tsurayuki*, 137.
35. Murase, *Kyūtei kajin Ki no Tsurayuki*, 171. This and his previous posting as *daikenmotsu* (warden of the palace storehouse) from 923 to 928 were both comfortable sinecures with few actual duties. As warden of the palace storehouse, Tsurayuki would have been simply required to keep track of its keys. Serving as magistrate of the capital's sparsely inhabited western half also entailed few responsibilities.

Even if he was in fact pleased with his appointment, however, *Tosa nikki*'s author would have sought to flatter his aristocratic readership by protesting that the distance from them made the experience akin to banishment. From their perspective, Tosa undoubtedly represented the most severe form of exile imaginable. The penal codes in *Engi shiki* designated the province a form of "distant banishment" (*onru*) representing the most punitive type of expulsion from the capital.[36] As far back as the eighth century it had been the destination of exiles such as Isonokami no Otomaro (d. 750), who was sent there in 739, and Ōtomo no Koshibi (695–777), who received the same sentence in 749. As we saw in chapter 2, the bones of Prince Nagaya suffered a similar fate. Although we only know the title of the tale *Tosa no otodo* (The Lord of Tosa) from the preface to *Sanbō ekotoba* (Illustrations and Explanations for the Three Treasures, 984), such associations make its use of the toponym sufficient to suggest the eponymous protagonist is also banished at some point.

The largest number of intertextual references to Tosa as an exilic space in the diary cluster around one of the author's immediate forebears, Ki no Natsui (fl. 858–866), who was sent there in the aftermath of the Ōtenmon Disturbance of 866. His biography in *Sandai jitsuroku* describes Natsui as a benevolent official who also excelled at medicine, calligraphy, and board games.[37] Like Tsurayuki, he had been a scribe in the Naiki office before becoming a provincial governor. Several other biographical details are also echoed in the diary. *Sandai jitsuroku*'s description of him gathering medicinal herbs in Tosa, for example, recalls the tonic produced by its provincial head doctor. Both texts also feature the death of female relatives (a mother in Natsui's case). The lengthy description of people in Higo province bidding him farewell when he finished serving as its governor may have also served as a foil to similar (albeit parodic) scenes in the diary.[38]

Tosa nikki's prose also gestures to Tosa's status as an exilic space by describing the ship's progress with the archaic verb *ou* (pursue)

---

36. *Engi shiki* section 29, KST 26:722. Unlike similar categories in the Tang penal codes specifying the relative severity of exile, these were not based on their actual distance from the capital (Stockdale, *Imagining Exile in Heian Japan*, 91).
37. *Nihon sandai jitsuroku* entry for Jōgan 8/9/22, KST 4:195.
38. Watanabe, "*Tosa nikki* no naimen-teki keisei," 30–34.

in a deliberate echo of a *Man'yōshū* poem by Otomaro lamenting his banishment:

chichi-gimi ni	To my lord father
ware wa anago zo	I am a cherished child.
haha-toji ni	To my lady mother
ware wa anago zo	I am a cherished child.
mai-noboru	On their way to the capital
yaso uji hito	the many clansmen in their myriads
tamuke suru	have made offerings to the gods,
kashiko no saka ni	at these fearsome cliffs,
nusa matsuri	worshipping with prayer slips,
ware wa zo oeru	where I myself pursue
tōki Tosa-ji o	the distant way to Tosa![39]

In fact, many of the instances where *ou* appears in *Tosa nikki* describe the ship's smooth progress over the gentle Inner Sea after "thrusting" (*sasu*) across the rough waters of the open Pacific.[40] Rather than replicate the original poem's sorrowful tone, therefore, Tsurayuki's prose marks the opposite trajectory away from Tosa's exilic space by using the same verb to represent the growing safety of the sea as he nears home.

All the historical allusions mentioned thus far begin and end with the diary's titular toponym. Within its text, by contrast, place names only begin to possess narrative contexts toward the end of the journey, after the party reaches the security of Izumi. There, the many rocky islets that had previously concealed treacherous reefs and pirates are now replaced by the level shoreline of the home provinces (*kinai*) adjoining the capital, making it possible to identify such threats in advance and either steer around them or flee overland. Within these more safely familiar environs, the same clan identity that Otomaro's poem moves away from begins to cohere around the travelers through references to Tsurayuki's ancestors, who originated in the eponymous province of Kii on Izumi's southern borders. This history extends all the way back to the landscapes of legend when the travelers reach the hallowed shores of Sumiyoshi, a site

39. Nakanishi, "Tsurayuki no hōhō," 114–15. *Man'yōshū* poem 6:1022, SNKBZ 7:156.
40. Yasuda, "*Tosa nikki* ni mochiirareta 'ofu,'" 58.

traditionally associated with the sovereign Jingū (169–269, r. 201–269), whose long-lived minister Takechi no Sukune (b. 84) was a distant ancestor of the author.

Place names connected to the Ki clan's more recent history appear when the ship advances up the Yodo-gawa. As signs of spring start to emerge in both prose and poetry, the party confronts a key turning point in the clan's fortunes at the Nagisa villa formerly owned by Prince Koretaka (844–897). When Koretaka was initially designated crown prince by his father, Montoku (827–858, r. 850–858), Tsurayuki's forebears had reason to hope that their kinship with his mother, Ki no Shizuko (d. 866), would gain them political preeminence at court. Instead, his sudden removal from the succession in 850 led to an equally dramatic fall from grace for his maternal kin. Tsurayuki's grandfather Motomichi was not elevated to the Fifth Rank until he was in his fifties, a full twenty years after his own father and grandfather had crossed this critical threshold into the upper echelons of the court. Unlike them, moreover, his death is ignored in official accounts. As we will see in the next chapter, Tsurayuki's treatment of Nagisa indicates, among other things, that he is well aware of this history.

Two days after passing Koretaka's former villa, one last locale obliquely marks Tsurayuki's clan on 2/11 when the party arrives in the environs of the Yawata shrine, also known as Iwashimizu Hachimangū. The head priest (*kannushi*) of this holy place dedicated to the deity of Otoko-yama was traditionally chosen from the Ki clan (TNZ 383–89). Even though it was customary for officials to pay their respects there when they returned to the capital, however, the diarist and her fellow travelers are unaware of its existence until a stranger points out the location. This omission is even more surprising in light of Otoko-yama's mention in the *kana* preface to the *Kokinshū* noted in the previous chapter. Perhaps the diary is being inspired rather by a *waka* from the anthology depicting a mist-shrouded mountain near the capital its speaker is approaching from the east.[41]

The presence of Tsurayuki's clan shrine is signified metonymically rather than literally in a tranquil space adjacent to the actual site, taking shape in one of the diary's most vividly depicted landscapes within an

---

41. Kikuchi, *Kokinshū igo ni okeru Tsurayuki*, 135; *Kokin wakashū* poem 413, SNKBZ 11:176.

anonymous poem that only hints at the presence of Yawata through an image of the willows on the opposite riverbank, where the party has halted at the temple of Sōō-ji:

sazare-nami	Rippling wavelets
yosuru fumi oba	approach in a pattern
ao-yagi no	of green willows
kage no ito shite	whose dappled threads
oru ka to zo miru	seem woven together!
(TN 53, 2/11)	

In this reimagining of the riverside as a textile, the reflected image of willow fronds and their rippling surface become the warp and weft weaving together a pattern of green land and blue water. Together, they provide a close-up view of the shoreline, where the trees had been planted in rows on the temple's earthen bulwarks. Ripples also mark the swollen springtime flow of the river lapping insistently against a shore dappled in sunlight and the long shadows cast by its willow fronds. The resulting atmosphere of refined tranquility in a watery borderland connecting clanscape to traveler conveys the sense of coming home to a familiar identity. The impact of such feelings is all the more powerful as a result of the characters having previously passed over a liquid landscape that was, by contrast, thoroughly alien.

Place Names as Poetic Fictions

Unlike many other Heian vernacular texts, in which storied place names mingled past with present, the majority of landscapes depicted in *Tosa nikki* lack ties to identifiable narratives.[42] This is particularly true of the locations passed during the first leg of the journey. It is this segment of the voyage that provides the diary with one of its most distinctive features. Unlike previous travelogues' shared concern with documenting an actual itinerary, *Tosa nikki* uses fictional place names to mark its route

---

42. Takahashi, "Heianchō bungaku 'fūkei' ron (ichi)," 19–20.

with notable frequency. In doing so, it draws on a poetic tradition that dates back to the earliest extant Japanese texts, in which otherwise unknown locations occasionally appear in songs on account of their descriptive qualities. Whereas this fictionalized treatment of toponyms was previously limited to poetry, however, the diary also adopts this approach in its prose. This fluid mingling of both forms of language is enabled at least in part by the foreignness of *Tosa nikki*'s liquid landscape.

The alien and terrifying nature of a maritime journey would have been sure to arouse horrified fascination in a readership who rarely left the capital's environs, as attested to by its dramatic treatment in such contemporaneous tales as *Taketori* and *Utsuho monogatari*. As we saw in chapter 3, *The Pillow Book* also describes the vulnerability of boats in such settings at some length. Fear of its dangers is further hinted at in *waka* likening waves to snow and blossoms within the diary, a formula often used in the *Man'yōshū* to pacify water spirits.[43] Because its Pacific coast was deemed to be especially treacherous, the terrors of a maritime journey from Tosa would have made it a particularly compelling setting in this regard. One popular twelfth-century *imayō* song gives us a striking description of this region's pelagic perils:

Tosa no funa-ji wa osoroshi ya	How fearsome the sea route of Tosa!
Murotsu ga oki narade wa	No way to avoid the offing at Murotsu.
shima-se ga iwa wa tate	Reefs near shore jut out like islands.
Saki ya Saki no ura ura	At Saki, ah Saki, bay after bay!
mikuriya no Hotsu misaki	The sacred mighty peninsula of Hotsu.
Kongō Jōdo no tsure nagoro	The Diamond Pure Land awash in waves.[44]

Like the diary, this song maps out a route dominated by waves and reefs, both of which forced boats to head far out into the ocean. Such dangers would explain why the return journey from Tosa could also take place partly by land across Iyo province. It is thus possible that Tsurayuki in fact substituted the Pacific coast for his actual route back to the capital in the interests of dramatic appeal.

43. Satō, *Heian waka bungaku hyōgen ron*, 82.
44. *Ryōjin hishō* song 348, SNKBZ 42:278.

The infinite expanse of the open Pacific also blurs the line between fact and fiction due to its liminal location at what was deemed to be the edge of the perceptible world. In its detailed account of governmental posts and procedures in Tsurayuki's day, *Engi shiki* treats Tosa as the southernmost border of the Heian realm.[45] The vanishing point on its horizon where sky and water merge also marked the border between this world and the mythic land of eternal life known as Tokoyo (Everworld) described in the legend of Urashimako, who, like the diarist, returns to a home changed beyond recognition.[46] One anonymous poem in the diary is a particularly powerful evocation of this alien setting. So vast is the oceanic space it describes that it erases normal spatial distinctions and reduces the viewing subject to a forlorn mote swallowed up by their surroundings:

kage mireba	Reflections reveal
nami no soko naru	beneath the waves
hisakata no	a far-off firmament,
sora kogi-wataru	rowing across whose sky
ware zo wabishiki	is this misery-filled I!
(TN 31, 1/17)	

Through a play on reflective images, the boat in this *waka* drifts over both waves and sky, bringing together real and imagined spaces in the same manner as the diary merges autobiographical fact with biographical fiction.[47]

In addition to removing distinctions between sky and water, the diary's ocean causes landscapes to appear the same from a distance or close up, for the cardinal directions to disappear, and for the seasons to blur as waves morph by turns into winter snow or spring blossoms.[48] Taken as a whole, such visual peculiarities unmoor *Tosa nikki*'s maritime setting from the tangible coordinates of physical space and seasonal time. The fictional quality of this liquid landscape is also suggested by the frequent foregrounding of language's role in its construction. Omnipresent wind

45. *Engi shiki* section 22, KST 26:566.
46. Higashihara, "'Nami no soko naru,'" 7–9.
47. Watanabe, "*Tosa nikki* shiron," 80.
48. Nishinoiri, "*Tosa nikki* no umi," 115–16.

and waves, representing a causal relationship between an invisible entity and its temporary manifestation in visible traces, can even be likened respectively to signified and signifier.[49] Language's capacity to represent the experience of travel also decreases in tandem with the contraction of the diary's liquid landscape from the open ocean at its beginning to a shrunken pond at its end.

These connections between liquid, language, and landscape all come together on 2/4 when the literal significance of Izumi's name as "wellsprings" inspires a verse about that location's paradoxical lack of fresh water:

te o hidete	Our dipped hands
samusa mo shiranu	do not know cold
izumi ni zo	at a wellspring which
kumu to wa nashi ni	we never once drew from
higoro henikeru	for all these many days!
(TN 44, 2/4)	

The poem's waterless landscape draws on the phrase "wellspring of words" (言泉) used to describe poetic language that is gushing forth from emotion. This same figure of speech, which originates in the sixth-century *Wenxuan* (Selections of Refined Literature), is also employed by Tsurayuki in the preface to *Shinsen waka*.[50] In this case, the association of liquid with language is further deepened through the poem's use of *kumu*, which can refer either to the actions of "scooping" liquids or "assembling" something, thereby making it a description of the many days at sea spent with nothing to do but put poems together to pass the time.[51] As such, the *waka* can therefore also be read as a metafictional reference to the process by which *Tosa nikki* took shape.

In the prose surrounding this poem, the same place name presents the single most puzzling geographical detail in the diary when it appears as Izumi no Nada on both 1/30 and 2/5. Beginning with the eminent linguist Yamada Yoshio (1875–1958), many scholars have suggested that

49. Kanda, "*Tosa nikki* ron no tame," 114–17.
50. *Shinsen waka*, 188.
51. Ogawa, "*Tosa nikki* ni okeru waka no seishō," 245.

Tsurayuki confused the first Nada chiasmatically with the Tana River, which the party passes earlier that same day.[52] Others view the place name's repetition as a rhetorical device for conveying stasis, since *nada* can refer to either a long stretch of beach or a location where the wind and waves are especially fierce. In fact, however, there is no such unbroken shoreline in the region.[53] The length it represents is thus likely to be temporal rather than spatial, reflecting the diary's tendency to map the passage of time through a succession of toponyms.

Other instances in which fictional aims appear to determine place names include the location of Fawn Cape (Kako no Saki) on 12/27, where we are first introduced to the deceased girl whose ghost subsequently haunts the voyage. Similarly, the name Ōminato (Great Harbor) marks the place where the vessel experiences the greatest amount of time at anchor. Toponyms are also put to poetic ends in prose through an orthographic twist on 2/5 when the first vowel in Ozu is written with を (thread) rather than the more typical お (little), in order to introduce a poem that seamlessly weaves together its endlessly onward-stretching shoreline with a lengthy skein.[54] At other points, the absence of place names in the diary appears to be as deliberate as their presence. Fear entirely subsumes geography, for example, when toponyms disappear for eight days beginning on 1/21 during the party's frantic flight from rumored pirates, as if to suggest the diarist no longer cares where she is as long as she can be elsewhere.

Although the above instances are typically viewed as anomalous, moreover, many other locations along the Pacific coast mentioned in *Tosa nikki* might very well be equally fictional. Beginning with such Edo-period tomes as *Tosa nikki chiri ben* and *Tosa nikki fune no tadaji*, much effort has been expended by generations of scholars in precisely identifying Tsurayuki's actual itinerary, an undertaking reflected in the maps that

52. Yamada, "*Tosa nikki* ni chiri no ayamari aru ka," 9. See also Mitani, *Tosa nikki*, 95–97.

53. Nakazato, "Kikō bungaku toshite mita *Tosa nikki*," 35. A useful overview of debates on this topic is provided in Higo, "*Tosa nikki* ni mirareru chimei sakuzatsu ni tsuite," 58–64.

54. TN 45, 2/5: "What we cannot go past, / however far forth we go, / is the lovely lady's skein / of Thread Bay's winding line / of shoreside groves of pine!" (*yukedo nao / yuki-yararenu wa / imo ga umu / ozu no ura naru / kishi no matsubara*).

invariably accompany modern annotated editions.[55] In fact, however, the majority of the diary's place names are first documented in early modern times, with only a handful that can be dated prior to the thirteenth century.[56] What is more, the chief exceptions appear in songs: Saki and Murotsu from the aforementioned *imayō*, and Nawa no Tomari as Nawa no Ura in the *Man'yōshū*.[57]

It is, in fact, highly unlikely that Tsurayuki's aristocratic readership would have possessed detailed knowledge of the locales the travelers pass by during the oceanic leg of their journey. This is perhaps why geographical references only become consistently reliable once the party enters the mouth of the Yodo-gawa. If anything, his aristocratic patrons' limited familiarity with the Pacific coastline would have given Tsurayuki free rein to select toponyms for their imagistic effects in that portion of the journey. The many descriptive names populating its itinerary—such as Ōtsu (Great Port), Urado (Bay Entry), Narashizu (Level Port), Ishizu (Stone Port), and Kurosaki (Dark Peninsula)—would have helped readers picture their landscapes.

This creative use of place names even extends to the diary's title, which, like the poetic wellspring of words mentioned at Izumi on 2/4, can be read as a metafictional comment on the discursive nature of its landscapes. Like Izumi, Tosa is both the historical name of a province the party passes through and a (likely) fictional site where poems are composed. Although its title is ostensibly derived from the party's point of departure, *Tosa nikki*'s eponymous place name appears only once on 1/29 as a "Tosa Anchorage" (Tosa no Tomari) the travelers reach after they have already left Tosa province. The toponym's chief purpose in this vignette is to provide the opportunity for a woman who has lived in another place with the same name to compose a poem. This preference for exploring the poetic possibilities of fictional place names over the prosaic ones of actual historical locations makes the episode emblematic of *Tosa*

---

55. An annotated edition of *Tosa nikki chiri-ben* is available in Ide and Hashimoto, *Tosa nikki o aruku*. Other book-length studies of *Tosa nikki*'s geography are Takemura, *Tosa nikki no chiri-teki kenkyū*; and Shimizu, *Tosa nikki no fūdo*.

56. Takata, "*Tosa nikki* no kyokō hōhō," 31.

57. *Man'yōshū* poems 3:354 and 357, SNKBZ 6:211 and 212. Ishizu also appears in *Sarashina nikki*.

nikki's divergence from the representational norms of earlier travelogues. The parodic appropriation of poem tales that this eponymous toponym also produces will be explored in the next chapter.

Fitting to the Setting

Whether historical or fictional, the landscapes that appear in *Tosa nikki* present a challenge for its poets, who must adapt language fostered in the capital region to spaces located far outside its boundaries. The capital's absent presence looms over the travelers throughout the journey as both an object of nostalgic longing (*miyako*) in *kana* and the locus of ritual and social order (*kyō*) in Sinographs.[58] According to Kikuchi Yasuhiko (1936–2001), the provincial setting that takes its place offered Tsurayuki with an opportunity for applying the *Kokinshū*'s courtly poetics to more informal and mundane situations. This aim may have also led him to make children responsible for the more unorthodox departures from poetic conventions that resulted in order to avoid readerly censure.[59] Even within this alien setting, however, social expectations based on distinctions in age, gender, and status often appear to inform the appraisals of poets. For example, the praise directed toward children's *waka* on 1/15 and 1/22 amounts to an assertion that their sentiments are suitably childish.

Many scholars believe *Tosa nikki*'s chief aim was to identify particular modes of poetic expression that conformed with such social distinctions. As noted in chapter 1, Hagitani famously viewed *Tosa nikki* as a poetic primer for the children of Tsurayuki's aristocratic patrons. Its intended audience may also have been adult male patrons or women seeking to master the popular practice of composing *waka* in a female

---

58. Kikuta, "*Tosa nikki* no bungei-teki kōzō," 53. For one view of this longing for the capital as the diary's primary focus, see Komachiya, "*Tosa nikki* to *Takamitsu nikki*," 58–59. My translation has rendered *miyako* and *kyō* as "the capital city" and "the capital" (or *The Capital*) respectively.

59. Kikuchi makes these two points respectively in *Kokinshū igo ni okeru Tsurayuki*, 164–65 and "*Tosa nikki* ni okeru uta no eisha," 34.

persona.⁶⁰ The diary's concern with poetic propriety has also been compared to the *ciyi* (etiquette manuals) and *shuyi* (writing models) popular in Tang China during the eighth and ninth centuries.⁶¹ Regardless of the particular audience it sought to address, or its primary purpose in doing so, *Tosa nikki*'s approach to depicting landscapes in *waka* stresses the importance of including natural imagery in travel poetry, of aligning scenes with their social contexts, and of conforming to convention in their ritualized representation. Because the clearest illustrations of success and failure in these areas are presented in parallel pairs of poems, one of the diary's aims appears to have been articulating criteria for *waka* fitting to their settings.

One indication the diary may have been informed at least in part by a pedagogical purpose is the unusual amount of prose it devotes to discussing the nature, purpose, and quality of *waka* in comparison to other *nikki* or *monogatari*.⁶² Many of the diarist's strongest interjections are found in the critical comments that follow poems, for example.⁶³ Yet her reasoning is rarely specified, nor does *Tosa nikki* employ the extensive critical vocabulary seen in later poetics treatises. Deciphering the diarist's ambiguously laconic responses to poems thus often requires reading them contextually. In many cases, the basis for her judgments can be deduced from contrasting examples. For example, the paramount importance of prioritizing landscape over artifacts in travel poetry is illustrated by a pair of *waka* appearing on 2/1. The first poem, composed by an anonymous figure at a place called Hako no Ura (Box Bay), creates a visually striking depiction of its landscape through the inventive treatment of the object that toponym denotes:

tama-kushige	Gem-sparkling is the comb
Hako no ura nami	in a Box Bay where waves
tatanu hi wa	do not rise on a day

60. This view can be found in Tsumoto, "*Tosa nikki* wa naze, nan no tame," 35; and Yamaguchi, *Ōchō kadan no kenkyū*, 632–52.
61. Kawaguchi, "*Tosa nikki* no seiritsu," 100–101. For an overview of their early history in China and Japan, see Rüttermann, "'So That We Can Study Letter-Writing,'" 60–64.
62. Shibuya, "*Tosa nikki* ni okeru waka," 88–89.
63. Hijikata, *Nikki no seiiki*, 132.

> *umi o kagami to* when the sea as a mirror
> *tare ka mizaramu* must surely seem to all.
> (TN 42, 2/1)

The absence of any other textual references to this "Box Bay" suggests it is one of the diary's fictitious locales. It is perhaps this fabrication that sanctions the poet's innovative approach to its representation. Although combs and mirrors were conventionally associated with the boxes that contained them in a metonymic manner, they instead function metaphorically here to signify the sparkling smooth surface of the bay's waters.

The diarist's positive evaluation of this poem is implied through its contrast with a second *waka* composed at the same place by the ex-governor that is overtly criticized for its lack of natural imagery:

> *hiku fune no* The boat is pulled along
> *tsunade no nagaki* with hempen ropes long
> *haru no hi o* as these spring days,
> *yosoka ika made* up to forty or fifty of which
> *ware wa henikeri* is the time I have spent!

You can get a sense of the impression this left on another listener who was definitely muttering, "Why is this so plain-worded?" under their breath. (TN 43, 2/1)

The term "plain-worded" (*tadagoto*) that is dismissively used by this anonymous critic refers to one of the six stylistic modes of poetry listed in the *kana* preface to the *Kokinshū*, where it represents *waka* that are devoid of natural imagery.[64] In keeping with this definition, the figural purpose behind the poem's ropes is to represent time rather than a landscape, as is also true of the days signified by its spring sun. Although Tsurayuki had previously employed hempen ropes to the same end at a poetry match, that *waka* included natural imagery.[65] More to the point, perhaps, the earlier poem was not composed during a journey.

---

64. Heldt, *The Pursuit of Harmony*, 232–33.
65. *Teiji'in uta-awase* poem 65, SNKBZ 11:507: "Lost amid reeds / in Naniwa's bay, / the boat pulled along / with hempen ropes long / as the time I have spent!" (*ashi mayou / Naniwa no ura ni / hiku fune no / tsunade nagaku mo / ware wa henikeri*).

The poems by provincial gentry who feed the party on 1/7 offer another informative contrast, in this case on the basis of the relative subtlety with which their speakers insert themselves into the landscapes they describe. The first of these two *waka* by the widow provides a positive model that is praised for its tactfully understated display of wit:

asajiu no	Choked with growth
nobe ni shi areba	are the fields they are from,
mizu mo naki	and so starved for sight of water
ike ni tsumitsuru	is the pond where plucked and piled
wakana narikeri	are these young herbs as my name!

How amusing! This "pond" she speaks of is the name of her place, of course. (TN 22, 1/7)

The diarist's explicit association of pond with poet seems at first glance to be labored and superfluous, given that the widow has already been identified by this location. Perhaps she is making clear that the *waka* is not referring to the Waterless Pond (Mizu-nashi no Ike) Sei Shōnagon includes in her list of famous poetic ponds.[66] Specifying its significance as a place name further implies the pond is a metonym for its resident, thus alerting readers to the presence of pivot-words in the last two measures: *wakana* as "young herbs" with *wagana* as "my name," and *tsumi* as both "to pluck" and "to pile up." These links turn the young herbs being gathered up into the growing number of years in the countryside that have obscured any memory of the speaker back in the capital. An additional play on *mizu* (water/did not see) as *mitsu* (satiated/saw) implies that her prospects of encountering a lover have dried up as a result.[67] The orthographic basis for two of these associations between the speaker's natural surroundings and her socially isolated situation, relying as they do on silent readings, explains why the poem is written, as well as why the diarist identifies the pond's metonymic meaning.

The second poem by the widow's boorish neighbor stands in stark contrast to the subtle wit that makes her discreet insertion of herself into a waterless landscape charming and sympathetic. The bombastic solecism

---

66. *Makura no sōshi* section 36, SNKBZ 18:88–89; see also McKinney, *The Pillow Book*, 41.
67. Morishita, "*Tosa nikki* ichigatsu nanuka," 25.

with which he describes his seascape is as egocentric and ill-considered in its off-putting boorishness as its predecessor was tactful and apt.

yuku saki ni	Greater than the roar
tatsu shiranami no	of white-crested waves
koe yori mo	rising in your path
okurete nakamu	are the abandoned wails
ware ya masaramu	of myself most of all.

That's what he recited! He must have a loud voice. (TN 23, 1/7)

The boor's conventional use of white-crested waves is only marginally more appealing than his meager gifts of food.[68] A more literate poet would know they were also an established euphemism for pirates and brigands, making what should be wishes for a safe voyage into a malapropism whose ominous implications are exacerbated by the wails he boastfully exaggerates. By simultaneously appearing to praise his delivery and mock his bombast, the diarist's speculative assessment of his voice that follows this performance displays masterfully understated sarcasm on her part.

In direct contrast to the boor's belabored failures, a child manages to offer a more subtle and suitable poetic reply with understated ease. Whereas the man's narcissism was juxtaposed with the widow's modest discretion, his assertive use of an adult "I" (*ware*) is now met with the more youthful and diffident first-person pronoun *maro*. In addition to meeting the requirements of a poetic reply by repeating the words *yuku* (to go) and *masaru* (to exceed) from the boor's *waka*, moreover, the child masterfully moderates his bombast by reducing the liquid setting from a vast ocean to the boundaries of a river.[69]

yuku hito mo	Both those who go
tomaru mo sode no	and stay bear sleeves whose
namida-gawa	streams of tears
migiwa nomi koso	do nothing but overflow
nure-masarikere	the riverbanks, it seems!
(TN 23, 1/7)	

68. Nitta, "*Tosa nikki* ni tsuite," 5–6.
69. Ogawa, "Zōtō o kyohi suru uta no sekai," 5–8.

This poem addresses both the travelers and their host from a distanced perspective that contains a hint of cool sarcasm in its assertion that it is *only* the riverbanks that overflow with tears. The river itself might also be a metonym for the boor standing beside it, further implying that he is the only one weeping.[70] Such precociousness led Kigin and Moribe to attribute this *waka* to a daughter of Tsurayuki who is identified in the early twelfth-century historical chronicle *Ōkagami* (The Great Mirror) as the author of an anonymous poem in *Shūi wakashū* (Anthology of Later Gleanings, 1007).[71] Regardless of the poem's source, its wit indicates the value *Tosa nikki* places on semantically complex landscapes containing subtly ambiguous allusions to the individuals within them.

Another two *waka* in the entry for 1/29 illustrate the difficulties that a landscape divorced from the geography of the capital presents to poetic celebrations of the new year demanding the reproduction of particular words and practices. The first poem by a little girl suggests a maritime substitute for the pine saplings that were customarily tugged on to celebrate the first Day of the Rat. By contrast, the second *waka* by an adult stresses the distance between this same setting and the traditional landscape in which the day's other rite of plucking young herbs was held.

> *obotsukana*   It is hard to tell that
> *kyō wa ne no hi ka*   today is the Day of the Rat.
> *ama naraba*   If I were a diver-girl
> *umi-matsu o dani*   I would be pulling up
> *hikamashi mono o*   strands of sea-pine at least . . .

That's what she said. How does it fare as a poem for *The Youngest Day of the Rat* at sea? Another person composed this verse:

> *kyō naredo*   Though today is the day,
> *wakana mo tsumazu*   we don't pluck young herbs

---

70. Morishita, "*Tosa nikki* ichigatsu nanuka," 48. See also Hasegawa, "*Tosa nikki* no zōtōka," 98–99.

71. See McCullough, *Ōkagami, The Great Mirror*, 222–23. Medieval and early modern genealogies such as the *Sonpi bunmyaku* and *Kishi keizu* specify she was a *naishi* (palace handmaid).

Kasuga-no no	in Kasuga's fields
waga kogi-wataru	which are not in the bay
ura ni nakereba	we now row across.
(TN 40, 1/29)	

The first *waka* is probably attributed to a child in order to excuse the *umi-matsu* (sea pine) it inventively derives from a literal reading of the Sinographs 海松 typically used to write the name of a type of seaweed called *miru* or *mirubusa* in poetry. The resulting poem is both odd and simplistic, leaving the diarist doubting its merits. By contrast, the second poem hews close to tradition by mentioning Mount Kasuga, which appears in earlier poetic celebrations of the same day. Here, once again, the diarist's silence indicates tacit approval, suggesting ritual demands require the precise reproduction of traditional tropes, if only to mark their absence from the setting in which the *waka* is composed.

The most acutely inconvenient gap between poetic language and landscape in *Tosa nikki* occurs at Sumiyoshi. Long celebrated in myth and song, this hallowed location provided a particularly dense site for poetic associations, two of which are invoked in *waka* recited by an anonymous figure and the bereaved mother addressing the place with its older, more descriptive name of Suminoe (Clear Cove):

kyō mite zo	Just the sight of it now
mi oba shirinuru	informs us of our estate:
Suminoe no	Suminoe's clear cove,
matsu yori saki ni	where pines have spent by far
ware wa henikeri	fewer years than myself!
Suminoe ni	To Suminoe's clear cove
fune sashi-yoseyo	set course in our ship!
wasure-gusa	Forgetting-herbs
shirushi ari ya to	they say hold powers surely worth
tsumite yuku beku	plucking before going onwards.
(TN 46, 2/5)	

The first *waka* evokes the shoreside pines at Sumiyoshi, viewed in *Man'yōshū* poems as tokens of the longevity blessing its hallowed shores, by echoing an anonymous *Kokinshū* poem whose speaker praises the ageless Princess Pine growing there.[72] In addition to ignoring this tree, the anonymous *waka* in *Tosa nikki* flouts convention by preposterously claiming its speaker is much older than Sumiyoshi's evergreens.

As was true of the poems commemorating the Day of the Rat, the second one in this pair appears to observe poetic convention more closely by mentioning the forgetting-herbs that, at least according to the diarist, were traditionally associated with Sumiyoshi. Whereas the evocation of Mount Kasuga matched its temporal setting, however, the flora mentioned in the mother's *waka* is out of season. Ultimately it is impossible to determine which poem is most at fault, in part because of the other possible causes for the subsequent onset of a storm mentioned in chapter 2. The diarist in any case appears to be oblivious of any such shortcomings when she exclaims indignantly: "This is a far cry from the god spoken of in poems mentioning the clear cove of Suminoe, forgetting-herbs, and the eternal shoreside Princess Pine!" (TN 47, 2/5). As we will see next, this recurring gap between poetic language and place in the diary opens up a new discursive space in prose where they can mingle.

Landscapes in Poetic Prose

The aforementioned challenges in depicting its scenes in travel poetry are one reason why the diary's representations of landscape are often critiqued. Indeed, they seem at first sight to merit being dismissed as little more than a repetitious recitation of pine trees, waves, and moonlight.[73] The narrator's impressions of them are equally limited, with *omoshiroshi* (enthralling) being the most frequent response to such scenes. Often used to describe song and dance in Heian texts, the adjective retains a performative dimension in the diary, where it typically precedes poetic composi-

---

72. *Kokin wakashū* poem 905, SNKBZ 11:343: "Since I last saw it / the years have grown long. / At Suminoe's clear cove / the shoreside Princess Pine / has lasted how many reigns?" (*ware mite mo / hisashiku narinu / Suminoe no / kishi no hime matsu / ikuyo henu ramu*).

73. Kondō, "*Tosa nikki* ni okeru shizen," 28.

tion. The other predominant adjective, *kurushi* (frustrating), plays a similar role in generating *waka* toward the end of the journey as the party's sluggish progress spurs on poems seeking to assuage their growing impatience.[74] More often than not, the waves, wind, and rain that predominate throughout are cause for vexation rather than aesthetic inspiration. This apparent lack of interest in depicting its surroundings is at least partly due to the diary's wintry waterborne setting, removed as it is in time and space from the autumnal and springtime gardens favored in Heian-period vernacular court literature. Even snow, the quintessential seasonal motif for winter and early spring in the *Kokinshū* anthology, only appears in *Tosa nikki* as a visual simile for surf.

Pine trees represent the landscape element in *Tosa nikki* that is most saturated with poetic connotations, yet even here his diary differs from the imperial anthology Tsurayuki helped compile. The pine saplings that bring the diary to a close with a final recollection of the dead girl occur only once in the *Kokinshū*, where they represent the future promise of a long life.[75] By contrast, *Tosa nikki* draws on less auspicious poetic conventions: pine saplings (*komatsu*) glossed as 子松 (child pine) appear in two *Man'yōshū* elegies.[76] This association with death is even more common in Heian elegiac *shi*, where the tree often appears beside graves.[77] At the same time as they constitute the most paradigmatically poetic natural object in the diary, however, pines seem to represent the limits of this representational mode in a famous vignette on 1/9 in which a poem is portrayed falling short of its setting:

> And so we passed by *The Uda* Pine-Tree Plains. It is beyond knowing how many pine trees are there, or how many millennia they have spent in this place. Waves lapped against each root and cranes alighted atop each branch. Overcome by the charm of this sight, someone on our ship composed this verse:

74. Yamada, "*Tosa nikki* ni okeru 'omoshiroshi' 'kurushi' sunkan," 2–6.
75. *Kokin wakashū* poem 907, SNKBZ 11:343: "Of catalpa bows / is the stony strand of the pine sapling. / In whose reign was it, / thinking of reigns to come, / that its seed was planted?" (*azusa yumi / isobe no komatsu / taga yo ni ka / yorozu yo kanete / tane o makikemu*).
76. *Man'yōshū* poems 2:146 and 228, SNKBZ 6:108 and 151.
77. Kojima, *Kokufū ankoku jidai no bungaku*, 433.

mi-wataseba	My gaze sweeps across
matsu no ure-goto ni	pines on whose every branch
sumu tsuru wa	there roost cranes who
chiyo no dochi to zo	I think must surely be
omou bera naru	millennium-old companions.

Or words to that effect. This poem cannot surpass seeing the place. (TN 25–26, 1/9)

In keeping with the diary's fictional treatment of toponyms in its prose, the otherwise unknown locale of Uda contains the posthumous name of the sovereign most responsible for the efflorescence of *waka* at court in Tsurayuki's day. Consequently, the diarist's declaration that the poem "cannot surpass seeing the place" (*tokoro o miru ni e-masarazu*) has been taken as a manifesto of sorts rejecting earlier court poetry's mannered conventions in favor of a spontaneous and unmediated response to the actual scene.[78] This presumed contrast between poetry and a more naturalistic form of prose has a long history in readings of the diary, going back to Mabuchi's praise for *Tosa nikki*'s avowed realism, mentioned in chapter 1.

However, the birds in this prose landscape clearly mark it as imaginary. Because cranes favor wetland areas, the party would have been more likely in reality to have seen storks on the coastline (TNZ 167).[79] On the other hand, cranes frequently appear on pine branches as felicitous symbols of long life in the screen *waka* Tsurayuki composed for the birthday celebrations of his patrons. One written in 915 to celebrate the fiftieth year of Tokihira's chief wife, Renshi (d. 935), is particularly close to the poem at Uda.[80] Rather than rejecting poetic convention out of hand in depicting landscapes, therefore, it could be argued that the diarist's comment points instead to the importance of also including *waka*'s formal features in prose. This is accomplished by the preceding description of the scene. The sentence "Waves lap against each root and cranes alight

---

78. Konishi, "Tsurayuki bannen no kafū," 982–87.
79. Porter in fact renders *tsuru* as "storks" (*The Tosa Diary*, 45).
80. *Tsurayuki shū* poem 51, SNKS 80:67: "In my garden / are pines on whose branch tips / there roost cranes who / I think must surely be / a millennium of snow" (*waga yado no / matsu no kozue ni / sumu tsuru wa / chiyo no yuki ka to / omou bera nari*).

atop each branch" provides a symmetrically pleasing picture of parallel juxtapositions in hue and motion by complementing the poem's implicit color combination of dark green pine needles and white birds with a similar one between sea-green water and white-crested waves. The prose also adds a further contrast between the stillness of the tree roots and the movement of the waves that is not overtly present in the poem. Perhaps a screen painting did in fact inspire this carefully balanced depiction.[81] Regardless of its original source, it is the poetic structures crafted through juxtapositions in the prose that expand on the *waka*'s imagery and imbue it with dynamic movement.

The incorporation of poetic structures into prose can already be seen in Tsurayuki's prefaces to the *Kokinshū* and *waka* for the Ōi-gawa procession, both of which drew on the venerable rhetorical figures of *makura-kotoba* and *jokotoba*, as well as parallelisms derived from Literary Sinitic, in order to convey a sense of gravitas. Unlike these earlier texts, *Tosa nikki*'s sentences at times also draw on the asymmetrical structures of *waka*. One strikingly vivid example can be found in a sentence on 2/1 that describes Kurosaki's landscape through an enumeration of the five colors (*goshiki*) associated with the cosmos' cardinal directions: "The name of the place is black and the color of the pines is green, while the waves of its reefs are like snow and the colors of its shells are red, leaving it just one short of all *Five Primary Colors*" (ところのなはくろく、まつのいろはあをく、いそのなみはゆきのごとくに、かひのいろはすはうに、五色にいまひといろぞたらぬ。) (TN 42, 2/1). The sentence intricately interweaves sound and meaning in a structure that is located somewhere between prose and poetry. End rhymes bind the first four clauses into couplets, as does the repeated use of the particles の and は. Both paired clauses also share a common spatial structure in which a locale is followed by an object situated within it. Although these parallelisms may at first sight appear to adopt the structure of a *kundoku* vernacularized rendition of a *shi* poem, it avoids their symmetry by introducing a simile for the color white in the third clause and by ending with the comment that a single color is missing in the final one.[82] This subtle yet insistent deferral of

---

81. Katagiri, *Kokin wakashū no kenkyū*, 50–52.
82. The one missing color, yellow, represents the center from which the other directions branch out.

precise parallelism through an asymmetrical structure of five clauses that differ internally in their wording makes the sentence reminiscent of *waka* in both a metrical and rhetorical sense.

The most concisely powerful example of this figural flow from parallelism to asymmetry occurs in the final entry's depiction of the river port of Yamazaki. The densest site of human habitation outside the capital, its thriving environs are famously portrayed by the literatus Ōe no Mochitoki (955–1010) several decades after *Tosa nikki* in a Literary Sinitic preface entitled "On viewing women entertainers" (見遊女) found in *Honchō monzui* (Literary Essence of Our Court, ca. 1058):

> The vicinity of Kaya lies between the three provinces of Yamashiro, Kawachi, and Settsu, making it the most important port in the realm. People traveling back and forth from west, east, north and south all follow its roads. As for its folk who sell the pleasures of women to people from all over the realm at exorbitant prices, both old and young mingle and support each other in towns and hamlets gazing out on one another.
>
> 河陽則介山河攝三州之閒。而天下之要津也。自西自東。自南自北。往反之者。莫不率由此路矣。其俗天下衒賣女色之者。老少提結。邑里相望。[83]

Unlike Mochitoki's relatively expansive prose—which dwells on Yamazaki's strategic location at the convergence of three provinces, the volume of its traffic, its rapacious economy, and the intimate proximity of its inhabitants to one another—*Tosa nikki*'s description of the river port deploys the poetic devices of metonymy and pivot-words to convey its physical density and bustling activity: "There was no change to the small sign depicting a chest at Yamazaki, or the large effigies of a conch-shaped rice cake and fishing hook off the great road curving along the riverbend at Magari" (やまざきのこびつのゑも、まがりのおほちのかたも、かはらざりけり。) (TN 53, 2/16). In addition to carrying more than one meaning, the individual objects represented in this noun-heavy sentence possess more than one spatial relation to one another. The picture is either

---

83. *Honchō monzui*, SNKBT 27:272. For a complete translation, see Kawashima, *Writing Margins*, 33–34. On Kaya and its female entertainers, see Goodwin, *Selling Songs and Smiles*, 15–20.

painted on a small chest or is the depiction of that chest on a shop sign (TNZ 410).[84] The second half of the sentence is even more ambiguous: まがり might refer to a place name, a rice cake, a water container, a fishing hook, or a prominent bend on a road or river next to those entities. Similarly, おほち (pronounced as either *ōchi* or *ōji*) could also indicate a place name, a wide road, rice cakes, or conch shells (TNZ 402–3).

The two most widely available translations of the diary address these ambiguities in different ways. Porter's version places the picture on the box and omits the place name of Magari no ōchi, instead rendering the two words as rice cakes twisted into the shape of shells in a fusion of both meanings.[85] McCullough's rendering, on the other hand, follows Hagitani in reading the sentence as a series of complementary relationships: Yamazaki and Magari are place names representing mountains and rivers respectively, while the small two-dimensional pictorial representation of a chest is contrasted with the large three-dimensional effigy of a hook.[86] This interpretation is consonant with the parallelisms favored in premodern East Asian texts, but it can also be augmented by following Porter's example and adding on other potential meanings to the translation of the second half of the sentence. In addition to marking a place name, in other words, the curved shape common to all meanings of まがり could simultaneously describe a fishhook, a rice cake, a turn in the road, and a riverbend, with all of these objects being both spatially similar and adjacent to one another. Such semantic ambiguities complicate and thicken the initial parallelisms of the sentence by forming an asymmetrical distribution of figural language in its second half through pivot-words that produce a wealth of objects and shapes packed into a few syllables whose semantic density and metonymic contiguity matches the spatial compactness of a site filled with human activity and its products.

Even when their sentences do not mingle parallelism with asymmetry, prose depictions of landscape in the diary at times draw on the spare

---

84. Hagitani further notes that the latter interpretation would make this the first mention of shop signs in Japan prior to the fourteenth century.

85. Porter, *The Tosa Diary*, 125: "He saw in the shops at Yamasaki the little boxes painted with pictures and the rice-cakes twisted into the shape of conch shells."

86. McCullough, *Kokin Wakashū*, 289: "We noticed there had been no changes in the pictures of small boxes at Yamazaki or in the shapes of the big fishhooks at Magari."

descriptiveness of poetic language, as can be seen in the following brief passage in which a single word that denotes the movement of water also metonymically connotes an adjacent landscape:

> Because the water's surface is the same as yesterday, the ship wasn't put out to sea. Since the blowing gusts didn't let up, waves rolled back from the shore in rising crests. A verse was composed about this:
>
> | | |
> |---|---|
> | *o o yorite* | Twining hemp strands |
> | *kai naki mono wa* | serves no purpose, |
> | *ochi-tumoru* | when piles of fallen |
> | *namida no tama o* | tears are the jewels |
> | *nukanu narikeri* | that remain unstrung! |
> | (TN 43, 2/3) | |

The seaside setting of this entry is outlined with masterful economy by introducing a single compound verb, *tachi-kaeru* (roll back), whose motion implies the existence of a level sandy shore nearby. If it had instead been a rugged coastline of the sort the ship had previously encountered elsewhere, the windswept waves would have dashed against its rocks to produce a fine spray.

Unlike the prose passages appearing in anthologies and poem tales, which typically introduce the wording of the poem that follows, the imagery in this sentence is entirely separate from that of the *waka*, whose words replace the rhythmic lapping of waves with the equally repetitive act of twining threads to form a necklace. Moreover, metonymy in the *waka* moves in the opposite direction from the prose: the poem's objects imply movement rather than the other way around. Hemp was a particularly time-consuming material to work with. After the plant was soaked to disentangle its fibers, they were twined together into threads of a similar thickness before being bundled into long loops piled up and stored in a wooden container (TNZ 308–9). The circular shapes produced by this repetitive process evoke the rhythmic movement of the waves and the swaying roll of a boat at anchor. As we shall see in the next section, the lack of forward movement characterizing both this entry and the diary overall is often conveyed through an unusual temporal structure that sets *Tosa nikki* apart from later Heian women's memoirs.

The Banality of Travel

The extended periods of stasis within *Tosa nikki* are another remarkable aspect of its travelogue prose, one sustained by a format that is unique among Heian vernacular diaries. Whereas later memoirs vary radically in the stretches of time between which they alternate, the diary consistently marks each day of the voyage with a calendrical date, even when nothing noteworthy occurs in the entry. By deploying non-events to move its narrative along, *Tosa nikki* also privileges fictionality over the facticity that otherwise would constitute the sole value in mentioning such details. Moments of uneventfulness in the diary are in fact so common that they play an essential role in creating a remarkably long journey, one whose fifty-five days are more than double the twenty-five that the *Engi shiki* allotted for a voyage from Tosa to the capital.[87] Frustration at the snail's pace of progress in an early spring setting suspended between wintry desolation and vernal promise is compounded by the additional delay imposed on the ex-governor's household when his replacement arrives late, forcing them to risk dangerous sailing conditions in a desperate attempt to make it back in time for the annual round of promotions at court. Fear of pirates and the girl's ghost subsequently gives added urgency to this frantic race back home.

In addition to providing a detailed chronology, the introduction of the date for each entry is presented in a remarkably uniform manner throughout the diary—with the exception of a few days in the early stages that involve ritual actions such as the prayers for safe travel that begin the voyage in the second entry, the observances on the seventh day of the new year, and the final round of farewells from provincial wellwishers two days later. A similar uniformity is used to mark non-events in the diaries of nobles. At times their language can be strikingly similar to that of *Tosa nikki*. For example, the opening sentence on 1/8 declaring "Something blocks our progress, so we are still in the same place" (TN 24, 1/8) is virtually identical to a comment made by Tadahira in his diary when a similar hindrance, likely to be a calendrical taboo particular to

---

87. *Engi shiki* section 24, KST 26:618.

him, effectively immobilizes the aristocrat.[88] Such terse expressions of annoyance, irritation, or disapproval caused by weather or astrology are quite common in later noblemen's journals.

Unlike these texts, however, *Tosa nikki* occasionally betrays signs that such expressions are deliberately intended to further fictional aims. One particularly telling example can be found in the brief entry for 1/12, which simply notes: "No rain falls. The ships of Fumutoki and Koremochi have finally come from the level port of Narashizu, where they had fallen behind, to join us here at the cave harbor of Murotsu" (TN 29, 1/12). The opening sentence's terse mention of the absence of rain is peculiar given that the same condition has implicitly obtained on preceding days without the need to note it overtly. As it happens, however, this turns out to be the last day with clear weather for an extended period. Through its connections with the entries before and after it, this simple and seemingly superfluous observation thus lays the groundwork for a bitterly ironic situation within *Tosa nikki*'s larger narrative arc, as it becomes apparent in hindsight that the party has foregone a critical opportunity to make forward progress. Other brief and seemingly trivial passages also seem carefully crafted. For example, the terse description of the weather on 1/28 contains a deadening rhythm as the growing disappointment at a lack of change in the traveler's situation is conveyed first through a negative verb and then by omitting verbs altogether: "All night long the rain didn't let up. Next morning too" (TN 39, 1/28). Similarly, the repetition of the phrase "the ship wasn't put out to sea" (*fune idasazu*) in the opening sentence for three days in a row beginning on 1/18 accentuates both the narrative's lack of forward movement and the diarist's growing frustration.

The attention to sequencing that is evident in the preceding examples of banal detail can also be seen in the distribution of non-events across *Tosa nikki*'s narrative structure as a whole. On the one hand, its daily entry format has been critiqued for hindering the sustained treatment of any single emotion.[89] However, it could also be argued that consecutive stretches of uneventful days are placed strategically throughout the diary

---

88. *Teishin kōki* entry for Engi 12/8/24, ZZGR 5:134: 有障無參 (Something blocked me from going).

89. Shibuya, "Bunshō kara mita *Tosa nikki*," 24. Suzuki Tomotarō briefly notes the alternating arrangement of short and long entries among the diary's dyads in "*Tosa nikki* no kōsei*," 84–85.

in order to structure the progression of emotions within *Tosa nikki* as a whole. For example, the longest periods of stasis—clustered around the diary's middle portions at Ōminato, Murotsu, and Izumi—delineate more eventful periods and establish a stark contrast with the sense of excited anticipation at returning home that characterizes the beginning and end of the journey. Simultaneously, smaller sequences within these larger units amplify the underlying sense of frustration, as can be seen in the series of days that are spent at Ōminato, in which brief banal entries build on one another to create narrative progressions in affect:

> *The Second.* Still anchored in this great harbor of Ōminato. *The Lector* has sent over food and saké.
> *The Third.* Still in the same place. Perhaps the wind and waves hope in their hearts for us to stay a while. The thought fills my heart with dread.
> *The Fourth.* A gale blows, making it impossible to put our ship out to sea. Masatsura offered up saké and various delicacies to the former governor. We could hardly stand by and do nothing in response to such generosity, and so we returned the kindness with some trifle. We have nothing of worth for that purpose. Everything seemed fine on the surface, but it feels somehow as though we have lost face.
> *The Fifth.* Since the wind and waves don't let up, we are still in the same place. People came to see us one after the other in an endless stream.
> *The Sixth.* Same as yesterday. (TN 21, 1/2–1/6)

Initially, perhaps, the diarist attempts to find humor in the delay. After noting the lector's solicitude in the first entry, the second one suggests a similar concern for the travelers on the part of the wind and waves, which "have a heart" (*kokoro aru*) befitting that of a well-wisher seeking to detain the party. The next entry, describing the awkward encounter with Masatsura (discussed in chapter 2), avoids monotony by omitting mention of the waves that accompany the windy weather in the entries before and after it. Their return with the wind in the fourth entry also heralds a return to witticism in a sentence likening the waves' endless movement to the stream of people visiting the ship, perhaps further suggesting both are equally undesirable. However, this renewed attempt at humor vanishes entirely in the final entry, whose jarringly sudden abruptness suggests the diarist is no longer able to continue making light of the situation.

Another series of brief entries from 1/23 to 1/25 also hints at an emotional progression by building dramatic tension through growing fear and frustration at the inability to advance despite the threat of pursuing pirates:

> *The Twenty-Third.* The sun shines and then is clouded over. Talk of pirates in the area leads us to pray to gods and buddhas.
> *The Twenty-Fourth.* The same place as yesterday.
> *The Twenty-Fifth.* That steersman fellow said, "The northerly looks ominous," so the ship wasn't put out to sea. All day our ears were filled with rumors of pursuing pirates. (TN 37, 1/23–25)

The arrangement of the two sentences in the first entry, in which clouds gather in the sky while rumors of pirates lead to entreaties for it to clear, succeeds at concisely enfolding the human world within its surroundings. The seemingly banal comment that nothing has changed in the single sentence of the next entry thus also implicitly contains a bitter observation that the previous day's prayers have gone unheard. The last entry then returns to paired observations of the heavenly and human realms as it contrasts the stillness of the boat with the perceptible movement of wind and the rumored one of pirates. Variety is thus maintained at the same time as tension builds for both diarist and her readers at the prospect that marauding pirates could appear at any moment.

The last lengthy period of stasis extends across three days from 2/12 to 2/14. As we saw in chapter 2, protracted negotiations with the steersman over his payment are likely to account for this prolonged stay in Yamazaki. Rather than specify the cause of delay, however, this sequence of entries focuses on seemingly minor details replete with narrative and affective repercussions:

> *The Twelfth.* We have stayed over in Yamazaki.
> *The Thirteenth.* Still in Yamazaki.
> *The Fourteenth.* Rain falls. Today we sent for carriages to take us to *The Capital.* (TN 53, 2/12–14)

Stasis in the first entry is amplified the following day by omitting verbs entirely. Growing impatience is then conveyed by the "today" in the succeeding entry. The downpour mentioned by the diarist on this day is another telling detail, suggesting as it does that the travelers' frustration at being cooped up in close quarters when they are so near to the end of the journey has reached the point where they cannot bear waiting any longer, regardless of the weather or the fact that the fourteenth would have been an ill-omened day of the month for travel (TNZ 392).

In fact, *Tosa nikki*'s historical author would have probably enjoyed staying in Yamazaki for some length of time on account of his friendship with Kintada, who was governor of Yamashiro province during that period and thus probably had a residence in the town where he could host Tsurayuki.[90] As with the fraught negotiations with its residents, described in chapter 2, these curt expressions of growing frustration are thus likely to be fictional and intentional. Like the other notations of non-events in the diary, the ex-governor's interlude in Yamazaki therefore endows the narrative with taut webs of suppressed affect that intermingle the terse language of aristocratic diaries with an anthological attention to sequencing in order to create dramatic progressions within the emotional arc of the narrative as a whole.

Conclusion

The static quality of so many entries in *Tosa nikki* is one example of the diary's tendency to organize its narrative spatially around the names of places the party moves to or stays in.[91] Travel provided a ready-made structure for narrative development by plotting time through the linear progression of contiguous spaces, and by possessing a clearly delineated beginning and end. Such characteristics would also have been ideally suited to the combination of visual and verbal elements favored in vernacular texts during this period. One scholar, for example, has suggested that the doubled perspective located simultaneously inside and outside the frame of a painted scene appearing in many of Tsurayuki's screen

90. Kubota, "*Tosa nikki* ni miru 'Yodo-gawa,'" 68–72. See chapter 1 for an account of Tsurayuki's relationship with Kintada after his return from Tosa.
91. Takahashi, "*Tosa nikki*," 110–11.

waka helped him develop the diary's distinctively twofold temporal structure. Its first layer consists of the single unified perspective framing each entry, which looks back retroactively on the sequence of episodic events that unfolded over the course of that one day. The second layer is the single unified perspective narrated in the prologue and epilogue framing the diary, which looks back retroactively on the entire sequence of entries as a single narrative progression.[92] Perhaps we can think of its readers occupying a similarly bifurcated narratorial perspective as they simultaneously observe its scenes inside and outside the textual frame as fiction and history respectively.

Another related possibility is that *Tosa nikki*'s prose was designed to complement pictures in a version such as the one mentioned in chapter 1. More precisely, the headnote from *Egyō hōshi shū* tells us that its poem was composed in the voice of a character who was depicted in an illustration of the diary's final scene:

On the feelings aroused by a house that had become dilapidated over the course of five years depicted in an illustration of Tsurayuki's *Tosa Diary*:

kurabe koshi	Even the waveborne path
nami-ji mo kaku wa	I came to compare it with,
arazariki	was never such as this.
yomogi no hara to	The weed-choked moorland
nareru waga yado	my grounds have become.[93]

Its combination of painting with poetry and prose could have made this version of *Tosa nikki* akin to the more detailed description of the journal created by Genji during his exile at Suma:

The appearance of various locales, bays and stony shores that were otherwise obscure to his audience were depicted for them in full. *Kana* writings were mingled with grass-style calligraphy here and there and, though it

---

92. Horikawa, "*Tosa nikki no hōhō*," 62–78. This dual narrative structure is also identified in Fukazawa, *Jiko genkyū tekisuto no keifugaku*, 63–65. Tsurayuki's screen *waka* likely also inspired the visual metaphor likening waves to snow in the diary (Iizuka, "*Tosa nikki* no waka," 15–19).

93. *Egyō hōshi shū* poem 192, KT 3:184.

lacked the details of a proper diary, it included many moving poems with great appeal.[94]

Like Genji's Suma journal, Tsurayuki's Tosa diary portrays a landscape of bays and beaches unfamiliar to its audience, omits many of the quantitative details found in a normal diary, and includes many poems designed to move the reader. Given the frequency with which Murasaki Shikibu mentions Tsurayuki in her tale, it is even possible she had this early illustrated version of *Tosa nikki* in mind when she envisaged her hero's journal.

We have no way of knowing if the picture Egyō mentions was originally made by Tsurayuki or added later by an early reader such as the priest. Nor is it certain whether it is from a picture scroll or a folding screen. Egyō's poem is clearly in the voice of a character from the diary, as is the case with *waka* from the roughly contemporaneous *Yamato monogatari* made by women viewing illustrations of the tragic tale of the maiden of Ikuta-gawa and her two rival suitors that are composed in the voices of all three protagonists.[95] Although it is typically assumed that these illustrations were painted on folding screens, there is nothing in the prose of the poem tale that specifically supports that assumption. Moreover, the fact that the headnote in *Egyō hōshi shū* describes the final scene in *Tosa nikki* suggests it is referring to a complete version of the text, which would have been easier to assemble and view as a picture scroll. Some of *Tosa nikki*'s stylistic peculiarities would be especially amenable to this format. Expressions such as *kaku aru uchi ni* (meanwhile) or *kakute* (so then) dividing separate locations within a day's entry, for example, could have provided cues for the unrolling of the next scene on a scroll. This format would yet again make it similar to Genji's Suma journal, which is explicitly described as a "scroll" (*maki*) when it is introduced.

Regardless of *Tosa nikki*'s precise material dimensions, the distinctive aspects of its prose identified above would have lent themselves to an

---

94. *Genji monogatari* (Eawase), SNKBZ 21:387–88; see also Tyler, *The Tale of Genji*, 328–29. One other illustrated diary is mentioned earlier in the Akashi chapter when Murasaki consoles herself in Genji's absence (SNKBZ 21:261; see also Tyler, *The Tale of Genji*, 271).

95. *Yamato monogatari* episode 147, SNKBZ 12:371–73. This episode is further discussed in chapter 5.

illustrated version of the diary. Fictional place names marking locations within the narrative would have augmented otherwise generic painterly depictions of landscapes, as would the attention to details of color and shape that the diary's more poetically structured sentences provide. Likewise, the brief enumeration of a sequence of days spent at the same place could convey temporal duration in an economical manner by combining multiple entries with a single picture. Although *Tosa nikki*'s continuing ability to attract a readership without illustrations in ensuing centuries is doubtless due at least in part to Tsurayuki's posthumous fame, it can also be attributed to the diary's innovatively fluid intermingling of poetic fictions with prosaic details in the vivid depiction of a voyage over liminal liquid landscapes that were far removed from the Heian court's familiar environs. This new representation of space is also a profoundly parodic one, insofar as it is enabled in part by the diary's willful disregard for the documentary demands met by earlier travelogues.

PART III

More Than a Poem

CHAPTER 5

Narihira's Poem-Tellings

One of the more unusual aspects of *Tosa nikki* is the attention it pays to the oral narration of anecdotes relating the circumstances in which *waka* were composed. Known as *uta-gatari* (poem-tellings), these poetic anecdotes occupy a central but largely invisible place within Japanese literary history. Although only a few fragmentary references to this practice have survived, the integral role played by poetry in vernacular Japanese narrative has led to its association with a broad array of texts. The first academic treatment of *uta-gatari*, for example only cites two instances in which the word appears while speculating at length on its relationship to the ship songs discussed in chapter 3.[1] Some histories of the practice extend back to the earliest myths and songs. One of the more influential formulations by Itō Haku (1925–2003) used the term to describe the production and reception of *Man'yōshū* poems.[2]

Uta-gatari is most typically associated with the development of poem tales (*uta monogatari*), a genre conventionally limited to three collections of vignettes describing the origins of particular *waka* that were anonymously compiled over the course of the tenth century in roughly the following chronological order: *Ise*, *Yamato*, and *Heichū monogatari*.[3] Stylistic

---

1. Masuda, "Uta-gatari no sekai," 15–22.
2. Itō, *Man'yōshū no hyōgen to hōhō*. Sasaki, *Uta-gatari no keifu* identifies a link to earlier texts.
3. There are several translations of *Ise monogatari* in English, reflecting its importance in the literary canon: Vos, *A Study of the Ise-Monogatari*; McCullough, *Tales of Ise*;

differences between *Ise* and *Yamato monogatari* have also been attributed to their purportedly more pronounced influence on the later poem tale.[4] The practice of poem-telling has even been posited as the medium through which individual episodes within *uta monogatari* later became *setsuwa* anecdotes.[5] By contrast, the term appears rarely and with little specificity in most Anglophone scholarship. The most precise definition, provided by Joshua Mostow, observes, "In *uta-gatari*, someone makes up a story to contextualize a pre-existing poem."[6]

Mentions of poem tales in premodern texts are even sparser than for poem-tellings. The words *uta monogatari* first appear together in *Eiga monogatari*, where they describe the textual patrimony Fujiwara no Michikane (961–995) leaves behind for his daughter after he dies.[7] However, most scholars believe this is a reference to "poems and tales" rather than a distinct genre—an assumption also made when the same words appear together in the *Sagami shū* (Sagami Anthology, eleventh century) devoted to *waka* by a colleague of Murasaki Shikibu and Sei Shōnagon named Sagami (ca. 998–1061), and in the voluminous compendium of poetic lore known as *Shūchūshō* (Sleeve Notes, ca. 1185–1190) compiled by Kenshō (ca. 1130–1210). When they make their first unambiguous appearance as a compound term in the diary of the poet Minamoto no Ienaga (1170–1234), *uta monogatari* refer to oral accounts of *waka*, in other words, *uta-gatari*.[8] It was not until modern times that they were first recognized as a specifically textual genre by the scholars Haga Yaichi (1867–1927) and Fujioka Sakutarō (1870–1910).[9] Despite this relatively recent provenance, *uta monogatari* remains a useful genre category insofar as *Ise*, *Yamato*, and *Heichū monogatari* share distinctive formal and

---

Harris, *The Tales of Ise*; Mostow and Tyler, *The Ise Stories*; and Macmillan, *Tales of Ise*. The other two texts only have one translation each: Tahara, *Tales of Yamato*; and Videen, *Tales of Heichū*.

4. Amagai, "Uta-gatari to uchigiki." See also the introductory essay by Takahashi for *Yamato monogatari* in SNKBZ 12:434–37.
5. Amagai, *Uta-gatari to setsuwa*; and Tsutsumi, "*Ichijō sesshō gyoshū* kara setsuwa e."
6. Mostow, *Courtly Visions*, 19.
7. *Eiga monogatari*, SNKBZ 32:142; see also McCullough and McCullough, *A Tale of Flowering Fortunes*, 479.
8. Gotō, "Uta-gatari to uta monogatari," 183–200.
9. Abe, *Uta monogatari to sono shūhen*, 10–13.

historical characteristics as *waka*-centered vignettes produced by the tenth-century court. Because the term was initially interchangeable with *uta-gatari*, moreover, their association with oral anecdotes appears to have been acknowledged early on.

This chapter will investigate poem-tellings' characteristics, as well as their connections to both poem tales and *Tosa nikki*, by focusing on a single *waka* Narihira composed at Nagisa. One reason for doing so is that his poems were particularly amenable to those aspects of *uta-gatari* that can be gleaned from the earliest references to the practice made by Murasaki Shikibu and Sei Shōnagon. Both women's interest in anecdotes about Narihira also offers a unique opportunity to bridge the historical gap between their descriptions of poem-tellings in the eleventh century and the tenth-century poem tales he appears in.

Within his oeuvre, the Nagisa poem also holds unique potential for understanding *uta-gatari*'s relationship to a diverse array of strategies for contextualizing *waka* due to the peculiar historical significance accorded its composer and recipient soon after their deaths. Its earliest iterations are especially amenable to comparison due to their shared connections with *Tosa nikki*'s author: the *Kokinshū* anthology, whose compilation Tsurayuki supervised; his curation of its contents in *Shinsen waka*; and an *Ise* episode that he is likely to have had a hand in writing. The diary's version of the Nagisa poem is particularly valuable for understanding *uta-gatari* because if offers us the only surviving example of their content through the diarist's transcription of an anecdotal reference to the *waka*. Among other things, its portrayal of poem-telling sheds light on the diary's own metafictional distinction between its version of parodic hybridity and the more common genre fluidity shared among vernacular Heian anthologies, memoirs, and poem tales.

Uta-gatari *and Murasaki Shikibu*

The word *uta-gatari* first appears in texts associated with the two foremost female authors of the mid-Heian period, Murasaki Shikibu and Sei Shōnagon. The most frequently cited such instance is the headnote to poems 88 and 89 in the *Murasaki Shikibu shū* (Murasaki Shikibu

Anthology), which describes its eponymous poet composing two *waka* after hearing a poem-telling about a pond named Kainuma no ike (Shell-Marsh Pond). Despite its brevity, the storyteller's quoted speech in the opening headnote to these poems, along with the content of its *waka*, offer some glimpses into the mechanics of *uta-gatari*.

> This came about when I thought to attempt a composition after hearing an unusual poem-telling by someone who had said "There's a place called Shell-Marsh Pond, you know . . ."

yo ni furu ni	Fallen old in the world,
nado Kai-numa no	what point is there in Shell-Marsh
ikeraji to	Pond holding hope of life?
omoi zo shizumu	So I think in gloom sinking
soko wa shiranedo	down into unfathomable depths.

Thinking to say something uplifting, there was also this:

kokoro yuku	In my heart it goes well
mizu no keshiki wa	as the water-filled scene
kyō zo miru	I perceive on this day!
ko ya yo ni kaeru	Hence this return to the world
Kai-numa no ike	with purpose at Shell-Marsh Pond.[10]

Kainuma is introduced with the same particle *namu* (you know) used by narrators in *monogatari* to gain their audiences' attention. Here, its declarative tone highlights the place name's importance as the subject of the tale and conveys assurance that it exists. Such an assurance would be especially warranted given its location on the realm's northernmost frontier province of Michinoku.[11] As such, it would not have been personally familiar to an imperial consort such as Murasaki Shikibu's mistress Fujiwara no Shōshi (988–1074), something further suggested by its absence from any extant *waka*. No doubt the storyteller was a fellow attendant of Murasaki Shikibu who sought to entertain her mistress with an

---

10. *Murasaki Shikibu shū* poems 88 and 89, SNKS 35:147.

11. One single reference to Kainuma, appearing in the dictionary *Wamyō ruijūshō* (Notes on Japanese Words by Topic, 938), describes it as a village in Michinoku province's Niita district but makes no note of a pond there (Yoshihara, *Waka no utamakura chimei daijiten*, 551).

exotic story about a strange locale she had come across during time spent in that distant province with a senior male relative or spouse. Such features help explain the reason for selecting the pond to create an "unusual poem-telling" (*ayashiki uta-gatari*).

Kainuma is also amenable to narrative expansion because its name combines a vivid landscape with intimations of human actions that took place there. The toponym's descriptive connotations would help an audience picture this "Shell Marsh Pond" as a small body of water, perhaps a lagoon whose reed-lined shores harbor bleached fragments of shell brought in by strong currents. The two pivot-words embedded in the place name that Murasaki Shikibu's poems explore—*kai* as "shells" or "purpose" and *ike* as "pond" or "life"—also suggest the story of an individual who lived there. Although it is possible she invented these associations, the earliest mytho-histories and *fudoki* gazetteers contain numerous onomastic narratives identifying the origins of place names in the actions of their protagonists, making it more likely the poems' connections between the two words come from a preexisting narrative.

The perspectives of the poem's speakers also hint at the outlines of the original anecdote. Both *waka* are often treated as first-person expressions of Murasaki Shikibu's own circumstances at the time on account of the sentence preceding them, which declares: "This was apparently at a time when she was suffering from some ailment" (*wazurau koto aru koro narikeri*).[12] However, its use of the auxiliary verb *keri*, which often indicates the speaker has no direct experience of the events they are relating, makes it more likely that this sentence was added after Murasaki Shikibu's death, along with many other changes in the content and organization seen in surviving variants of the anthology.[13] Moreover, the rarity with which sentences ending in *keri* appear in *Murasaki Shikibu shū* suggests they fulfill a different purpose from the headnotes to its poems. One such would be to provide supplementary information as an "after-comment" (*sachū*) appended by a later reader.[14] In fact, the reference to an illness

---

12. See, for example, Bowring, *Murasaki Shikibu*, 247.
13. On these changes, see Tokuhara, *Murasaki Shikibu shū no shinkaishaku*, 123–44; and Hirota, *Murasaki Shikibu shū uta no ba*, 318–21.
14. Tokuhara, *Murasaki Shikibu shū no shinkaishaku*, 6–7.

here makes more sense when it is read after the *waka* preceding the Kainuma pair in the anthology.

> My response when asked if something was troubling me at the end of the Ninth Month:
>
> | *hana susuki* | Plumed pampas |
> | *ha wake no tsuyu ya* | leaves parted carry dew. |
> | *nani ni kaku* | For what reason does it |
> | *kare-yuku nobe ni* | remain there without vanishing |
> | *kie-tomaru ramu* | on moors that go on withering? |
>
> This was apparently at a time when she was suffering from some ailment.[15]

By responding to the inquiry about her circumstances in the headnote with a landscape reflecting the autumnal period in which the *waka* was composed, Murasaki Shikibu appears to couch her poetic reply in allegorical terms, something further suggested by the conventional association between its central image of dew and the fragility of human life. In other words, the reference to her illness appears to be an attempt by a later reader to identify the source of her suffering as physical rather than mental.

If anything, the speaker's claim that she can actually see the pond in the second *waka* makes it more likely both Kainuma poems are expressing the feelings of characters in the poem-telling rather than those of Murasaki Shikibu herself. A similar imaginative stance can be seen in *Yamato monogatari*'s account of a maiden who throws herself into the Ikuta-gawa when she is unable to choose between two men. After telling us that this tragic tale was subsequently depicted in a painting, the narrator proceeds to cite ten poems by later viewers of the painting that are composed in the voices of all three protagonists.[16] Although the second headnote's description of its poem as having been composed "to say something uplifting" (*kokochi yoge ni iinasamu tote*) is more ambiguous, it can be read as an indication Murasaki Shikibu is seeking to raise the spirits of herself and the other audience members by imagining a

---

15. *Murasaki Shikibu shū* poem 87, SNKS 35:146–47.
16. *Yamato monogatari* episode 147, SNKBZ 12:371–73; see also Tahara, *Tales of Yamato*, 93–98.

heroine who emerges triumphantly from previous challenges ready to face life again.

This reading of the second poem is further confirmed by the link between their liquid locales and the word for "living" made in both the Ikuta-gawa narrative and the Kainuma poem-telling, which suggests both stories involve a woman's attempt to drown herself when she is unable to choose between two suitors. In addition to the tale of Ikuta-gawa, and that of "the Maiden of Unai" (Unai Otome) recounted by two separate *Man'yōshū* poets, this same narrative trope appears in the story of Ukifune.[17] Like *Genji*'s final heroine, the Kainuma poems progress from questioning the purpose of living to finding value in continuing to do so. Perhaps the seed of Ukifune's tale, which inspired such later readers as the author of *Sarashina nikki*, can be found in these *waka*, making them an example of the role *uta-gatari* played in shaping later *monogatari*. Regardless, both the content of the Kainuma poems and their prose contexts suggest that in addition to describing the circumstances surrounding preexisting *waka*, *uta-gatari* could inspire their audience to add poems of their own.

Additional insights into this practice can be gleaned from three other mentions Murasaki Shikibu makes to *uta-gatari* in *Genji*. The first of these appears in the Sakaki chapter's description of a conversation between Genji and Suzaku in which they regale one another with "amorous poem-tellings" (*sukizukishiki uta-gatari*) about *waka* they have exchanged with various women.[18] The second mention appears in the Yadorigi chapter, when a woman who had attended on his mother recounts anecdotes about her to Kaoru that include "poem-tellings concerning Her Majesty's fleeting compositions on seeing the colors of blossoms or autumn foliage."[19] Between them, these brief passages indicate poems in *uta-gatari* could range from romantic to seasonal topics, and their poets could be either dead or living.

---

17. The story of the Maiden of Unai appears in *Man'yōshū* poems 9:1801–3 (SNKBZ 7:444–45) and 9:1809–11 (SNKBZ 7:448–51).

18. *Genji monogatari* (Sakaki), SNKBZ 21:124; see also Tyler, *The Tale of Genji*, 208.

19. *Genji monogatari* (Yadorigi), SNKBZ 24:458; see also Tyler, *The Tale of Genji*, 958.

One other reference to poem-tellings in *Genji* appears in the Tokonatsu chapter as an example of the sort of courtly modes of speech lacking in Tō no Chūjō's uncouth daughter Ōmi no Kimi. In addition to being the longest description of *uta-gatari* in the tale, this passage provides an intriguing description of their performative features: "When done with a suitable voice, even an uninteresting poem-telling can incite curiosity by obscuring the beginning or ending in the delivery, intriguing an audience all the more and making them wonder what profounder points they may have missed while they were straining to hear the story."[20] The "beginning or ending" (*moto-sue*) that is obscured in this description of a skillful poem-telling is usually taken to refer to the first and final measures of *waka*.[21] Members of the court were frequently challenged to identify poems from such partial allusions. Other riddles might be raised, however, by a muffled delivery of the introduction or conclusion of the surrounding story. When we turn to the Nagisa poem later in this chapter, we will see that the structure of individual episodes in *Ise* lent itself to precisely such forms of guesswork.

Uta-gatari *and Sei Shōnagon*

Additional information about poem-tellings can be found in *The Pillow Book*, a text whose content and form both reveal its author's fascination with stories about *waka*. Defying as it does the conventional taxonomies of its own time, *Makura no sōshi* has been especially open to an association with the equally amorphous concept of *uta-gatari*. One authority, for example, defines it as a parodic rhetorical mode used by Sei Shōnagon to treat historical fact in a humorous or fictionalized manner.[22] A particularly influential formulation characterizes her entire text as "a self-produced and self-staged poem-telling" (*jisaku jien no uta-gatari*).[23] One example of this connection between *uta-gatari* and *The Pillow Book*'s

---

20. *Genji monogatari* (Tokonatsu), SNKBZ 22:247; see also Tyler, *The Tale of Genji*, 476.
21. Tamagami, *Genji monogatari hyōshaku* 5:410.
22. Mitamura, *Makura no sōshi hyōgen no ronri*, 118–38.
23. Nomura, "Kyūtei bungaku toshite no *Makura no sōshi*," 8–17.

structure can be seen in its author's female homosocial fantasy of a house occupied by off-duty women attendants: "Everyone gathers each day to sit down together in one place when the occasion presents itself and exchange stories with one another, or talk about a poem they remember someone having composed."[24] Insofar as *Makura no sōshi* represents its author's community in ahistorical terms by replacing chronological time with an accumulation of discrete narratives, as Naomi Fukumori has pointed out, the equally nonlinear nature of unrelated anecdotes circulating among the inhabitants of this house can be seen as a synecdoche for the entire text.[25]

Another connection between *The Pillow Book*'s structure and *utagatari* can be seen in its tendency to link adjacent sections, or items within them, when poem-tellings are mentioned. For example, a description of their performative context in "The Home of a Lady in Court Service" (*Miyazukae-bito no sato nado mo*) is followed by an illustration of their content in "At the Place of Someone Said to Be a Lord of Some Sort" (*Aru tokoro ni, nani no kimi tokaya iikeru hito no moto ni*). The first of these sections tells us that nighttime offers an ideal occasion for poem-tellings: "How charming it is to fall asleep while listening to people tell each other about particular poems!"[26] No doubt a dark nocturnal soundscape of this sort would have fueled the imagination by requiring an audience to visualize the story in their minds. When such a tale is then presented in the next section, its female protagonist also illustrates the Tokonatsu chapter's recommendation for obscuring a poem-telling's contents by having her "softly whispering to herself *at daybreak the moon / lingers with me waiting*," in an allusion to a poem attributed to Kakinomoto no Hitomaro (fl. ca. 690).[27]

24. *Makura no sōshi* section 284, SNKBZ 18:438; see also McKinney, *The Pillow Book*, 241.
25. Fukumori, "Sei Shōnagon's *Makura no sōshi*."
26. *Makura no sōshi* section 172, SNKBZ 18:302; see also McKinney, *The Pillow Book*, 166.
27. *Makura no sōshi* section 173, SNKBZ 18:302; see also McKinney, *The Pillow Book*, 166. The full poem is as follows: "In the longest month / at daybreak the moon / lingers with me waiting. / If milord were to come, / would I be longing like this?" (*nagatsuki no / ariake no tsuki no / aritsutsu mo / kimi shi kimasaba / waga koime ya mo*) (*Shūi wakashū* poem 795, SNKBT 7:231).

The *Pillow Book*'s most detailed description of activities connected with *uta-gatari* appears in a sequence of four items within its list of "Pleasing Things" (*Ureshiki mono*). Their order of appearance offers a powerful example of the text's artistry by mimetically representing the complex ways in which oral and written modes of narration intersected.

> When poems composed for an occasion or in an exchange with others are talked about and noted down in writing. Although I have never known what this is like personally, I can still imagine how it would be to experience it.
>
> How pleasing it is to hear the old words of a story or poem from a stranger and then come across it again in another conversation! How entertaining it is to then discover it in something. "So *that* is where it comes from," you say to yourself, recalling the one who had drawn your attention to it.
>
> Getting hold of paper from Michinoku, or even the regular sort if it is good quality.
>
> How happy it makes me to suddenly remember the beginning or end of a poem when I am asked to supply it by someone who shames me with their own brilliance. There are so many cases where you have clean forgotten something someone else asks you about.[28]

By moving from the act of inscribing *waka* to their reception in an oral narrative that is followed by reading a written version, the initial pair of items reproduces one route by which poem-centered narratives circulated. In the first item, Sei Shōnagon expresses the hope that her own *waka* might be written down by others in a brief "notation" (*uchigiki*) constituting the first step in writing a poem-centered anecdote. We are also told that the poem must be mentioned widely for this initial inscription to occur, something more likely to happen if it was composed at a social gathering or as part of an epistolary correspondence. Insofar as most *waka* in *monogatari* appear in such settings, this observation indicates one of the ways in which poem-tellings and poem tales were connected.

Although the notation that is mentioned in this first item seems to follow the same trajectory from speech to writing shared by most scholarly accounts of *uta-gatari*'s role in shaping *uta monogatari*, the second

---

28. *Makura no sōshi* section 258, SNKBZ 18:388–89; see also McKinney, *The Pillow Book*, 211.

item moves in the opposite direction by portraying a reader who discovers the written source of a story or poem they had previously only heard in an oral recounting. It is easy to imagine that Sei Shōnagon would have been pleased at such a discovery because it could help her to remember the poem. As she goes on to note in the final item cited above, members of the court were frequently challenged to identify *waka* from the sort of partial allusion described in both the Tokonatsu chapter's account of *uta-gatari* and the vignette involving Hitomaro's *waka*. Her pleasure might also result from an ability to appreciate subtle differences between the two versions, or result from satisfaction at having questions that arose from hearing the poem-telling answered in the written account. Regardless, the relationship described here between "old words" (*furuki koto*) in spoken accounts and material "things" (*mono*) revealed to a reader's eye should caution against assuming oral anecdotes about *waka* always preceded textual ones.

This complex relationship between textuality and orality is also alluded to in the third and fourth items, which appear to place equal value on precisely replicating the contents of a story and on adapting them to suit new circumstances. The terse reference to the acquisition of blank paper making up the third item suggests that the unexpected discovery of the written source for a poem should lead to the creation of a new copy. Read in this light, the constant need to remember old poems that is mentioned in the fourth item indicates the practical value such copies served as reference sources. New copies could also adapt or alter the source material, thereby providing the basis for new oral recountings. In sum, all four items hint at the process by which oral and textual anecdotes about *waka* shaped one another.

Many of these elements in the practice of poem-telling can also be seen when the story of a *waka* Narihira's mother wrote to him is told in another section of *The Pillow Book*. The manner in which her poem is introduced, narrated, and evaluated are all reminiscent of an *uta-gatari*: "How terribly moving and special it was when the princess who was the mother of the middle captain Narihira sent word to his place in that poem with the line *more and more to see you*. I can just imagine what it must have been like for him to open the message and see it there."[29] Sei Shōnagon's partial citation is a clear indication that she expects her

---

29. *Makura no sōshi* section 289, SNKBZ 18:444; see also McKinney, *The Pillow Book*, 244.

readers to recognize the entire poem.[30] Her conversational tone also resembles that used to introduce the Kainuma poem-telling. Another aspect of this anecdote that suggests a relationship to *uta-gatari* is its placement before a section that describes the author jotting down memorable poems in the *uchigiki* format that *uta monogatari* initially built on: "It's awful to find some unmentionably lowly serving woman casually singing a poem you had thought charming enough to note down in a booklet."[31] This depiction of a female servant singing a *waka* previously recorded by the narrator offers yet another example of the porous boundaries between song and poetry discussed in chapter 3. Coming as it does after the anecdote about Narihira, moreover, it also hints at the different channels through which his verse reached multiple strata of court society.

The narrator's desire to assume Narihira's gaze as he read his mother's *waka* is emblematic of the pronounced scopophilia Edith Sarra identifies as one of *The Pillow Book*'s most distinctive characteristics.[32] Such voyeuristic tendencies make it all the more surprising that Sei Shōnagon makes no mention of his romantic liaisons, particularly because they would have involved the sort of content described in her list of "Pleasant Things" (*Kokoro yuku mono*) as "entertaining, distasteful, or strange occurrences from the recent past that cross the line between public and private."[33] This unsanctioned blurring of different social arenas succinctly encapsulates one of the chief reasons for interest in stories about Narihira, insofar as scandals involving him and royal consorts would have encouraged speculation of the sort *uta-gatari* encouraged by hinting at their identities and motives. Because such stories were so numerous, however, Sei Shōnagon's decision to focus rather on his feelings for his mother is in keeping with the deliberately eccentric stance adopted throughout *The Pillow Book*.

---

30. The full poem is as follows: "When they say that / parting is inevitable / as we grow old, / more and more to see you / do I desire milord!" (*oinureba / saranu wakare mo / ari to ieba / iyo iyo mimaku / hoshiki kimi kana*) (*Kokin wakashū* poem 900, SNKBZ 11:341).

31. *Makura no sōshi* section 290, SNKBZ 18:444; see also McKinney, *The Pillow Book*, 244.

32. Sarra, *Fictions of Femininity*, 222–64.

33. *Makura no sōshi* section 29, SNKBZ 18:71; see also McKinney, *The Pillow Book*, 30–31.

Sei Shōnagon's enthusiastic speculation about Narihira's response to his mother's *waka* also gives us a glimpse into the process by which individual poem-tellings expanded as answers were provided to questions arising from earlier versions. Both the *Kokinshū* and *Ise* versions of the prose prefacing this same anecdote offer details of time, place, and medium that would have contributed to the emotional impact Sei Shōnagon tries to envisage.[34] By noting that his mother sent her poem to Narihira at the end of the calendar year, they convey her sense of urgency as her life also approaches its end; by specifying that she was residing in the abandoned former capital, they indicate her isolation from the court society her son is now immersed in; and by revealing that her letter had no other content, they mark the powerfully condensed form into which the *waka* distills those two details. But *Ise*'s additional mention of her son's anxiety upon receiving the poem and his tears after reading it are significant expansions on the content of the *Kokinshū* headnote. Whereas the anthology tends to omit such responses in its versions of Narihira's *waka*, the poem tale typically includes them in order to create causal connections between individual poetic vignettes. Sei Shōnagon's speculation about his reaction to his mother's poem thus suggests the critical role such conjectures played in creating poem tales from poems. Invitations to such expansions are in fact made explicit in the last poem tale, *Heichū monogatari*, which ends many of its episodes with the narrator wondering what happened next.

Sei Shōnagon's anecdote also illustrates the difficulties entailed by any attempt to identify consecutive stages in the development of poem-centered narratives. It is easy to imagine that she is alluding to the *Kokinshū* version, since the author notes elsewhere that members of the court were expected to be thoroughly familiar with the anthology's contents. On the other hand, extensive allusions to *Ise* in Murasaki Shikibu's writings indicate the poem tale was also widely known in this period.[35] It is also possible, as many scholars have suggested, that Narihira's personal *waka* anthology was the original source for all these versions.

---

34. *Kokin wakashū* poem 900, SNKBZ 11:341; *Ise monogatari* episode 84, SNKBZ 12: 187–88.

35. A detailed account of these intertextual links is provided in Takahashi, "Allusion to and Transformation of the *Ise monogatari*."

However, differences in the contents and organization of the oldest surviving versions of *Narihira shū* (Narihira Anthology) from the mid-Heian period make it impossible to reconstruct a putative ur-text. The futility of any such attempt is further underlined by the complex interplay between oral and textual iterations in *uta-gatari* illustrated by *The Pillow Book*. As we will see, however, the distinctive early history of the Nagisa poem makes it an exception in this regard.

Narihira and Koretaka in Sandai jitsuroku

The unusually diverse array of contexts in which Narihira's Nagisa poem appears can be attributed at least in part to the equally unusual treatment accorded its composer and recipient in *Sandai jitsuroku*. The completion of this historical chronicle a few years before the Nagisa *waka* emerges makes it an especially valuable source of information on the poem's immediate context. Like other such biographies in *Sandai jitsuroku*, Narihira's is more detailed than those in earlier court histories.[36] In addition to the information its predecessors included—such as an individual's parentage, court rank, posts held, and new surnames bestowed by a sovereign—the last official court chronicle mentions particular proclivities or pursuits that distinguished their subjects.[37] An unusual number of such characteristics in Narihira's obituary, two of which are entirely unique to his biography, made it fertile ground in which to cultivate the diverse accounts of his life that developed in later centuries.

The unusually lofty pedigree Narihira possessed as the grandson of two sovereigns provides one such narrative seed. His father, Prince Abo (792–842), was a son of Emperor Heizei (774–824, r. 806–809), while his mother, Princess Ito, was the same daughter of Kanmu who added her palm print to the prayer mentioned in chapter 3. This doubly royal lineage distinguishes Narihira from other commoners, a notion *Ise* develops by hinting at his proclivity for affairs with imperial consorts. His

---

36. A complete translation of the obituary is provided in Newhard, *Knowing the Amorous Man*, 31–32.
37. Noguchi, "*Sandai jitsuroku* no kōsotsu kiji," 131–204.

mother's pedigree played a key role in this regard by elevating Narihira above both his father and paternal half-siblings, all of whose own mothers were commoners. This distinguished maternal background explains why she is the only one of his parents mentioned in the *Kokinshū* and *Ise*, as well as why the poem tale stresses her royal status.

His paternal background, by contrast, put Narihira at a double disadvantage. He was born after his disgraced father had returned to the capital from a fourteen-year exile in Kyushu, where Prince Abo had been sent as punishment for his alleged involvement in a failed attempt to restore his own father to the throne in 810. As the youngest of five sons, moreover, Narihira was such a peripheral addition to his father's already marginalized male offspring that his own obituary fails to include him among the sons Prince Abo names when it cites his request that they be given the hereditary title of "Ariwara Lords" (Ariwara no asomi) to mark their royal descent. References to Narihira as *zaigo* (the fifth Ariwara son) in later narratives suggest both this youth and marginality elicited sympathy from readers in equal measure.

Other narrative seeds are provided by the summary of Narihira's qualities that follows this account of his parentage. In a tacit nod to his poetic skills, this is one of only two such character sketches in *Sandai jitsuroku* that take the form of a quatrain. Its four sentences, each consisting of four Sinographs, form complementary pairs describing first his external and internal qualities before ending with his writerly abilities in both formal and informal contexts:

體貌閑麗	Form and features were elegant and handsome.
放縱不拘	Self-indulgent no matter the circumstance.
畧無才學	Practically without talent or training.
善作倭歌	Well-skilled in making Yamato verse.[38]

The first sentence, which is unique to his obituary, highlights Narihira's erotic appeal for both genders in the same manner as his successor Genji. The second sentence, on the other hand, had been used in earlier court histories to describe men who flouted social norms or indulged in the

---

38. *Nihon sandai jitsuroku* entry for Tenchō 6/5/28, KST 4:475–76.

pleasures of sex, falconry, and drinking to excess. As it happens, these same pleasures appear in the erotic poem-tellings Genji and Suzaku exchange as well as in *Ise*'s account of the hunting and drinking that accompanies Narihira's excursion to Nagisa. Between them, the two first sentences in his obituary identify the external qualities that made Narihira an attractive object for readers to desire and the internal ones making his amorous adventures a source of vicarious pleasure.

The catalyst that transforms these characteristics into stories is provided by the reference to Narihira's abilities as a writer in the third and fourth sentences. Although the third sentence at first sight appears to indicate a lack of facility with Literary Sinitic, his skills as a *shi* poet in fact led Narihira to participate in a formal reception for emissaries from Parhae in 872 mentioned in the same court history.[39] The phrase "practically without talent or training" is used in earlier histories to describe men who have advanced on the basis of birth or royal patronage rather than through a formal education.[40] Although this assessment implies princely privilege, it also suggests Narihira possessed the poetic skills of a talented amateur. In this regard he again resembles Genji, whose effortless mastery of Literary Sinitic is favorably contrasted with the acceptable but uninspired abilities his son gains through a formal education. Like the opening reference to Narihira's pansexual appeal, the fourth one describing his skill at Japanese poetry only appears in his obituary. The singular nature of both sentences framing this thumbnail sketch of Narihira thus highlights the unique qualities that made him such a compelling protagonist.

Equally unique narrative seeds accompany *Sandai jitsuroku*'s portrayal of the person to whom the Nagisa poem is addressed. Like Narihira, Prince Koretaka suffered politically from paternal actions when his father, Montoku, replaced him as crown prince with Yoshifusa's grandson. This change in the succession is traditionally attributed to the machinations of the Fujiwara patriarch, who subsequently became the first regent outside the imperial family after his grandson was enthroned as the sovereign Seiwa (850–881, r. 858–876). The significance of this change in the succession can be seen in the fact that it inaugurates not

---

39. *Nihon sandai jitsuroku* entry for Jōgan 14/5/17, KST 4:307.
40. Watanabe, "Narihira denki kai hoketsu," 95–106.

only *Sandai jitsuroku*'s account of Seiwa's reign but also the entirety of the chronicle as well. Tellingly, Koretaka's political fate is only mentioned in an oblique allusion cloaked in the ambiguously allegorical imagery of a song.

The sovereign's personal name was Korehito. He was the fourth son of Sovereign Montoku. His mother was an imperial consort of the Fujiwara clan and daughter of the Grand Minister of Senior First Rank Lord Yoshifusa. He was born in Kashō 3/3/25 at the First Avenue residence of the Grand Minister in the eastern part of the capital. On the twenty-fifth day of the Eleventh Month in that same year he was made Crown Prince. He was nine months old at the time. Earlier, there had been a song of foretelling that said:

天皇諱惟仁。文德天皇之第四子也。母太皇大后藤原氏。太政大臣贈正一位良房朝臣之女也。嘉祥三年歲在庚午三月廿五日癸卯。生天皇於太政大東京一條第。十一月廿五日戊戌。立爲皇太子。于時誕育九月也。先是有童謠云

大枝ヲ超エテ	Passing over the bigger branches,
走リ超テ	passing over in a rush,
躍ドリ騰ガリ超テ	passing over while dancing and leaping,
我ヤ護モル田ニヤ	here in these paddies that we guard,
捜アサリハ食ム志岐ヤ	a snipe searches for food to eat,
雄々イ志岐ヤ	a snipe so brave and bold!

People in the know took the "bigger branches" as references to his older brothers. At the time, Sovereign Montoku had four royal sons. First was Prince Koretaka, second was Prince Koresuji, and third was Prince Korehiko. The Crown Prince was the fourth son. It is because the royal will had passed over the elder three that "passing over" appears thrice in the song.

識人以爲。大枝謂大兄也。是時文德天皇有四皇子。第一惟喬親王。第二惟條親王。第三惟彥親王。皇太子是第四皇子也。天意若曰超三兄而立。故有三超之謠焉。[41]

The abovementioned verse is the last of four "songs of foretelling" (J. *waza-uta*, C. *tongyao*) appearing in the court histories written after

---

41. *Nihon sandai jitsuroku*, KST 4:3.

Nihon shoki, all of which concern crown princes (the last two of whom were demoted at Yoshifusa's urging). As mentioned in chapter 2, such songs represent a rare example of an explicitly satirical genre in premodern East Asia. Characterized by allegorical imagery and wordplay, their contents spread rapidly by word of mouth after originating with children or individuals possessed by *kami*. This combination of sacral authority, anonymity, and coded language allowed *waza-uta* to safely comment on fraught social conditions.[42] Placing such a song at the start of a historical chronicle whose compilation was overseen by his own grandson, Tokihira, thus acknowledges the widespread outrage that resulted from Yoshifusa's actions.[43]

By portraying all three older brothers as victims, however, the song's puns and repetitions divert attention from the particular injustice Koretaka suffered. Restoring the prince's place in history is thus one motive for his appearance in *Ise*. Formal similarities between the poem tale and the historical account make the *uta monogatari* a particularly fitting medium for redressing the chronicle's shortcomings. The prose in both narratives explains the circumstances leading to the creation of verses, includes remarks about the identities of the individuals involved, and presents their narrators as an anonymous community of "people in the know," as *Sandai jitsuroku* puts it. Like many *waka* in *Ise*, this *waza-uta* also encourages further speculation, in this case by making it possible to view its evaluation of Yoshifusa as either negative or positive. Although the snipe's theft of rice from a guarded paddy suggests he has improperly intruded on Montoku's prerogative to determine the succession, the "brave and bold" nature of these actions also suggests admiration for his audacity in doing so. The figural capacity of this *waza-uta* to accommodate the perspectives of both sides in the succession struggle ultimately serves to legitimize *Sandai jitsuroku* by demonstrating that it represents the views of the court as a whole. Consequently, the entire historical narrative relies on the song's erasure of Koretaka as a discrete figure in order to legitimate its account. It is precisely because the song fails to do the prince

---

42. On the use of *waza-uta* in the official court histories and their Sinitic precedents, see Nishimura, "Retrospective Comprehension."

43. Sakamoto, *The Six National Histories of Japan*, 180.

justice in this respect that another figural representation of him in *waka* would appear soon afterward.

Nagisa in Anthologies

As Richard Okada has noted, one reason why Narihira's *waka* became a favored subject for *uta-gatari* soon after his death was their tendency to incite readerly speculation through semantic ambiguities, rhetorical questions, implicit metaphors, and counterfactual hypotheses.[44] Such characteristics led Tsurayuki to make his famous appraisal of the poet in his *Kokinshū* preface: "As for Ariwara no Narihira, there is too much heart and too few words, like a wilted flower whose color has faded while its scent lingers."[45] The use of essentially identical language to describe his poetry in the *mana* preface suggests this view was widely shared.[46] By employing a faded flower to mark the temporal gap between the youthful desires animating Narihira's poems and the lingering scent of their textual afterlife, both prefaces indicate that additional narrative contexts were necessary to recover the motivations generating his *waka*.

This need for further contextualization makes the Nagisa poem a notable exception to the *Kokinshū* editors' general tendency to lavish the longest headnotes in the anthology on Narihira's *waka*. In addition to hinting at the fraught history represented in the poem, the headnote's brevity powerfully illustrates the critical role played by naming poet and place in constructing *waka*-centered narratives.

Composed upon seeing cherries at Nagisa Villa. By Narihira of the Ariwara Lords.

yo no naka ni   If only our world
taete sakura no   were to cease having cherries

---

44. Okada, *Figures of Resistance*, 143–46.
45. *Kokin wakashū* kanajo, SNKBZ 11:26.
46. *Kokin wakashū* manajo, SNKBZ 11:426: "The poems of the Ariwara Middle Captain possess an excess of feeling and a dearth of words, like flowers that have wilted but still show some hint of color and retain their fragrant scent" (在原中將之歌。其情有餘。其詞不足。如萎花雖少彩色。而有薰香。).

nakariseba	in existence ever more,
haru no kokoro wa	then springtime hearts
nodokekaramashi	would be at ease.[47]

The contextual information represented by its headnote's terse mention of the sight and location that inspired this poem is supplemented only slightly by its placement early on in the sequence of spring verses addressing cherry blossoms, which indicates the trees at Nagisa have only just begun to bloom.[48] As is typical in *waka* anthologies, the lack of subjects in its headnote makes the prose narrative neither first- nor third-person, placing it in a liminal position between an autobiographical account by Narihira that originated in his personal *waka* anthology and a biographical one that was added later by its editors. The authorial attribution supplied by the *Kokinshū*'s compilers thus plays a critical role in turning this ambiguous fragment of life-writing into a narrative that is explicitly third-person. Its reference to Narihira's princely lineage as a "lord" (*asomi*) further situates this biography within official historical discourse in the same manner as it does when it appears in *Sandai jitsuroku*'s obituary.

It is the place name in the headnote, however, that is critical to establishing a narrative context. Like Kainuma, Nagisa Villa becomes the seed for a poetic anecdote by signifying a setting and subject. Nagisa's literal meaning of "strand" provides readers with a picture of waves lapping against the Yodo-gawa riverbank, while its designation as a "villa" (*in*) metonymically marks the complicated family history of its resident, who received it from the same father who had removed him from the succession. Both aspects of the prince's history are conveyed by the term *in*, which refers to residences supporting royalty in comfortable retirement from public life.

This narrative context gains additional dimensions through similarities and contrasts created by the parallel structure used in the headnote to the preceding poem composed by Yoshifusa to celebrate Seiwa's mother Fujiwara no Meishi (829–900). In each case, the poet views cherry blossoms at a mansion whose name marks that space as a source of paternal support for its inhabitant, thereby transforming the sight into an allegori-

---

47. *Kokin wakashū* poem 53, SNKBZ 11:48.
48. Komatsu, *Koten sainyūmon*, 303.

cal representation of that resident's relationship to the royal line. Whereas Montoku's villa marks his role in removing Koretaka from the succession, Yoshifusa's mansion signals the part he plays in fostering his daughter Meishi's perpetuation of the same ruling line through her son.

> Composed upon seeing flowering cherries that had been placed in a vase before the consort at Somedono. By the former chancellor.

toshi fureba	As the years pass
yowai wa oinu	I have grown ever older.
shika wa aredo	Yet though this be so,
hana o shi mireba	when I see these blossoms
mono-omoi mo nashi	my gloom disappears.[49]

Although their headnotes connect the flowers in both poems by depicting their composers engaging in the same act of gazing upon them at aristocratic mansions, the blossoms' different spatial relationships to those locations suggest different degrees of figural distance between those cherries and their residences' inhabitants. Because their allegorical significance depends in both cases on a complex operation involving both metonymical and metaphorical modes of signification, moreover, it is expressed first in a relatively explicit manner within Yoshifusa's poem in order to ensure its implicit presence within the one Narihira composes. The interior location of the vase and its proximity to Meishi's body leaves no room for the blossoms to represent anything other than her body metonymically and its fertility metaphorically. By comparison, their external location on the trees at Nagisa creates more space between them and Koretaka, allowing the flowers to represent someone or something other than the prince.

These rhetorical maneuvers reveal their political purpose through the contrasting emotional responses each poet has to the same sight. As a source of joy at Somedono and sorrow at Nagisa, the blossoms typify what Susan Klein has identified as a tendency for secular political allegory in Heian *waka* to occur "in the context of eulogistic congratulations to those stationed above the author or in public poetry expressing the author's

---

49. *Kokin wakashū* poem 52, SNKBZ 11:48.

discontent."⁵⁰ Through their complementary differences, the paired *waka* allegorically accommodate both sides of the succession struggle in the same manner as the *waza-uta* in *Sandai jitsuroku*. The critical role played by Yoshifusa's *waka* in reproducing the same political arrangement within the imperial anthology that had been recently established in the imperial history accounts for its author's singular status as the only *Kokinshū* poet who is a high-ranking nobleman. Tokihira's involvement in producing both texts further implies the interests of Yoshifusa's grandson are at work here.

Figural language's capacity to generate multiple meanings also poses dangers for the poet and/or compiler by creating the potential for disrupting the political order being upheld by this allegory for the Fujiwara clan's flowering fortunes. Narihira's use of the verb *taete* (to cease abruptly or break off) in his *waka* could in fact be interpreted as enjoining his audience to stage a violent coup that would bring an equally swift and decisive end to Fujiwara influence.⁵¹ The poet's reputation for employing counterfactual hypotheses thus seems deliberately intended in this case to avoid implying that he is plotting to overthrow the regency. Rather, the impossibility of extinguishing the Fujiwara—something as improbable as a world without cherry blossoms—turns the Nagisa poem into an acknowledgment of Yoshifusa's power. The regent's triumph is also endowed with a sense of inevitability by placing Narihira's regret after Yoshifusa's joy, in keeping with the anthology's overall tendency to represent negative outcomes as the natural course of events in human affairs.

By decisively departing from the figural logic Narihira employs, the *waka* that follows it plays an essential role in confining its predecessor's meaning to the political binary of victor and vanquished. Its figural, affective, and historical characteristics all mark a decisive break from the Nagisa poem in this regard.

Topic unknown. Poet unknown.

ishi-bashiru   How I wish rock-racing
taki naku mogana   falls were not here!

50. Klein, *Allegories of Desire*, 26.
51. For a more literal interpretation of *taete*, see Takeoka, *Kokin wakashū zenhyōshaku*, 1:352.

> *sakura-bana* The cherry blossoms
> *ta orite mo komu* would I pluck and bring back
> *minu hito no tame* for people who have yet to see them.⁵²

Cherry blossoms are now cherished rather than abhorred, and the allegorical implications of an abrupt rupture in the political status quo are now literalized as the purely physical act of breaking off branches. The anonymous nature of this poem also removes it from the narrative frameworks of biography and history sustaining the allegorical significance of the preceding pair. Like other such *waka* in the *Kokinshū*, its headnote implies that this poem originated with a historical person and context. Without knowing either, however, there is no way of assigning it political significance. Conversely, the existence of such information, however minimal, in the paratexts provided for its two predecessors underscores the critical role proper nouns play in establishing their historical significance.

The importance of such paratextual apparati as authorial attribution and anthological placement for producing political allegory within the Nagisa poem is also attested to by their deliberate removal from its iteration in *Shinsen waka*. Overall, the later anthology subsumes its poems' individual histories under purely aesthetic principles by removing any mention of their creators and compositional contexts, and by replacing the associative progressions governing their narrative sequencing in earlier anthologies with symmetries that are consistently contrastive and static.⁵³ Traditional references to time are also rejected when its preface uses the expression "blossom and fruit in balance" (花實相兼) to describe *Shinsen waka*'s structure. Whereas this botanical binary had previously referred to new and old forms of poetry respectively in such texts as *Kakyō hyōshiki* (A Formulary for Verse Based on the Canons of Poetry, 772) and *Shinsen man'yōshū* (Newly Selected *Man'yōshū*, 893), *Shinsen waka* rejects this historical valence in favor of purely formal contrasts.⁵⁴ As a result, each poem is imbued with intimations of its ultimate fate without detailing an intermediate narrative

---

52. *Kokin wakashū* poem 54, SNKBZ 11:49.
53. Satō, *Heian waka bungaku hyōgen ron*, 103.
54. On the use of this term in *Kakyō hyōshiki*, see Rabinovitch, "Wasp Waists and Monkey Tails," 527.

progression: spring flowers fade in fall and birthday blessings turn to mourning rites.[55]

Shinsen waka's relative brevity also makes its selections significant in their own right. Many of its poets are related to Tsurayuki in a configuration famously described by the historian Mezaki Tokue (1921–2000) as the "Ki Clan Mountain Range" (*Kishi sanmyaku*), whose members in this anthology even include the compiler's humble father.[56] By contrast, it contains only a third of the *Kokinshū*'s poems by the more famous half of its "six poetic immortals" (*rokkasen*): Narihira, Ono no Komachi (fl. ninth century), and Henjō (816–890).[57] These biases make it all the more significant that Tsurayuki includes both the Nagisa poem and the one by Yoshifusa. Although the regent's *waka* is placed well after Narihira's in a deliberate avoidance of any historical link between them, however, the decision to put other poems by Tsurayuki and Koretaka respectively before and after the Nagisa verse in *Shinsen waka* parallels the prominent place all three men occupy when Narihira's poem reemerges in *Tosa nikki* and *Ise*.[58]

Nagisa in Ise

The *Ise* episode in which the Nagisa poem appears takes full advantage of the opportunities for greater narrative contextualization presented by the unusually brief prose that accompanied it in the *Kokinshū*. By fleshing out its surrounding geography and immediate audience, the poem tale also lays the groundwork for one of its most celebrated and structurally complex episodes. In addition to inaugurating one of the largest multi-episodic narratives within *Ise*, the account of a hunting party at Nagisa involving Narihira and Koretaka displays the full range of techniques employed by the poem tale's anonymous authors to

---

55. Tesaki, "*Shinsen waka* no henshū ni okeru Tsurayuki no ito," 7.
56. Mezaki, *Ki no Tsurayuki*, 21.
57. Yamaguchi, *Ōchō kadan no kenkyū*, 590–91.
58. These *waka* by Tsurayuki, Narihira, Koretaka, and Yoshifusa are poems 67, 69, 71, and 91 respectively in *Shinsen waka*.

create individual episodes, several of which also suggest a connection to *uta-gatari*.[59]

In combination with the Nagisa poem, the prose that prefaces it represents a comparatively lengthy version of the simplest narrative unit common to all *Ise* episodes. An equally simple strategy is then used to build on this nucleus of poem and preface by adding an anonymous poetic response. Further connections based on similarities in person, place, and time weave other poetic exchanges into one large episode by creating a travel narrative out of complementary movements in poetry and prose. Its poetic topics progress from springtime cherry blossoms to the autumnal Tanabata lovers in a partial evocation of the seasonal cycle whose circular temporality is reproduced spatially in prose, tracing an itinerary that frames the entire episode by beginning and ending at Nagisa.

Like the other twenty-four *waka* by Narihira it shares with the *Kokinshū*, the Nagisa poem plays a pivotal role in creating multi-episodic structures within *Ise* as well, the largest of which encompasses its entire text through the placement of such poems in its first and last episodes. Episode 83 further explores the relationship between Koretaka and Narihira through two poetic exchanges that also take place at Minase, before concluding with one final visit to Koretaka's winter retreat in Ono. Together with another such visit to Ono in episode 85, the poetic exchanges in episodes 82 and 83 form one of the most extended accounts of the hero's engagement with a single individual in the tale. The politics of imperial succession doubtless inspire this length, which is only surpassed by *Ise*'s depictions of its hero's transgressive affairs with two other older imperial figures connected to Seiwa's rule: his chief consort, Fujiwara no Kōshi (824–910), and his older half-sister Tenshi (d. 913), who served as Ise Shrine priestess during her younger sibling's reign.[60] In addition to being Tenshi's full brother, Koretaka completes this set of multi-episodic narratives by providing the male complement to the female pair. Together

---

59. For a detailed account of *Ise*'s complex textual history in English, see Vos, *A Study of the Ise-Monogatari* 1:13–48 and 76–100. All subsequent citations are from the standard Teika-bon text.

60. The imputation of scandalous conduct to both women probably originated with the replacement of Montoku's patriline by that of Kōkō in the imperial succession (Imanishi, "The Formation of the *Ise monogatari*," 21–23).

with Narihira's amorous pursuit of the two imperial women, his participation in the hunts and feasts the prince engages in thus encompasses the range of activities typically associated with the phrase "self-indulgent no matter the circumstance" (放縦不拘) that was used in his obituary to describe Narihira's impulsive actions.

These micro- and macro-structural aspects of the Nagisa vignette explain the notable length of episode 82's opening section. In order to fulfill the multiple aims of contextualizing Narihira's poem, initiating an episode consisting of three separate vignettes, and launching a multi-episodic narrative, this prose expands on the *Kokinshū*'s spare headnote by adding information about the surroundings, primary recipient, social context, and the narrator's own relationship to the account.

> Once, they say, there was a prince named His Highness Prince Koretaka. It's said he had a royal residence in a place called Minase across from Yamazaki. Every year when the cherry blossoms were in full bloom, they say that royal residence is where His Highness would go. At such times His Highness would always bring along another person who is said to have been a chief equerry. With so much time and so many reigns having passed long since, the name of that person has apparently been lost to memory! Lacking any passion for the hunt, it is said they just drank saké while pursuing Yamato verse. Now, too, the cherry trees of that villa, at the Nagisa residence by the Katano hunting fields, are particularly enthralling. Dismounting to sit under the trees and breaking off branches to adorn their hair, they say everyone composed verse, high, middling, and low alike. This was composed by the person who is said to have been a chief equerry.[61]

The aura of political defeat surrounding Nagisa is given historical depth by expanding its setting to include the surrounding fields of Katano, where Kanmu frequently led hunting expeditions that established the sacral boundaries of his new Heian capital. The decision to abandon hunting in favor of saké and poetry thus establishes a contrast between the prince's position and that of his royal ancestor. Even though Koretaka's royal status grants him the right to hunt, the purposelessness of enacting this privilege—like his comfortable retirement at the Nagisa villa—only serves to underscore the prince's political marginalization. This melan-

---

61. *Ise monogatari* episode 82, SNKBZ 12:183–84.

cholic irony is further spelled out in the next poetic performance at Ama no Kawa on the same day. At least one of Kanmu's hunts at Katano concluded with a banquet where his retinue recited poems at his command.[62] Although Koretaka orders Narihira to compose a poem in similar fashion, a more egalitarian ethos at the *Ise* banquet leads the prince to make an unsuccessful attempt at replying with one of his own.

Because Koretaka's presence is central to all these political implications, it is revealing that the prose opening to episode 82 provides key details whose obfuscation through a muffled or faint vocalization would have encouraged the sort of speculation *uta-gatari* sought to incite, in this case by leaving an audience wondering about his identity. Such speculation is further encouraged by the narrator's insistence on subsequently referring to him exclusively through honorific verbs or the generic designation of *miko* (prince) over the course of the entire episode. The same purpose appears to be at work in the unusual decision to identify Narihira by the post of *uma no kami* (chief equerry), which seems to offer the prospect of successfully identifying the year he was at Nagisa.[63] In the absence of any other clues, however, readers then and now are left with a considerable span of time between Narihira's appointment to that post in 864 and Koretaka's retirement to Ono in 872. The narrator's claim that his name has been forgotten is even more noteworthy for being the only such interjection in the entire poem tale. Perhaps this aside is intended to draw still further attention to the question of his identity, as Takeoka Masao (1919–1985) argued.[64] Because these narratorial anomalies all but openly challenge us to identify Narihira, the presence of Nagisa in this vignette becomes essential to deciphering it. Perhaps for this same reason, we will subsequently see *Tosa nikki* also treating the toponym as a trigger for recalling not only the poem but also the identities of its composer and addressee.

---

62. On the ritualized poetic performance of rulership at Kanmu's hunting banquets, see Heldt, *The Pursuit of Harmony*, 36–38.

63. Historical discrepancies entailed by the appearance of other named individuals alongside this "chief equerry" in episodes 77 and 78 suggest their contents are later additions (Mostow and Tyler, *The Ise Stories*, 164–66).

64. Takeoka, *Ise monogatari zenhyōshaku*, 1180–81.

Like other *uta-gatari*, the episode also inspires an additional *waka* that represents either a later reader's reaction or the imagined one of another person at Nagisa. Like the poem that follows his in the *Kokinshū*, the deliberately literal approach of this response has the paradoxical effect of underscoring the earlier *waka*'s allegorical implications through its purposeful disavowal of any such insinuation.

Another verse by someone else:

chireba koso	Because they scatter
itodo sakura wa	cherries are all the more
medetakere	moving a sight!
ukiyo ni nani ka	What in this sorrowful world
hisashikaru beki	can we expect to last long?[65]

By indicating how the Nagisa poem was received, this anonymous *waka* exemplifies one of the key differences between Narihira's portrayal in the *Kokinshū* and *Ise*. Its refusal to engage with his poem in any but the most minimal manner through its repetition of the word for cherry trees, coupled with its assertion that their blossoms should be treasured, together foreground the violation of poetic protocol Narihira commits in failing to praise his host's residence. This anonymous response to his poem thus further underscores the original *waka*'s allegorical implications by drawing attention to its dissociation from the immediate social context in which Narihira recites it.

The anonymous rejoinder's connection to Narihira's poem is made even more tenuous by simply marking it as another verse by someone else, instead of specifying that it is a reply. Because it appears nowhere else in the written record, this anonymous *waka* was likely designed for episode 82 at a later date, making it similar to those that were subsequently added to an initial poem-telling by its audience. In other words, it can be read as either the response of a person who is located within the narrative frame, or that of an outside observer. Coupled with the strategic way in which its characters are introduced, this mode of poetic accretion therefore hints at the episode's origins in *uta-gatari*. As we will see next, how-

---

65. *Ise monogatari* episode 82, SNKBZ 12:184–85.

ever, *Tosa nikki*'s treatment of the Nagisa poem suggests its poem-telling appeared after the *Ise* version.

Nagisa in Tosa nikki

Although *Tosa nikki* is largely ignored in accounts of Narihira's poetry, its status as one of the earliest texts in which his *waka* appears offers a rare opportunity to expand our understanding of their handling in the *Kokinshū* and *Ise*. Because Tsurayuki was involved with both these other texts, moreover, comparing their versions of the Nagisa *waka* with the one in *Tosa nikki* also gives us a sense of the ways in which such narratives circulated simultaneously. Perhaps most significantly of all, *Tosa nikki*'s self-reflexive attention to the diarist's own actions makes its depiction of the Nagisa poem a remarkably vivid snapshot of the complex ways poem-tellings intersected with both oral and textual narratives. This remarkable level of detail is achieved with a surprisingly small number of sentences in which the diarist cites an oral anecdote and the responses to it, while also indicating through her transcription of this exchange how such elements helped shape written anecdotes about *waka*.

One noteworthy aspect of the Nagisa poem's treatment in *Tosa nikki* is its temporal context. The narrator's repeated references to an immediate present draw our attention to the fact that she is transcribing other people's speech that same day. In this regard the entry, like others that specify the time in which they are being written, departs from the standard practice of recording events on the following morning that was mentioned in chapter 1. This stress on the present in its portrayal of Nagisa is perhaps inspired by *Tosa nikki*'s status as a travelogue, insofar as encounters with storied locales in such narratives conventionally contrasted their current appearance with their fabled past. Regardless of the reasons for this choice, the resulting account is remarkable not only for its deviation from diaristic norms but also due to the portrayal of inscription that results. By representing the diarist writing in the narrative present, in other words, her transcription of the anecdotal references that are made to Narihira's *waka* provides us with the only example of a poem-telling's content and mode of presentation. Together with the poems added to it, this transcription also brings to mind the *uchigiki*-style notations mentioned in *The Pillow Book* as an initial stage in the transformation of spoken anecdotes into written vignettes. As we will see, however, other aspects of the account echo *Makura no sōshi*'s description of oral anecdotes that originate in written texts.

Taken as a whole, the entry echoes many of the features that were identified by Sei Shōnagon and Murasaki Shikibu in their references to *uta-gatari*. The temporal contrast between past and present that informs the account also reveals a new aspect of this practice in the influence it exerts on the wording of the Nagisa poem.

> While our ship is dragged upstream, a place called "*The Villa* by the Strand" comes into view. Thinking back on *The Villa*'s past, I recall it being said to be an enthralling place. Pines stand on the hills behind it, and a plum has bloomed in the courtyard within. People now speak, saying: "This place possesses an exalted history, you know!" "*The Late Middle Captain* Ariwara no Narihira was accompanying *The Late* Prince Koretaka here when he said:
>
> | *yo no naka ni* | 'If only our world |
> | *taete sakura no* | were without cherries |
> | *sakazaraba* | ever blooming in it, |
> | *haru no kokoro wa* | springtime hearts |
> | *nodokekaramashi* | would feel at ease.' |
>
> This is the very same place where he composed that poem!" (TN 50–51, 2/9)

Because the diarist goes out of her way to indicate that more than one person is speaking, its two sentences are likely being uttered by different individuals. The dialogic manner in which this discourse unfolds recalls *Makura no sōshi*'s description of a house whose occupants spend their time conversing about such stories. Like the fragmentary citation from the Kainuma poem-telling, the first speaker here introduces the place name in a preamble. Although minimal in comparison with *Ise*'s account of the Nagisa poem, the second speaker's observation that Koretaka was its initial recipient and Narihira was his attendant at the time are both significant expansions on the content of the *Kokinshū* headnote, which did not specify whether Narihira's *waka* was directly addressed to the prince in his presence or was simply about him. These comparisons between *Tosa nikki* and the other two texts in which the Nagisa poem appears thus suggest that both poem-tellings and poem tales differed from anthologies in the stress they laid on the social context in which a *waka* was initially composed and the relationship of its audience to the poet. Their importance is also subtly emphasized in the diary by marking place and person with the Sinographs for *in* 院 (villa) and *ko* 故 (late) respectively.

On the other hand, the citation of the entire Nagisa *waka* in this entry offers no opportunity for the sort of guesswork we saw in previous examples of *uta-gatari*. This anomaly is perhaps due to the fluid nature of its midmost measure, which plays a critical role in both identifying the entire poem and establishing its significance. Although standard modern editions of the *Kokinshū* and *Ise* make the third measure *nakariseba* (if there were none), other versions have *sakazaraba* (if none bloomed) instead.[66] As it happens, Tsurayuki can be seen deliberately employing both options in different texts: all extant versions of *Shinsen waka* use *nakariseba*, while all versions of *Tosa nikki* favor *sakazaraba*.

Several reasons have been given for the diary's unambiguously deliberate choice of wording. Hagitani suggests the more conceptual and abstract nature of *nakariseba* would have confused young readers learning how to compose their own *waka* (TNZ 367). Perhaps the intention was to parody the original by reducing the novel description of cherry trees never existing to the more quotidian one of them not blooming.[67] The simplest explanation is that *sakazaraba* echoes the preceding comment noting that "a plum has bloomed" (*mume no hana sakeri*) in the courtyard of the villa.[68] The seeming simplicity of the reasoning informing this last explanation in fact adds ironic depth to the poem's wording. Because *Tosa nikki*'s early springtime setting literally fulfills Narihira's desire for there to be no blooms on the villa's cherries, this choice of verb ends up lending ironic poignancy to the Nagisa anecdote for the travelers who are viewing its villa in the narrative present.

---

66. Fukui, "*Tosa nikki* to Ariwara no Narihira," 34. Along with the Nurigome-bon version of *Ise*, *sakazaraba* is used in the only surviving *Kokinshū* manuscript from the Heian period, the Gen'ei-bon, as well as in the Shunzei-bon and Kiyosuke-bon variants.
67. Satō, "*Tosa nikki* ni okeru 'parodi,'" 30.
68. Tanaka, "Ki no Tsurayuki ni miru kana sanbun no kokoromi," 54.

Thus, the wording of the diary's version of this poem indicates the value placed on adapting *waka* to the audience and context in which each poem-telling was performed in order to shape its desired impact. The impression of an implicitly ironic gap between Narihira's past and the diarist's present that *sakazaraba* represents is accordingly rendered explicit in both of the *waka* that follow this anecdote, and by the mention of both "now" and "today" in the sentence introducing them.

Just now someone has composed a verse resembling the place as it is today.

chiyo hetaru	Millennia have passed
matsu ni wa aredo	for these pines, and yet
inishie no	the chilling voice
koe no samusa wa	of days long gone by
kawarazarikeri	remains unchanged!

And another person has composed:

kimi koite	In longing for milord,
yo o furu yado no	ages pass at this lodging
mume no hana	where plum blossoms
mukashi no ka ni zo	even now put forth
nao nioikeru	their past fragrance!
(TN 51, 2/9)	

Between them, these *waka* confirm two central aspects of *uta-gatari* inferred from their description by Murasaki Shikibu and Sei Shōnagon: the role played by audiences in adding their own *waka*, and the importance laid on identifying the anecdote's original poet and audiences. Both *waka* appear to echo the preceding anecdote's focus on the composer and initial recipient of the original poem by replicating their order of appearance in the *uta-gatari*, with the "chilling voice" in the first poem alluding to Narihira's recitation, and the "milord" in the second one gesturing to the villa's former resident, Koretaka. The plum blossoms' lingering scent in the second poem additionally recalls the imagery used to describe the textual traces that preserve Narihira's sentiments in the *Kokinshū* prefaces. Between them, the two *waka* thus also seem to mimic the diarist's transcription by representing first vocal and then textual forms of poetry.

The first of these two *waka* is also noteworthy for its use of an expression that appears nowhere else to portray the wind blowing through

Nagisa's pines: *koe no samusa* (the chilling voice). The closest equivalent to this singular synesthesia appears in a headnote from the Tameuji-bon version of *Tsurayuki shū* describing "the sound of the chilling wind blowing through pine and bamboo" (*kaze samuku fukite, matsu take no oto*) that Tsurayuki hears at Kanesuke's deserted Awata villa when he visits it shortly after returning from Tosa.[69] The second *waka* this headnote refers to clearly connects its wind to Tsurayuki's former poetic community.

kage ni tote	For its cover
tachi-kakurureba	I stand here concealed,
kara-koromo	this robe of Cathay
nurenu ama furu	unsoaked by rain falling
matsu no koe kana	with the pine's cries![70]

The soughing wind blowing through pine trees within the headnote becomes the sound of rain falling on their branches in the poem, turning the *waka* into a tearful elegy for the shelter Kanesuke's patronage once provided. This poignancy deepens when the elegy reappears later in the same anthology with a headnote claiming Tsurayuki first composed it at Awata while Kanesuke was still alive.[71] Through this repetition, the same voice that once represented the lively music accompanying a banquet now grieves for its loss.

Like the wind in this poem, the blooming plum in *Tosa nikki* produces pathos by repeating the same word in different contexts. This similarity also creates a connection between the two mansions, each of which represents the last physical trace of a male homosocial community that once gathered there to create poetry. Yet another, subtler link to Narihira's poetic legacy is suggested by the singular synesthesia that appears in the first anonymous *waka* at Nagisa: like the vision of a world without cherry trees, the combination of sound with temperature is as imaginative as it is counterintuitive. In this sense, the Nagisa *waka* provides an additional indication that poem-tellings sought to foster speculative

---

69. Hirasawa, *Ōchō bungaku no shihatsu*, 315–17. For the full text of this headnote, see *Tsurayuki shū* poem 767, SNKS 80:266.
70. *Tsurayuki shū* poem 768, SNKS 80:266.
71. *Tsurayuki shū* poem 821, SNKS 80:284.

ingenuity on the part of their audiences. As we will see in the next section, this aspect of *uta-gatari* is made more explicit when another poem by Narihira is referenced in the diary.

The appearance of this *uta-gatari* only a few decades after the Nagisa poem was included in the *Kokinshū* further begs the question as to whether it represents an intermediate stage between the anthology's version of the *waka* and the one given such an extensive narrative context in the poem tale.[72] One possible answer lies in a subtle difference between the villa's description in *Ise* and *Tosa nikki*. When it asserts the cherries are "particularly enthralling" (*koto ni omoshiroshi*), episode 82 draws attention to their allure in a narratorial interjection that is as unusual as the one casting doubt on Narihira's identity. Whereas every other sentence prefacing the Nagisa poem in *Ise* uses the auxiliary verb *keri* to convey the narrator's distance from the content of their narration, this one adopts a declarative tone intimating that its speaker has seen Nagisa's blossoms in person. By contrast, the diarist uses *keri* in an identical description when she notes: "I recall now that this is a place said to be enthralling" (*omoshirokarikeru tokoro*). This phrasing thus seems to be alluding to the portrayal of Nagisa in *Ise* or a poem-telling based on it. In other words, *Tosa nikki*'s description of Nagisa is more likely to be citing an earlier narrative rather than expanding on it.

This reading can accommodate several of the functions scholars attribute to *keri*. Its broadest definition, provided by Takeoka Masao, famously described the auxiliary verb as a means of indicating speakers' temporal, spatial, or psychological distance from the content of their utterances.[73] In temporal terms, *keri* often marks either the speaker's sudden realization of something that has already been taking place, or a past event they have not directly experienced.[74] Both meanings can operate simultaneously in cases where the speaker suddenly recalls someone else's

---

72. Others posit *Tosa nikki* is citing Narihira's personal *waka* anthology or an *uta-gatari* tradition handed down through the Ki clan. A helpful overview of these theories can be found in Ichihara, "*Tosa nikki* nigatsu kunichi."

73. Yoda, *Gender and National Literature*, 151–53.

74. An extended account of debates over *keri*'s functions can be found in Okada, *Figures of Resistance*, 35–42. Okada concludes by stating *keri* can bolster a narrator's authority by indicating it is citing an earlier source. This intertextual aspect is also noted in Watanabe, *Flowering Tales*, 40.

past experience in the present moment of narration. We can see this dual usage of *keri* being deployed in the Nagisa entry, for example, by the diarist when she introduces the villa by recalling the allure of its cherry blossoms. It is also employed this way by the narrator of the *uta-gatari*, who concludes by excitedly declaring: "This is the very same place where he composed that poem!" (*to iu uta yomeru tokoro narikeri*). Because both narrators in the diary echo *Ise*'s descriptions of Nagisa while establishing their own distance from it, they are in all likelihood referring to a preexisting anecdote. The relationship between these two Nagisa narratives thus confirms Sei Shōnagon's description of *uta-gatari* as a practice that could draw on either written stories or oral ones.

Ise *and* Tosa nikki

In addition to their chronological order of appearance, a related question scholars have often raised concerning the historical connection between *Ise* and *Tosa nikki* is whether they share the same author. There is both circumstantial and textual evidence to suggest Tsurayuki was involved in creating the poem tale, including his documented dealings with Narihira's descendants, similarities between the two men's poems, and the close resemblance between *Ise*'s prose and the corresponding *Kokinshū* headnotes to Narihira's poems.[75] In an intriguing parallel with *Tosa nikki*'s diarist, one of Tsurayuki's own *waka* is even attributed to an anonymous woman in episode 108 within the poem tale. Perhaps the strongest evidence for his involvement with *Ise* comes from its possession of numerous lexical and syntactic features that are not found in any tenth-century texts other than ones Tsurayuki wrote.[76]

Although there is no way of knowing the exact nature of these contributions to *Ise*, there are a number of reasons to think that episode 82 was entirely his creation. It is the only text aside from the *Kokinshū* and

---

75. Yoshiyama, "'Koretaka shinnō monogatari,'" 42–43; and Fukui, *Zōho Ise monogatari seisei-ron*, 350–51. Hagitani notes *Tosa nikki* and *Ise*'s shared tendency to blur the line between fact and fiction in "*Ise monogatari* no sakusha wa," 37.

76. Yamada, *Ise monogatari seiritsu-ron josetsu*, 21–40.

Tosa nikki, for example, that refers to *waka* as *yamato uta* (Yamato verse). Tsurayuki's extensive experience as a compiler of anthologies, as well as the attention he pays to sequencing *Tosa nikki*'s entries that we saw in the previous chapter, is perhaps also reflected in the *Ise* episode's singular attention to micro- and macro-structural intricacies. Another possible indication of Tsurayuki's connection with episode 82 is the prominent place it accords to Ki no Aritsune (815–877), whose name is repeatedly invoked both to bind together its individual vignettes and connect it to episode 83.[77] Aritsune's dual position as Narihira's father-in-law and Koretaka's maternal uncle also places him at the center of the kinship ties connecting the two main characters in the multi-episodic narrative.[78] Although Aritsune was only distantly related to Tsurayuki as a cousin of the latter's grandfather, his role in episode 82 as a proxy poet speaking for Koretaka resembles that of Tsurayuki vis-à-vis his own aristocratic patrons.

On the other hand, Aritsune's absence from *Tosa nikki*'s poem-telling is perhaps because his connection to Tsurayuki would have presented an uncomfortable reminder of their clan's past rivalry with the Fujiwara (TNZ 378). Perhaps because it is recited at a safe remove from this history, a *waka* composed by the bereaved mother shortly after Nagisa recedes from sight further hints at these tensions. The phrase *arishi* (I recall them) through which she refers to her deceased daughter in this *waka* also appears in episode 101 of *Ise*, where it creates a graphological pun on 在氏 (Ariwara clan) as part of a thinly veiled poetic allusion to the growing political influence of Yoshifusa's family.[79]

saku hana no	Blooming flowers
shita ni kakururu	beneath which hide
hito o ōmi	so many people,
arishi ni masaru	more than I recall there being
fuji no kage kamo	under the wisteria's shade![80]

77. Fujihara, "The Historical Reality of Ki no Aritsune and the *Ise monogatari*," 59–61.

78. At the time, Aritsune, Narihira, and Koretaka would have been in their fifties, forties, and twenties respectively (Schalow, *A Poetics of Courtly Male Friendship in Heian Japan*, 37–76).

79. Hasegawa, "Hyōgen, sono senryaku-teki na *Tosa nikki*," 136–37.

80. *Ise monogatari* episode 101, SNKBZ 12:202.

The deliberately ambiguous way in which this poem hovers between praising the Fujiwara and criticizing them causes the listeners in *Ise* to wonder aloud about its intended meaning, something that must also have been done by the episode's readers (and a poem-telling's audience).[81] Perhaps *Tosa nikki*'s allusion to this *waka* and the Nagisa poem were designed with a similar response in mind.

Another possible indication that Tsurayuki authored episode 82 is provided by the diary's one other reference to a poem by Narihira on 1/18. Like *The Pillow Book*'s anecdote about his mother, its partial presentation of the original *waka* suggests a link with *uta-gatari*.[82] Another such link is hinted at when the imaginative speculation this citation excites in the diarist subsequently inspires an anonymous poem.

> Something blocks our progress, so we are still in the same place. This evening the moon sank into the sea. Seeing this brought to mind that poem by milord Narihira in which he said: *May the mountain rim retreat, so it will not retire!* If he had composed it at sea, he might instead have said: *May the waves rise up to block it, so it will not retire!* Recalling that verse now, someone recited:
>
> | *teru tsuki no* | The shining moon |
> | *nagaruru mireba* | flows by to reveal |
> | *Ama no gawa* | Heaven's River, |
> | *izuru minato wa* | whose mouth issues into |
> | *umi ni zarikeru* | this very same sea! |
>
> (TN 24, 1/8)

In a notable departure from the deferential attitude toward Narihira that the Nagisa poem-teller conveyed in the stiffly formal language that identified him posthumously by post and family name, the diarist refers to him here in much more familiar and affectionate terms as "milord Narihira" (*Narihira no kimi*). Perhaps this presumption of intimacy facilitates her imaginary identification with him when she surmises that he would

---

81. Mostow and Tyler, *The Ise Stories*, 212–13. A less ambiguously critical reading is provided in Marra, *The Aesthetics of Discontent*, 45.

82. *Kokin wakashū* poem 884, SNKBZ 11:336: "Will the moon swiftly / hide away / with us unsated? / May the mountain rim retreat / so it will not retire!" (*akanaku ni / madaki mo tsuki no / kakururu ka / yama no ha nigete / irezu mo aranamu*).

have replaced the original poem's mountains with waves if he had been at sea.

By illustrating the precedence a poem's setting takes over precedents in its wording, her musings in this passage explicitly reveal the logic implicitly at work in the Nagisa poem-telling. In addition to its maritime content, the wording she proposes is further shaped by its setting: the intransitive verb *sawaru* (be blocked by something) that was used in the preceding prose to describe the situation of enforced stasis being experienced by her now reappears in her *waka* as its transitive counterpart *saeru* (to block something) in order to depict the action she wishes for the waves to perform on the moon. Its thoroughly implausible nature makes the resulting vision of rising waves blocking a sinking moon an entirely plausible one to associate with a poet who desired mountains to leave the moon behind or cherry trees not to bloom. In other words, the entry suggests that Narihira's poetic proclivity for improbable scenarios facilitated their imaginative refashioning in poem-tellings.

As with the previous *uta-gatari* at Nagisa, this recollection of an earlier poem also inspires new *waka* that comment on the original. Like the maritime measures the diarist proposed, this new poem takes the other remaining *waka* Narihira recites in episode 82 and adapts it to the travelers' current seaside setting. Its celestial Ama no Kawa (Heaven's River), designating the Milky Way, appears to evoke both the poet's own liquid locale and the terrestrial one at Ama no Kawara (Heaven's Riverbed) that Narihira mentions in the poem he composes within the second of three vignettes that comprise episode 82.[83] In a thorough-going analysis of this passage, however, Fukui Teisuke argues that the diary is instead citing the three *Kokinshū* poems preceding his Nagisa *waka*.[84]

futatsu naki	There are no two
mono to omoishi o	I had thought, and yet,
mina-soko ni	in watery depths
yama no ha narade	lacking mountain peaks
izuru tsuki-kage	the moon's reflection rises.

---

83. *Kokin wakashū* poem 418, SNKBZ 11:179: "At the end of the hunt / with the Weaver Maid / let us ask to lodge / here at Heaven's Riverbed / where we have just come." (*kari-kurashi / Tanabata tsume ni / yado karamu / Ama no kawara ni / ware wa kinikeri*).

84. Fukui, "*Tosa nikki* to Ariwara no Narihira," 26–29.

Ama no kawa	In Heaven's River
kumo no mio nite	the waterway of clouds
hayakereba	races by so rapidly
hikari todomezu	that its light never lingers
tsuki zo nagaruru	as the moon flows by.
akazu shite	While yet unsated
tsuki no kakururu	the moon is hidden by
yama-moto wa	mountains at whose base
anata omote zo	for that distant visage
koishikarikeru	do I keep yearning![85]

The first of these three poems, composed by Tsurayuki himself, shares the diarist's excitement at seeing a mountain-less moonlit waterscape; the second one envisions the same streaming moonlight as the diary's anonymous *waka*; and the third poem amplifies the counterfactual tenor of Narihira's entreaty for the moon not to sink behind the mountains by depicting one that has already done so. In light of the close relationship between the Nagisa poem-telling and episode 82, however, it seems more likely that Tsurayuki is drawing on the same source in this entry. Regardless of its original source of inspiration, the entry illustrates the opportunities that Narihira's imaginative poetics afforded for further treatment by the audience of an *uta-gatari*.

Questions of authorship and dating aside, the number and variety of characteristics *Tosa nikki* shares with *Ise* overall would seem to indicate a close historical relationship between the two texts. Both appraise the *waka* they introduce, embrace anonymous characters, make vague gestures to historical time, deploy episodic structures, and employ short sentences eschewing honorific and auxiliary verbs.[86] Just as *Tosa nikki*'s longest entries simply tack one location onto another with the brief deictic *kaku* (while thus), the travel narratives making up *Ise*'s longer episodes (including the outing to Nagisa) are organized as a succession of

---

85. *Kokin wakashū* poems 881–83, SNKBZ 11:335. All three verses also appear sequentially in *Shinsen waka* as poems 260, 264, and 266.

86. Poem and prose are also linked in *Tosa nikki*'s manuscripts by merging the final measures of its *waka* with the latter (Sakakura, "*Tosa nikki* no uta to ji no bun," 401; and Kanechiku, "Waka and Media," 380–81). See Teika's description of the text in chapter 1.

toponym-centered vignettes.⁸⁷ In both texts, words in the preceding prose that represent phenomena or situations reappear in the poems with their speakers' emotional responses to them.⁸⁸ As we will see in the next section, this final aspect is also parodied in *Tosa nikki*, thus offering yet another indication that the poem tale preceded the diary.

Genre Fluidity and Parodic Titling

Ultimately, the process by which *Ise* took shape through countless additions, omissions, rearrangements, and amendments made by an unknown number of anonymous individuals over an unknown period of time in the tenth century makes it more useful to regard its similarities with *Tosa nikki* as symptomatic of the general predilection for stylistic hybridity and taxonomic flexibility in Heian vernacular texts. At the same time, the singular and parodic nature of the diary's title distinguishes its precise and intentional form of hybridity from other such manifestations of genre fluidity. Tellingly, this hybridity is articulated through a metafictional allusion to *Tosa nikki*'s titular toponym that takes the shape of a comically underwhelming *uta-gatari*, making it one of many ways in which the text resembles a fictional narrative more than it does any contemporaneous diary.

Unlike her counterparts in later women's memoirs, the diarist tends to downplay her own personal relationship to the events and phenomena she relates. As a result, she rarely uses the auxiliary verb *ki* marking the speaker's direct experience of a past event, and generally prefers marking grammatical aspect with the more impersonal auxiliary verb *nu* rather than its transitive counterpart *tsu*. Both *nu* and *keri* combine, for example, to mark the diarist's recognition of turning points on the journey that hold equal significance for all the travelers: the number of days spent at sea on 1/16, their arrival at Izumi on 1/30, and the start of the last leg of

---

87. On this use of *kaku*, see Watanabe, *Heianchō bunshō shi*, 60–66.
88. Murofushi, "*Tosa nikki* to Tsurayuki," 43. This relationship is described as a balance between the two forms of language in Akimoto, "*Tosa nikki* no bunshō," 5.

the journey upriver to the capital on 2/7.[89] This means of distinguishing subsections within the narrative is also characteristic of *Taketori*, where *keri* clusters around the beginning and end of the quests undertaken by each of its heroine's suitors.[90] These similarities are likely due to the tight linear structure resulting from both texts' possession of a clearly delineated beginning and end, which makes them more amenable to such internal divisions than *Ise*'s loose assemblage of episodes. In the case of *Tosa nikki*, such demarcations also offer a clear indication that its text was shaped as a single artistic whole.

Many other aspects of the diary bear a strikingly close resemblance to fictional tales. Like *Ise* (and unlike later vernacular memoirs), the auxiliary verb *keri* often appears in *Tosa nikki* together with the particle *namu* as a means of stressing the content of a sentence. This narrational style also makes it different from contemporaneous diaries in Literary Sinitic, which were more concerned with leaving a record to posterity than engaging the interest of their audience.[91] The diary's similarities with *monogatari* also include its material dimensions, such as the inclusion of pictures in Egyō's version that was discussed in the previous chapter. Its earliest manuscripts even use the same square-shaped paper format (*masugata-bon*) commonly employed for fictional narratives.[92] Taken as whole, these characteristics recall the *kana* record kept by the character Toshikage in *Utsuho monogatari*, which consisted of "events just as they had happened, recorded in writing after the manner of a tale with poems appended at various junctures."[93] The supposed facticity of *Tosa nikki*'s content relating "events just as they had happened" (*aritsuru koto*) resembles a diary, while the presentation of those events "after the manner of a tale" (*monogatari no yō ni*) could reflect any or all of the above-mentioned characteristics.

---

89. On the diary's use of *ki*, see Katō, "Ki to keri ga shimesu jishō," 31. On its use of *nu*, see Takeuchi, "*Tosa nikki* no tensu, asupekuto," 63 and 66. The latter's distribution in combination with *keri* is noted in Ogawa, "*Tosa nikki* ni okeru 'nanuka,'" 93.

90. Sakakura, "*Taketori* ni okeru 'buntai.'"

91. These pairings of *namu* with *keri* are noted in Ishihara, "*Tosa nikki* no sōzō," 19. The resulting difference from *kanbun* diaries is observed in Kamitani, *Kana bungaku no bunshōshi-teki kenkyū*, 152.

92. Higashihara, *Tosa nikki kyokō ron*, 190–91.

93. *Utsuho monogatari* (Kurabiraki-chū), SNKBZ 15:475.

Such forms of genre fluidity were further facilitated by several features common to the language of all Heian vernacular texts. As modern scholars have often noted, ambiguities in tense, deixis, and grammatical person made it possible for Heian readers to approach the same work in very different ways. As a *monogatari*, they might treat its characters as historical individuals; as a *nikki*, they might focus on one such figure in the narrative present; and as an anthology, they might focus on the poems. Different genre filiations could also result from varying perceptions of the narrators' proximity to their protagonists. As *monogatari*, they became distanced observers; as *nikki*, they were closely identified with the protagonists; and as anthologies either option was possible.[94] Characteristics associated with all three genres in these schemes are also present in *Tosa nikki*. Like other diaries, its daily entry format provides a sense of immediacy. Like *monogatari*, on the other hand, its historical setting is ambiguous and its interest in a single individual less pronounced. Like the short sentences in anthologies, its lack of clearly delineated subjects makes them equally attributable to the poet or a later compiler.

This tendency toward genre fluidity probably originated with the omission of grammatical subjects in the prose portions of anthologies that were compiled by their subject and thus implicitly all first-person.[95] Subsequent alterations by later readers eventually made it difficult to differentiate these perspectives from third-person ones. Modern scholarship has often favored a first-person reading, as reflected in its use of the neologism *shikashū* (personal *waka* anthology) to describe these texts. As Morimoto Motoko has pointed out, however, they were referred to in their own time as *ie no shū* (household anthologies).[96] The collective and anonymous nature of authorship implied by this latter designation meant there was no perception of a need to determine when and how (or even if) any given anthology transitioned from being more like an autobiographical *nikki* to being more like a biographical *monogatari*.

---

94. The first of these two typologies is presented in Konishi, *A History of Japanese Literature*, 256, while the second one is articulated in Ishihara, *Heian nikki bungaku no kenkyū*, 556.
95. Katagiri, *Ise monogatari no kenkyū*, 1:6–8.
96. Morimoto, "Shikashū to wa nani ka," 4–5.

Confronted with this fluidity, modern attempts at classifying vernacular Heian texts have often turned to the final element in their titles. One example of the tripartite division discussed above is provided by *Ise*, which was also called *Zaigo ga monogatari* (Tales of the Fifth Ariwara), *Zaigo chūjō no nikki* (Diary of the Fifth Ariwara Middle Captain), and *Chūjō no shū* (The Middle Captain's Anthology). However, it is also possible that their opening portions reflected taxonomic logics as well. Most scholars believe the toponym that begins *Ise*'s title refers synecdochally to the Ise Shrine whose priestess's affair with the hero in episode 69 of the standard edition is currently thought to have opened the poem tale's oldest iterations.[97] The prominence given to Narihira in all the aforementioned titles, on the other hand, could indicate the episodes in those versions were treated more like life-writings, perhaps by arranging them chronologically, designating the protagonist with greater precision and consistency, or even representing them as overtly autobiographical. By contrast, poem tales whose titles begin with toponyms such as Ise and Yamato eschew a single narrative frame in favor of more localized organizational schemes involving one or two adjacent episodes, perhaps reflecting their origins in such site-specific *uta-gatari* as the ones connected to Kainuma or Nagisa. Accordingly, the appearance of a place name at the head of *Tosa nikki*'s title may signal its filiation with both *uta monogatari* and *uta-gatari*.[98]

Other distinctive aspects of the diary's designation acquire added significance in this light. Like *Tosa nikki*'s attribution to a single historical individual, the stability of its title is as striking in a Heian context as it is unremarkable in a modern one. Because readers were using this appellation within a few years of Tsurayuki's death, moreover, there is a distinct possibility that it was his own creation, and thus integral to the diary's intended purpose. The curious stress laid on consistently titling it with two words denoting poem tales and diaries thus suggests a desire to make the deliberately distinctive nature of *Tosa nikki* apparent to Heian readers

---

97. Mostow and Tyler, *The Ise Stories*, 3. A comprehensive list of explanations for its title can be found in Vos, *A Study of the Ise-Monogatari*, 1:66–70.

98. For an intriguing account of another toponymic connection between the titles of *Tosa nikki* and *Yamato monogatari* as narratives that decenter the capital, see Kawashima, *Itineraries of Power*, 46–48.

who would have otherwise viewed its hybridity as unremarkable and incidental. Whereas its designation as a *nikki* reflects the text's consistent use of the daily entry format common to contemporaneous diaries, the rural place name may signal both its episodic *waka*-centered contents and the critical role played by toponyms in creating the illustrated narrative mentioned in chapter 4.

Tosa nikki's titular toponym signals another form of hybridity in its simultaneous evocation of and dissociation from a specific historical context. The names "Ise" and "Yamato" anchor their eponymous poem tales' amorphous amalgams of fact, fiction, and hearsay in some form of historicity by referring to actual provinces. By contrast, Teika's version of *Tosa nikki*'s title uses the Sinographs 土左 to mark its toponym instead of the compound 土佐 used to designate the province. By casting its own referentiality into doubt, therefore, this title appears to parody poem tales' reliance on such proper nouns in making their own claims to veracity. In addition to confirming the parodically fictional nature of many place names in the diary that was discussed in chapter 4, Teika's subtle graphological pun suggests its contents are both similar to and distinct from the lived experience of its author in a manner resembling its ambiguous designation by Egyō as "Tsurayuki's *Tosa Diary*."

This parodic doubling of *Tosa nikki*'s eponymous toponym is also evident at the one point where it appears within the text. Rather than being mentioned at the beginning of the diary—which would follow the metonymic logic used in the earliest iterations of *Ise*, or the autobiographical logic implied by its connection to Tsurayuki's own provincial posting—the toponym appears roughly midway through the journey when the travelers come across a place called "Tosa Anchorage" (Tosa no Tomari). Immediately after its appearance, however, the word's significance is undermined by a clumsy attempt at toponymical poem-telling that is farcically redundant.

> Our ship drew near an intriguing place. I gather that someone asking where we are was told the place is called "Tosa Anchorage." Apparently a woman who lived long ago in a place said to bear the name of "Tosa" is with us now here on board! She spoke, saying: "Why, it is the same name as that of a place where I once lived for a while in the past! How poignant!" Then she recited this verse:

toshigoro o	Since it bears the name
sumishi tokoro no	of a place I had lived in
na ni shi oeba	for many long years,
ki-yoru nami o mo	even approaching waves
aware to zo miru	are a poignant sight to see!

That is what she said! (TN 40–41, 1/29)

In the space of a few words, this brief episode manages to evoke the language of *monogatari* in its question-and-answer format, its formulaic introduction of the woman's speech, its insistent use of *keri* to mark actions the diarist only hears about, and the placement of its toponym within a vaguely quasi-historical past: "long ago in a place said to bear the name of Tosa" (*Mukashi, Tosa to iikeru tokoro*). Even the limited duration of the female character's residence at this other Tosa alludes to poem tales in which women accompany their husbands to a province.

Although we can perhaps designate this narrative at Tosa Anchorage as a poem-telling in a technical sense on account of the *waka* that follows it, the vignette is parodically redundant in its presentation of the poem's affective content and the response to it, both of which are essential to *uta monogatari* and *uta-gatari* alike. The woman's *waka* fails to add new emotional or intellectual perspective to the content of her preceding speech. Nor is any additional significance provided when the diarist responds by exclaiming "That is what she said!" (*to zo ieru*), which draws attention to the powerful reaction elicited by the poem without specifying whether it is negative or positive, thus ending up being equally superfluous. Insofar as such obliqueness on the diarist's part typically stems from a desire to avoid accountability for her opinions, however, this comment likely conveys surprise at the wasted opportunity to exploit the toponym's twofold signification of the poet's current location and her earlier residence. In other words, the incident is only remarkable enough to be treated as a poetic vignette by the diarist because it is such a remarkably poor poem-telling. By exemplifying how *uta-gatari* should *not* be conducted, this episode functions as the inverse of the poem-telling at Nagisa. Because the diary's title is implicated in this failure, moreover, the episode also carries the humorous and metafictional message that *Tosa nikki* is parodically undermining both diaries' conventional claims to utility and *monogatari*'s more oblique claims to historical veracity by including purposeless anecdotes containing frivolous fictions within its text.

Conclusion

My frequent reliance on hypotheses in this account of *uta-gatari* reflects their sparse presence in the written record. At the same time, their speculative nature is in keeping with the imaginative forms of engagement poem-tellings sought to incite in an audience through evocative place names or the partial obfuscation of their content in performance. This imaginative speculation also spurred on the audience's own creation of poems that were then expanded and/or altered in each subsequent poem-telling. Such accretions were further fueled by the dual role textual versions played as both the source of *uta-gatari* and their product. This circular relationship between poem-tellings and poem tales requires us to revise the standard linear developmental model that has been used to argue for the oral practice's vital role in Heian literary history as a precursor to its written counterpart.

All these aspects of *uta-gatari* can be seen in *Tosa nikki*'s transcription of the Nagisa poem's anecdotal recounting. As the only surviving example of their content, moreover, this transcription also illustrates poem-tellings' emphasis on the *waka*'s original audience, a characteristic they also share with poem tales. Comparison with other texts in which the Nagisa *waka* appears also reveals that *uta-gatari* shaped the poem to fit its performative context. The similar treatment that *Tosa nikki* gives to another *waka* by Narihira suggests that his poems were particularly amenable to such adaptations because their embrace of hypothetical, ambiguous, and counterfactual rhetoric invited further speculation. The Nagisa *waka* is an exemplary instance of such characteristics, both on account of its attempt to imagine a world without cherry trees, and on account of the resulting political allegory whose ambivalence led to differing responses in the *Kokinshū*, *Shinsen waka*, and *Ise*. By contrast, the lack of any such stimulating ambiguities in the *uta-gatari* that anchors *Tosa nikki*'s title indicates it is a failure, thereby marking the diary's parodic divergence from the claims to facticity made by *monogatari* and *nikki* alike, even as it combines other characteristics of the two genres in a manner that makes its similarity to *Ise* so pronounced it seems likely to have resulted from Tsurayuki's prior involvement with the famed poem tale.

CHAPTER 6

Nakamaro's Cosmopolitanisms

The most elaborate and ambitious poetic anecdote in *Tosa nikki* depicts Abe no Nakamaro explaining *waka* to foreigners. As with Narihira, the diarist frequently punctuates her account with the storytelling auxiliary verb *keri* to comment on poetic praxis by engaging in speculation about a famous historical figure. Differences in their social status, however, entail differences in the scope of that commentary. Whereas *Tosa nikki*'s initial readership resembled the aristocratic Narihira, Nakamaro is described as a "master" (*nushi*) possessing specialist skills acquired through a foreign education. This cosmopolitan background enables his anecdote to comment on language and culture in a comparative context whose expansive scope has attracted the interest of many modern readers.

The eighth century in which Nakamaro lived represents a high point in Japan's engagement with the outside world, one in which both objects and people crossed greater distances to reach the archipelago than at any other point in its premodern history. Mediterranean artifacts can still be seen in the Shōsōin treasure house. Immigrants and visitors hailed from as far away as present-day Iran and Cambodia.[1] New evidence of people moving in the opposite direction continues to be uncovered. In 2004 the grave marker of a Japanese émigré who came with Nakamaro to study in

---

1. Schafer, "Fusang and Beyond," 178.

the Tang capital in 717 was discovered in Xian bearing the naturalized name of Jing Zhencheng (699–734). No other eighth-century Japanese émigré, however, possesses a life documented so extensively that the most exhaustive and authoritative modern biography by Sugimoto Naojirō (1890–1973) exceeds 800 pages in length.

This remarkable detail is largely due to the equally distinctive life as a government official Nakamaro would embark on when he became the only Japanese individual to ever pass the Tang civil service examination eleven years after arriving in Chang'an. His subsequent career under the Sinicized name of Chao Heng would take him from the Tang empire's cultural core as the palace librarian of Emperor Xuanzong (658–762, r. 712–756) to its southernmost territories as governor of Annam. From a poetic perspective, Nakamaro's relationship to the palace is particularly significant in a peculiarly paradoxical fashion. It was during this time that he established ties with Wang Wei (699–759) and Li Bai (701–762), whose own periods of service there overlapped with his. Although the life of a Tang official would have entailed numerous occasions for composing poetry, Xuanzong's patronage of these two literary giants must have made Nakamaro's term as a palace librarian particularly productive in this regard.

It is therefore striking that his only surviving poems express the desire to forsake this milieu for the land of his birth. Nakamaro's eventual failure to do so would make them a particularly poignant and powerful expression of cosmopolitanism. Insofar as an unknown number of his writings traveled back to Japan without him, Nakamaro's historical legacy exemplifies the tendency for premodern textual traversals to surpass those of their creators. The portability and replicability that enabled them to cross the greatest distances with the most enduring impact also made texts the most effective medium for creating cosmopolitanism prior to modernity. Such characteristics have led scholars to adopt the term "cosmopolis" in order to describe the uniquely transcultural and transpolitical forms of community created by the circulation of prestige literary languages such as Sanskrit, Greek, Latin, Arabic, Persian, and Literary Sinitic. Apart from one recent history of world literature that views the preservation of his poems in China as an exception to the overwhelmingly Sinocentric circulation of texts within the East Asian cosmopolis, however, the potential Nakamaro's textual legacy possesses for furthering our understanding of that community's contours remains largely unexplored.[2]

This chapter will trace the process by which the earliest depictions of Nakamaro would contribute to *Tosa nikki*'s uniquely detailed depiction of premodern East Asian cosmopolitanism. I will begin by illustrating the ways in which *shi* by and about the historical individual reveal the political stakes involved in his positioning vis-à-vis his palace colleagues' Sinocentric visions of Japan. The significance this poetic legacy holds for the *waka* he was subsequently associated with in the ninth century will be addressed next. I then shift from this larger historical context to the more immediate one in which *Tosa nikki* alters that *waka* to reflect Tsurayuki's own engagement with East Asian diplomacy and his vision of a translingual maritime poetics. Finally, I will explore the ways in which *Tosa nikki* mobilizes these two aspects to articulate a vision of vernacular cosmopolitanism based on a broad notion of translation encompassing transcription, interpretation, and adaptation. Taken as a whole, these insights help us to appreciate the diary's distinctive placement of Japan within a wider world.

Nakamaro in Shi *Poems*

Like his later *waka*, the small number of extant *shi* composed by and about the historical Nakamaro depict him attempting to return to Japan. These include the only two poems attributed to him, both of which were probably composed in the Tang capital at Chang'an. Both also exhibit his mastery of the complex tonal regulations for *jintishi* (new style *shi* poems) popular at the time, thus demonstrating the talent that enabled him to participate in poetic intercourse with the greatest literati of his day. The second one in particular also illustrates Nakamaro's tendency to represent himself in spatially liminal language accommodating more than one identity. By contrast, the *shi* his fellow literati address to him repeatedly place him beyond the recognizable borders of their world.

2. Beecroft, *An Ecology of World Literature*, 124.

Nakamaro's earliest surviving poem, likely composed in 733, is a pentasyllabic quatrain seeking Xuanzong's permission to leave palace service and return to Japan. At once formally flawless and rhetorically plain, it is the poem's genre and historical context rather than its contents that are most significant with respect to the development of his later poetic legacy.

慕義名空在	While yearning to do right, my reputation is empty.
輸忠孝不全	While fulfilling loyalties, my filial piety is lacking.
報恩無有日	There is no final day I can fully repay your royal favor.
歸國定何年	In what year am I sure to return home to my land?[3]

Nakamaro's quatrain lacks the metaphorical imagery this brief poetic form typically relied on to create multiple layers of meaning. Nonetheless, it adheres to the genre's formal requirements in its tonal patterning and syntax, which moves from strict parallelisms in the first couplet, which balances the conflicting demands of political loyalty and filial piety, to syntagmatic sentence-structures conveying an emotional climax in the second couplet. Perhaps the most noteworthy aspect of this poem is its later textual history. Although it was evidently composed in Chang'an, the quatrain only survives in the twelfth-century *Kokin wakashū mokuroku*, which cites an unknown ninth-century Japanese history as its source.[4] As we will see, its genre and the historical period it can be traced back to both play critical roles in the development of Nakamaro's poetic biography within *Tosa nikki*.

Nakamaro's one other surviving *shi* was composed twenty years later for a farewell banquet in the capital after Xuanzong had finally granted him leave to depart with a returning Japanese diplomatic mission led by Fujiwara no Kiyokawa (d. 778). It provides a fuller picture of his poetic propensity for tact than the earlier quatrain, both by virtue of being three times longer and because it is accompanied by the farewell poems of three palace colleagues in the largest surviving anthology of Tang prose and poetry, *Wenyuan yinghua* (Literary Garden of Splendid Blossoms,

---

3. *Kokin wakashū mokuroku*, GR 16:116.
4. The quatrain's history is detailed at length in Sugimoto, "Abe no Nakamaro no shi," 58–64.

ca. 1204).⁵ The complicated textual history of this Song-dynasty anthology, which underwent four major transformations over two hundred years, makes it impossible to know if the current version alters these poems' original order of appearance or omits others composed for the occasion.⁶ They are even further decontextualized in the *Quan Tangshi* (Complete Tang Poems, 1706), where each *shi* appears separately under the name of its respective poet. Faced with these challenges in reconstructing the event, my reading will begin with Nakamaro and end with Wang Wei, in recognition of their respective roles as the one departing and the one commemorating the occasion.

Like his earlier quatrain, Nakamaro's banquet poem adopts a diplomatic stance balancing his eagerness to see his parents with reluctance to leave the palace community. His reluctance is also conveyed metrically through a *pailu* (extended regulated verse), which doubled the two couplets at the core of a standard *lushi* (regulated verse). A different sort of ambivalence is also suggested by the poet's liminal position within it.

銜命將辭國	With His Majesty's permission, I take leave of the realm.
非才忝侍臣	Lacking talent, I have disgraced my position as minister.
天中戀明主	At the center of Heaven is the shining master I long for.
海外憶慈親	On the outer sea are the loving parents I think of.
伏奏違金闕	Reporting to the throne, then leaving the golden palace.
騑驂去玉津	Driving my steed out, then heading for the jeweled harbor.
蓬萊鄉路遠	The Isle of Immortals lies distant on my homeward road.
若木故園鄰	The Sun Tree is adjacent to my old garden's borders.
西望懷恩日	Westward I gaze, cherishing His Majesty's favor this day.
東歸感義辰	Eastward I return, moved by your goodness this hour.
平生一寶劍	A lifetime's cherished blade do I
留贈結交人	leave as token of friendship's ties.⁷

5. Nakamaro is not mentioned in a poem by Xuanzong bidding farewell to the Japanese delegation that was subsequently preserved in *Tōdaiji yōroku* (Essential Records of Tōdaiji, 1106).
6. On the complex textual history of this anthology, see Tahmoresi, "The *Wenyuan yinghua*," 27–49.
7. QTS 732.8375.

The "shining master" (明主) who Nakamaro longs for in the second couplet evokes a transpolitical space through hybridized diction containing tropes from both languages simultaneously. Although the parallel structures of his couplet imply this ruler's radiance refers to Xuanzong's enlightened reign, that same luminousness also evokes the Japanese sovereign's divine descent from the sun goddess Amaterasu. The penultimate couplet likewise places Nakamaro in a liminal zone between the two men as his gaze moves between an increasingly distant Tang ruler to the west and the growing proximity of his Japanese sovereign to the east.

After this adroit use of parallel constructions to convey his shifting identity, the poem concludes with Nakamaro citing history to convey the arc of his life on the continent and the sorrowful finality with which he now parts from his friends there. The sword he leaves behind in the final couplet alludes to the one Prince Ji Zha (576–484 BCE) of Wu hangs on the tree by an old friend's grave in *Shiji* (Records of the Historian, ca. 91 BCE). This historical analogy also references the prince's reputation as a model student of classical culture who, according to *Zuo zhuan* (The Zuo Tradition, ca. late fourth century BCE), visited Confucius's home state of Lu to learn the classical music, dances, and songs of the Zhou dynasty (ca. 1046–256 BCE).[8] Nakamaro's colleagues also refer to this prince and other historical figures who journeyed long distances to pursue learning, perhaps indicating that their poems reply to his.

Among these colleagues, Zhao Hua (d. 783) is the only one not to express reluctance at parting through a prosodically prolonged poem. As Nakamaro's successor in the post of palace librarian, it may have seemed more appropriate to adhere strictly to metrical standards rather than appear overly effusive.

西掖承休浣	From the palace's western annex receiving leave to bathe.
東隅返故林	From the capital's eastern margins returning to former groves.
來稱郯子學	Arriving like the Master of Tan to study.
歸是越人吟	Returning like the Folk of Yue to chanting.

---

8. For a translation of this account, see Watson, *The Tso Chuan*, 149–53.

馬上秋郊遠	On horseback autumn suburbs will grow distant.
舟中曙海陰	By boat the dawn-lit seas will be shadowed.
知君懷魏闕	I know milord will long for the capital's gate-towers
萬里獨搖心	from a myriad miles away alone with heart atremble.[9]

The bureaucratic nature of Zhao Hua's relationship to Nakamaro is foregrounded by opening with the former colleague's point of departure at the Bureau of Central Writings (Zhongshusheng). In using the expression "leave to bathe" (休浣), which indicated a temporary absence from official duties, this line also observes the rhetorical conventions governing such an occasion by asserting that Nakamaro will doubtless return. At the same time as he asserts the centripetal pull of Chang'an, however, Zhao Hua also historicizes and relativizes Sinitic civilization in his second couplet. Like the aforementioned Ji Zha, the ruler of the state of Tan visited Lu in order to study the classical cultural legacy of the Zhou dynasty. Coupled with the ensuing mention of the formerly barbarian southern land of Yue, this historical allusion becomes a reminder that the forebears of Nakamaro's compatriots were originally no more civilized than his countrymen.

Another poem, by Bao Ji (d. 792), is simultaneously more expansive and chauvinistic than those of the other Tang officials. Although he engages with the content of Nakamaro's poem by attempting to describe his destination, Bao Ji also exoticizes and marginalizes Japan in equal measure:

上才生下國	Superior talent born in a lesser realm.
東海是西鄰	The Eastern Sea its western border.
九譯蕃君使	Envoy to a vassal lord with ninefold translators.
千年聖主臣	Minister to a sage master thousandfold in years.
野情偏得禮	Wild in temperament, you fully mastered ritual.
木性木含仁	A tree by nature, your trunk harbored benevolence.
錦帆乘風轉	Brocade sails will mount whistling winds.
金裝照地新	Gilded hulls will shine back anew onto land.

9. QTS 129.1320.

孤域開蜃閣	A lonely outpost raised on seafoam pavilions.
曉日上車輪	The dawn sun rising as a chariot wheel.
早議來朝日	Surely you will hasten to return to the morning audience,
塗山玉帛均	On Mount Tu again precious silks will be distributed.[10]

Japan now becomes an eastern vassal realm so distant from Tang civilization that its language requires multiple interpreters to make it intelligible. Nakamaro's destination is now a barbarian frontier from which he is sure to return to the Tang capital, where he will once again participate in government, represented by the legendary Mount Tu on which the sage king Shun (ca. 2294–2184 BCE, r. 2255–2205 BCE) held court.

The most extensive means for gauging how Nakamaro and Japan were viewed at Xuanzong's court is provided by the preface Wang Wei appended to his own banquet poem. At 545 characters, its 105 sentences make this the longest such text extant.[11] Because it incorporates Nakamaro's mention of Ji Zha, Wang Wei likely wrote it to memorialize the banquet some time afterward. He begins by praising Xuanzong's reign as a glorious era whose civilizing influence surpasses even those of the legendary sage rulers Yao (2324–2206 BCE, r. 2333–2234 BCE) and Shun in its scope, which extends from the Queen Mother of the West to the Isle of Women representing Japan in the east.[12] Gifts are exchanged with envoys who come from every cardinal direction. In a succinct description of Tang cosmopolitanism, Wang Wei depicts the flow of objects and people fostered through Xuanzong's encouragement of foreign trade, a monetary economy, and urbanization: "Barriers are abolished, and prohibitions relaxed. Those above promulgate learning and culture. No one reaches here only to return without treasures. Therefore, people live where they will, coming and going as though in a market" (廢關弛禁。上敷文教。虛至實歸。故人民雜居。往來如市。).

After lauding Xuanzong's reign as a golden age of commerce and culture, the preface proceeds to describe Nakamaro's destination. Japan is

---

10. QTS 205.2142.

11. Ueno, *Kentōshi Abe no Nakamaro no yume*, 137. Subsequent citations from this preface are taken from Kobayashi and Harada, *Ō I*, 299–302.

12. This gendering of Japan likely alludes to the legendary queen Himiko (d. 247), who the *Weizhi* (Chronicles of Wei, 297) famously described sending an embassy to that Sinic kingdom in 238.

upheld as "the greatest of all realms bordering the Eastern Sea" (海東國日本爲大) and the most faithful to Sinitic culture in adopting the Xia dynasty's calendar and Han dynasty's formal garb, thereby epitomizing the Confucian idea that rites should be selected to match historical circumstances. In his homeland, Wang Wei declares, Nakamaro will literally embody cosmopolitanism politically and poetically: "Parting from old colleagues in the capital, you will gain audience to lords and ministers of your former court. Recite poems by the seven masters of the Jian'an era and gird yourself with the seals of both lands" (去帝鄉之故舊。謁本朝之君臣。詠七子之詩。佩兩國之印。). Dual political allegiances are bridged by the literary tradition of the Jian'an era (196–220), which represented the advent of briefer poetic forms focused on the speaker's personal experiences in Tang literary history. All of these features, as we will see, uncannily foreshadow Nakamaro's textual afterlife.

Wang Wei must have been assigned this preface at least in part due to his reputation as a poet. Although his own *shi* matches that of his friend in length, however, it appears to fall short of the cosmopolitanism expressed in his preface by placing Japan beyond the world's visual and verbal boundaries.

積水不可極	Massed waters extend beyond measurable end.
安知蒼海東	What is known of the blue-green sea to the east?
九州何處遠	In all nine lands, is any further than your Kyushu?
萬里若乘空	Thousands of leagues away, it lies astride the sky.
向國惟看日	Facing your realm, all one sees is the sun.
歸帆但信風	Homebound sails can only trust to the wind.
鰲身映天黑	Leviathan's girth reflects a Heaven darkened.
魚眼射波紅	Fishes' eyes cast rays into waves glowing crimson.
鄉樹扶桑外	Your rustic groves grow beyond the Sunrise Tree.
主人孤島中	Your lord and master in isolation amid islands.
別離方異域	Leaving here, you head on to foreign parts.
音信若爲通	How will we send word to one another?[13]

---

13. QTS 127.1288.

The sea Wang Wei focuses on is described in vivid language. His characteristic love of color contrasts informs its striking juxtaposition of the darkly glistening bulk of the *ao* (Leviathan), a gigantic sea turtle large enough to bear three mountains on its back, with waves turned red by sunlight reflected in the darting eyes of tiny fish. For all its beauty, however, Wang Wei's vision ends on the horizon, with Japan located somewhere out of sight beyond the mythical Fusang tree from which the sun rose and sank.

This inability to visualize Japan is foregrounded in the rhetorical question that opens his second couplet by asking if there is anywhere in the world farther away. Beneath its surface, however, the same word used to refer to the entire world as "all nine lands" (九州) in this question might also refer to Kyushu, where Nakamaro could expect to make his first landfall in Japan. The seeming rudeness of such a statement has led some to doubt that Kyushu is being referred to at all.[14] Given the warm tone Wang Wei evinces in his preface, however, this line can be read in a more positive light as a statement of cultural kinship with Nakamaro's homeland, one reflecting the Tang poet's possible awareness of a love for homophones that *waka* poetry shared with quatrains (a poetic form at which Wang Wei excelled, and to which *waka* were often likened in later Heian texts). As we shall see, the Sinographic (il)legibility of Japanese place names reappears in *Tosa nikki*'s depiction of translation and vernacular identity. Wit is also evident in the decision to place this pun within the same line that Nakamaro chose for his own ambiguously doubled reference to a longed-for lord. Read this way, Wang Wei's rhetorical question becomes a knowing riposte to his friend's vague reference to political allegiances and to the diplomatic necessities shaping their ambiguity.

With the possible exception of Bao Ji, the sentiments expressed by Nakamaro's well-wishers exemplify the overall tendency for eighth-century Tang literati to view their Northeast Asian neighbors as cultural peers.[15] Despite acknowledging a historically and geographically unstable notion of Sinitic civilization, however, both Wang Wei and Zhao Hua locate its present political and discursive center at Chang'an, an orientation that leads them to spend more time describing the Tang capital than

---

14. Nakakōji, "Ō I ga Abe no Nakamaro ni okutta shi," 18–23.
15. Abramson, *Ethnic Identity in Tang China*, 160–61.

Japan. Nakamaro's home only appears at the end of Zhao Hua's poem as an intangible entity vanishing into the distance. It is thus particularly revealing that the archipelago's most detailed depiction is provided by the most chauvinistic poet, who uses imagery that is simultaneously concrete and fantastical in its portrayal of a land whose dwellings rest on the frothy exhalations of exotic mollusks.

This inability to visualize Japan also characterizes Nakamaro's final appearance in Tang poetry. Shortly after the banquet's conclusion, he embarked for home in the eleventh month of 753 with the returning diplomatic delegation led by Kiyokawa. At an early point in the voyage, however, Nakamaro's ship was separated from the rest of the convoy by a severe storm (the three other vessels eventually managed to make their way to Japan). News of Nakamaro's disappearance seems to have somehow also reached Li Bai, who prematurely mourned his friend in a quatrain that cast his former palace colleague as a moon sinking into the sea somewhere beyond the floating island of Penglai and its immortal inhabitants.

日本朝卿辭帝都	As minister of Japan's court he left the imperial capital.
征帆一片繞蓬壺	With a slip of a sail he rounded the Isle of Immortals.
明月不歸沈碧海	His bright moon will not return, sunk in jade seas.
白雲愁色滿蒼梧	White clouds in somber hues shroud Cangwu.[16]

Li Bai demonstrates his mastery of the discursive economy mandated by this brief poetic form in his simultaneously literal and figural use of lunar imagery. The moon often represented Japanese priests and envoys in Tang poems seeing them off, probably because it rises in the east, and because it traditionally accompanied lonely travelers and exiles in poetry.[17] As we will see, this same moon went on to gain additional layers of significance in *Tosa nikki*.

The failure of both Wang Wei and Li Bai to envisage Japan is particularly noteworthy given their respective reputations for visual acuity and imaginative capacity. As such, they eloquently testify to the bound-

16. QTS 184.1885.
17. Kakehi, *Ri Haku*, 166.

aries placed on cosmopolitan visions of their eastern borders in the poetry of Tang literati. As Edward Schafer (1913–1991) notes in his appraisal of these and other similar poems depicting Japan, "all of these fanciful accounts describe a place that is not of our world—nor completely another. It emerges from nowhere only to fade beyond the reach of perception."[18] Although their vision of Japan shares these limits, these two poems, along with Wang Wei's preface, would journey there to shape Nakamaro's poetic legacy through both their language and their intimations of a common poetics shared by *shi* and *waka*.

Nakamaro's Waka *in Ninth-Century Japan*

Although the historical Nakamaro's poetic biography ends with Li Bai's premature elegy, a much richer textual legacy began to arrive in Japan within his own lifetime. After making landfall in the southernmost extremity of the Tang world in Annam (present-day Vietnam), both he and Kiyokawa eventually returned to Chang'an in 755. That same year marked the beginning of the An Lushan Rebellion (755–763) that would end Xuanzong's reign and usher in a protracted period of political decline. Insofar as word of his survival would eventually reach the Nara court via Parhae and Silla, Nakamaro's later years also indicate the role that other Northeast Asian states would increasingly play in mediating relations with the continent. According to the official court history *Shoku Nihongi* (Continued Chronicles of Japan, 797), a letter written by Nakamaro in Chang'an shortly before his death in 770 was brought to the Nara capital by Sillan envoys that same year.[19] No doubt his earliest surviving quatrain traveled to Japan via this same diplomatic postal route, along with an unknown number of other writings by him.

Both the extent of this textual legacy and the reasons for its preservation in Japan are hinted at when Nakamaro reappears in an entry

---

18. Schafer, "Fusang and Beyond," 392.
19. *Shoku Nihongi* entry for Hōki 1/3/4, KST 2:519. Silla would sever all diplomatic ties with the Nara court less than a decade later, in 779.

from another official court history, *Shoku Nihon kōki* (Continued Later Chronicles of Japan, 869), which mentions his posthumous promotion to the Second Rank in 836. The enumeration of five separate posts he held in the Tang government within this entry, some granted posthumously, indicates that Nakamaro's career was thoroughly documented at the ninth-century Heian court. A similar degree of familiarity with his *shi* is suggested when *Shoku Nihon kōki* follows this biographical sketch with an encomium whose eight sentences in archaic quadrisyllabic meter evoke Nakamaro's poetic legacy through both their form and content.

> He crossed over whale-haunted waves. His masterful achievements were rare as *kirin* horn. His words as peaks soared skyward. His learning called out over the sea. Displaying such quality he rose accordingly. The reputation of his voice has spread far and wide. How could we not pity him? In the end there was no word of his return. Only his writings remain in a narrowed heaven. Long will the tale of his life resonate over a bereft land.
>
> 身涉鯨波。業成麟角。詞峰聳峻。學海揚涉。顯位斯昇。英聲已播。如何不愍。莫遂言歸。唯有挾天之章。長傳擲地之響。[20]

Of particular interest here is the way in which the opening description of the "whale-haunted waves" (鯨波) Nakamaro crossed appears to reference both of the poetic traditions he was affiliated with. Because the same phrase can be found in Wang Wei's preface, where it echoes the oceanic Leviathan in his own poetic farewell, this encomium suggests Heian readers were familiar with the Chang'an banquet poems. The phrasing might also gesture to Nakamaro's dual poetic heritage by evoking the pillow-word *izana-tori* (whale-hunted) used as an epithet for maritime spaces in early Japanese poetry.

Both this hybridized diction and the motives behind Nakamaro's posthumous promotion also have a bearing on the *Kokinshū* poem he became synonymous with around this same time. Many scholars believe it accompanied his other writings back to Japan.[21] However, the existence

---

20. *Shoku Nihon kōki* entry for Jōwa 3/5/10, KST 3:52.
21. Kamiyasu, "Abe no Nakamaro no zaitōka o megutte," 41–42; Tōda, "Aounabara furisake mireba," 29. For the most comprehensive account of theories about the *waka*'s provenance, see Kitazumi, "Abe no Nakamaro 'Ama no hara' no uta shikō."

of only one other *waka* composed in Tang China (*Man'yōshū* poem 1:63 by Yamanoue no Okura), suggests there was little interest in either composing or preserving such poems. Its association with Nakamaro is more likely to be a product of later tradition, something perhaps suggested by the auxiliary verb *keri* (they say) appearing in its *Kokinshū* headnote.

They say this was composed on the continent while gazing at the moon. By Abe no Nakamaro.

ama no hara	Heaven's high plains
furisake mireba	my gaze sweeps over to see
Kasuga naru	Kasuga, where stands
Mikasa no yama ni	Mount Mikasa, where
ideshi tsuki kamo	this moon rose over me![22]

Its formulaic wording suggests this poem may have originated as an anonymous song predating Nakamaro. The first two measures are shared with eight *Man'yōshū* poems, as well as a shrine song (*kagura uta*) that further hints at sacral origins.[23] A similarly ritualistic quality is apparent in its depiction of a moon rising over Mount Mikasa, which also appears in a *Man'yōshū* poem by Nakamaro's kinsman Abe no Mushimaro (d. 752):

ama-gomoru	Shrouded by rain
Mikasa no yama o	is Mount Mikasa,
takami kamo	whose heights surely
tsuki no idekonu	hinder the moon's rise
yo wa fukenitsutsu	as night deepens.[24]

Mushimaro's poem praises the might of the Abe clan deity enshrined on its slopes by elevating Mount Mikasa to such heights that it can block the moon's passage across the heavens. This numinous aura is further reinforced in Nakamaro's *waka* by adding the locative particle *ni* after the mountain's name to emphasize the stability and solidity of its presence.

22. *Kokin wakashū* poem 406, SNKBZ 11:172.
23. Takeoka, *Kokin wakashū zenhyōshaku*, 1:939. For the *kagura uta*, see song 85, SNKBZ 42:88.
24. *Man'yōshū* poem 6:980, SNKBZ 7:139.

Only the Heian-period Shin'in gyohon manuscript of the *Kokinshū* uses the particle *wo* instead to stress the movement of objects across its space in the same manner as Mushimaro. This remarkable consistency in its wording is thus another indication the *waka* possesses ritual qualities.

Drawing on both the court's official histories and *Shinsen shōjiroku* (Newly Selected Record of Clan Names and Hereditary Titles, 815), Hasegawa Masaharu has made a convincing argument that both *waka* were originally recited by priests at the Abe clan shrine as part of the rites conducted there to protect Japanese envoys before they headed overseas.[25] In other words, Nakamaro's *waka* began as a public prayer rather than a private lamentation. Given the pronounced interest in mollifying spirits at the ninth-century court through posthumous promotions such as the one granted to Nakamaro in *Shoku Nihon kōki*, it is easy to imagine the *Kokinshū* poem became associated with him at that time as a means for placating his resentful ghost in order to ensure envoys enjoyed the safe return he had been denied.

In addition to these ritual implications, the spatial contours of this *waka* echo the diplomatic posture adopted in the opening line of his *shi*. Just its declaration of fealty to a "shining master" referenced both a Tang sovereign and a Japanese one, the celestial zone that opens his *waka* can accommodate the realms of "all under heaven" both rulers presided over. Like the "whale-haunted waves" traversed in *Shoku Nihon kōki*, in other words, the "plains of heaven" his gaze crosses over in his *waka* can be read as a hybrid form of language combining a traditional *waka* epithet with Literary Sinitic diction in order to create a space that is transpolitical and transcultural.

Its complex configuration of politics and ritual makes Nakamaro's *waka* a suitably formal and multivalent opening for the *Kokinshū*'s Travel section, which is devoted to journeys beyond the capital on official business. By recalling the ritual space in which he began his voyage to the continent from the point at which he would embark on his return, Nakamaro's poem succinctly condenses the poetic vectors representing court-sponsored travel as either a movement to or from the capital. The

---

25. Hasegawa, "Abe no Nakamaro zaitōka," 21–24. These same rites were held before the mission that took Nakamaro to Tang China and the one he attempted to return with (*Shoku Nihongi* entries for Yōrō 1/2/1 and Hōki 8/2/6; KST 2:67 and 432).

placement of this poem also aligns the spatial syntax organizing its internal structure with that organizing Travel as a whole. Just as Nakamaro moves from a borderless celestial zone to a specific terrestrial one, so too does this section of the *Kokinshū* begin outside the realm before moving to specific spaces within its borders.

Given the Heian court's evident familiarity with Nakamaro's biography, the *Kokinshū* headnote only needed to situate this *waka* overseas for it to imply that he composed it in Tang China. In fact, however, the term used to describe this setting was as open to different political interpretations as the heavens Nakamaro gazes across. Although it was written with the Sinographs 大唐 in Japanese diplomatic letters addressing the Tang sovereigns, in order to convey respect for the power and majesty of Da Tang (Great Tang), "Morokoshi" was more typically glossed as 諸越 in Japanese texts, where it originally indicated a region in southern China from which "various" (*moro*) imports "came over" (*koshi*).[26] This commercial inflection also appears in a lengthy after-comment (*sachū*) appended to the *Kokinshū* poem in the eleventh century.

> The following story has been passed down about this poem. Long ago, they say, Nakamaro was sent to the land of the Tang to study its ways. However, many years passed, and he was no longer able to return home. But when another embassy from this land made its way there, he thought to return with them and set out to do so. By the seaside at a place called Mingzhou the people of that land held a farewell banquet. Night fell, and he composed this while gazing out on the moonlight streaming enthrallingly over the scene.[27]

Although the farewell banquet and synopsis of Nakamaro's career appearing here may be citing *Tosa nikki*, its commercial urban context is particular to this narrative. Due to its central location between China's northern and southern littoral zones, Mingzhou was one of the largest trading ports in East Asia from the eighth to twelfth centuries. By moving Nakamaro from the Tang capital to its premier entrepôt, this anecdote overlays the political terms representing Morokoshi as a static terrestrial

---

26. Wang, *Ambassadors from the Islands*, 173–74.
27. *Kokin wakashū* poem 406, SNKBZ 11:172–73.

imperial territory with commercial ones defining it as a dynamic maritime trading network. In this context, in other words, the space it represented expands to include the northeastern polities that bordered the archipelago as well. As we will see, it is this last incarnation of Morokoshi that informs *Tosa nikki*'s depiction of Nakamaro.

The mercantile relationships represented in the preceding anecdote offer an important supplement to traditional views of the period in which Nakamaro's poetic afterlife began taking shape. Conventional histories typically treat the years after his failed attempt to return home as the beginning of a decisive turn away from cosmopolitanism in Tang China. Over the course of the next century, economic anxieties, xenophobia, and state persecution of Buddhism contributed to a noticeable decline in attitudes toward non-Han ethnicities, replacing earlier celebrations of cultural differences with anxieties over political allegiance.[28] At the same time, the development of new agricultural technologies during this period fed rural demand for foreign imports, leading private traders from the Shandong peninsula and southern coast of central China to sail as far as Hakata in Kyushu, where customs officials made an initial selection of goods to send on to the Heian court before selling the remainder. In exchange, these continental merchants would bring back textiles and other finely crafted objects.[29] These activities also supported the movement of diplomats and priests in the ninth century, as well as the establishment of multilingual communities at nodal points along this maritime network. The flow of goods and people in both directions was often facilitated, for example, by coastal enclaves of Korean-speakers who provided transporters, hosts, and translators for Japanese travelers to the continent.[30]

These trading relations also fostered a transnational poetic culture exemplified by the works of Bai Juyi, whose celebrations of an eighth-century world filled with foreign peoples and exotic artefacts would shape East Asian poetry for centuries afterward. His collected works first en-

---

28. Schafer, *The Golden Peaches of Samarkand*, 10; Abramson, *Ethnic Identity in Tang China*, xiv–xv.

29. Batten, *Gateway to Japan*, 105–23. An informative overview of Japanese trading relations in this period can be found in von Verschuer, *Across the Perilous Sea*, 23–40.

30. Reischauer, *Ennin's Travels in T'ang China*, 272–94.

tered the Heian court around 838 after being discovered by a customs official inspecting merchandise at Dazaifu. Private trading vessels also transported later editions of his oeuvre acquired by the monks Ennin and Egaku. One poem by Bai Juyi, in which a merchant returning from Japan assures him that he would enjoy a rapturous reception there, suggests he was keenly aware of the role commerce played in establishing his poetic reputation.[31]

This maritime trading network also began to displace the Sinocentric structures that had previously organized both the circulation of *shi* poems and their depictions of Japan. As Gian Piero Persiani has noted, commerce enabled Japanese *shi* to reach the continent by the beginning of the tenth century.[32] Unlike Wang Wei, moreover, ninth-century Heian travelers to Tang China—such as Tachibana no Hayanari, Ennin, Kūkai (774–835), and Ensai (d. 877)—could place Kyushu precisely in their *shi* poems by situating it to the east of Zuzhou and Danzhou islands.[33] Unlike their precursors, Tang poets in this same period were also capable of depicting Japan in quotidian terms, as is evident in the following *lushi* by the monk Jia Dao (779–843) seeing off a Japanese colleague who was returning home.

懸帆待秋水	Spread sails await autumn waters.
去入杳冥關	Departing into distant murky borders.
東海幾年別	Eastward is the sea for so many years forsaken.
中華此日還	Central is our splendor on this day when you return.
岸遙生白髮	Shores in the distance will birth white hairs.
波盡露青山	Waves at their end will reveal green mountains.
隔水相思在	Separated by waters while thinking of each other.
無書也是聞	Without letters how will we hear of one another?[34]

The Buddhist context in which this poem takes shape as a message from one monk to another helps explain the remarkably unremarkable language

31. Waley, *Life and Times of Po Chü-I*, 198–99 and 212–13.
32. Persiani, "China as Self, China as Other," 52–56.
33. Nakakoji, "Tōshi no Nihon kodai shizō, hosoku." The present-day location of these two islands has yet to be identified.
34. QTS 573.6667.

describing Japan in its penultimate couplet. The generic and universal quality of the landscape it creates by juxtaposing white-capped waves with verdant slopes embodies what Charles Holcombe has characterized as a transregional Buddhist perspective on landscapes succinctly conveyed by the scriptural passage "The mountains and streams of different lands share the wind and moon of the same heaven," which *Tōdaiwajō tōseiden* (Record of the Great Tang Priest's Eastward Expedition, 779) claims Prince Nagaya had embroidered on the robes of a thousand monks.[35]

Comparison of Jia Dao's poetic farewell for a Japanese friend with that of Wang Wei highlights the difference between this Buddhist view of Japan as simply one of many similar locales, and an imperial one that places it beyond the visible world. Although both poets bemoan the barriers to future communication with their friends posed by an intervening sea, Jia Dao is at least able to envisage what lies on its other side. In this sense, the ninth-century poet's perspective can be considered more thoroughly Buddhist than that of his eighth-century predecessor, despite the religious sensibility that is often associated with Wang Wei's poetry. At the same time, however, Jia Dao's poem also shares the Sinocentric logic of its predecessors when it places Japan on the eastern margins of Tang China's "central splendor" (中華). Nonetheless, his poetry would also contribute to *Tosa nikki*'s depiction of a more neutral seascape at a time when the maritime networks that had sustained such language were in danger of disappearing.

Nakamaro's Cyan Sea Plains

The remarkable consistency with which Nakamaro's *waka* appears in virtually every version of the *Kokinshū* makes it particularly significant that *Tosa nikki* transforms its plains from those of a high heaven into the expanses of a blue-green sea. Like Narihira's Nagisa poem, this choice places a past landscape within that of a poetic present, in this case by referring to the fraught historical currents shaping tenth-century Japan's relation-

---

35. Holcombe, "Trade-Buddhism," 283.

ship to Northeast Asia. In the process, Tsurayuki transforms Nakamaro from a figure representing the collapse of eighth-century Sinocentric cosmopolitanism into someone situated within an equally unstable but more diffused relationship to the continent in his own time.

The diary introduces Nakamaro's *waka* in similar terms to those framing its anthological predecessor. Like the *Kokinshū* headnote to his poem, the diarist places Nakamaro in a vaguely continental setting, while its latent ritual characteristics in the imperial anthology are now rendered overt through a preamble outlining *waka*'s mythical origins and palliative function:

> I don't sleep, and now the moon on the night of the twentieth has risen. It appears from the middle of the sea rather than over mountain rims! I wonder if this was what that man of old called Abe no Nakamaro witnessed when he was about to set back for home after having crossed over to the continent. At the place where he was to board ship, they say, the people of that land held a farewell banquet at which they crafted continental verses to express their regret at seeing him leave. They must have not yet felt satisfied, for it is said that they stayed there until the moon on that night of the twentieth rose right out of the sea. Seeing it there, Master Nakamaro is said to have said: "In my land, verses such as these were first recited by gods in the age of the gods. High, middling, and low alike now recite them at partings from loved ones such as this, and also when feeling sorrow or joy." Then he composed this verse:

aounabara	Over cyan sea plains
furisake mireba	my gaze sweeps out to see
Kasuga naru	Kasuga, in which lies
Mikasa no yama ni	Mount Mikasa, where
ideshi tsuki kamo	this moon once rose over me!
(TN 33–34, 1/20)	

In addition to locating its historical origins in mythical times, Nakamaro's speech highlights *waka*'s incantatory aspects through the compositional contexts it enumerates. The occasions of separation from loved ones, sorrow, and joy he lists are associated in the *Kokinshū* with the categories of Partings (*ribetsu*), Travel (*kiryo*), Lamentations (*aishō*), and Blessings (*ga*), each of which implies a ritual purpose. Travel and Parting poems are designed to ensure the reunion with loved ones by safeguarding the traveler, while Lamentations and Blessings were composed for mourning rites and birthday celebrations respectively.

Despite these connections with the *Kokinshū*, the distinctive and precise history of the epithet that opens his poem in the diary points to an equally distinct and precise version of Morokoshi in *Tosa nikki*. The phrase *aounabara* (cyan sea plains) only appears once previously in a *Man'yōshū* poetic prayer for safe passage composed by Ono no Tamori (fl. 750) at a farewell banquet held prior to his departure at the head of a diplomatic delegation to Parhae.

aounabara	Over cyan sea plains,
kaze nami nabiki	wind-lashed waves calmed,
yuku sa ku sa	both going and coming
tsutsumu koto naku	without any mishap
fune wa hayakemu	may the vessel speed.[36]

Though Tamori was ultimately unsuccessful in his mission to enlist Parhae as a military ally against Silla, Brendan Morley notes that he was the first member of the Japanese court to bring back news of both the An Lushan Rebellion and Nakamaro's survival.[37] With his extensive knowledge of the *Man'yōshū* acquired at the palace library, Tsurayuki must have deliberately singled out this phrase for its connection to the diplomatic postal route that conveyed Nakamaro's writings to Japan. Even if the diary's readership were unaware of the connection to Tamori, their own familiarity with the *Kokinshū* version would make it readily apparent Tsurayuki had altered the original. By turning this opening line into a signature of sorts marking his own presence in the poem, the diary's author is in fact signaling his participation in similar diplomatic exchanges.

The cyan sea plains in their *waka* represented a politically fluid region for both Tsurayuki and Tamori. Constantly shifting alliances among the multiple polities occupying Northeast Asia produced an unusually complex diplomatic situation that has been characterized by the histo-

---

36. *Man'yōshū* poem 20:4514, SNKBZ 9:458–59.
37. Morley, "Poetry and Diplomacy," 348–49.

rian Wang Zhenping as "dynamic and unpredictable."[38] In Tamori's time, for example, Parhae took advantage of unrest in the aftermath of the An Lushan Rebellion to replace Silla as Japan's chief commercial and political partner on the continent, thereby assuming a central place in East Asian maritime trading relations.[39] The fragility of these political relations became particularly acute in the decades between the appearance of Nakamaro's *waka* in the *Kokinshū* and its reemergence in *Tosa nikki*, during which time the aftershocks that rippled across East Asia in the wake of the Tang empire's collapse in 907 effectively upended the unipolar political order it had promulgated as a framework for international relations.

The effects of this unrest were most keenly felt by the Heian court when Parhae collapsed in 926, followed ten years later by Silla. As Japan's last remaining diplomatic partner and chief conduit for information about events on the continent, Parhae's dissolution and its violent aftermath abruptly severed Japan's official channels of communication with the continent. For the next half century, the land was wracked by political and social upheavals as the regime of Dong Qidan (Eastern Kitan) established under the Liao dynasty (907–1125) attempted to prevent uprisings among their new subjects by transferring up to a quarter of the population to other parts of their empire. Up until its final dissolution in 1003, remnants of the Parhae regime would also continue to pose a threat to this new polity.[40]

In the 920s and 930s, the Heian court refused to establish official ties with all of its neighbors on the newly volatile continent. Parhae's last ruler had unsuccessfully sought aid from Japan as well as the Korean peninsular states of Silla and Koryŏ in the face of the Liao threat.[41] The court also rejected multiple diplomatic overtures from the successor states who had inherited portions of the Tang empire—Later Liang (907–923) in northern China and Wuyue (907–978) on its central coast—along with

38. Wang, *Tang China in Multi-Polar Asia*, 1. On Northeast Asian multipolarity, see 55–96.
39. Yun, "Parhae as an East Asian Maritime Power," 118.
40. Crossley, "Bohai/Parhae Identity," 31–32; Lim, "The Movement to Restore Parhae," 65.
41. Kim, "The Fall of Parhae," 57.

the states of Later Paekche (900–935) and Later Koryŏ (935–1392) on the Korean peninsula.[42] This new stance may have partly been due to the difficulty of re-establishing the traditional ritual order previously governing diplomacy. Commerce, by contrast, offered an easier and more informal means of maintaining connections to the continent. Such considerations probably explain why, when a merchant from Wuyue arrived at court in 936 bearing gifts and a letter from its ruler, Suzaku refused to receive the trader while having Tadahira write a reply to that sovereign.[43]

Any efforts to establish contacts of either a diplomatic or commercial nature would have been severely hampered in any case by the significant rise in piracy that accompanied political turmoil on the continent. In response to this growing menace, the court established the military office of *tsuibushi* (envoys for pursuit and capture) in 932. Although raiders would eventually encroach on the neighboring province of Iyo by the end of Tsurayuki's time in Tosa, the historical record makes no mention of his own response to this growing threat. What is certain is that the situation had become so severe by the end of his term that, according to the *Geki bunin* (Record of Court Appointments, ca. 1500), it caused his successor Shimada no Kimiaki to delay his own voyage to Tosa for three months after being appointed governor in Shōhei 4/4/29 (934).[44]

Its flagrant fictionality makes *Tosa nikki*'s mentions of pirates obviously unreliable as a historical source of information about this period. The deliberate way in which the diary casts doubt on its references to such threats suggests that Tsurayuki, being all too aware of the potential pitfalls entailed by an attempt to defend his record as governor, turns them to his advantage in order to amuse his readers instead. On the one hand, the diarist's intermittent references to the possibility that pirates are pursuing her ship suggests a desire to avenge fallen comrades on their part that would seem to indicate her master had vigorously attempted to suppress them during his governorship. On the other hand, her growing skepticism towards these rumors proves justified in the end when they ultimately fail to appear. *Tosa nikki* thus sidesteps questions about its au-

---

42. Batten, *Gateway to Japan*, 78; von Verschuer, *Across the Perilous Sea*, 23–40.
43. Jun, *History of Sino-Japanese Cultural Exchange*, 95.
44. *Geki bunin*, ZGR 4:51.

thor's actions with typically self-reflexive irony by reminding readers that rumors are often unreliable sources of information.

If anything, Tsurayuki's lack of military accomplishments is sardonically underscored by alluding to his more capable forebears through the titles identifying the two men in *Tosa nikki* most responsible for making decisions. In what seems to be a deliberate parody of the patrilineal principle allowing sons to partially inherit their fathers' names, the designations of "the lord on board" (*funagimi*) and "the steersman" (*kajitori*) partially overlap with the names of Funamori and his son Kajinaga (754–806), the only members of Tsurayuki's clan who reached the aristocratic Third Rank.[45] The gap between these fictional characters and their historical counterparts is particularly acute in the case of the senior pair of figures. In his frantic flight from pirates across the southern fringes of the realm, the ex-governor could not be more different from the martial Funamori, who was himself made governor of Tosa in 778 after previously being catapulted into the Fifth Rank as a reward for his many military victories on the realm's northeastern frontier.

Within two years of Tsurayuki's return from Tosa, a senior member of his clan would fail to match Funamori's competence in an even more spectacular manner. In 936, the court sought to quell the growing threat of piracy by making Ki no Yoshihito grand governor (*taishu*) of Iyo overseeing all the *tsuibushi* forces in the South Sea Circuit (Nankaidō). With a jurisdiction that encompassed Shikoku and the Kii peninsula, the military and commercial responsibilities of this post were second in scope only to those of Dazaifu's administrator.[46] Although Yoshihito's background as a son of the distinguished scholar official Haseo may have theoretically prepared him for such weighty responsibilities, subsequent events suggest otherwise. In 939, one of his nominal subordinates, Fujiwara no Sumitomo (893–941), resigned his post in Iyo province and proceeded to lead several hundred ships in raids along the entire length of the Inland Sea. The situation escalated rapidly into a macabre version of the diary's own itinerary when Sumitomo's forces first overran Tosa

---

45. On these conventions, see Plutschow, *Japan's Name Culture*, 55–57. Tsurayuki may have engaged in a similar form of wordplay by reversing syllables in Tokifumi's name to designate the character "Fumutoki" appearing on 2/12.

46. Kobayashi, "Fujiwara Sumitomo no ran sairon," 4–8.

province in 940 and then rowed up the Yodo-gawa to burn Yamazaki soon afterwards.⁴⁷ Only after much effort, including multiple attempts at negotiation, was Sumitomo finally vanquished in 941.

Tsurayuki was intimately involved in two events that were connected to the end of this rebellion. When a victory celebration was held on 4/27 at the Iwashimizu Hachimangū shrine affiliated with his clan the year after Sumitomo's demise, he performed a dance in offering to the martial deity before reciting a *waka* praising Sumiyoshi at the concluding banquet.⁴⁸ Another gathering he participated in soon afterwards suggests that Sumitomo's disruption of the court's connections to the continent had inspired a renewed interest in developing diplomatic ties. According to a brief entry in *Nihon kiryaku*, a formal reception was held in 942 for envoys from some unspecified country: "Rites for visitors from afar who had come to court were held in the hall, including a banquet with poetry" (於殿上有遠客來朝之禮。是爲催詩興也。).⁴⁹ As head of the department of Buddhist and foreign affairs (*genba no kami*) at the time, Tsurayuki would have been tasked with overseeing this gathering.

The challenges posed to maritime travel during this period make it likely that the envoys he received came to Japan's northwestern shores. As Joan Piggott notes, the court was still grappling with piracy in the Inland Sea as late as 948.⁵⁰ By comparison, passage across the cyan sea plains of Nakamaro's *waka* might have posed less difficulties for envoys originating in Parhae's former territories, particularly since this route had long been favored by such diplomatic missions to Japan. The delegation could have been sent by either the Liao or the surviving remnants of Parhae's regime in a bid to establish formal recognition from the Heian court. *Nihon kiryaku*'s vague description of these envoys as simply "visitors from afar" (遠客) would seem to indicate that

---

47. An informative outline of key events in the rebellion is provided in Friday, *Hired Swords*, 149–52.

48. *Shūi wakashū* poem 456, SNKBT 7:129: "By word alone / had I long heard / of Sumiyoshi's / millennia-old pine / now seen this day!" (*oto ni nomi / kiki-wataritsuru / Sumiyoshi no / matsu no chitose o / kyō mitsuru kana*). The connection between Sumiyoshi in this poem and the shrine where Tsurayuki recited it remains unclear.

49. *Nihon kiryaku* entry for Tengyō 5/5/17, KST 10:831. An earlier banquet of this sort is described in great detail in Horton, "Literary Diplomacy in Early Nara."

50. Piggott, "Court and Provinces Under Fujiwara no Tadahira," 54.

the ambiguous status of the realm they represented was, in fact, precisely what was at issue.

Taken as a whole, these events in the years shortly after Tsurayuki's return from Tosa suggest the uncertain state of Japan's links to the continent would have been very much in the minds of his initial readership. Nakamaro's *waka* deftly acknowledged this politically fluid context by invoking a maritime space without the distinctions between center and periphery represented by the "Eastern Sea" (東海) that Bao Ji, Wang Wei, and Jia Dao all mention. The political stakes informing such designations is perhaps most apparent back at the farewell banquet in Chang'an, where Nakamaro's placement of Japan "adjacent" (鄰) to the Sunrise Tree of Fusang contrasts starkly with its location "beyond" (外) it in Wang Wei's poem. Such language evokes a diplomatic taxonomy familiar to both men, in which "adjacent lands" (鄰國) were equal in stature while "outer vassals" (外蕃) were politically subordinate.[51] Whereas Nakamaro defines his homeland through a non-hierarchical set of relations, in other words, its marginalization by Wang Wei carries the same political implications as the more explicit description of a realm whose ruler is a "vassal lord" (蕃君) in Bao Ji's poem. Insofar as they eschew any such larger set of spatial relations, the diplomatic implications conveyed by the cyan seas in Tsurayuki's version of Nakamaro's *waka* are consistent with the delicate diplomatic positions both Japanese poets found themselves in.

The portion of mainland Northeast Asia facing those cyan sea plains provides a particularly powerful illustration of the political stakes entailed by such spatial schemes. The literal meaning of "Parhae" as "bursting forth from the sea" (渤海) suggests it sought to define itself at the center of a maritime mercantile world, even as those same qualities rendered it peripheral in Tang sources that described it as "a flourishing realm by the Eastern Sea" (海東盛國). The territories comprising this premodern polity have also been defined differently within the competing histories of modern nation-states that have claimed all or part of them at some point.[52] These rival claims are at least as charged in the

---

51. Kang, *Diplomacy and Ideology in Japanese-Korean Relations*, 42; Wang, *Ambassadors from the Islands*, 175–76.

52. On modern national histories of Parhae, see Sloane, "Parhae in Historiography and Archaeology"; Hamada, "Transition of Understanding Parhae in Japan"; Yun,

case of its adjoining maritime zone. Both politics and history have led China and South Korea to propose reviving the name "Eastern Sea" in order to reclaim this space from the history of imperialism shaping its current international designation as the "Sea of Japan." By contrast, Tsurayuki's cyan sea plains avoid potential conflict by drawing on the same tendency to exhibit diplomatic tact through spatial ambiguities present in Nakamaro's poems.

Cosmopolitan Currents at Sea

In addition to marking its own historical moment, Nakamaro's *waka* in *Tosa nikki* also celebrates the cosmopolitan poetics that had been nurtured through trade up until that time by immersing his poem within a larger sea of hybridized diction. This transcultural maritime zone partly reflects the overall preference for generic imagery over toponymic specificity in the diary's poetic landscapes mentioned in chapter 4. Unlike their terrestrial counterparts, however, *Tosa nikki*'s maritime *waka* display extensive familiarity with Literary Sinitic poetry in three respects. First, they typically invert the binary spatial relations structuring earlier *shi*. Second, the criterion for selecting those earlier poems indicates extensive familiarity with their creators' biographies. Third, they reveal a nuanced understanding of Tang poetics by focusing on particular portions of a single genre. In aggregate, these characteristics create a remarkably detailed and diverse picture of the poetic corpus that had been imported to Japan in the ninth century, one which also furthers our understanding of the shape Nakamaro's *waka* takes within the diary.

The practice of generating *waka* from *shi* in Tsurayuki's day is now synonymous with the anthology *Kudai waka* (Poetic Lines as Waka Topics, 894) written by the scholar Ōe no Chisato (fl. 890s). As its title suggests, the 110 vernacular Japanese poems Chisato produced for the anthology adapted individual "lines" (*ku*) from Literary Sinitic poetry,

---

"Chinese Perceptions of Parhae"; and Park, "Perceptions of Parhae in North Korea, Japan, and Russia."

often by reproducing binary structures such as the two consecutive actions depicted in the anthology's second poetic pair:

Drawn by the voice of a bush warbler, coming beneath the blossoms.
鶯聲誘引 / 來花下

Drawn by the voice of a bush warbler crying, I have come beneath these blossoms!
鶯の / 啼きつる聲に / 誘はれて / 花の下にぞ / 我は來にける[53]

Aside from their grammatical and lexical peculiarities, the two forms of poetry differ most in the placement of caesura within them. Whereas the *shi* line hews to strict metrical conventions by creating a separate clause from the final three syllables, the position of caesura in *waka* could vary considerably.

Most of the individual lines used to produce *waka* in *Tosa nikki* and *Kudai waka* are taken from quatrains that had originated as individual contributions within larger sequences of "linked lines" (C. *lianju*, J. *renku*) composed in a group setting. As indicated by their genre designation, quatrains were thought of as "cut-off lines" (C. *jueju*, J. *zekku*) that had been severed from these original contexts. The more general predilection in Tang China and Heian Japan for cutting off portions of poems are manifestations of what Wiebke Denecke has called a "couplet culture" consisting of "interrelated poetic practices that centered on the poetic couplet as the smallest, most significant poetic unit."[54] In *Tosa nikki*, poetic significance is also assigned to the binaries produced by caesura within couplet's individual lines, and to the positioning of couplets within quatrains.

The importance of caesura in both *waka* and *shi* is stressed when the only lyrics to a *kara uta* appear in *Tosa nikki*. Scholars' longstanding failure to identify their source is an eloquent testament to our limited understanding of the full corpus of Sinitic poems familiar to a Heian readership. Although she is equally ignorant of their provenance, the diarist is nonetheless able to discern a discrete poetic unit within the

---

53. *Kudai waka*, 452.
54. Denecke, "'Topic Poetry Is All Ours,'" 14.

words she hears by identifying binary patterns that are semantic and syntactic rather than prosodic.

> A woman composed this poem after hearing the words *When I gaze towards The Sun, the capital lies in the distance*, or the gist of some such phrase uttered by the men who have been seeking solace in continental verses:
>
> | | |
> |---|---|
> | *hi o dani mo* | Even the sun itself |
> | *ama kumo chikaku* | near heaven's clouds |
> | *miru mono o* | I seem to see, and yet |
> | *miyako e to omou* | these longings for the capital city |
> | *michi no harukesa* | stretch over a distant path! |
>
> Another person composed this:
>
> | | |
> |---|---|
> | *fuku kaze no* | As long as there is no end |
> | *taenu kagiri shi* | to the gusting wind, |
> | *tachi-kureba* | the rising swell comes in, |
> | *nami-ji wa itodo* | making the waveborne path |
> | *harukekarikeri* | grow ever more distant! |
>
> (TN 39, 1/27)

Despite replicating the *kara uta*'s lyrics to very different degrees—with the first poem re-using its words in all but one measure and the second only echoing it in the final one—all three examples of verse are alike in their reliance on asymmetrical pairings. The concessive and causal constructions uniting both halves of these *waka* represent two of the most common means by which such pairings were produced in vernacular poetry. The latter construction also appears in the fragment of *kara uta* lyrics, whose speaker first gazes on the sun before realizing their distance from the capital. Their common reliance on such asymmetrical binarisms, by implication, makes it possible for *waka* and *shi* to share the same *sama* (gist or outline) that the diarist identifies as common to both genres.

The Tang poetic sources *Tosa nikki* draws on to create such asymmetrical binarisms are far more varied than those *Kudai waka* uses. Like many other Heian texts, the overwhelming majority of Tang *shi* cited in Chisato's anthology are by Bai Juyi and his friend Yuan Zhen (779–831). Their ubiquity makes it all the more noteworthy that *Tosa nikki* only cites a single couplet by the former poet:

| 誰言南國無霜雪 | Who said southern lands lack frost and snow? |
| 盡在愁人鬢髮閒 | There is nothing else amid these grieving locks.⁵⁵ |

In a rhetorical move that is repeated throughout the diary, the first half of this couplet is transformed into an overtly maritime setting in *waka*.⁵⁶ The second half subsequently appears the day after Nakamaro's tale in a barbed complaint about the voyage's hardships.⁵⁷ This couplet is also noteworthy for its connection to the life of Bai Juyi, who composed it when he was assistant governor of the southern prefecture of Jiangzhou. By singling out this one allusion, as Nishinoiri Atsuo notes, *Tosa nikki* signals its affiliation with an earlier tradition of poets who lament their exile to the south.⁵⁸ Nakamaro doubtless participated in this same tradition when he became governor of Annam after the An Lushan Rebellion. Because Heian readers had access to far more of his written legacy than is available to us now, it is entirely possible Tsurayuki was also familiar with some of those poems.

The biography of another ninth-century Tang poet is alluded to one day after Bai Juyi's couplet is first cited. In this case, the couplet by Jia Dao that the diarist recalls marks both his maritime connection to Northeast Asia and his reputation as a wordsmith: "During this time, both the clouds above and the sea below looked exactly the same. This must have been why some man of olden times said *a pole pierces the moon above waves; a ship presses against a sea in the sky*. I heard words to that effect from a poem once" (TN 31, 1/17). The syntactic parallelisms linking the two sentences the diarist cites make it clear that she is referencing the vernacularized version of a *shi* couplet. The original is likely to be the closing couplet of a quatrain that Jia Dao contributed to a *lianju* sequence composed at a banquet honoring the ambassador of Koryŏ.

---

55. As cited in TNZ 203.

56. TN 31, 1/16: "Not even frost / is found in this region, / they say, and yet / amid these waves / snow now falls!" (*shimo dani mo / okanu kata zo to / iu naredo / nami no naka ni wa / yuki zo furikeru*).

57. TN 36, 1/21: "The sea's terrors have turned my hairs completely white. A full seventy- or eighty-years' worth of suffering do I now see in the sea!"

58. Nishinoiri, "*Tosa nikki* no umi," 116. On Bai Juyi's exilic poetic persona in this period, see Shields, "Remembering When," 7 and 28. Tang poetic lamentations over southern postings are addressed at length in Schafer, *The Vermilion Bird*.

水島浮還沒	On water islands float before sinking.
山雲斷復連	On mountains clouds part then gather.
棹穿波底月	A pole pierces waves beneath the moon.
舟壓水中天	A ship presses against waters in the sky.[59]

Like the landscape that appeared in his *lushi* bidding farewell to a Japanese monk, this one is resolutely generic. Also like that poem, the allusion to it in *Tosa nikki* is ultimately the product of Northeast Asia's maritime networks. Perhaps it was the same monk he bade farewell to who first brought Jia Dao's works to Japan, or it may have been the ambassador for whom he composed this quatrain. Between them, both of Jia Dao's poems attest to the role played by priests and diplomatic intermediaries in fostering Japanese poetic cosmopolitanism.

Another allusion to the Tang poet's biography is perhaps intended by beginning the diarist's citation with the opening depiction of a pole being thrust into water. This application of force echoes a famous anecdote in which Jia Dao is said to have debated whether the priest in a poem should "rap" on a moonlit gate or "push" it. Perhaps not coincidentally, the first of two *waka* inspired by the ninth-century poet's couplet creates a barrier as firm as the gate in that anecdote by replacing a liquid surface that is easily pierced by the pole in the original quatrain with a solid object that repels it.

minasoko no	In watery depths
tsuki no ue yori	lies the moon above which
kogu fune no	rows by this ship
sao ni sawaru wa	whose pole comes up against
katsura naru rashi	what seems to be its laurel tree.
kage mireba	Reflections reveal
nami no soko naru	beneath the waves
hisakata no	a far-off firmament
sora kogi-wataru	sailing across whose sky
ware zo wabishiki	is this misery-filled I!
(TN 31, 1/17)	

---

59. QTS 791.8915.

While the first *waka* increases the force encountered by the pole in the opening line of Jia Dao's closing couplet, the second one departs from this source by directly voicing the melancholic sentiments the Tang poet only hints at. Like the poem that adapted Bai Juyi's couplet on the previous day, these two represent practical strategies for transforming *shi* lines into vernacular poems, leading Hagitani to argue that all three *waka* serve a pedagogical function (TNZ 212). Regardless of their purpose, the common emphasis on maritime and exilic spaces these two *shi* couplets share with *Tosa nikki*'s *waka* are likely to be intentional.

This assured grasp of the Tang poetic corpus demonstrated by the diary's author becomes far more tenuous in the case of its narrator. Her version of Jia Dao's closing couplet differs in small but significant ways from both its lines, first by placing the moon above waves rather than below them, and then by making the scene overtly maritime. The tentative manner in which she presents the couplet and the *kara uta* lyrics mentioned previously also contrasts starkly with the confidence on display when women recall lines from *shi* in *The Pillow Book*, whose author goes so far as to assert: "It is women who don't forget such things. With men that is not the case."[60] This contrast is likely to be a product of the narrator's relatively humble status, which would have normally precluded her participation in the venues where vernacularized *shi* were heard and memorized. Her distance from such settings is stressed the first time *kara uta* appear in the diary during a banquet she is excluded from: "I gather continental verses were uttered in raised voices, and Yamato verses were also apparently uttered by host and guest. I cannot write down the continental verses here" (TN 16, 12/26). It is probably her dependence on the memories of others that leads the diarist to refrain from writing down the *kara uta* recited on this occasion, an ironic decision in light of her own faulty recollection of Jia Dao's couplet. Like other aspects of *Tosa nikki*'s language, then, the narrator's imperfect grasp of *shi* parodies discursive practices that were familiar to its aristocratic readers.

The diarist's comparative lack of familiarity with *shi* is underscored the day after this banquet at the governor's mansion, when the sight of

---

60. *Makura no sōshi* section 155, SNKBZ 18:285; see also McKinney, *The Pillow Book*, 157. Women other than the author identify *shi* from their chanted renditions in sections 74 and 79 (SNKBZ 18:131 and 145; see also McKinney, *The Pillow Book*, 64 and 72).

another group of well-wishers leads one of her fellow passengers to recall the closing couplet from another quatrain representing southern exile. Edo-period scholars such as Bokuyū and Kigin identified several correspondences between this scene and one depicted in a *jueju* by Li Bai in which he bids farewell to a local magistrate, one Wang Lun, who had hosted him for three days at a village named after the Daoist paradise of Taohua-tan (Peach Blossom Lake).

李白乘舟將欲行	Li Bai boards the boat seeking to set forth.
忽聞岸上踏歌聲	Foot-stamping songs sound suddenly from the shore.
桃花潭水深千尺	Peach Blossom Lake's waters are a thousand feet deep.
不及汪倫送我情	Nowhere near Wang Lun's feelings seeing me off.[61]

The division of this quatrain into couplets that describe first a shore and then its adjacent waters is replicated on 12/27 in prose and poetry respectively. There, the diarist begins by describing a chorus of well-wishers singing by a shoreline in a manner that recalls the songs mentioned by Li Bai.[62] As though in recognition of this connection between the scene at hand and the opening couplet in his quatrain, one of the travelers proceeds to compose a *waka* that replicates the closing couplet's tropological link between the profundity of a host's solicitude and the depths of their watery surroundings.

sao sasedo	Though poles be plunged
sokoi mo shiranu	fathomless is the bottom
watatsumi no	of the mighty ocean god,
fukaki kokoro o	whose depths the hearts
kimi ni miru kana	of milords do show!
(TN 19, 12/27)	

At the same time as this poem recalls Li Bai's couplet, the spatial relations organizing that verse are expanded and inverted in the *waka* by transforming the lake into the sea, and by making the watery depths equal to the well-wishers' feelings rather than inferior to them. It also preserves the *jueju*'s supernatural undertones while transforming their refer-

61. QTS 171.1765.
62. This passage is cited in chapter 3.

ent by replacing the legendary riparian paradise of Peach Blossom Spring with the mythical maritime realm of the sea god.

The targeted and subtle nature of these alterations points to Tsurayuki's thorough familiarity with the original. In itself, this is not surprising. Li Bai's poetry, which is first listed in the *Nihon koku genzaisho mokuroku* (Catalog of Writings Currently in Japan, 891), had been circulating in Japan for more than four decades when *Tosa nikki* was written. In this particular context, however, the allusion is also significant for indicating that the Tang poet's biography was also known at the time. Because Li Bai visited Taohua-tan during a southern journey he made in his later years, the circumstances in which the quatrain was composed echo those endured by the ex-governor, who we saw previously alluding to Bai Juyi's couplet in order to lament his journey to the realm's southernmost borders in Tosa as an old man. Such erudition on Tsurayuki's part would explain why a variant of the anonymous *waka* was subsequently preserved under his name in *Kokin waka rokujō*.[63]

In addition to these biographical details, *Tosa nikki*'s preference for the closing lines in *jueju* is another noteworthy aspect of the Tang poetry it cites. The implicit formal equivalence it establishes between *waka* and quatrains' closing couplets suggests Tsurayuki is making a metalinguistic commentary on correspondences between the two genres that goes beyond their shared brevity. By virtue of their close relationship to love songs, quatrains characteristically deployed deictic pronouns, modal expressions of desire, homophonous wordplay, and a forward-moving syntax.[64] All these characteristics were shared by Heian *waka*, particularly anonymous love verses, which typically employed pivot-words or implicit metaphors to bind an initial description of a landscape to a human situation in the closing line. As we saw already, Wang Wei's punning reference to Kyushu in his farewell poem may have been inspired by this shared propensity for homophones, just as the reference to Jian'an-era poetry in his preface may indicate a common interest in direct expressions of affect. Given Tsurayuki's evident familiarity with Tang poetry,

---

63. *Kokin waka rokujō* poem 3:32611. The final measure in this version replaces "milords do show" (*kimi ni miru kana*) with "milords must surely know" (*kimi wa shiranamu*).

64. Egan, "Recent-Style Shi Poetry," 199–203 and 219–22; Lin, "The Nature of the Quatrain," 308.

the particular attention he pays to the closing couplets of *jueju* also suggests he is aware they are the focus of interest in quatrains.[65]

All the aforementioned characteristics shared by *Tosa nikki*'s maritime *waka* also obtain in its version of Nakamaro's poem. The cyan sea plains that open it are as vivid and politically neutral as the jade sea in Li Bai's elegy for Nakamaro and the blue-green sea in Wang Wei's farewell to him. The former poem is particularly reminiscent of Nakamaro's *waka*. Both possess a similar "outline" (*sama*) that moves from sea to mountains and past to present. Following a suggestion first made by Arthur Waley (1889–1966), many scholars believe Nakamaro had previously composed a *shi* for Li Bai that inspired both his *waka* and his friend's elegy.[66] However, the diary's familiarity with Li Bai's poetic biography, coupled with its propensity for producing *waka* from the closing couplets in quatrains, makes it at least as likely that Tsurayuki added the cyan seas in order to link Nakamaro's poem to Li Bai's. Like its other maritime *waka*, the diary's version of Nakamaro's verse adapts this continental counterpart by inverting the spatial relationships organizing it. Instead of sinking into the sea, the moon now rises from it, in the process transforming this celestial object from the representation of an absolute break between past and present in the quatrain into a celebration of temporal continuity in the *waka*. Perhaps this transformation also celebrates a suture of the recent rupture in mercantile relations that had previously supported the flow of poems enabling the rich intertextuality of *Tosa nikki*'s maritime *waka*. As we will see next, these connections between the poems of Li Bai and Nakamaro, together with the political context mentioned in the previous section, also inflect the ending to *Tosa nikki*'s account.

Translation and Difference

Both the intertextual links with Li Bai's quatrain and the allusion to diplomatic receptions obtaining in Nakamaro's cyan seas also shape the reception of his *waka* in *Tosa nikki*. By portraying his poetic recitation

---

65. On this latter characteristic, see Owen, *The Great Age of Chinese Poetry*, 48.
66. Waley, *Poetry and Career of Li Po*, 61; Kurokawa, "Abe no Nakamaro no uta," 994; Ogawa, "Mikasa no yama ni ideshi"; Tōda, "Aounabara furisake mireba," 46.

alongside the acts of transcription, commentary, and adaptation, Tsurayuki's diary produced the first detailed account of translation in Japan. Its metalinguistic scope and sophistication are perhaps only to be expected from a man whose *Kokinshū* preface had already provided an account of *waka*'s history, purposes, and stylistic characteristics. At the same time, Tsurayuki is possibly distancing himself from the diary's views by attributing its opinions to a flawed and fictional narrator in much the same manner as Murasaki Shikibu does when she has Genji defend fiction.

Regardless, it seems likely that one of the reasons why Tsurayuki's account of cultural and linguistic difference is so vivid is because it is grounded in his own historical experience. The passage in question employs simple language to avoid an entirely abstract discussion for an audience who had little reason to engage in translation themselves. One way this is achieved is through repeated deixis that maps cultural and political difference spatially as here/there, this land/that land, and our land/the continent while Nakamaro's poem moves from recitation to inscription and then explication.

> It occurred to him that the people of that land would probably not be able to understand this poem just by hearing it. He nonetheless wrote down an outline of its contents in the letters used by all men everywhere and explained their full import to an interpreter who could convey our language. On account of this, they must have been able to hear what was in his heart, for it is said that they were moved beyond all expectation. Although the words of the continent differ from those of this land, the hearts of people must surely be the same, for the moon's light shines the same everywhere. (TN 34, 1/20)

Because translation has played a central role in Japanese literary history, this final portion of the Nakamaro anecdote is the only passage in the diary other than its prologue that has attracted sustained commentary in Anglophone scholarship.[67] The first of these analyses, by Tomiko Yoda, argues that the transcription of Nakamaro's *waka* is designed to convey its formal structures, whereas the oral translation that follows is intended to convey the entirety of its content.[68] This reading makes a convincing

---

67. Accounts of the role translation has played in developing modern Japanese literature include Levy, *Sirens of the Western Shore*; and Saito, *Kanbunmyaku*.
68. Yoda, *Gender and National Literature*, 93.

case for the ability of writing to preserve poetic parallelisms that might be obscured in speech, something that would also be true of the outline (*sama*) revealing binary structure in the *kara uta* lyrics. As we saw in the previous section, such binaries also reveal similarities between the physical and temporal configurations structuring both Nakamaro's *waka* and Li Bai's *jueju*.

A subsequent reading of the same passage by Atsuko Sakaki inaugurates her sweeping history of the role an imagined China played in defining Japan. Within this context, Sakaki views the diary's depiction of Nakamaro as an assertion of Japanese bilingualism's superiority to its more culturally impoverished monolingual Chinese counterpart.[69] Her description of Nakamaro as a teacher in this scene is particularly noteworthy in light of the patronizing manner in which his achievements as a student of Sinitic culture were praised in the farewell poems of his Tang peers. The ability to move between languages that enables this pedagogical authority, like translation, is a process of negotiation between cultures that entails "a politics as well as a poetics, an ethics as well as an aesthetics," as the comparative literature scholar Bella Brodzki has put it.[70] It is particularly telling in this regard that their identification with a monolingual empire led Nakamaro's Tang peers to view the need for multiple interpreters as a sign of barbarism. Such implications are absent from *Tosa nikki*, which views translation as neutral means for conducting relations among adjacent states within the multilingual and multipolar configuration of East Asia that arose after the collapse of the Tang empire.

Whereas Sakaki and Yoda place Nakamaro's story at the beginning of broad historical accounts that take the Heian period as their point of departure, a later analysis of this passage by David Lurie situates it at the end of the process through which Japanese writing systems initially developed. In this context, Nakamaro's *waka* confirms the long-standing capacity for Sinographs to simultaneously represent multiple languages through the operation of *kundoku* reading strategies.[71] Lurie's characterization of Japanese Sinographs as an inherently multilingual written medium has led Ross King to argue that their plasticity as a read sign made

---

69. Sakaki, *Obsessions with the Sino-Japanese Polarity*, 24.
70. Brodzki, *Can These Bones Live?*, 2.
71. Lurie, *Realms of Literacy*, 328.

the East Asian cosmopolis distinct from its peers in the premodern world.[72] As we saw in the case of "Morokoshi," such plasticity offered a flexible means for articulating and negotiating relations among different political, linguistic, and cultural groups within this cosmopolis, making Sinographs a particularly effective mechanism for calibrating the potentially conflicting demands of different parties within a multipolar region. The hybrid diction and diplomatic spatial ambiguities of his poetry would have made Nakamaro an especially fitting means for representing such multilingual malleability.

Additional insights can be gleaned from this passage by considering the interpreter's role within it. Because the need for such a person runs counter to the commonly held assumption (both now and in his own time) that Nakamaro was fully proficient in spoken and written Sinitic, the blatant ahistoricity entailed by their appearance in this passage precludes a literal reading. Rather, the interpreter's presence is both justified and necessary if we regard the scene as a historical allegory for Tsurayuki's own experience composing *shi* with foreign envoys in 942. Like the version of Nakamaro portrayed in *Tosa nikki*, its author would have needed a translator to communicate with his foreign guests even if they were capable of comprehending his written poems.[73] Although it is of course possible that Tsurayuki envisaged this exchange before enacting it, the specificity of *Tosa nikki*'s depiction suggests the reverse is more likely. Perhaps he even discussed *waka* at the diplomatic banquet hosting continental envoys in the same manner as Nakamaro does in the diary. Although it is often assumed that *Tosa nikki* was completed immediately after its author had returned to the capital, this connection would imply he was in fact still revising it within his final four years, making the historical world it represents that much broader and richer as a result.

The interpreter's presence in this account indicates that the translation of his poem does not end with Nakamaro's own inscription but is rather continued over into and supplemented by another's speech. Because the diarist does not reproduce either Nakamaro's inscription or a transcription of the interpreter's words, we are forced to guess what form they

---

72. King, "Ditching 'Diglossia,'" 4–6.
73. Kanda, *Ki no Tsurayuki*, 236. On the role played by these interpreters in conducting diplomacy, see Duthie, *Man'yōshū and the Imperial Imagination*, 206–9.

took.[74] One way of identifying the manner in which Nakamaro's textual translation might have differed from its oral interpretation is through a comparison of the *waka* with the closing couplet from Li Bai's elegy. *Tosa nikki*'s deliberate attempt to adapt the elegy in its version of Nakamaro's poem makes their differences apposite indicators of the ways in which *waka* diverged from Literary Sinitic poetry. On the one hand, as we have seen, the outline (*sama*) of a poem could be transferred from one language to the other. On the other hand, certain aspects of this same *sama* in Nakamaro's *waka* were not transparent in Literary Sinitic, and would therefore have represented such a fundamental challenge to foreign readers that an oral commentary in their spoken language would be needed in order to convey the poem's full import to them.

The first of these challenges becomes evident when we compare the mountain in Nakamaro's *waka* to the one in Li Bai's *jueju*. Mount Cangwu was a classical topos instantly recognizable throughout East Asia as the resting place of the legendary sage rulers Yao and Shun. These mythical associations made it synonymous with the death of royalty and travelers alike.[75] In the passage from his preface to *Shinsen waka* cited in chapter 1, Tsurayuki himself marks the passing of Uda and Daigo by alluding to this mythological topos when he refers to the nearby Xiang River, where Shun's wives were said to have drowned themselves after his death. By contrast, Mount Mikasa and Kasuga were both located outside the poetic geography of *shi*. Even the toponymic status of Kasuga within Nakamaro's inscription of his poem could not have been evident to foreign readers, who would most likely have taken the Sinographs 春日 to be a literal reference to the sun in springtime rather than the name of a place. It is at least as unlikely that such readers would have grasped Mount Mikasa's dual significance as the site of the deity protecting overseas missions and the poet's clan shrine, incantatory aspects of his poem that Nakamaro alludes to in the speech introducing it. By requiring an interpreter to supplement the *waka*'s transcription with additional contextual information, *Tosa nikki* indicates that such historical and cultural

---

74. Hagitani offers the following as a potential inscription of Nakamaro's poem: 青海原 / 振放見 / 春日之 / 三笠山乎 / 月出哉 (TNZ 231).

75. Wang, *Spatial Imaginaries in Mid-Tang China*, 210–11.

aspects of the poem's landscape cannot be conveyed through Sinographs alone.

In addition to the scene's numinous qualities, the speaker's subjective relationship to it is not automatically rendered transparent through Sinographs. The auxiliary verb *ki* and exclamatory final particles *kamo* that conclude the *waka* mark the current recollection of an event that Nakamaro had personally experienced, thereby producing a parallel between past and present moons in the final measure. Although tense is provided implicitly by negating the moon in Li Bai's couplet, the affirmation of its existence in Nakamaro's poem would not in itself automatically imply a particular tense. Even if a grammatical marker such as 嘗 (in the past) was employed in the Sinographic rendering of this *waka*, its use would preclude the doubled vision of a moon simultaneously rising in the present within the original poem. The possibility that a foreign audience might not have grasped this dual tense is indirectly confirmed by Waley's own translation, which represents Nakamaro's vision of the moon rising over Kasuga as something he is speculating about in the present moment rather than something he is recalling from memory.[76]

The need for someone who can explain Nakamaro's *waka* to an audience lacking the contextual knowledge of language, religion, and history required to understand it thus marks an absolute form of cultural difference that resists cosmopolitanism. As Lawrence Venuti has noted, representing the translator as a visible presence foregrounds the "foreignness" of a text, one that cannot be fully domesticated by the target culture into forms that are transparent and equivalent.[77] The interpreter's presence in this anecdote further serves as an important reminder that translation is also a process involving the movement of people. As Michael Cronin has observed, "The translating agent like the traveler straddles the borderline between the cultures."[78] Nakamaro's anonymous interpreter likewise reflects the concrete historical conditions that enabled people to move among languages, cultures, and political affiliations within

---

76. "Across the fields of Heaven / Casting my gaze I wonder / Whether over the hills of Mikasa also, / that is by Kasuga, / The moon has risen." (Waley, *Poetry and Career of Li Po*, 61).
77. Venuti, *The Translator's Invisibility*, 1–2.
78. Cronin, *Across the Lines*, 2.

a multipolar Northeast Asia. In addition to the professional translator Tsurayuki employed, Nakamaro's interpreter could represent a Japanese monk who had lived abroad, an immigrant fleeing unrest in the former territories of Parhae, or a multilingual merchant. As a third-party intermediary, the interpreter might also represent the roles played by continental intermediaries in transmitting *shi* by Nakamaro and Tang poets to Japan.

Although this anecdote stresses distinct aspects of *waka* that are lost in translation, it also demonstrates the ease with which their imagery can be appropriated and transformed by people of different times, places, and languages. In this regard, Nakamaro's tale resembles modern accounts of translation that regard it as a creative act involving recontextualization, rearrangement, and supplementation rather than simply a literal word-for-word substitution.[79] These multiple linguistic mediations can all be seen in *Tosa nikki*'s treatment of Nakamaro's *waka*. It is initially presented in the diary with the wording altered to represent Tsurayuki's own experience; its contents are then rearranged through transposition into the syntax of Literary Sinitic when it is inscribed; this text is then supplemented by an extended explanation of its significance; and its words are then repurposed in a *waka* composed by another passenger whose recollection of the same story leads them to eschew toponyms in order to portray a seascape bridging both poets' experiences in different times and places.

And then, thinking on that past in the present moment, someone composed this verse:

miyako nite	In the capital city,
yama no ha ni mishi	at the mountain's rim I saw
tsuki naredo	this moon, though now
nami yori idete	it rises from waves
nami ni koso ire	and sinks into waves!
(TN 35, 1/20)	

Like Nakamaro's *waka*, this one moves from the speaker's memory of a mountaintop moon to the present vision of a maritime one. Unlike his

---

79. Bassnett, *Translation Studies*, 36–37.

poem, however, the absence of toponyms in this anonymous *waka* would have also made a Sinographic version fully transparent, thereby obviating the need for an interpreter. In this sense, the new adaptation represents a return from Nakamaro's poem to the more cosmopolitan register of Li Bai's elegy. Its significance is reshaped yet again when, as we saw in chapter 1, this poem's *Gosenshū* headnote establishes other equivalences between past and present by portraying its author Tsurayuki gazing out to sea in the same manner as Nakamaro. Moreover, the same *waka* provides yet another example of translation in this broad sense when it reappears in *Kokin waka rokujō* with "sea" (*umi*) instead of "waves" (*nami*).

By enfolding the localized landscape in Nakamaro's poem within a larger maritime space, *Tosa nikki* also provides a powerfully succinct illustration of the symbiotic relationship between cosmopolitan and vernacular forms of language common to premodern times. Perhaps the most dramatic demonstration of this symbiosis can be seen in the diary's own inscription. Although often celebrated as a pioneering attempt to convey the sounds of speech in prose by relying on *kana* script, *Tosa nikki* also employs thirty-four Sinographs in either a phonographic or logographic capacity on forty-one different occasions. Their rarity within a sea of roughly 2,500 *kana* makes the use of these Sinographs appear all the more motivated. It is therefore significant that they are only used once for a proper noun. When "Uda" is written with the compound 宇多 on 1/9, it signifies the name of the place the party passes by and the posthumous designation of a sovereign. It also echoes the compound 宇陀 (*uta*) used as *hentaigana* (variant *kana*) to phonetically represent the most common word designating *waka*.

By folding two categories of proper noun and a general term into this one Sinographic compound, *Tosa nikki* turns it into a metalinguistic comment on the connections obtaining among politics, place, and poetics in its vision of vernacularism. These three elements are also connected in Pollock's account of the South Asian regional language of Kannada through which he initially formulated the idea of a cosmopolitan vernacular. Kannada first appeared as a literary language in panegyric court poetry that drew on aesthetic critical discourses originating in a transregional Sanskrit poetics of kingship, while also articulating the concept of a vernacular alternative by appealing to a sense of local place as "that which does not travel" (*desi*) within the larger cosmopolis.⁸⁰ These same connections among poetry, politics, and place that Pollock identifies in Kannada texts also obtain in Nakamaro's *waka*. Mount Mikasa becomes a place that "does not travel" due to its numinous and ritual qualities. By establishing the ritual boundaries of the realm through the observances held there to see off diplomatic envoys, the mountain also articulates a court-centered social order whose presence in a vernacular poem creates a form of cultural identity that is simultaneously geographical, political, and aesthetic. But Nakamaro's tale also expands on this succinct formulation of vernacular identity by placing the localized landscape that represents it within the directionless expanse of a moonlit maritime space whose generic characteristics could be readily expressed in Sinographs, and whose outline (*sama*) could be conveyed in both *jueju* and *waka*.

The significant role translation plays in mediating between the cosmopolitan and vernacular registers represented by this larger landscape in Nakamaro's tale also reflects its central place in creating an East Asian cosmopolis. Writing a few years before Pollock, Victor Mair also posited *desi* as a concept that contributed to the development of East Asian vernaculars. At the same time, he identified its source in the Buddhist acceptance of transcription, transliteration, and translation as means for conveying religious doctrine.⁸¹ Because Buddhism rejected the idea of an authoritative scriptural language, it embraced these technologies, making translation an activity that could be associated with proselytizing missionaries instead of barbarian supplicants. Like its approach to landscape, in other words, the religion adopted a neutral perspective on language that rejected political hierarchies and cultural particularities.

Given the moon's long-standing associations with Buddhism in East Asian poetry, therefore, it is perhaps not coincidental that it plays a central role in mediating between times, languages, and landscapes in this anecdote. Lunar imagery appears within each of the multiple narrative frames that make this the single most complex entry within the diary: the diarist's opening description of that day's scene, the poem-telling triggered by the sight of it, the poem at that anecdote's core, the diarist's commentary that the anecdote inspires, and, finally, the *waka* resulting

---

80. Pollock, "The Cosmopolitan Vernacular," 18–19.
81. Mair, "Buddhism and the Rise of the Written Vernacular," 724–28.

from another individual's recollection of that same anecdote. The moon's recurring appearance in this narrative thus aptly conveys language's infinite capacity for expansion and recontextualization through a common visual experience shared among peoples of different times and places. The diarist's description of a moon that looks the same in the words of any land also suggests Sinographs' capacity to accommodate multiple languages through a single set of visual signs that could simultaneously offer a means of transcription and translation. Moonlight thus represents a cosmopolitan language that extends beyond the bounds of a particular time or place in much the same manner as *Tosa nikki*'s cyan seas, creating a fluid poetic space fostered by the circulation of texts carried by the merchant traders, diplomatic envoys, and Buddhist priests who crossed its liquid landscapes. It is in this movement between spaces and languages that the anecdote acquires metalinguistic dimensions as a comment on vernacular Japanese poetry's place within a larger world by drawing on the singularly hybrid language that Nakamaro's poetic legacy provided.

Conclusion

In choosing to represent Japan's place within a larger world through Nakamaro, *Tosa nikki* was able to draw on the rich textual legacy of an individual whose life embodied linguistic, cultural, and political forms of hybrid identity expressed poetically in the creation of liminal spaces blending the vocabulary of *waka* with that of *shi*. This rhetorical strategy was also a diplomatic one designed to accommodate the Sinocentric discourse surrounding him. Even though the Tang empire welcomed the historical Nakamaro into the heart of its cultural and political life, his colleagues proved incapable of admitting Japan within even the outermost mythical borders of the world they envisaged in poetry. These discursive boundaries are most powerfully demonstrated at their limits through the spatially ambiguous language Nakamaro resorts to in signaling his dual political identity, and the equally ambiguous pun Wang Wei relies on to reference Japanese place names and poetry in seeming appreciation of his friend's maneuvers. When both poems reappear in ninth-century Japan, their hybrid rhetoric would also facilitate Nakamaro's association with a *waka* poem that met the court's ritual needs for ensuring the safe passage of its diplomatic envoys to the continent. Both these ritual and rhetorical aspects ensured a prominent place for Nakamaro's *waka* within the *Kokinshū*, where later narrative accretions would also mark a parallel shift from diplomacy to commerce as the chief means for establishing connections with the outside world.

When the same *waka* reappears in *Tosa nikki* a few decades later, Tsurayuki adapts it to represent a new vision of cosmopolitanism inspired by his involvement in an attempt to reestablish ties with a continent whose political contours were even more volatile than in Nakamaro's lifetime. Consequently, the cyan seas he now gazed across represented a more complex and fluid world than the fixed unipolar framework in which his Tang colleagues had grounded their *shi*. In addition to reflecting new political realities in the aftermath of the Tang empire's disintegration, these cyan seas turn Nakamaro's poem into an adaptation of Li Bai's elegy, thereby demonstrating an extraordinarily erudite appreciation of Tang poetry's biographical and rhetorical contexts shared with other *waka* depicting maritime spaces in the diary. This larger cosmopolitan space also represents the historical conditions that produced it through diplomatic and commercial activities in the region that facilitated the introduction of *shi* by such figures as Nakamaro, Li Bai, Bai Juyi, and Jia Dao into Japan. Similarities between the poems of Nakamaro and Li Bai also serve to accentuate their differences when the diary draws on Tsurayuki's own experience hosting foreign diplomats to portray an interpreter who explains the full significance of Nakamaro's *waka* to literate foreigners. Through the different modes of translation represented in this anecdote, cosmopolitanism becomes the context in which a vernacular poetic and political identity takes shape in the same manner as the sea surrounds and defines the mountain in Nakamaro's poem.

Later depictions of Nakamaro would never approach this scope and sophistication. Even though the narrative appended to his *Kokinshū* poem in the eleventh century appears to draw on *Tosa nikki*, the intricacies of translation at the core of his depiction in the diary are conspicuously absent. When Nakamaro next appears in anecdotal *setsuwa* literature, the capacity to imagine his participation in a larger cosmopolitan community had shrunk still more. In *Konjaku*, for example, he addresses his poem to Japan instead of engaging in dialogue with his well-wishers. The extensive historical documentation of his life also appears to have disappeared at this time, judging from the anecdote's concluding assertion that his *waka* was handed down by people who heard it from Nakamaro after his return.[82] Even its banquet setting is subsequently stripped away when the poem reappears in the twelfth-century *Kohon setsuwa shū* (A Collection of Anecdotes from Old Books) and the fourteenth-century *Yotsugi monogatari* (Tales of Successive Reigns), both of which depict Nakamaro reciting it to himself in lonely exile.[83] The steadily shrinking stage on which Nakamaro is depicted after *Tosa nikki* may appear inevitable in hindsight, insofar as tenth-century Japan has often been treated as a decisive turn away from the continent. Yet the fact that intercultural connections are being depicted in *Tosa nikki* at a time when they were endangered suggests how much they continued to matter. It was precisely these stresses, combined with *Tosa nikki*'s overall self-reflexivity and the poetic legacy of Nakamaro, that enabled the unprecedented sophistication and ambition with which the diary articulates a uniquely cosmopolitan vision of the relations among politics, language, and culture.

82. *Konjaku monogatari shū* story 24:44, SNKBZ 37:357–58. Nakamaro's biography in *Xin Tangshu* (New Tang History, 1060) also claims he returned to Japan (Araki, "Abe no Nakamaro kichō densetsu no yukue," 51–58).

83. *Kohon setsuwa shū* story 45, SNKBT 42:450; *Yotsugi monogatari* story 39. For later pictorializations of Nakamaro reciting his poem, see Mostow, *Pictures of the Heart*, 163–64.

EPILOGUE

This book has focused on the historical context in which *Tosa nikki* was written in order to better understand how and why it affords so many unique insights into Heian culture by simultaneously evoking and displacing the world familiar to its aristocratic readers. I would like to end, however, by suggesting how these remarkable features allow us to place the diary within two broader intertwining histories. The first and more immediate of these directly links it to the vernacular prose written by Heian court women that begins to appear soon afterward. The same innovative qualities that made it a potential source of inspiration for these writers also makes it possible to put *Tosa nikki* within a second, much broader history of world literature, where its brief fictional form has a strong claim to being the earliest novella.

We can begin tracing the first of these two histories by returning to the phrase "Tsurayuki's *Tosa Diary*" initially used to describe *Tosa nikki*. In addition to its antiquity, I have employed this phrase in the subtitle of my study because it highlights the uniquely unmediated relationship between author and text around which my approach has taken shape. At the same time, however, this phrase can be read in two other ways that mark even more pronounced degrees of intimacy and estrangement between its contents and author. In one rendering, it indicates that he is the actual subject of the diary, a view espoused by many readers who believe the female narrator is merely a vehicle for conveying his personal experiences and emotions. At the other extreme, it could simply indicate he copied a text authored by someone else. This last reading offers a point of departure for considering some alternate histories in which we might situate the diary.

My attempts to contextualize *Tosa nikki* have proceeded from the assumption that its authorship can be attributed to an identifiable historical individual. Even the remarkably strong basis we have for making such an assertion in this case, however, ultimately amounts to circumstantial evidence. In addition to the empirical hurdles posed by a manuscript culture that only affords access to Heian texts through later copies and citations, and that did not consistently distinguish between the roles of author and calligrapher, the challenges posed to identifying any text as the creation of a single person become even more acute in the case of poems and fictional narratives that were frequently altered by later readers. We should therefore not be entirely surprised to find Masaari asserting in the thirteenth century that *Tosa nikki* was originally written by a woman, nor automatically discount the possibility that this view was shared by Tameie and others interested in such texts. Regardless of its ultimate veracity, this belief formed one strand of the diary's reception history, and thus its possible impact on other texts, in ways that merit consideration.

There are in fact hints contained within the writings of earlier Heian women suggesting that they not only shared Masaari's belief in the diary's female authorship but also viewed it as a source of inspiration. The strongest such intimation is found in *Sarashina nikki*, a diary that suggests Masaari's view of women's memoirs as a distinct genre was already nascent less than a century after *Tosa nikki* was written. Its author, Sugawara no Takasue no Musume (b. 1008), seems to have perceived herself as belonging to a lineage of female writers through her connections to three of the most celebrated women authors in the Heian period. Her mother was a half-sister of *Kagerō nikki*'s author, another female relative served the daughter of Sei Shōnagon's mistress, and her stepmother's uncle was married to a daughter of Murasaki Shikibu.[1] By placing her diary at the end of his list, Masaari appears to reflect its author's own view of *Sarashina nikki* as the culmination of this textual genealogy. According to the same logic, *Tosa nikki*'s position at the beginning of his list sug-

---

1. Arntzen and Itō, *The Sarashina Diary*, 10–11; also 44 and 61–66 on its intertextual links with *Makura no sōshi*, *Kagerō nikki*, and *Murasaki Shikibu nikki*.

gests they both viewed the diary as its ancestral matrix. *Sarashina nikki* appears to intimate as much itself by beginning with a return journey to the capital from a provincial posting, and by choosing a title that, unlike that of any other Heian women's memoir, begins with a toponym.

This estimation of *Tosa nikki*'s role in inaugurating a female literary tradition is further confirmed by the traces of its influence we can detect in the works of the other women writers affiliated with Sugawara no Takasue no Musume, including the authors of the other two memoirs Masaari lists. The distinctively self-reflexive prologue with which *Kagerō nikki* begins may have drawn inspiration from its opening passage. Murasaki Shikibu's diary bears an even closer resemblance to *Tosa nikki* in its narrator's preference for describing external events, its judgments of people, and the attention it pays to the disbursement of gifts. The other outstanding female author to whom Sugawara no Takasue no Musume was connected, Sei Shōnagon, may have also been influenced by the diary. Despite possessing structures that are diametrically opposed, with one adhering to a strict linear narrative and the other rejecting any overarching structure whatsoever, both *Tosa nikki* and *Makura no sōshi* depict popular songs and other aspects of Heian life ignored in vernacular works. Insofar as many scholars view all of these texts as a complex blend of fact and fiction, they might have been inspired by *Tosa nikki* in this regard as well.[2] These connections offer us a means to bypass our modern ambivalence over the ambiguous place Tsurayuki's diary occupies within a group of texts that are valued as much for being all-too-rare examples of premodern female authorship as they are for their stylistic achievements. Although our awareness of the diary's masculine authorship may make it difficult to escape the feeling that *Tosa nikki* is an inherently unconvincing and insincere attempt at representing a female subject, Heian women writers who viewed it as genuine could find inspiration in its innovations for their own experimental forays into new narrative forms.

Extending this line of enquiry to include *Tosa nikki*'s possible influence on *Genji* raises the stakes significantly due to the global historical preeminence often accorded the latter text as the world's first novel. Such claims are arguably made even more powerful by what Michael Emmerich

---

2. For one influential articulation of this view, see Kimura, "Nikki bungaku no hōhō," 13.

identifies as the relative weight given to critical discourses about *Genji* in comparison to actual engagements with its text.[3] Perhaps for the same reason, its critics have articulated the criteria for making this assertion with at least as much clarity as its proponents. The most sustained example is offered by Masao Miyoshi (1928–2009), who stated: "I believe that *Genji* is not at all a novel, a modern narrative form that weaves its incidents into a plot and presents autonomous and discrete characters that supposedly refer to imagined individualities. The Aristotelian concept of the beginning, middle and end hardly applies to *Genji*, nor does the clarity of modern ironic vision."[4] The last of these characteristics is in fact evident in what Amanda Stinchecum identifies as "an increasing refinement in the uses of aesthetic difference and irony" within *Genji*'s final chapters.[5] Irony also results from the undermining of her protagonists that Virginia Woolf (1882–1941) produces by blurring individual voices in the psychological novels *Mrs. Dalloway* (1925) and *To the Lighthouse* (1927), works that Miyoshi considered the closest English-language equivalents to *Genji*'s fluid narrative perspective. In addition to the formal features and psychological content shared by their works, Valerie Henitiuk has noted that both writers also appropriated masculine forms of knowledge in order to explore the "truth" of fiction.[6]

Although *Tosa nikki* appears at first sight to have little in common with *Genji*'s sprawling narrative, it in fact anticipates many of the features identified above. The use of masculine modes of knowledge to depict historical truths in fiction that Henitiuk mentions can be seen in the imaginary narrator's appropriation of a masculine genre in order to portray otherwise invisible social realities such as commerce and popular culture. The lack of clearly delineated characters Miyoshi stresses also characterizes the diary's longer sentences. Like free indirect discourse in Woolf's novels, these ambiguities also produce ironies, such as when the subject of desires becomes confused with their object in the complex interplay of thoughts and speech that accompany the consumption of sweetfish. *Tosa nikki* is unique, however, in rendering the writer's ironic

---

3. Emmerich, *The Tale of Genji*, 230–31.
4. Miyoshi, "Translation as Interpretation," 300.
5. Stinchecum, "Who Tells the Tale?," 403.
6. Henitiuk, "Going to Bed with Arthur Waley," 43–44.

stance explicit through the deliberate scribal choices preserved in medieval manuscripts. In addition to the various Sinographs discussed in previous chapters, scholars have identified many others that are clearly intended to convey irony. A poignant reminder of the dead girl, for example, is conveyed by writing the first calendrical Day of the Rat as 子日 (*The Youngest Day of the Rat*) on 1/29, while the chronic nature of the ex-governor's ailments is underscored by using the Sinographs 病者 (*The Ailing*) to establish a pointed contrast with the temporary indisposition of another passenger on 2/7.

This singular focus on the writer and the act of inscription distinguishes *Tosa nikki*'s resemblance to the novel from that of *Genji*. The abovementioned graphological nuances, for example, suggest the diary was meant to be savored through silent readings in order to fully appreciate its scribal choices. This difference in emphasis can also be seen in the psychological complexities it possesses. One major aspect of the novel that critics often identify in *Genji* is the nuanced interiority it bestows on its characters by endowing them with conflicting desires, or motives that remain semi-opaque to themselves and others. By contrast, it is the narrator in *Tosa nikki* who displays such complexities in a sustained manner through her wordy denials, inconsistent treatment of characters, willful ignorance, and hesitation to ascribe opinions to either herself or others. These devices make her a fully fleshed character in her own right, complete with a richly varied psyche whose depths are further conveyed by hinting to the reader that they are only being partially articulated in her discourse. In addition to making the diarist a relatively less transparent narrator than her counterpart(s) in *Genji*, the complications these features introduce into the epistemological underpinnings of her narrative also make it more sophisticated in a metafictional sense. All these self-reflexive gestures to writer and writing are highlighted from the very start by opening the diary with a prologue that indicates it is the doubly parodic product of a man writing like a woman writing like a man.

The historical narrative suggested by these differences, in which the shorter parodic work of fiction represented by *Tosa nikki* influenced the lengthier sober work of fiction represented by *Genji*, echoes the developmental model Bakhtin posited for Western literature. As we have seen, many stylistic aspects of medieval European parody that the Russian critic famously identified as precursors to the novel are also evident in *Tosa nikki*: its creative combination of elements that are usually particular to distinct genres (such as autobiographical diaries and biographical tales), its eclectic assemblage of different spoken sociolects, its obsession with consumption, and its interest in non-elite people and practices. Such historical equivalences also inevitably entail larger political implications, however. As Reginald Jackson points out, *Genji*'s designation as a novel can imply a cultural hierarchy privileging the West and excluding any textual aspects that resist assimilation.[7] At the same time, I would argue, such comparisons can decenter a master narrative whose teleological endpoint in the modern West is naturalized by projecting its self-identical origins onto the past. Insofar as the above-mentioned characteristics in *Tosa nikki* both prefigure and in some regards surpass their novelistic counterparts in *Genji*, the diary can deepen and extend its successor's displacement of Eurocentric or presentist accounts of world literature. For this reason, the same novelty, psychological complexity, and eclecticism that put the diary on a par with *Genji* also merit considering its role in pioneering another related genre that is ostensibly the product of Western literature. That is to say, if we can call *Genji* the world's first novel, we can also refer to *Tosa nikki* as its first novella.

Although their relative length provides the most obvious basis for respectively likening *Genji* and *Tosa nikki* to novel and novella, their distinctive formal characteristics are not solely due to this material difference. *Genji*'s sprawling narrative results from a cosmology with no connection to Aristotle as much as from the lack of strict conventions that might place limits on its length. The diary's contained linear structure, on the other hand, rejects the expandable episodic form favored by most Heian forms of vernacular prose fiction. Compared to its peers, this distinctive aspect of *Tosa nikki* bears a much closer resemblance to classical formulations of the novella in nineteenth-century German literary criticism, which defined it as a prose narrative whose brevity led it to focus on a single character, event, or situation. Thus, in contrast to the comparative formlessness of novels, the novella's monolinear plot tends to focus on an "extreme situation" in the words of the literary critic György Lukács.[8] In nineteenth-century German novellas, these conditions are

---

7. Jackson, *A Proximate Remove*, 185.
8. Lukács, *Solzhenitsyn*, 8.

often enabled spatially through a setting that is removed from the urban centers their readers were most likely to identify with.[9] Such characteristics also distinguish *Tosa nikki*, insofar as its focus on a return voyage represents a single self-contained set of circumstances far removed from the familiar parameters of its aristocratic readers' lives in the capital.

Other characteristics of the novella later critics have identified suggest additional points of intersection. *Tosa nikki*'s liminal position between *nikki* and *monogatari*, for example, resonates with more recent descriptions of the novella as a genre defined by its relations with others, a view most pithily expressed in its common shorthand definition as a narrative that is longer than a short story but shorter than a novel.[10] Less tangibly, but perhaps more tellingly, the diminutive and feminine associations shared between *Tosa nikki* and the novella have led to similar treatments in modern literary criticism. Just as scholars of Japanese literature have tended to treat the longer versions of memoir literature with greater weight and at greater length, so too have scholars of Western literature typically lavished much more critical attention on the novel.

Combined with these formal similarities, the critical role ascribed to the novella in histories of Western prose fiction places *Tosa nikki* in a uniquely pivotal position from which to reconfigure conventional accounts of world literature. It was the integration of their short stories into episodes populated by a recurring cast of characters that drove the initial development of novels from novellas.[11] The rejection of established genre conventions in both forms of prose fiction that enabled this relationship is traditionally traced to the fourteenth-century *Decameron*, a collection of brief fictional narratives whose distinguishing characteristics include novelty, verbal wit, socially diverse characters, a preference for female narrators, and the self-conscious narrative framing of its content.[12] As we have seen, all these features also characterize *Tosa nikki*. We could also add to this list the lingering threat posed by the Black Plague, which pervades the *Decameron*'s entire story cycle with the same menacing atmosphere provided by the dead girl in the diary.

9. Gailus, "Form and Chance," 774.
10. Fuchs, "Novella," 399–400.
11. Good, "Notes on the Novella," 197–209.
12. Allaire, *The Italian Novella*, 1–13.

Like parody and satire, however, the novella's history in Asia is coterminous with modernity and its immediate antecedents.[13] In the case of Japan, for example, Richard Lane compared Saikaku's short stories with the *Decameron*'s novellas due to their shared interest in money, sexuality, urbanism, and poetic prose.[14] Because these same elements are also present in *Tosa nikki*, its claim to being the world's earliest novella profoundly realigns Japanese literary histories ascribing unprecedented forms of representation to the early modern period just as much as it calls into question the larger history of an ostensibly modern Western genre that currently begins in Italy four centuries after Tsurayuki's *Tosa Diary* was written. Taken as a whole, the wide range of characteristics that appear together in such detail and subtle complexity at such an early date within this remarkable piece of prose fiction provides a powerful argument for recognizing *Tosa nikki*'s singular place in the history of literature writ large.

---

13. Examples of this approach in an Asian context include Allen, "The Novella in Arabic"; and Wang, *Ming Erotic Novellas*.

14. Lane, "Saikaku and Boccaccio," 8–19.

APPENDIX I

Tosa nikki *Translation and Text*

Italics in the following translation mark allusions to lines from poems and to Sinographs, with the latter also capitalized. Place names whose discursive nature is highlighted by the diarist are rendered literally and in quotes. The accompanying Japanese text reproduces the original mix of *kana* and Sinographs in the Seikeisho'oku-bon, complete with orthographical anomalies, along with the punctuation and diacritics that Hagitani supplies in *Tosa nikki zenchūshaku*. In a few cases, quotations have been altered to reflect my own demarcations of dialogue.

I am attempting this out of curiosity about what it would be like for a woman to try her hand at keeping one of those so-called *Daily Journals* I hear men keep. One year, at around eight in the evening one day past the twentieth of the final month, we set out from the gate of the governor's mansion to prepare for our journey home. I will scrawl down a few jottings regarding that affair on what I have to hand. Someone who, having spent four or five years as a provincial governor, completed the usual affairs associated with his post, received official clearance to return after undergoing an audit and such, set out from the governor's residence, and crossed over to the place where the boat would be boarded. This person and that, both ones familiar and unfamiliar, came to make their goodbyes. Those with whom he had had extensive intercourse over the past few years were especially loath to leave, and while they made a fuss all *Day* over those departing, night fell.

をとこもすなる日記といふものを、をむなもしてみむとて、するなり。それのとしの、しはすの、はつかあまりひとひのひの、いぬのときにかどです。そのよし、いささかに、ものにかきつく。あるひと、あがたのよとせいつとせはてて、れいのことどもみなしをへて、げゆなどとりて、すむたちよりいでて、ふねにのるべきところへわたる。かれこれ、しるしらぬ、おくりす。としごろ、よくくらべつるひとびとなむ、わかれがたくおもひて、日しきりに、とかくしつつのゝしるうちに、よふけぬ。

&

On *The Twenty-Second* we raised *Prayers* in level tones for smooth seas at least as far as Izumi province. Though the path before us lies on the sea, Fujiwara no Tokizane bade farewell to our steeds at the traditional banquet seeing us off. High, middling, and low all had more than their share of saké. It made for a bizarre spectacle to see their riotously rotten behavior here by the brine of the sea.

廿二日に、いづみのくにまでと、たひらかに、願たつ。ふぢはらのときざね、ふなぢなれどむまのはなむけす。かみなかしもゑひあきて、いとあやしく、しほうみのほとりにてあざれあへり。

&

The Twenty-Third. A person named Yagi no Yasunori was here. He is not someone who serves in the governor's office, I gather, and yet he has given us such an impressive farewell banquet! Could this be a result of the governor's qualities? I am told that it is typical for people in the provinces to say, "Well, this is it," and then vanish from sight, yet here was someone with a heart coming over to us without concern for what others might think! My praise is not in any way based on the things we were given.

廿三日。やぎのやすのりといふひとあり。このひと、くににかならずしもいひつかふものにもあらざなり。これぞ、たたはしきやうにて、むまのはなむけしたる。かみからにやあらむ、くにびとのこころのつねとして、いまはとてみえざるを、こころあるものは、はぢずになむきける。これは、ものによりてほむるにしもあらず。

&

The Twenty-Fourth. The Lector graced us with his presence at a farewell banquet held in our honor. Everyone attending, high and low alike, right down to the young ones, became silly with drink. Even performers who don't know how to make the single stroke in *The Letter "One"* stamped out *The Letter "Ten"* in crisscross patterns with their feet as they swayed to the music.

廿四日。講師、むまのはなむけしにいでませり。ありとあるかみしも、わらはまでゑ
ひしれて、一文字をだにしらぬものしが、あしは十文字にふみてぞあそぶ。

The Twenty-Fifth. I heard that a letter of invitation came from the governor's residence. Having been summoned thus, we make our way all the way back there, where they say that what passed for entertainment continued all day and all night until dawn.

廿五日。かみのたちより、よびに、ふみもてきたなり。よばれていたりて、ひひとひよ
ひとよ、とかくあそぶやうにて、あけにけり。

The Twenty-Sixth. We are still at the governor's residence, whose master has made a great fuss, going so far as to give out things to even our *Men-at-Arms*. I gather continental verses were uttered in raised voices, and Yamato verses were also apparently uttered by host and guest. I cannot write down the continental verses here. As for the Yamato ones, I gather the governor who was hosting composed:

廿六日。なほかみのたちにて、あるじしののしりて、郎等までにものかづけたり。か
らうたこゑあげていひけり。やまとうた、あるじもまらうども、ことひともいひあへり
けり。からうたは、これにえかかず。やまとうた、あるじのかみのよめりける、

みやこいでて	Leaving the capital city
きみにあはむと	to be with you, milord,
こしものを	I came here, and yet
こしかひもなく	I came here to no avail
わかれぬるかな	as we now part ways!

And with that, they say, the former governor now going home composed:

となむありければ、かへるさきのかみのよめりける、

しろたへの	White as bleached hemp
なみぢをとほく	is the waveborne path
ゆきかひて	we cross in the distance.
われににべきは	In resemblance to me
たれならなくに	who else might there be?

I gather there were also ones by other people, but none of them seem worth mentioning. After saying this and that, I am told that both the previous governor and the current one descended to the courtyard, whose current master clasped hands with its former one and exchanged niceties in slurred speech before the one set out and the other went inside.

ことひとびとのもありけれど、さかしきもなかるべし。とかくいひて、さきのかみいまのも、もろともにおりて、いまのあるじもさきのも、てとりかはして、ゑひごとにこころよげなることして、いでいりにけり。

The Twenty-Seventh. We set out from the great port of Ōtsu heading for the bay entry of Urado. There was a girl born in *The Capital* who had suddenly died in this province. Not a single word was spoken about her amid the bustle of our hasty preparations for departure. Now that we are on our way back to *The Capital*, her loss leaves only grief and longing. It is beyond what some people can endure. During this time someone wrote out this poem:

廿七日。おほつよりうらどをさしてこぎいづ。かくあるうちに、京にてうまれたりしをむなご、くににてにはかにうせにしかば、このごろのいでたちいそぎをみれど、なにごともいはず。京へかへるに、をむなごのなきのみぞ、かなしびこふる。あるひとびともえたへず。このあひだに、あるひとのかきていだせるうた、

みやこへと	Towards the capital
おもふをものの	thoughts turn while
かなしきは	haunted by this grief
かへらぬひとの	for one not returning
あればなりけり	with us here and now!

And then at another time there was this:

また、あるときには、

あるものと	We think her with us,
わすれつつなほ	as we carry on forgetting
なきひとを	that person is no more,
いづらととふぞ	until asking where she is
かなしかりける	brings on this fresh grief!

I gather that was what was said. Meanwhile, the governor's maternal brothers and some other people caught up with us at a place called "Fawn Cape," bringing saké and such, and so we disembarked and seated ourselves on the pebble-strewn shore to exchange words of fond farewell. We couldn't help but whisper among ourselves that, out of all the people from the governor's mansion, it is those who had come here to put in a brief appearance who seem to truly have a heart. While words of regret at parting were being exchanged, those people all lined up their mouths and strained together to haul out a song on the seashore:

といひけるあひだに、かこのさきといふところに、かみのはらから、またことひとこれかれ、さけなにともておひきて、いそにおりゐて、わかれがたきことをいふ。かみのたちのひとびとのなかに、このきたるひとびとぞこころあるやうには、いはれほのめく。かくわかれがたくいひて、かのひとびとの、くちあみももろもちにて、このうみべにてになひいだせるうた、

をしとおもふ	Thinking to detain those
ひとやとまると	we hold dear in our hearts,
あしがもの	like ducks in the reeds
うちむれてこそ	flocking all together,
われはきにけれ	have we come here!

They stayed on after uttering this, I gather. Greatly moved, one of the people departing apparently composed:

といひてありければ、いといたくめでて、ゆくひとのよめりける、

さをさせど	Though poles be plunged,
そこひもしらぬ	fathomless is the bottom
わたつみの	of the mighty ocean god,
ふかきこころを	whose depths the hearts
きみにみるかな	of milords do show!

While all this was being said, the steersman had been guzzling down saké, oblivious to the poignancy of the moment. Suddenly desiring a speedy departure, he bellowed, "The tide is already in. The wind will soon blow." So we proceeded to get back on board. Meanwhile, people took every available opportunity to utter verses from the continent they deemed suitable to the occasion. Despite being in a western province, one person uttered a song from the eastern province of Kai. I actually heard someone say, "with such singing, dust is sure to scatter from the cabin roof and clouds waver in the sky!" Tonight we are staying in the bay entry of Urado. Fujiwara no Tokizane, Tachibana no Suehira, and others have caught up with us.

といふあひだに、かぢとりもののあはれもしらで、おのれしさけをくらひつれば、はやくいなむとて、「しほみちぬ。かぜもふきぬべし」とさわげば、ふねにのりなむとす。このをりに、あるひとびと、をりふしにつけて、からうたども、ときにつかはし

きいふ。またあるひと、にしくになれど、かひうたなどいふ。「かくうたふに、ふなや
かたのちりもちり、そらゆくくももただよひぬ」とぞいふなる。こよひうらどにとまる。
ふぢはらのときざね、たちばなのすゑひら、ことひとびとおひきたり。

The Twenty-Eighth. We set out from the bay entry of Urado in pursuit of the great harbor of Ōminato. Meanwhile, Yamaguchi no Chimine, the son of a previous governor, came on board bearing saké and side-dishes. We did nothing but drink and eat while the ship went onward.

廿八日。うらどよりこぎいでて、おほみなとをおふ。このあひだに、はやくのかみのこ、
やまぐちのちみね、さけよきものどももてきて、ふねにいれたり。ゆくゆくのみくふ。

The Twenty-Ninth. We have anchored at the great harbor of Ōminato. The provincial head doctor has gone to the trouble of bringing us the new year's tonic, along with other *Medicines* and saké to steep them in. It's as though he holds good will towards us.

廿九日。おほみなとにとまれり。くすしふりはへて、とうそ白散、さけくはへてもてき
たり。こころざしあるににたり。

New Year's Day. We are still anchored in the same place. Because the person who was in charge of the *Medicines* apparently propped them up against the cabin overnight, they blew out to sea when a howling wind whipped up, so we ended up not taking them. We are even without dried taro stems or rough-skinned kelp, nothing of that sort for the day's teeth-firming rite. Our present land lacks all such things. No one even thought to find them ahead of time. We simply sucked on the mouths of dried sweetfish pressed flat to our lips. "What feelings does it stir up in them to have people's lips sucking on theirs?" "I imagine they must be saying to one another such things as, 'I find all my thoughts turning toward the capital city today,' or, 'I wonder how it is for the heads of those dear mullet fellows stuck on *Sprigs* of holly tied to the festive straw ropes festooning the gates of tiny city tenements?'"

元日。なほおなじとまりなり。白散をあるもの、よのまとて、ふなやかたにさしはさめ
りければ、かぜにふきならさせて、うみにいれて、えのまずなりぬ。いもし、あらめ

も、はがためもなし。かうやうのものなきくになり。もとめしもおかず。ただ、おしあゆのくちをのみぞすふ。「このすふひとびとのくちを、おしあゆもしおもふやうあらむや。」「『けふはみやこのみぞおもひやらるる』『こへのかどのしりくべなはのなよしのかしら、ひひら木らいかにぞ』とぞいひあへなる」。

The Second. Still anchored in this great harbor of Ōminato. *The Lector* has sent over food and saké.

二日。なほおほみなとにとまれり。講師、ものさけおこせたり。

The Third. Still in the same place. Perhaps the wind and waves hope in their hearts for us to stay a while. The thought fills my heart with dread.

三日。おなじところなり。もし、かぜなみの「しばし」とをしむこころやあらむ。こころもとなし。

The Fourth. A gale blows, making it impossible to put our ship out to sea. Masatsura offered up saké and various delicacies to the former governor. We could hardly stand by and do nothing in response to such generosity, and so we returned the kindness with some trifle. We have nothing of worth for that purpose. Everything seemed fine on the surface, but it feels somehow as though we have lost face.

四日。かぜふけば、えいでたたず。まさつら、さけよきものたてまつれり。このかうやうにものもてくるひとに、なほしもえあらで、いささけわざせさす。ものもなし。にぎははしきやうなれど、まくるここちす。

The Fifth. Since the wind and waves don't let up, we are still in the same place. People came to see us one after the other in an endless stream.

五日。かぜなみやまねば、なほおなじところにあり。ひとびとたえずとぶらひにく。

The Sixth. Same as yesterday.

六日。きのふのごとし。

It is now *The Seventh* of the new year. We are in the same port. How it grates to think about the white steeds that were presented with new government posts at the palace today! The only white we could see was that of the waves. During this time, one long chest after another was sent from the home of a person living in a place named "Pond" which, though lacking handsome ornamental carp, include the crucian variety, as well as all manner of other things from rivers and sea. The young herbs remind us that today indeed is the day for plucking shoots in the capital. There was a poem as well. Here it is:

七日になりぬ。おなじみなとにあり。けふは、あをむまをおもへどかひなし。ただ、なみのしろきのみぞみゆる。かかるあひだに、ひとのいへの、いけとなあるところより、こひはなくて、ふなよりはじめて、かはのもうみのも、こどものども、ながびつににないつづけて、おこせたり。わかなぞけふをばしらせたる。うたあり。そのうた、

あさぢふの	Choked with growth
のべにしあれば	are the fields they are from,
みづもなき	and so starved for sight of water
いけにつみつる	is the pond where plucked and piled
わかななりけり	are these young herbs as my name!

How amusing! This "pond" she speaks of is the name of her place, of course. Apparently, she is a well-bred personage who has lived there after having accompanied a man down from the capital to this province. The contents of the chests were passed out to everyone, down to the youngest child. We all ate our fill, and the sailors' stomachs stretched so taut that the sound of them drumming on their bellies was loud enough to startle the sea itself. No doubt we are in for big waves. Many other things happened the same day. Someone came over bringing lunch boxes . . . what was their name again? At any rate, his heart seems to have been set on reciting a verse. After speaking about this and that, he sorrowfully declared: "How the waves rise!" and recited this poem:

いとをかしかし。このいけといふは、ところのななり。よきひとの、をとこにつきてくだりて、すみけるなり。このながびつのものは、みなひと、わらはまでにくれたれば、あきみちて、ふなこどもは、はらつづみをうちて、うみをさへおどろかして、なみたてつべし。かくて、このあひだにことおほかり。けふ、わりごもたせてきたるひと、その

ななどぞや。いまおもひいでむ。このひと、うたよまむとおもふこころありてなり
けり。とかくいひいひて、「なみのたつなること」とうるへいひて、よめるうた、

ゆくさきに	Greater than the roar
たつしらなみの	of white-crested waves
こゑよりも	rising in your path
おくれてなかむ	are the abandoned wails
われやまさらむ	of myself most of all.

That's what he recited! He must have a loud voice. How could we compare this verse with the things he brought? Everyone made a show of being moved, but not a single person offered a verse in reply. Even though there are some among us who are certainly capable of doing so, we did nothing but praise his poem and go on eating until night fell. Finally, the poem's owner said: "Another time, then" and got up to leave. Someone's little child whispered: "I'll offer a reply." Surprised, someone said: "How charming! Does she really think she can do it? If she is going to recite it, she should do so at once!" I gather there was a search made for the person who had said "Another time," with the thought of waiting until he had returned before reciting it, but it seems that he had already left for home, perhaps thinking the night was growing late. "Well, then. How did you fare with your composition?" someone asked, but the child was shy at first and said nothing until, pressed further, she uttered this verse:

とぞよめる。いとおほごゑなるべし。もてきたるものよりは、うたはいかがあらむ。こ
のうたを、これかれあはれがれども、ひとりもかへしせず。しつべきひともまじれれ
ど、これをのみいたがり、ものをのみくひて、よふけぬ。このうたぬし、「まだまから
ず」といひてたちぬ。あるひとのこのわらはなる、ひそかにいふ。「まろ、このうたの
かへしせむ」といふ。おどろきて、「いとをかしきことかな。よみてむやは。よみつべ
くば、はやいへかし。」といふ。「まからず」とて、たちぬるひとを「まちてよまむ」と
てもとめけるを、「よふけぬ」とにやありけむ、やがていにけり。「そもそもいかがよ
んだる」と、いぶかしがりてとふ。このわらは、さすがにはぢていはず。しひてとへ
ば、いへるうた、

ゆくひとも	Both those who go
とまるもそでの	and stay bear sleeves whose
なみだがは	streams of tears
みぎはのみこそ	do nothing but overflow
ぬれまさりけれ	the riverbanks, it seems!

That's what she recited. What a thing to say! Was it because the poet is so pretty that it came as such a surprise? It was certainly most unexpected. "Still, what are we to do with a child's verse?" "An older male or female relative should sign it with a hand print." "It might not be the best thing to do, but regardless, let's send it over to him when we have a chance." After this was said, it looks like the poem was written down and set aside.

となむよめる。かくはいふものか。うつくしければにやあらむ、いとおもはずなり。「わらはごとにてはなにかはせむ。」「おむな、おきな、ておしつべし。」「あしくもあれ、いかにもあれ、たよりあらばやらむ」とて、おかれぬめり。

The Eighth. Something blocks our progress, so we are still in the same place. This evening the moon sank into the sea. Seeing this brought to mind that poem by milord Narihira in which he said: *May the mountain rim retreat, so it will not retire!* If he had composed it at sea, he might instead have said: *May the waves rise up to block it, so it will not retire!* Recalling that verse now, someone recited:

八日。さはることありて、なほおなじところなり。こよひ、つきはうみにぞいる。これをみて、なりひらのきみの「やまのはにげて、いれずもあらなむ」といふうたなむおもほゆる。もし、うみべにてよまましかば、「なみたちさへて、いれずもあらなむ」とも、よみてましや。いま、このうたをおもひいでて、あるひとのよめりける、

てるつきの	The shining moon
ながるるみれば	flows by to reveal
あまのがは	Heaven's River,
いづるみなとは	whose mouth issues into
うみにざりける	this very same sea!

Or words to that effect.

とや。

Early at morning on *The Ninth* we finally row out from this great harbor of Ōminato in pursuit of the net anchorage of Nawa no Tomari! Thinking to themselves that we are now at the border of the province, many people came in turn to see us off. Out of them all, it is only Fujiwara no Tokizane, Tachibana no Suehira, and Hasebe no Yukimasa who have pursued us without ceasing since the day his lordship departed the governor's residence, thus proving themselves true-hearted. The depth of their concern must surely rival that of the sea itself! From now on, our ship leaves them behind. Yet I hear that they still pursue us, thinking to see us off up until the very last moment. And so we rowed onwards. Those by the sea shrank into the distance, and those on the boat faded from sight. There must surely be things left unsaid ashore, as there are things left in our thoughts on board, but nothing can be done about it. Even so, I muttered the following verse to myself before breaking off:

九日のつとめて、おほみなとより、「なはのとまりをおはむ」とて、こぎいでけり。これかれたがひに、「くにのさかひのうちは」とて、みおくりにくるひとあまたがなかに、ふぢはらのときざね、たちばなのすゑひら、はせべのゆきまさらなむ、みたちよりいでたうびしひより、ここかしこにおひくる。このひとびとぞ、こころざしあるひとなりける。このひとのふかきこころざしは、このうみにもおとらざるべし。これより、いまはこぎはなれてゆく。これをみおくらむとてぞ、このひとどもはおひきける。かくて、こぎゆくまにまに、うみのほとりにとまれるひともとほくなりぬ。ふねのひともみえずなりぬ。きしにもいふことあるべし。ふねにもおもふことあれど、かひなし。かかれど、このうたをひとりごとにして、やみぬ。

おもひやる	Thoughts cast back
こころはうみを	from hearts over the sea
わたれども	might make the passage,
ふみしなければ	but without brush traces,
しらずやあるらむ	who would fathom them?

And so we passed by *The Uda* Pine-Tree Plains. It is beyond knowing how many pine trees are there, or how many millennia they have spent in this place. Waves lapped against each root and cranes alighted atop each branch. Overcome by the charm of this sight, someone on our ship composed this verse:

かくて、宇多のまつばらをゆきすぐ、そのまつのかずいくそばく、いくちとせへたりとしらず。もとごとになみうちよせ、えだごとにつるぞとびかよふ。おもしろしとみるにたへずして、ふなびとのよめるうた、

みわたせば	My gaze sweeps across
まつのうれごとに	pines on whose every branch
すむつるは	there roost cranes who
ちよのどちとぞ	I think must surely be
おもふべらなる	millennium-old companions.

Or words to that effect. This poem cannot surpass seeing the place. While we looked at such scenes as we rowed onward, both the mountains and the shore slipped into dark as night fell. Unable to tell west from east, we are now entirely dependent on what the steersman's heart tells him about the weather. Being unused to such a situation, even the men are anxious. How much more so the women, who press heads to the bottom of the ship with voices given over to weeping! While we were feeling thus, the crew and steersman sang boat songs without a care in the world. Here are some of the verses they sang:

とや。このうたは、ところをみるに、えまさらず。かくあるをみつつこぎゆくまにまに、やまもうみもみなくれ、よふけて、にしひむがしもみえずして、てけのこと、かぢとりのこころにまかせつ。をのこもならはぬは、いともこころぼそし。ましてをむなは、ふなぞこにかしらをつきあてて、ねをのみぞなく。かくおもへば、ふなこ、かぢとりは、ふなうたうたひて、なにともおもへらず、そのうたふうたは、

はるののにてぞ	In springtime fields
ねをばなく	is the sound of weeping.
わがすすきに	By blades of pampas grass
てきるきる	are hands sliced and slashed,
つんだるなを	plucking greens that will go
おややまほるらむ	to some hungry parent eager to feed,
しうとめやくふらむ	or a mother-in-law's gobbling greed?
かへらや	Oh, to be home!
よんべの	Where is that little one
うなゐもがな	who spent last night with me?
ぜにこはむ	Could I get those coins?
そらごとをして	Their tall tale I heeded,
おぎのりわざをして	to pay later what was needed.
ぜにももてこず	But no coins are they bringing.
おのれだにこず	Nor are they themselves coming.

There were many more, but I won't write them down. Hearing people laugh, hearts calmed a bit despite the rough sea. And so we spent the whole day rowing onward to reach anchorage. Feeling queasy, the elderly man and dame ended up going to sleep without touching a bite of food.

これならずおほかれども、かかず。これらをひとのわらふをききて、うみはあるれども、こころはすこしなぎぬ。かくゆきくらして、とまりにいたりて、おきなびとひとり、たうめひとり、あるがなかに、ここちあしみして、ものもものしたばで、ひそまりぬ。

The Tenth. Today we have anchored at the net anchorage of Nawa no Tomari.

十日。けふは、このなはのとまりにとまりぬ。

The Eleventh. Just before daybreak our ship set out in pursuit of the cave harbor of Murotsu. Because everyone else was still asleep, they couldn't tell what the sea looked like. It is only by gazing at the moon that one can distinguish west from east! Meanwhile, dawn broke forth in all its glory as we washed our faces and set about our morning routines until noon. Just now we have arrived at a place called "Wings." After being told the name of the place, a child who is still quite immature said: "I wonder if this place called 'Wings' actually resembles bird wings." People laughed at these childishly naïve words. Then a girl who is apparently with us here recited this verse:

十一日。あかつきにふねをいだして、むろつをおふ。ひとみなまだねたれば、うみのありやうもみえず。ただ、つきをみてぞ、にしひむがしをばしりける。かかるあひだに、みなよあけて、てあらひ、れいのことどもして、ひるになりぬ。いまし、はねといふところにきぬ。わかきわらは、このところのなをききて、「はねといふところは、とりのはねのやうにやある」といふ。まだをさなきわらはのことなれば、ひとびとわらふ。ときに、ありけるをむなわらはなむ、このうたをよめる、

まことにて	If it is truly the case
なにきくところ	that there are wings
はねならば	in this place whose name I hear,
とぶがごとくに	then let us fly like birds
みやこへもがな	back to the capital city!

That's what she said! Men and women alike are thinking in their hearts how much they would like to return to *The Capital* and so, although this verse cannot be said to be a good one, it nonetheless rang true, and has not been forgotten by other people. The child's query about the place named "Wings" brings back memories of the one who once was. Is she ever forgotten? Still, these words bring fresh grief to the mourning mother as she observes the rites required of her on this particular day. Being short one person from the number that originally came out to the provinces, those words from the old song that go *a smaller number now appear homeward bound* come to mind, inspiring someone to compose this:

とぞいへる。をとこもをむなも、いかでとく京へもがなとおもふこころあれば、このうたよしとにはあらねど、「げに」とおもひて、ひとびとわすれず。この、はねといふところとふわらはのついでにぞ、また、むかしへびとをおもひいでて、いづれのときにかわする。けふはまして、ははのかなしがらるることは、くだりしときのひとのかずたらねば、ふるうたに、「かずはたらでぞかへるべらなる」といふことをおもひいでて、ひとのよめる、

| よのなかに | In our thoughts we may imagine |
| おもひやれども | all the relationships in this world, |

こをこふる	but there are no thoughts
おもひにまさる	that surpass the thoughts
おもひなきかな	of one longing for a child!

That's what they uttered over and over again.

といひつつなむ。

The Twelfth. No rain falls. The ships of Fumutoki and Koremochi have finally come from the level port of Narashizu, where they had fallen behind, to join us here at the cave harbor of Murotsu.

十二日。あめふらず。ふむとき、これもちがふねのおくれたりし、ならしづよりむろつにきぬ。

At daybreak on *The Thirteenth* rain fell for a bit. After a while it ceased. Thinking to bathe in the river, several of the women descended from the ship and headed off to a spot that would do for that purpose. Gazing out over the sea:

十三日のあかつきに、いささかにあめふる。しばしありてやみぬ。をむなこれかれ、ゆあみなどせむとて、あたりのよろしきところに、おりてゆく。うみをみやれば、

くももみな	The clouds all
なみとぞみゆる	look like waves!
あまもがな	Oh, for a diver-woman!
いづれかうみと	I would know from asking her
とひてしるべく	which one is the sea.

That's the poem I composed. Now that the tenth has passed, the moon in the dawn sky makes for an enthralling sight. Since the ship first set out, no woman has once worn fine robes of dark red silk for fear of attracting the sea god. Saying this, some took refuge in the scanty excuse of a few reeds and hitched their skirts up to their knees, seemingly untroubled by the thought that they were displaying the sort of abalones and mussels whose inner flesh makes a tasty coupling with pickled sea squirts!

となむうたよめる。さて、とをかあまりなれば、つきおもしろし。「ふねにのりはじめしひより、ふねには、くれなゐこくよききぬきず。それは「うみのかみにおぢて」とい

ひて、なにのあしかげにことづけて、ほやのつまのいずし、すしあはびをぞ、こころにもあらぬ、はぎにあげてみせける。

The Fourteenth. Rain began to fall at break of dawn, so we stayed in the same place. The lord on board observed a vegetarian fast. Since we lack appropriate food, his lordship desisted in the afternoon after bestowing rice and saké on the steersman, since we have no coins, in exchange for some sea bream caught yesterday. This sort of thing happens more than once. The steersman brings over more sea breams. We give out rice and saké other times. The steersman does not seem displeased with this arrangement.

十四日。あかつきよりあめふれば、おなじところにとまれり。ふなぎみ、せちみす。さうじものなければ、むまときよりのちに、かぢとりのきのふつりたりしたひに、ぜになければ、よねをとりかけて、おちられぬ。かかることなほありぬ。かぢとり、またたひもてきたり。よね、さけ、しばしばくる。かぢとりけしきあしからず。

The Fifteenth. There was no azuki bean porridge simmering today, to our mouths' bitter regret. The day continued to go poorly as time crawled by with us scuttling back and forth on our knees across the rolling deck. It is now the twentieth day of this journey! Over all that time people have been gazing listlessly out to sea. A little girl uttered:

十五日。けふ、あづきがゆにず。くちをしく、なほひのあしければ、ゐざるほどにぞ、けふはつかあまりへぬる。いたづらにひをふれば、ひとびと、うみをながめつつぞある。めのわらはのいへる、

たてばたつ	Rising with each other.
ゐればまたゐる	Sitting with each other.
ふくかぜと	With the blowing wind
なみとはおもふ	are these waves as close
どちにやあるらむ	as friends? I wonder . . .

Quite fitting, considering the childish source.

いふかひなきもののいへるには、いとにつかはし。

The Sixteenth. Since the wind and waves show no sign of letting up, we are still at rest in the same place. All I can do is wonder impatiently when the waves will vanish from the sea so that we can cross over to some place called the "Mighty Peninsula." The wind sweeping over them shows no sign of relenting any time soon. Someone recited this poem upon looking out at their foaming crests:

十六日。かぜなみやまねば、なほおなじところにとまれり。ただ、うみになみなくして、いつしかみさきといふところわたらむとのみなむおもふ。かぜなみとににやむべくもあらず。あるひとの、このなみたつをみてよめるうた、

しもだにも	Not even frost
おかぬかたぞと	is found in this region,
いふなれど	they say, and yet,
なみのなかには	amid these waves
ゆきぞふりける	snow now falls!

I have just realized now to my dismay that we have been at sea twenty-five days!

さて、ふねにのりしひよりけふまでに、はつかあまりいつかになりにけり。

The Seventeenth. Shrouds of cloud vanished to reveal the moon just before dawn. I gather its intriguing allure has drawn our ship out to sea. During this time, both the clouds above and the sea below looked exactly the same. This must have been why some man of olden times said *a pole pierces the moon above waves; a ship presses against a sea in the sky.* I heard words to that effect from a poem once. Someone else has composed this verse:

十七日。くもれるくもなくなりて、あかつきづくよいともおもしろければ、ふねをいだしてこぎゆく。このあひだに、くものうへもうみのそこも、おなじごとくになむありける。むべも、むかしのをとこは、「さをはうがつなみのうへのつきを。ふねはおそふうみのうちのそらを」とはいひけむ。ききざれにきけるなり。また、あるひとのよめるうた、

みなそこの	In watery depths
つきのうへより	lies the moon above which
こぐふねの	rows by this ship
さをにさはるは	whose pole comes up against
かつらなるらし	what seems to be its laurel tree.

Hearing this, someone has also composed:

かげみれば	Reflections reveal
なみのそこなる	beneath the waves
ひさかたの	a far-off firmament,
そらこぎわたる	rowing across whose sky
われぞわびしき	is this misery-filled I!

While these were being uttered, night gradually turned to dawn. That steersman fellow said: "Dark clouds have suddenly appeared. The wind will be blowing soon. We should turn his lordship's vessel back to the harbor." And with that the ship went back. Meanwhile, rain has begun to fall. What misery!

かくいふあひだに、よやうやくあけゆくに、かぢとりら、「くろきくもにはかにいできぬ。かぜふきぬべし。みふねかへしてむ」といひて、ふねかへる。このあひだにあめふりぬ。いとわびし。

The Eighteenth. We are still in the same place. The waters are rough, so the ship wasn't put out to sea. This anchorage looks enthralling both from a distance and close up, and yet I am too frustrated to even think of composing anything. The menfolk seem to have been uttering continental verses among themselves, no doubt to raise their spirits. The time wasted here instead of setting out to sea led someone to compose:

十八日。なほおなじところにあり。うみあらければ、ふねいださず。このとまり、とほくみれども、ちかくみれども、いとおもしろし。かかれども、くるしければ、なにごともおもほえず。をとこどちは、こころやりにやあらむ、からうたなどいふべし。ふねもいださでいたづらなれば、あるひとのよめる、

いそぶりの	Boulder-breaking waves
よするいそには	crash against reefs where,
としつきを	without concern
いつともわかぬ	for year or month,
ゆきのみぞふる	nothing but snow falls!

This poem is by someone who doesn't usually do such things. Some other person composed:

このうたは、つねにせぬひとのことなり。また、ひとのよめる、

かぜによる	Whipped up by the wind
なみのいそには	is this wave-swept reef where
うぐひすも	neither nightingales
はるもえしらぬ	nor spring could know
はなのみぞさく	the only flowers blooming.

Taking these poems to be little better than average, the foremost elderly man on board sought to alleviate his frustrations of the past few months and days, and has composed:

このうたどもを、すこしよろしとききて、ふねのをさしけるおきな、つきひごろのくるしきこころやりによめる、

たつなみを	Are these rising waves,
ゆきかはなかと	snow or blossoms?
ふくかぜぞ	The wind that blows
よせつつひとを	again and again on people
はかるべらなる	surely deceives them all.

Listening intently to what people say about these poems, someone else composed one. The syllables composed for that verse came to thirty-seven letters. Everyone looked like they were barely able to keep from laughing. The poem's owner seemed very put out and grumbled. Though they emulated others, they weren't able to truly absorb anything. Even if the poem were written out, it would be very hard to manage a properly arranged composition. Today alone it is embarrassing. One can only imagine what it will be like later!

このうたどもを、ひとのなにかといふを、あるひとききふけりてよめり。そのうた、よめるもじ、みそもじあまりななもじ。ひとみなえあらでわらふやうなり。うたぬしいとけしきあしくて、ゑず。まねべどもえまねばず。かけりともえよみすゑがたかるべし。けふだにいひがたし。ましてのちにはいかならむ。

The Nineteenth. The day boded ill, so our ship wasn't put out to sea.

十九日。ひあしければ、ふねいださず。

The Twentieth. It looked the same as yesterday, so our ship wasn't put out to sea. We are all sighing mournfully. In my frustration and anxiety I have been counting out the days that have passed over and over again. How many is it today?

Twenty? Thirty? I would surely sprain my fingers counting every single one. It all makes me feel quite miserable. I don't sleep, and now the moon on the night of the twentieth has risen. It appears from the middle of the sea rather than over mountain rims! I wonder if this was what that man of old called Abe no Nakamaro witnessed when he was about to set back for home after having crossed over to the continent. At the place where he was to board ship, they say, the people of that land held a farewell banquet at which they crafted continental verses to express their regret at seeing him leave. They must have not yet felt satisfied, for it is said that they stayed there until the moon on that night of the twentieth rose right out of the sea. Seeing it there, Master Nakamaro is said to have said: "In my land, verses such as these were first recited by gods in the age of the gods. High, middling, and low alike now recite them at partings from loved ones such as this, and also when feeling sorrow or joy." Then he composed this verse:

廿日。きのふのやうなれば、ふねいださず。みなひとびとうれへなげく。くるしくこころもとなければ、ただ、ひのへぬるかずを、けふいくか、はつか、みそかとかぞふれば、およびもそこなはれぬべし。いとわびし。よるはいもねず。はつかのよのつきいでにけり。やまのはもなくて、うみのなかよりぞいでくる。かうやうなるをみてや、むかし、あべのなかまろといひけるひとは、もろこしにわたりて、かへりきけるときに、ふねにのるべきところにて、かのくにびと、むまのはなむけし、わかれをしみて、かしこのからうたつくりなどしける。あかずやありけむ、はつかのよのつきいづるまでぞありける。そのつきは、うみよりぞいでける。これをみてぞ、なかまろのぬし、「わがくにに、かかるうたをなむ、かみよよりかみもよんたび、いまはかみなかしものひとも、かうやうにわかれをしみ、よろこびもあり、かなしびもあるときには、よむ」とて、よめりけるうた、

あをうなばら	Over cyan sea plains
ふりさけみれば	my gaze sweeps out to see
かすがなる	Kasuga, in which lies
みかさのやまに	Mount Mikasa, where
いでしつきかも	this moon once rose over me!

That's what he composed, they say! It occurred to him that the people of that land would probably not be able to understand this poem just by hearing it. He nonetheless wrote down the gist of its contents in the letters used by all men everywhere and explained their full import to an interpreter who could convey our language. On account of this, they must have been able to hear what was in his heart, for it is said that they were moved beyond all expectation. Although the words of the continent differ from those of this land, the hearts of people must surely be the same, for the moon's light shines the same everywhere. And then, thinking on that past in the present moment, someone composed this verse:

とぞよめりける。かのくにびとききしるまじく、おもほえたれども、ことのこころを、をとこもじにさまをかきいだして、ここのことばつたへたるひとに、いひしらせければ、こころをやききえたりけむ、いとおもひのほかになむめでける。もろこしとこのくにとは、ことことなるものなれど、つきのかげはおなじことなるべければ、ひとのこころもおなじことにやあらむ。さていま、そのかみをおもひやりて、あるひとのよめるうた、

みやこにて	In the capital city
やまのはにみし	at the mountain's rim I saw
つきなれど	this moon, though now
なみよりいでて	it rises from waves
なみにこそいれ	and sinks into waves.

The Twenty-First. Around six in the morning our ship put out to sea. All the other ships also set out. Looking around, it seemed as though the leaves of autumnal trees were scattered over the spring sea. Our *Prayers* appear to have worked, perhaps due to their earnestness. The wind wasn't blowing, and a fine sun appeared in the sky as we set out. Meanwhile, a youth who has come with us intending to find employment in the capital sang this ship song:

廿一日。うのときばかりに、ふねいだす。みなひとびとのふねいづ。これをみれば、はるのうみにあきのこのはしもちれるやうにぞありける。おぼろけの願によりてにやあらむ。かぜもふかず、よきひいできて、こぎゆく。このあひだに、つかはれむとて、つきてくるわらはあり。それがうたふふなうた、

なほこそ	All the more
くにのかたは	back towards land
みやらるれ	is my gaze drawn,
わがちちはは	my father and mother
ありとしおもへば	being there in my thoughts.
かへらや	Oh, to be home!

What poignant singing! While listening to this, our ship came to a place where birds called "black birds" were huddled together atop some rocks. Waves crashed whitely against the base of the rocks. The steersman said something to the effect of "by black birds approach white waves." Though nothing special in itself, his manner of saying things catches the ear. "Since such words are a poor fit with a person of his standing, they feel at fault somehow," someone said as we went onwards. The person who is our lord on board now looks at the waves: "Ever since we left the province there have been concerns raised by rumors that vengeful pirates pursue us. On top of that, the sea's terrors have turned my hairs completely white. A full seventy or eighty years' worth of suffering do I now see in the sea!"

とうたふぞあはれなる。かくうたふをききつつこぎくるに、くろとりといふとり、いはのうへにあつまりをり。そのいはのもとに、なみしろくうちよす。かぢとりのいふやう、「くろとりのもとに、しろきなみをよす。」とぞいふ。このことば、なにとにはなけれども、ものいふやうにぞきこえたる。「ひとのほどにあはねば、とがむるなり」かくいひつつゆくに、ふなぎみなるひと、なみをみて、「くによりはじめて、かいぞくむくいせむといふなることをおもふへに、うみのまたおそろしければ、かしらもみなしらけぬ。ななそぢやそぢは、うみにあるものなりけり。」

わがかみの	Is it my mane
ゆきといそべの	of snow or the reef's
しらなみと	white-crested waves
いづれまされり	that outdoes the other,
おきつしまもり	o distant island sentinel?

Say something, steersman!

かぢとりいへ

The Twenty-Second. We set out from last night's anchorage in pursuit of another. Mountains were visible in the distance. With us is a boy who is immature even for a nine-year-old. The child looked out at the mountains moving with our onward-rowing ship and, much to everyone's amazement, composed a verse. That verse was:

廿二日。よんべのとまりより、ことどまりをおひてゆく。はるかにやまみゆ。としここのつばかりなるをのわらは、としよりはをさなくぞある。このわらは、ふねをこぐまにまに、やまもゆくとみゆるをみて、あやしきこと、うたをぞよめる。そのうた、

こぎてゆく	Looking out from a ship
ふねにてみれば	rowing onwards,
あしひきの	even the foot-dragging
やまさへゆくを	mountains are moving.
まつはしらずや	Don't the pines know it?

That's what he said! Fitting words for such a childish youth. Today, the sea has taken on a rough appearance. Snow falls on the rocky strand and waves bloom in blossoms. Someone recited this:

とぞいへる。をさなきわらはのことにては、につかはし。けふ、うみあらけにて、いそにゆきふり、なみのはなさけり。あるひとのよめる、

なみとのみ	Waves are the only
ひとつにきけど	thing I hear, and yet,
いろみれば	looking at their colors,
ゆきとはなとに	with snow and blossoms
まがひけるかな	have I confused them!

The Twenty-Third. The sun shines and then is clouded over. Talk of pirates in the area leads us to pray to gods and buddhas.

廿三日。ひてりて、くもりぬ。「このわたり、かいぞくのおそりあり」といへば、かみほとけをいのる。

The Twenty-Fourth. The same place as yesterday.

廿四日。きのふのおなじところなり。

The Twenty-Fifth. That steersman fellow said, "The northerly looks ominous," so the ship wasn't put out to sea. All day our ears were filled with rumors of pursuing pirates.

廿五日。かぢとりらの、「きたかぜあし」といへば、ふねいださず。「かいぞくおひく」といふこと、たえずきこゆ。

The Twenty-Sixth. Can it be true? Word has it that pirates are pursuing us, and so we set out around the middle of the night, rowing to a place where placatory offerings for safe passage are made. We had the steersman do his thing with the prayer slips, which scattered to the east, after which he entreated thusly: "If it please you o gods, grant this fair ship leave to proceed with all haste in the direction towards which these prayer slips may scatter." Thus did he pray. Hearing his words, a girl child composed this:

廿六日。まことにやあらむ。「かいぞくおふ」といへば、よなかばかりより、ふねをいだしてこぎくるみちに、たむけするところあり。かぢとりして、ぬさたいまつらするに、ぬさのひむがしへちれば、かぢとりのまうしてたてまつることは、「このぬさのちるかたに、みふねすみやかにこがしめたまへ」とまうしてたてまつる。これをききて、あるめのわらはのよめる、

わたつみの	May the wind chasing prayers
ちぶりのかみに	scattered in offering
たむけする	to gods granting safe passage
ぬさのおひかぜ	over the sacred sea
やまずふかなむ	blow without ceasing!

That's what she recited! During this time we caught a good wind, causing the steersman to swell with pride as he joyfully issued commands to raise the sail and such. Hearing his voice, the children and women were very pleased, no doubt in anticipation now of a swift journey. One among them, a person known as the dame of Awaji, composed this verse:

とぞよめる。このあひだに、かぜのよければ、かぢとりいたくほこりて、「ふねにほあげ」などよろこぶ。そのおとをききて、わらはもおむなも、いつしかとしおもへばにやあらむ、いたくよろこぶ。このなかに、あはぢのたうめといふひとのよめるうた、

おひかぜの	Now that a tailwind
ふきぬるときは	has begun to blow at last,
ゆくふねの	the onward moving boat's
ほてうちてこそ	sail ropes snap as hands clap
うれしがりけれ	for the happiness it brings!

That was it! The weather offers many opportunities for prayer.

とぞ。ていけのことにつけつつ、いのる。

The Twenty-Seventh. A wind blew and the waves were rough, so the ship wasn't put out to sea. Here and there people have been heaving long sighs. A woman composed this poem after hearing the words *When I gaze toward The Sun, the capital lies in the distance,* or the gist of some such phrase uttered by the men who have been seeking solace in continental verses:

廿七日。かぜふきなみあらければ、ふねいださず。これかれ、かしこくなげく。をとこたちの、こころなぐさめに、からうたに、「日をのぞめば、みやことほし」などいふなることのさまをききて、あるをむなのよめるうた、

ひをだにも	Even the sun itself
あまぐもちかく	near heaven's clouds
みるものを	I seem to see, and yet
みやこへとおもふ	these longings for the capital
みちのはるけさ	stretch over a distant road!

Another person composed this:

また、あるひとのよめる、

ふくかぜの	As long as there is no end
たえぬかぎりし	to the gusting wind,
たちくれば	the rising swell comes in,
なみぢはいとど	making the waveborne path
はるけかりけり	grow ever more distant!

All day long the wind didn't let up. We fell asleep snapping our fingers to ward off misfortune.

ひひとひ、かぜやまず。つまはじきして、ねぬ。

❦

The Twenty-Eighth. All night long the rain didn't let up. The next morning too.

廿八日。よもすがら、あめやまず。けさも。

❦

The Twenty-Ninth. The ship was put out to sea. We rowed onward through a beautiful bright shiny day. I looked at the length my nails have grown, counting the days. Since today is apparently *The Youngest Day of the Rat* in the calendar year, I don't cut them. Because it is the first one of the new year, there is talk of the annual festivities being observed for the Day of the Rat back in *The Capital*. But however much we might say we wish for pine seedlings, it would be difficult to manage such a thing here at sea. A woman wrote out this verse:

廿九日。ふねいだしてゆく。うらうらとてりて、こぎゆく。つめのいとながくなりにたるをみて、ひをかぞふれば、けふは子日なりければ、きらず。むづきなれば、京のね

のひのこといひいでて、「こまつもがな」といへど、うみなかなれば、かたしかし。あるをむなのかきていだせるうた、

おぼつかな	It is hard to tell that
けふはねのひか	today is the Day of the Rat.
あまならば	If I were a diver-girl
うみまつをだに	I would be pulling up
ひかましものを	strands of sea-pine at least ...

That's what she said! How does it fare as a poem for *The Youngest Day of the Rat* at sea? Another person composed this verse:

とぞいへる。うみにて、子日のうたにては、いかがあらむ。また、あるひとのよめるうた、

けふなれど	Though today is the day,
わかなもつまず	we don't pluck young herbs,
かすがのの	in Kasuga's fields
わがこぎわたる	which are not in the bay
うらになければ	we now row across.

While such things were said we rowed onward. Our ship drew near an intriguing place. I gather that someone asking where we are was told the place is called "Tosa Anchorage." Apparently a woman who lived long ago in a place said to bear the name of "Tosa" is with us now here on board! She spoke, saying: "Why, it is the same name as that of a place where I once lived for a while in the past! How poignant!" Then she recited this verse:

かくいひつつこぎゆく。おもしろきところにふねをよせて、「ここやいどこ」ととひければ、「とさのとまり」といひけり。むかし、とさといひけるところにすみけるをむな、このふねにまじれりけり。そがいひけらく、「むかし、しばしありしところのなたぐひにぞあなる。あはれ」といひて、よめるうた、

としごろを	Since it bears the name
すみしところの	of a place I had lived in
なにしおへば	for many long years,
きよるなみをも	even approaching waves
あはれとぞみる	are a poignant sight to see!

That is what she said!

とぞいへる。

The Thirtieth. No rain or wind. Hearing that pirates fear to roam about after dark, we set out around twelve at night across Awa Straits. Since it was the middle of the night, we were unable to tell west from east. Men and women were frantically praying to gods and buddhas until we finally made it across the narrow channel. Around five in the morning we passed by a place called "Marsh Isle," and crossed over somewhere called "Tana River." Hastening frantically past it, we finally reached a place called "Onward Stretch of Izumi." All day there was nothing even remotely resembling a wave in sight. It's as if we had received the blessings of gods and buddhas. Counting back from today to the day when we first boarded this ship, I realize it is the thirty-ninth one spent on this journey! Now that we have made it to Izumi province, there is no further threat of pirates.

卅日。あめかぜふかず。「かいぞくは、よるあるきせざなり」とききて、よなかばかりにふねをいだして、あはのみとをわたる。よなかなれば、にしひむがしもみえず。をとこをむな、からくかみほとけをいのりて、このみとをわたりぬ。とらうのときばかりに、ぬしまといふところをすぎて、たながはといふところをわたる。からくいそぎて、いづみのなだといふところにいたりぬ。けふ、うみになみににたるものなし。かみほとけのめぐみかうぶれるににたり。けふ、ふねにのりしひよりかぞふれば、みそかあまりここぬかになりにけり。いまは、いづみのくににきぬれば、かいぞくものならず。

The First of the Second Month. Rain fell throughout the morning. It stopped around noon and so we set out from the place called "Onward Stretch of Izumi." Just as yesterday, no winds or waves could be seen on the water's surface. We went on past the pine groves at the dark peninsula of Kurosaki. The name of the place is black and the color of the pines is green, while the waves of its reefs are like snow and the colors of its shells are red, leaving it just one short of all *Five Primary Colors.* During this time we started to be towed along at a place called "Box Bay." While we were going onward in this manner, someone composed this verse:

二月一日。あしたのま、あめふる。むまときばかりにやみぬれば、いづみのなだといふところよりいでて、こぎゆく。うみのうへ、きのふのごとくに、かぜなみみえず。くろさきのまつばらをへてゆく。ところのなはくろく、まつのいろはあをく、いそのなみはゆきのごとくに、かひのいろはすはうに、五色にいまひといろぞたらぬ。このあひだに、けふは、はこのうらといふところより、つなでひきてゆく。かくゆくあひだに、あるひとのよめるうた、

<blockquote>

たまくしげ	Gem-sparkling is the comb
はこのうらなみ	in a Box Bay where waves

</blockquote>

たたぬひは	do not rise on a day
うみをかがみと	when the sea as a mirror
たれかみざらむ	must surely seem to all.

Also, the lord on board heaved a sigh and said: "To think our journey has taken us into this month!" Unable to bear his frustration any longer, he then said, "Others have spoken of it after all . . ." and then sought to brighten his mood by uttering:

また、ふなぎみのいはく、「このつきまでなりぬること」となげきて、くるしきにたへずして、「ひともいふこと」とて、こころやりにいへる、

ひくふねの	The boat is pulled along
つなでのながき	with hempen ropes long
はるのひを	as these spring days,
よそかいかまで	up to forty or fifty of which
われはへにけり	is the time I have spent!

You can get a sense of the impression this left on another listener who was definitely muttering, "Why is this so plain-worded?" under their breath. "The lord on board must actually think these are fine words he has managed to spin out!" "Careful! Our master can be touchy . . ." With such muffled whispers we let it pass. The wind and waves rose up again, so we stopped here.

きくひとのおもへるやう、「なぞ、ただごとなる」と、ひそかにいふべし。「ふなぎみの、からくひねりいだして、よしとおもへることを」「ゑじもこそしたべ」とて、つつめきてやみぬ。にはかにかぜなみたかければ、とどまりぬ。

The Second. The rain and wind don't let up. All day long and well into the night we prayed to gods and buddhas.

二日。あめかぜやまず。ひひとひ、よもすがら、かみほとけをいのる。

The Third. Because the water's surface is the same as yesterday, the ship wasn't put out to sea. Since the blowing gusts didn't let up, waves rolled back from the shore in rising crests. A verse was composed about this:

三日。うみのうへ、きのふのやうなれば、ふねいださず。かぜのふくことやまねば、きしのなみたちかへる。これにつけてよめるうた、

ををよりて	Twining hemp strands
かひなきものは	serves no purpose,
おちつもる	when piles of fallen
なみだのたまを	tears are the jewels
ぬかぬなりけり	that remain unstrung!

And with that, night fell.

かくて、けふくれぬ。

The Fourth. Our steersman says: "Today's wind and rain have a baleful look about them." And so he ended up not putting the ship out to sea. However, neither waves nor wind rose all day long. The steersman is a blockhead who has no idea how to gauge the weather! The shore by our anchorage is filled with all sorts of lovely shells and pebbles. And so someone on board who has been doing nothing but longing for the one who once was composed this:

四日。かぢとり、「けふ、かぜくものけしきはなはだあし」といひて、ふねいださずなりぬ。しかれども、ひねもすに、なみかぜたたず。このかぢとりは、ひもえはからぬかたゐなりけり。このとまりのはまには、くさぐさのうるわしきかひいしなどおほかり。かかれば、ただむかしのひとをのみこひつつ、ふねなるひとのよめる、

よするなみ	Approaching waves,
うちもよせなむ	may we approach still closer!
わがこふる	In my longing for
ひとわすれがひ	that one forgetting-shells
おりてひろはむ	would I disembark to gather.

These words led someone who was unable to endure the situation any longer to compose this in order to put the hearts of everyone on board at ease:

といへれば、あるひとのたへずして、ふねのこころやりによめる、

わすれがひ	Forgetting-shells
ひろひしもせじ	will we never gather,
しらたまを	but the gleaming pearl alone
こふるをだにも	will we long for rather
かたみとおもはむ	as a keepsake in our thoughts!

That's what they said! The girl has caused the parent to become childish. Some might have reason to claim she was no such poetic pearl in real life. Then again, you often seem to hear people say they remember the features of a dead child being fair. Bemoaning our having spent yet another day here, a woman composed this verse:

となむいへる。をむなごのためには、おやをさなくなりぬべし。「たまならずもありけむを」とひといはむや。されども、「ししこかほよかりき」といふやうもあり。なほ、おなじところにひをふることをなげきて、あるをむなのよめるうた、

てをひでて	Our dipped hands
さむさもしらぬ	do not know cold
いづみにぞ	at a wellspring which
くむとはなしに	we never once drew from
ひごろへにける	for all these many days!

The Fifth. Today at last we leave the Onward Stretch of Izumi in pursuit of the thread-bay anchorage of Ozu no Tomari. Pine groves stretch out as far as the eye can see. Here and there people grow frustrated, leading to this composition:

五日。けふ、からくして、いづみのなだよりをづのとまりをおふ。まつばら、めもはるばるなり。これかれ、くるしければ、よめるうた、

ゆけどなほ	What we cannot go past,
ゆきやられぬは	however far forth we go,
いもがうむ	is the lovely lady's skein
をづのうらなる	of Thread Bay's winding line
きしのまつばら	of shoreside groves of pine!

While this was said we came along. The lord on board urged the steersman onward, saying, "Hasten the ship while we have good weather!" The steersman then spoke to his crew, saying: "His lordship has spoken. Pull on the sail-ropes of this fair ship so it may go, before the morning northerly begins to blow!" The poetic quality possessed by these words lies precisely in their spontaneity on the steersman's part. It's not that the steersman had any intention of speaking in verse or anything of that sort. One person who was listening said: "How strange! What he said sounded like a poem!" and wrote it out to reveal that it does in fact come to thirty-one syllables! People's prayers for the waves to subside today seem to have had some effect, for the wind does not stir them up. Right then we found ourselves in a place where gulls frolicked about in a flock. A youth composed this verse in excessive joy at drawing near *The Capital*:

かくいひつつくるほどに、「ふねとくこげ。ひのよきに」とも よほせば、かぢとり、ふなこどもにいはく、「みふねより、おふせたぶなり。あさぎたの、いでこぬさきに、つなではやひけ」といふ。このことばのうたのやうなるは、かぢとりのおのづからのことばなり。かぢとりは、うつたへに、われ、うたのやうなることいふとにもあらず。きくひとの、「あやしく。うためきてもいひつるかな」とて、かきいだせれば、げにみそもじあまりなりけり。けふ、「なみなたちそ」と、ひとびとひねもすにいのるしるしありて、かぜなみたたず。いまし、かもめむれゐてあそぶところあり。京のちかづくよろこびのあまりに、あるわらはのよめるうた、

いのりくる	I think the lull in the wind
かざまともふを	comes from our prayers.
あやなくも	It makes no sense
かもめさへだに	for even these gulls
なみとみゆらむ	to look like waves!

While this was uttered we went on to a place called "Stone Port," whose pine groves are most enticing to behold and whose beach stretches on into the distance. Then we rowed across Sumiyoshi. Someone composed this verse:

といひてゆくあひだに、いしづといふところのまつばらおもしろくて、はまべとほし。また、すみよしのわたりをこぎゆく。あるひとのよめるうた、

いまみてぞ	Just the sight of it now
みをばしりぬる	informs us of our estate:
すみのえの	Suminoe's clear cove,
まつよりさきに	where pines have spent by far
われはへにけり	fewer years than myself!

Now the mother of that past person, who has not once forgotten her for a single day, composed this:

ここに、むかしへびとのははは、ひとひかたときもわすれねば、よめる、

すみのえに	To Suminoe's clear cove
ふねさしよせよ	set course in our ship!
わすれぐさ	Forgetting-herbs
しるしありやと	they say hold powers surely worth
つみてゆくべく	plucking before going onwards.

Although it is certainly not the case that she intends to completely forget her child, a brief respite from her pangs of longing should help her pour strength into them again. At these words, I gazed out listlessly as we came along, until the wind began to blow without any warning. As we pressed onward bit by bit, it pushed us farther and farther back, until it seemed as though our ship would break apart and founder. The steersman said: "*The Deity* of Sumiyoshi is your typical god. There must be something desirable in your lordship's possession." How very in keeping with the times this is! Then he said: "Please, your lordship, make an offering of prayer slips." Following his words, an offering of prayer slips was made. But though we did this, the gale didn't let up in the slightest. Winds gusted ever stronger and threatening waves towered ever higher, leading the steersman to speak again: "The prayer slips do not seem to have satisfied the god. Your lordship's vessel will not advance. Please, your lordship, offer up something that will bring happiness to the god's heart." Once again we follow his words, thinking there is nothing else we can do. The decision was made to offer up a single mirror, more precious than either eye, much to our bitter regret. All at once, the surface of the sea turned mirror-smooth, leading someone to compose this verse:

となむ。うつたへにわすれなむとにはあらで、こひしきここちしばしやすめて、またもこふるちからにせむとなるべし。かくいひて、ながめつつくるあひだに、ゆくりなくかぜふきて、こげどもこげども、しりへ、しぞきにしぞきて、ほとほとしくうちはめつべし。かぢとりのいはく、「このすみよしの明神は、れいのかみぞかし。ほしきものぞおはすらむ」とはいまめくものか。さて、「ぬさをたてまつりたまへ」といふ。いふにしたがひて、ぬさたいまつる。かくたいまつれれども、もはらかぜやまで、いやふきに、いやたちに、かぜなみのあやふければ、かぢとりまたいはく、「ぬさにはみこころのいかねば、みふねもゆかぬなり。なほ、うれしとおもひたぶべきものたいまつりたべ」といふ。また、いふにしたがひて、「いかがはせむ」とて、「まなこもこそふたつあれ。ただひとつあるかがみをたいまつる」とて、うみにうちはめつれば、くちをし。されば、うちつけに、うみはかがみのおもてのごとなりぬれば、あるひとのよめるうた、

ちはやぶる	Fierce and mighty
かみのこころを	the god whose heart
あるるうみに	we glimpse
かがみをいれて	upon casting a mirror
かつみつるかな	into the rough sea!

This is a far cry from the same god spoken of in poems mentioning the clear cove of Suminoe, forgetting-herbs, and the eternal shoreside Princess Pine! The god's heart could be glimpsed in the mirror all too clearly. The heart of this steersman is in fact the mighty heart of a god!

いたく、「すみのえ」「わすれぐさ」「きしのひめまつ」などいふかみにはあらずかし。めもうつらうつら、かがみにかみのこころをこそはみつれ。かぢとりのこころは、かみのみこころなりけり。

The Sixth. We set out from the channel markers to arrive at Naniwa, then entered the Yodo-gawa where it empties into the bay. Nothing could approach the joy everyone felt, including the women and elderly men, who put hands to foreheads as though genuflecting. The grand dame of Awaji Isle, who has been suffering from seasickness, is overjoyed at hearing we are nearing the capital city and, raising her head from the bottom of the ship, she uttered this:

六日。みをつくしのもとよりいでて、なにはにつきて、かはじりにいる。みなひとびと、おむな、おきな、ひたひにてをあててよろこぶこと、ふたつなし。かのふなゑひのあはぢのしまのおほいご、「みやこちかくなりぬ」といふをよろこびて、ふなぞこよりかしらをもたげて、かくぞいへる。

いつしかと	Wondering when,
いぶせかりつる	filled with impatience
なにはがた	at Naniwa's lagoon,
あしこぎそけて	reeds are parted by the oars
みふねきにけり	of the fair ship come here!

Coming as they do from *A Person* who is an utterly unexpected source, everyone was surprised by these words. The lord on board, who has been feeling unwell, is especially moved, and I gather he said: "There's not even the slightest resemblance to milady's seasick features!"

いとおもひのほかなる人のいへれば、ひとびとあやしがる。これがなかに、ここちなやむふなぎみ、いたくめでて、「ふなゑひしたうべりしみかほには、にずもあるかな」といひける。

The Seventh. Today the ship entered the river mouth. The water level is low, making it slow going upstream. Meanwhile, *The Ailing* lord on board, who is said to have always been an uncultivated person with no proclivity for such things, is nonetheless moved by the dame of Awaji's verse and, no doubt encouraged by the proximity of the capital city, he finally manages after much effort to spin out a peculiar verse. That verse went:

七日。けふ、かはじりにふねいりたちて、こぎのぼるに、かはのみづひて、なやみわづらふ。ふねののぼること、いとかたし。かかるあひだに、ふなぎみの病者、もとよりこちごちしきひとにて、かうやうのことさらにしらざりけり。かかれども、あはぢたうめのうたにめでて、みやこぼこりにやあらむ、からくして、あやしきうたひねりいだせり。そのうたは、

きときては	Having finally come
かはのぼりぢの	to the upstream route,
みづをあさみ	so shallow are its waters
ふねもわがみも	that both ship and self
なづむけふかな	stagger slowly today!

His ills must have led to such a composition. This single poem didn't suffice to express what he was feeling, so now there was this other one:

これは、やまひをすればよめるなるべし。ひとうたにことのあかねば、いまひとつ、

とくとおもふ	Hoping for haste,
ふねなやますは	the ship slowly struggles,
わがために	for it is on my account
みづのこころの	that the water's heart
あさきなりけり	now proves shallow!

No doubt he uttered this poem because he was unable to hold back his joy at drawing near to the capital city. "It falls short of the verse by my lady of Awaji. How awful. If only I hadn't said it!" he exclaimed. I gather he continued to regret this until he fell asleep in the night.

このうたは、みやこちかくなりぬるよろこびにたへずして、いへるなるべし。「あはぢのごのうたにおとれり。ねたき。いはざらましものを」と、くやしがるうちに、よるになりてねにけり。

The Eighth. We were still struggling upstream at a sickly pace when we stopped in the vicinity of a place supporting cormorant fishermen that is called "Royal Birdkeeper's Pasturage." Tonight the lord on board has been suffering greatly from a recurrence of his chronic ailment. Someone brought over a fresh catch. We exchanged rice for it. The men seemed to be muttering under their breath. I think I heard someone say: "That's what you'd call, 'hooking a big globefish with a few grains of parched rice,' I suppose." The same thing happened in other places. We were observing a vegetarian fast today, rendering the fish *Of No Use.*

八日。なほ、かはのぼりになづみて、とりかひのみまきといふほとりにとまる。こよひ、ふなぎみ、れいのやまひおこりて、いたくなやむ。あるひと、あざらかなるものもてきたり。よねしてかへりごとす。をとこども、ひそかにいふなり。「『いひぼして、もつつる』とや」かうやうのこと、ところどころにあり。けふ、せちみすれば、いを不用。

The Ninth. Our fretfulness grew at dawn as the ship was dragged along upstream, but because there was practically no water, the most we could manage was to inch forward at a crawl. During this time we found ourselves at a place where a sandbar protrudes into the river at a shallow crossing called "Wada Anchorage." We practiced almsgiving when begged for such things as rice and fish. While our ship is dragged upstream, a place called "*The Villa* by the Strand" comes into view. Thinking back on *The Villa*'s past, I recall it being said to be an enthralling place. Pines stand on the hills behind it, and a plum has bloomed in the courtyard within. People now speak, saying: "This place possesses an exalted history, you know!" "*The Late Middle Captain* Ariwara no Narihira was accompanying *The Late* Prince Koretaka here when he said:

九日。こころもとなさに、あけぬから、ふねをひきつつのぼれども、かはのみづなければ、ゐざりにのみぞゐざる。このあひだに、わだのとまりのあかれのところといふところあり。よね、いをなどこへば、おこなひつ。かくて、ふねひきのぼるに、なぎさの院といふところをみつつゆく。その院、むかしをおもひやりてみれば、おもしろかりけるところなり。しりへなるをかには、まつのきどもあり、なかのにはには、むめのはなさけり。ここに、ひとびとのいはく、「これ、むかし、なだかくきこえたるところなり」「故これたかのみこのおほむともに、故ありはらのなりひらの中將の、

よのなかに	'If only our world
たえてさくらの	were without cherries
さかざらば	ever blooming in it,
はるのこころは	springtime hearts
のどけからまし	would feel at ease.'

This is the very same place where he composed that poem!" Just now someone has composed a verse resembling the place as it is today.

といふうたよめるところなりけり」いまけふあるひと、ところににたるうたよめり。

ちよへたる	Millennia have passed
まつにはあれど	for these pines, and yet
いにしへの	the chilling voice
こゑのさむさは	of days long gone by
かはらざりけり	remains unchanged!

And another person has composed:

また、あるひとのよめる、

きみこひて	In longing for milord,
よをふるやどの	ages pass at this lodging
むめのはな	where plum blossoms

むかしのかにぞ	even now put forth
なほにほひける	their past fragrance!

While this is being said, our joy grows ever greater as we draw ever closer to the capital city upstream. Among those now returning to *The Capital* are some who had no *Children* when they departed, but gave birth to *Children* after arriving in the provinces. All of them now carry their children in their arms as they disembark from the ship to walk about before coming back on board again. Seeing this, the mother whose child died is unable to contain her grief.

といひつつぞ、みやこのちかづくをよろこびつつ、のぼる。かくのぼるひとびとのなかに、京よりくだりしときに、みなひと、子どもなかりき。いたれりしくににてぞ、子うめるものども、ありあへる。ひとみな、ふねのとまるところに、こをいだきつつ、おりのりす。これをみて、むかしのこのははは、かなしきにたへずして、

なかりしも	Recalling them without
ありつつかへる	those they now return with,
ひとのこを	other people's children,
ありしもなくて	without the one I recall,
くるがかなしさ	comes with such grief!

That's what she said while she wept! How must the father feel to hear this? Such words and poems are surely not the product of idle whim. It is said both overseas and here that they are undertaken when thoughts are beyond enduring. Tonight we stay at a place called "Cormorant Hall."

といひてぞなきける。ちちもこれをききて、いかがあらむ。かうやうのことも、うたも、このむとてあるにもあらざるべし。もろこしもここも、おもふことにたへぬときのわざとか。こよひ、うどのといふところにとまる。

The Tenth. Some hindrance prevented us from going upstream.

十日。さはることありて、のぼらず。

The Eleventh. Rain fell for a bit and then stopped. As we pushed on upstream, we saw a mountain range spreading out to the east. When asked about it, someone told us the shrine of Yawata is there. Hearing this, people were overjoyed and bowed down in prayer. The bridge of Yamazaki could also be seen. Our happiness knew no bounds. Here in the vicinity of *Sōō-ji*, our ship rests for a bit, there being some matters to settle. There are many willow trees on the riverbank by the temple. Someone looking down at the reflections of the willows in the watery depths composed this verse:

十一日。あめいささかにふりて、やみぬ。かくてさしのぼるに、ひむがしのかたに、やまのよこほれるをみて、ひとにとへば、「やはたのみや」といふ。これをききてよろこびて、ひとびとをがみたてまつる。やまざきのはしみゆ。うれしきことかぎりなし。ここに、相應寺のほとりに、しばしふねをとどめて、とかくさだむることあり。このてらのきしほとりに、やなぎおほくあり。あるひと、このやなぎのかげのかはのそこにうつれるをみて、よめるうた、

さざれなみ	Rippling wavelets
よするあやをば	approach in a pattern
あをやぎの	of green willows
かげのいとして	whose dappled threads
おるかとぞみる	seem woven together!

The Twelfth. We have stayed over in Yamazaki.

十二日。やまざきにとまれり。

The Thirteenth. Still in Yamazaki.

十三日。なほやまざきに。

The Fourteenth. Rain falls. Today we sent for carriages to take us to *The Capital*.

十四日。あめふる。けふ、くるま、京へとりにやる。

The Fifteenth. Today the carriages came. Tired of our difficulties aboard the ship, we left the ship and have moved to the house of some people. The people in this house seemed pleased to be acting as hosts. Seeing these hosts being such fine hosts felt overwhelming. We returned the kindness in various ways. The people in this house were leaving and entering without giving offense. All was as it should have been.

十五日。けふ、くるまゐてきたり。ふねのむつかしさに、ふねよりひとのいへにうつる。このひとのいへ、よろこべるやうにて、あるじしたり。このあるじの、またあるじのよきをみるに、うたておもほゆ。いろいろにかへりごとす。いへのひとのいでいり、にくげならずゐややかなり。

The Sixteenth. Today at sunset we were on the verge of heading off to *The Capital*. There was no change to the small sign depicting a chest at Yamazaki, or the large effigies of a conch-shaped rice cake and fishing hook off the great road curving along the river-bend of Magari. Someone said: "There's no way of knowing what lies in the shop-owners' hearts." On our way to *The Capital*, a person hosted us at Shimasaka. This was a most unexpected deed on their part. People have been doing much more for us on our return than they ever did when we departed. Here yet again we returned the kindness. Thinking to enter *The Capital* at night, we traveled onward in a leisurely manner while the moon was rising. As we crossed the laurel river of Katsura-gawa under shining moonlight, people said: "Unlike the uncertain course of tomorrow's stream at Asuka-gawa mentioned in poems, the calms and rapids of this river remain unaltered!" And with these words, the following verse was composed:

十六日。けふのようさつかた、京へのぼる。ついでにみれば、やまざきのこびつのゑも、まがりのおほちのかたも、かはらざりけり。「うりびとのこころをぞしらぬ」とぞいふなる。かくて京へいくに、しまさかにて、ひとあるじしたり。かならずしもあるまじきわざなり。たちてゆきしときよりは、くるときぞ、ひとはとかくありける。これにもかへりごとす。よるになして、京には、いらむとおもへば、いそぎしもせぬほどに、つきいでぬ。かつらがは、つきのあかきにぞわたる。ひとびとのいはく、「このかは、あすかがはにあらねば、ふちせさらにかはらざりけり」といひて、あるひとのよめるうた、

ひさかたの	Far off in the firmament,
つきにおひたる	lies the moon bearing
かつらがは	the laurel whose river
そこなるかげも	holds a reflection in its depths
かはらざりけり	revealing no change!

Another person uttered:

また、あるひとのいへる、

あまぐもの	Grown as distant
はるかなりつる	as heaven's clouds
かつらがは	is the laurel whose river
そでをひでても	I now have crossed
わたりぬるかな	with wetted sleeves!

And yet another person composed this:

また、あるひとよめり。

かつらがは	Laurel River
わがこころにも	does not share the path
かよはねど	of my heart, and yet
おなじふかさに	it seems to flow
ながるべらなり	at the same depth.

Excessive joy at the prospect of being in *The Capital* led to an excessive number of poems. Night fell and the places we came across were no longer visible. What joy to be finally entering *The Capital*! We reached home and went through the main gate. Under the bright moonlight every detail is visible. The place is hopelessly dilapidated and in far worse shape than we had heard. Clearly, the heart of the person to whom we had entrusted it has likewise deteriorated! "Since we had always viewed the fence between us as no barrier to seeing our two houses as one, they had actually volunteered to look after it." "That's right! And we never failed finding an opportunity to send them things." "And now to see it like this tonight!" But we can't very well allow ourselves to say such things in raised voices. Despite this glaring evidence of disregard, we will make an earnest show of gratitude with something. At any rate, the garden now has a water-filled depression resembling a pond. I recall there being many pines in that area. Only half now remain, as though the past five or six years had been *A Thousand* years instead! New ones now grow among those remaining. The general state of utter deterioration inspired people to say how poignant everything is. Among those pangs of longing that come ceaselessly to mind, how great the grief at returning unaccompanied by the girl born in this house! Others from the ship gather their children to them and bustle about. A person understanding the unendurable grief this brings whispered a verse:

京のうれしきあまりに、うたもあまりぞおほかる。よふけてくれば、ところどころもみえず。京にいりたちてうれし。いへにいたりて、かどにいるに、つきあかければ、いとよくありさまみゆ。ききしよりもまして、いふかひなくぞこぼれやぶれたる。いへに、あづけたりつるひとのこころも、あれたるなりけり。「なかがきこそあれ、ひとついへのやうなれば、のぞみてあづかれるなり」「さるは。たよりごとにものもたえずえさ

せたり」「こよひ、かかること」と、こわだかにものもいはせず。いとはつらくみゆれど、こころざしはせむとす。さて、いけめいてくぼまり、みづつけるところあり。ほとりにまつもありき。いつとせむとせのうちに、千とせやすぎにけむ、かたへはなくなりにけり。いまおひたるぞまじれる。おほかたの、みなあれにたれば、「あはれ」とぞ、ひとびといふ。おもひいでぬことなく、おもひこひしきがうちに、このいへにてうまれしをむなごの、もろともにかへらねば、いかがはかなしき。ふなびとも、みなこたかりてののしる。かかるうちに、なほかなしきにたへずして、ひそかにこころしれるひとといへりけるうた、

むまれしも	Remembering the birth
かへらぬものを	of one not returning,
わがやどに	great is the grief at seeing
こまつのあるを	pine saplings growing
みるがかなしさ	here on our grounds!

Those are the words they uttered. It must not have sufficed, for there was also this:

とぞいへる。なほあかずやあらむ、またかくなむ、

みしひとの	If only I could still see and
まつのちとせに	pine for a thousand years
みましかば	over the one I once saw,
とほくかなしき	would we have parted
わかれせましや	grieving into the distance?

There are many other bitterly regretful matters that are hard to forget, but I cannot cover them all. In any case, I will soon rip this up.

わすれがたく、くちをしきことおほかれど、えつくさず。とまれかうまれ、とくやりてむ。

APPENDIX 2

Tsurayuki's Chronology

This chronological summary of Tsurayuki's life lists events for which a specific year can be identified, each indicated in bold with the era name and corresponding year in the Gregorian calendar. Individual events within each year are also listed in bold in chronological order when such information is available.

Jōgan 12 (871): likely born this year or next to Ki no Mochiyuki by a palace performer.

Kanpyō 5 (893): on 9/25 first dated *waka* appears in *Shinsen man'yōshū* from poetry matches **at some point** that year hosted by Uda's older brother Koresada (d. 903) and their mother Hanshi (833–900).

Shōtai 1 (898): in 7th month contributes *waka* to a maidenflower contest at the Teiji'in.

Engi 1 (901): first known screen *waka* composed to celebrate Prince Motoyasu turning seventy.

Engi 2 (902): in 5th month composes screen *waka* for Rear Palace.

Engi 5 (905): on 2/21 composes screen *waka* on behalf of Fujiwara no Mitsuko (874–937) celebrating the fortieth year of her older brother Sadakuni; **on 2/29** contributes *waka* to poetry match hosted by Taira no Sadabumi (d. 923); **on 4/18** formally presents *Kokinshū* to Daigo; **at some point** becomes *gosho-dokoro no azukari*.

Engi 6 (906): in 2nd month also becomes *gon-shōjō* of Echizen; **at some point** composes screen *waka* depicting monthly court rites for Daigo.

Engi 7 (907): on 2/27 becomes *naizenshi no tenzen*; **on 9/10** writes preface to *waka* commemorating the Ōi-gawa excursion; **at some point** contributes to a maidenflower poetry match hosted by Uda.

Engi 8 (908): **at some point** this year or next composes *waka* mourning Narihira's grandson Kaisen.

Engi 10 (910): **in 2nd month** becomes *shōnaiki*.

Engi 12 (912): **in 12th month** composes screen *waka* on behalf of Daigo when Mitsuko becomes *naishi no kami*; **at some point** this year or next composes *waka* celebrating Sadakata turning forty.

Engi 13 (913): **on 3/13** contributes *waka* to Teiji'in poetry match; **in 4th month** becomes *tainaiki*; **on 10/13** contributes *waka* to palace chrysanthemum match; **next day** composes screen *waka* celebrating Mitsuko turning forty.

Engi 14 (914): **on 2/25** composes screen *waka* on behalf of Uda celebrating the skirt-donning (*mogi*) ceremony of Daigo's eldest daughter, Kanshi (b. 899).

Engi 15 (915): **on *2/5** composes screen *waka* on behalf of Daigo for his daughter Kyōshi (902–915) as Kamo priestess; **on 9/22** composes screen *waka* on behalf of Fujiwara no Kazuko for Fujiwara no Michiakira (856–920); **on 12/3** composes screen *waka* on behalf of Fujiwara no Yasutada (890–936) celebrating the fiftieth year of his mother, Renshi.

Engi 16 (916): **at some point** composes screen *waka* on behalf of Daigo for his daughter Senshi (902–920) as Kamo priestess.

Engi 17 (917): **on 1/7** raised to Junior Fifth Rank, lower grade; **in 1st month** becomes *suke* of Kaga; **in 8th month** composes *waka* at the command of Daigo; **in winter** composes screen *waka* for Daigo's younger brother Atsuyoshi (888–930); **at some point** composes screen *waka* requesting promotion to *suke* of Mino.

Engi 18 (918): **in 2nd month** becomes *suke* of Mino; **also** composes screen *waka* celebrating the *mikuji-age* (hair-binding) ceremony for Daigo's daughter Kinshi; **on 4/26** composes screen *waka* for crown prince Yasuakira (903–923); **in 7th month or earlier** composes screen *waka* for Daigo's consort Minamoto no Washi (d. 947).

Engi 19 (919): **in spring** composes screen *waka* on behalf of Daigo for either Yasuakira's consort or his mother, Onshi.

Engi 21 (921): **at some point** composes *waka* celebrating Kanesuke's promotion to *sangi*.

Engi 22 (922): **on 3/10** avoids attending court during the death anniversary of Kanmu's consort Fujiwara no Otomuro (760–790).

Enchō 1 (923): **in 6th month** becomes *daikenmotsu*.

Enchō 2 (924): **in 5th month** composes screen *waka* on behalf of Daigo for Onshi; **in 8th month** composes screen *waka* on behalf of Tadahira to celebrate his chief wife, Minamoto no Junshi (875–925), turning forty.

Enchō 4 (926): on 8/24 composes screen *waka* on behalf of Tsunesuke celebrating the sixtieth year of his father, Kiyotsura (867–930), the fourth son of Yasunori; **on 9/24** composes screen *waka* celebrating Uda turning sixty on behalf of his consort Fujiwara no Hōshi.

Enchō 5 (927): in 9th month composes *waka* for a *suhama* display presented by the losing side at Tadahira's garden match.

Enchō 6 (928): at some point composes proxy screen *waka* on behalf of Saneyori for Onshi.

Enchō 7 (929): in 9th month becomes *ukyō no suke*; **on 10/14** composes screen *waka* on behalf of Daigo's daughter Shūshi (d. 933) celebrating the fortieth year of her husband, Prince Motoyoshi (890–943).

Enchō 8 (930): in 1st month becomes governor of Tosa; **at some point** sends *waka* from Tosa to Kanesuke mourning the latter's mother; **at some point** sends *waka* composed on behalf of Sadakata to celebrate the cap-donning (*genpuku*) of Daigo's son Shōmei (924–990).

Shōhei 3 (933): on 8/27 sends screen *waka* from Tosa on behalf of Mitsuko or Suzaku celebrating the skirt-donning of Onshi's daughter Kōshi (920–957).

Shōhei 4 (934): on 12/21 likely leaves the governor's mansion in Tosa.

Shōhei 5 (935): on 2/16 likely back in the capital; **in summer** contributes to fan match hosted by Fujiwara no Tsunesuke (879–938); **in 9th month** composes screen *waka* on behalf of Prince Sadatoki (874–929) celebrating his mother Kazuko turning eighty; **on 12/2** composes screen *waka* on behalf of Saneyori celebrating the coming-of-age of three offspring; **in 12th month** composes screen *waka* for palace; **at some point** composes *waka* at Tadahira's Shirakawa residence; **at some point** visits Kanesuke's deserted Awata mansion; **at some point** composes *waka* at the residence of Kinshi, now Morosuke's wife; **repeatedly** seeks official appointment in *waka* to Tadahira and Morosuke.

Shōhei 6 (936): on 1/10 writes preface to *waka* for the Day of the Rat celebration at Tadahira's residence; **in spring** inscribes *waka* on fixed screen for Tadahira; **in spring** composes screen *waka* for Saneyori; **in summer** composes *waka* celebrating Renshi turning seventy; **at some point** composes screen *waka* for Tadahira's fifth son, Morotada (920–969).

Shōhei 7 (937): in 1st month composes screen *waka* for palace; **at some point** composes screen *waka* on behalf of Tsunesuke.

Tengyō 1 (938): repeatedly seeks a post in *waka* to Tadahira, Saneyori, and Morosuke.

Tengyō 2 (939): **on 2/28** hosts poetry match in Suō; **in 4th month** composes screen *waka* for Saneyori; **in *7th month** composes screen *waka* for Yōzei's son, Minamoto no Kiyokage (884–950); **at some point** this year or next composes screen *waka* for Tokihira's son Atsutada (906–943).

Tengyō 3 (940): **in 3rd month** becomes *genba no kami*; **on 5/14** renewed as a *bettō* for Suzaku'in.

Tengyō 4 (941): **in 1st month** composes screen *waka* for Saneyori; **in 3rd month** composes screen *waka* for palace; **on 3/28** composes *waka* seeing Kintada off to Ōmi.

Tengyō 5 (942): **on 4/27** recites *waka* at Iwashimizu Hachimangū; **in 4th month** composes screen *waka* for Tadahira's eldest daughter, Kishi (904–962), as *naishi no kami*; **on 5/17** hosts poetry banquet for foreign envoys; **in 9th month** composes screen *waka* for palace; **at some point** composes screen *waka* for Teiji'in.

Tengyō 6 (943): **on 1/7** raised to the upper grade of Junior Fifth Rank; **in 1st month** composes proxy *waka* for Morosuke to thank his father for lending him a belt ornament; **in 4th month** composes screen *waka* celebrating Kishi turning forty; **at some point** this year or next writes *Shinsen waka* preface.

Tengyō 8 (945): **in 2nd month** composes screen *waka* for palace; **on 3/28** becomes *mokugon no kami*.

Tengyō 9 (946): **in fall** sends *waka* to Kintada shortly before dying.

Bibliography

Abbreviations are as listed in the front matter. Primary sources are listed by title to distinguish them from secondary ones, and to reflect the uncertainties typically surrounding their authorial attribution. Only those editors responsible for particular texts are mentioned in volumes containing multiple texts. Translations are listed under their translators' names.

Abe Toshiko. *Uta monogatari to sono shūhen*. Tokyo: Kazama Shobō, 1969.
Abrahamson, Marc S. *Ethnic Identity in Tang China*. Philadelphia: University of Pennsylvania Press, 2008.
Akimoto Morihide. "*Tosa nikki* no bunshō." *Kokugo to kokubungaku* 62, no. 10 (1985): 1–12.
Akiyama Ken. "Kodai ni okeru nikki bungaku no tenkai." In *Heianchō nikki* I, edited by Nihon bungaku kenkyū shiryō kankō-kai, 16–23. Tokyo: Yūseidō, 1971.
Allaire, Gloria, ed. *The Italian Novella: A Book of Essays*. London: Routledge, 2003.
Allen, Roger. "The Novella in Arabic: A Study in Fictional Genres." *International Journal of Middle East Studies* 18, no. 4 (November 1986): 473–84.
Amagai Hiroyoshi, ed. *Uta-gatari to setsuwa*. Tokyo: Shintensha, 1996.
———. "Uta-gatari to uchigiki." *Bungaku gogaku* 151 (June 1996): 19–26.
Andō Yasuji. "*Tsurayuki shū* ni okeru Saneyori zōtōka o megutte: *Tosa nikki* shūshō no nishu no eika ni yosete." *Reitaku daigaku kiyō* 57 (December 1993): 347–58.
Angles, Jeffrey. "Watching Commoners, Performing Class: Images of the Common People in *The Pillow Book of Sei Shōnagon*." *Japan Review* 13 (2001): 33–65.
Arai Eizō. "Ōchō kannin Ki no Tsurayuki no shokumu." *Bungaku* 54, no. 2 (February 1986): 141–50.
Araki Hiroshi. "Abe no Nakamaro kichō densetsu no yukue: *Shintōsho* to *Konjaku monogatari shū* soshite *Tosa nikki* e." In *Nichietsu kōryū ni okeru rekishi, shakai bunka no shokadai*, edited by Liu Jianhui, 45–58. Kyoto: Kokusai Nihon Bunka Kenkyū Sentaa, 2015.

Arntzen, Sonja, and Moriyuki Itō. *The Sarashina Diary: A Woman's Life in Eleventh Century Japan*. New York: Columbia University Press, 2014.
Aston, W. G. "An Ancient Japanese Classic (The 'Tosa nikki,' or Tosa Diary)." *Transactions of the Asiatic Society of Japan* 3, no. 2 (1875): 109–17.
———, trans. *Nihongi: Chronicles of Japan from the Earliest Times to A.D. 697*. Rutland, VT: Tuttle Publishing, 1972.

Bachelard, Gaston. *The Poetics of Space*. Boston: Beacon Press, 1994.
Bakhtin, M. M. *The Dialogic Imagination*. Translated by Caryl Emerson and Michael Holquist. Austin: University of Texas Press, 1981.
———. *Rabelais and His World*. Translated by Helene Iswolsky. Bloomington: Indiana University Press, 1984.
Bal, Mieke. *Narratology: Introduction to the Theory of Narrative*. Toronto: University of Toronto Press, 1997.
Bassnett, Susan. *Translation Studies*. 3rd ed. London: Routledge, 2002.
Batten, Bruce. *Gateway to Japan: Hakata in War and Peace, 500–1300*. Honolulu: University of Hawai'i Press, 2006.
Beecroft, Alexander. *An Ecology of World Literature: From Antiquity to the Present Day*. London: Verso, 2015.
Bialock, David T. "Voice, Text, and the Question of Poetic Borrowing in Late Classical Japanese Poetry." *Harvard Journal of Asiatic Studies* 54, no. 1 (June 1994): 181–231.
Bock, Felicia. *Engi Shiki: Procedures of the Engi Era*. 2 vols. Tokyo: Sophia University, 1970.
Borgen, Robert. *Sugawara no Michizane and the Early Heian Court*. Cambridge, MA: Harvard Council on East Asian Studies, 1986.
Bowring, Richard John. *Murasaki Shikibu: Her Diary and Poetic Memoirs*. Princeton, NJ: Princeton University Press, 1985.
Branham, Robert B. *Unruly Eloquence: Lucian and the Comedy of Traditions*. Cambridge, MA: Harvard University Press, 1989.
Brannen, Noah. "Ancient Japanese Songs from the *Kinkafu* Collection." *Monumenta Nipponica* 23, no. 4 (1968): 275–320.
Brodzki, Bella. *Can These Bones Live? Translation, Survival, and Cultural Memory*. Stanford, CA: Stanford University Press, 2007.
Brower, Robert H., and Earl Miner. *Japanese Court Poetry*. Stanford, CA: Stanford University Press, 1961.
Bundy, Roselee. "A Format of Their Own: The Hundred-Poem Sequences of Sone no Yoshitada, Minamoto no Shitagō, and the Priest Egyō." *Monumenta Nipponica* 75, no. 1 (2020): 1–44.
Burns, Susan L. *Before the Nation: Kokugaku and the Imagining of Community in Early Modern Japan*. Durham, NC: Duke University Press, 2003.
Busujima Yukiko. "*Tosa nikki* no hyōgen: 'wasure-gai,' 'wasure-gusa' o chūshin ni." *Gakuai* 12 (March 1996): 59–69.
Butterfield, Ardis. *Poetry and Music in Medieval France: From Jean Renart to Guillaume de Machaut*. Cambridge: Cambridge University Press, 2002.

Carpenter, John T., ed. *Reading Surimono: The Interplay of Text and Image in Japanese Prints*. Leiden: Hotei Publishing, 2008.

Cavanaugh, Carole. "Text and Textile: Unweaving the Female Subject in Heian Writing." *positions* 4, no. 3 (Winter 1996): 593–636.

Ceadel, E. B. "The Ōi River Poems and Preface." *Asia Major* 3, no. 1 (1953): 65–106.

Chaiklin, Martha, ed. *Mediated by Gifts: Politics and Society in Japan, 1350–1850*. Leiden: Brill, 2016.

Chen, Jack W. "Sovereignty, Coinage, and Kinship in Early China." *positions* 21, no. 3 (2013): 637–58.

Chōya gunsai. By Miyoshi no Tameyasu. Edited by Kuroita Katsumi. KST 29. Tokyo: Yoshikawa Kōbunkan, 1964.

Commons, Anne. *Hitomaro: Poet as God*. Leiden: Brill, 2009.

Cronin, Michael. *Across the Lines: Travel, Language, Translation*. Cork: Cork University Press, 2000.

Crossley, Pamela Kyle. "Bohai/Parhae Identity and the Coherence of the Dan gur Under the Khitan/Liao Empire." *International Journal of Korean History* 21, no. 1 (February 2016): 11–45.

De Certeau, Michel. *The Practice of Everyday Life*. Berkeley: University of California Press, 1984.

Denecke, Wiebke. *Classical World Literatures: Sino-Japanese and Greco-Roman Comparisons*. Oxford: Oxford University Press, 2014.

———. "'Topic Poetry Is All Ours': Poetic Composition on Chinese Lines in Early Heian Japan." *Harvard Journal of Asiatic Studies* 67, no. 1 (June 2007): 1–49.

Derrida, Jacques. *Given Time: I. Counterfeit Money*. Chicago: University of Chicago Press, 1992.

Dustin, Griffin. *Satire: A Critical Reintroduction*. Lexington: University Press of Kentucky, 1994.

Duthie, Torquil. *Man'yōshū and the Imperial Imagination in Early Japan*. Leiden: Brill, 2014.

Egan, Charles H. "Recent-Style Shi Poetry: Quatrains (*jue ju*)." In *How to Read Chinese Poetry: A Guided Anthology*, edited by Zong-qi Cai, 199–225. New York: Columbia University Press, 2007.

———. "Were *Yüeh-fu* Ever Folk Songs? Reconsidering the Relevance of Oral Theory and Balladry Analogies." *Chinese Literature* 22 (2000): 31–66.

Egyō hōshi shū. Edited by Shinpen kokka taikan henshū iin-kai. In KT 3:1. Tokyo: Kadokawa Shoten, 1983.

Eiga monogatari. Edited by Yamanaka Yutaka, Akiyama Ken, Ikeda Naotaka, and Fukunaga Susumu. SNKBZ 31–33. Tokyo: Shōgakukan, 1997.

Emmerich, Michael. *The Tale of Genji: Translation, Canonization, and World Literature*. New York: Columbia University Press, 2013.

Endō Yoshimoto. "Tsurayuki no 'buntai to hyōgen ishiki:' *Tosa nikki* no bunshō o tōshite." In *Heianchō nikki* I, edited by Nihon bungaku kenkyū shiryō kankō-kai, 103–12. Tokyo: Yūseidō, 1971.

Engi shiki. Edited by Kuroita Katsumi. In KST 26. Tokyo: Yoshikawa Kōbunkan, 1937.

Fernández-Armesto, Felipe. *Civilizations: Culture, Ambition, and the Transformation of Nature.* New York: Simon & Schuster, 2001.
Foucault, Michel. "Of Other Spaces." *Diacritics* 16, no. 1 (Spring 1986): 22–27.
———. "What Is an Author?" In *Language, Counter-Memory, Practice: Selected Essays and Interviews,* edited by D. F. Buchard, 113–38. Ithaca, NY: Cornell University Press, 1977.
Friday, Karl. *Hired Swords: The Rise of Private Warrior Power in Early Japan.* Stanford, CA: Stanford University Press, 1992.
Fuchs, Florian. "Novella." *New Literary History* 50, no. 3 (Summer 2019): 399–403.
Fujihara Mika. "The Historical Reality of Ki no Aritsune and the *Ise monogatari.*" In *An Ise monogatari Reader: Contexts and Receptions,* edited by Joshua Mostow, Tokurō Yamamoto, and Kurtis Hanlon, 42–63. Leiden: Brill, 2021.
Fujioka Tadaharu. *Ki no Tsurayuki: utakotoba o tsukuru.* Tokyo: Shūeisha, 1985.
Fujiwara no Yasunori den. By Miyoshi no Kiyoyuki. In *Nihon shisō taikei* 8, edited by Yamagishi Tokuhei, Takeuchi Rizō, Ienaga Saburō, and Ōsone Shōsuke, 59–72. Tokyo: Iwanami Shoten, 1979.
Fukazawa Tōru. *Jiko genkyū tekisuto no keifugaku: Heian bungaku o meguru nanatsu no danshō.* Tokyo: Shinwasha, 2002.
———. "*Tosa nikki* jikūron: sono tassei to genkai." *Nihon bungaku* 32, no. 6 (June 1983): 59–68.
Fukuda Yoshikazu. "*Tosa nikki* kanken: iwayuru bōchi aishōka ni tsuite." *Nagasaki daigaku kyōikubu kiyō: jinbun kagaku* 15 (January 1975): 1–9.
Fukui Teisuke. "*Tosa nikki* to Ariwara no Narihira." *Bunkei ronsō* 3 and 7 (1968 and 1971): 19–38 and 1–17.
———. *Zōho Ise monogatari seisei-ron.* Tokyo: Parutosu-sha, 1997.
Fukumori, Naomi. "Sei Shōnagon's *Makura no sōshi*: A Re-visionary History." *Journal of the Association of Teachers of Japanese* 31, no. 1 (1999): 1–44.
Furuhashi Nobuyoshi. "Warai no bungaku, kaigyaku no seishin." *Kokubungaku kaishaku to kanshō* 44, no. 2 (February 1979): 114–20.

Gailus, Andreas. "Form and Chance: The German Novella." In *The Novel,* vol. 2, *Forms and Themes,* edited by Franco Moretti, 739–76. Princeton, NJ: Princeton University Press, 2006.
Geki bunin. Edited by Inoue Kōji. ZGR 4. Tokyo: Gunsho Ruijū Kansei-kai, 2004.
Genji monogatari. Edited by Abe Akio, Imai Gen'e, Akiyama Ken, and Suzuki Hideo. SNKBZ 20–25. Tokyo: Shōgakukan, 1994–98.
Gill, Robin D. *"Rise, Ye Sea Slugs!": A Theme from In Praise of Olde Haiku, with Many More Poems and Fine Elaboration.* Key Biscayne, FL: Paraverse Press, 2003.
Gilmore, John T. *Satire.* London: Routledge, 2018.
Glassman, Hank. "Chinese Buddhist Death Ritual and the Transformation of Japanese Kinship." In *The Buddhist Dead: Practices, Discourses, Representations,* edited by Bryan J. Cuevas and Jacqueline I. Stone, 378–404. Honolulu: University of Hawai'i Press, 2007.

Good, Graham. "Notes on the Novella." *NOVEL: A Forum on Fiction* 10, no. 3 (Spring 1977): 197–211.
Goodwin, Janet R. *Selling Songs and Smiles: The Sex Trade in Heian and Kamakura Japan*. Honolulu: University of Hawai'i Press, 2007.
Gosen wakashū. Edited by Katagiri Yōichi. SNKBT 6. Tokyo: Iwanami Shoten, 1996.
Gotō Shōko. "Uta-gatari to uta monogatari." In *Kokinshū*, edited by Ueno Osamu, 183–200. Tokyo: Benseisha, 1993.
Gundry, David J. *Parody, Irony and Ideology in the Fiction of Ihara Saikaku*. Leiden: Brill, 2017.
Gurevich, Aron. *Medieval Popular Culture: Problems of Belief and Perception*. Cambridge: Cambridge University Press, 1988.

Hagitani Boku. *Heianchō uta-awase taisei* 1. Kyoto: Dōhōsha Shuppan, 1995.
———. "*Ise monogatari* no sakusha wa Tsurayuki naru beshi." *Nihon bungaku kenkyū* 42 and 43 (February 2002): 23–38 and 50–56.
———. *Tosa nikki zenchūshaku*. Tokyo: Kadokawa Shoten, 1967.
Hamada Kosaku. "Transition of Understanding Parhae in Japan." *Journal of Northeast Asian History* 4, no. 2 (December 2007): 173–89.
Harich-Schneider, Eta. *Roei, the Medieval Court Songs of Japan*. Tokyo: Sophia University Press, 1965.
Harries, Phillip. "Personal Poetry Collections: Their Origin and Development through the Heian Period." *Monumenta Nipponica* 35, no. 3 (1980): 299–317.
Harris, Florence Best, trans. *Log of a Japanese Journey from the Province of Tosa to the Capital*. Meadville, PA: Flood & Vincent, 1891.
Harris, H. Jay, trans. *The Tales of Ise*. Rutland, VT: Tuttle Publishing, 1972.
Harusame monogatari. By Ueda Akinari. Edited by Nakamura Yukihiko, Nakamura Hiroyasu, and Takada Mamoru. In SNKBZ 78. Tokyo: Shōgakukan, 1995.
Hasegawa Kiyoyoshi. "*Tosa nikki* no zōtōka no kaishaku ni tsuite no shiken: omo toshite gohō- teki tachiba kara." *Gogaku bungaku* 10 (March 1972): 93–99.
Hasegawa Masaharu. "Abe no Nakamaro no zaitōka no seiritsu: uta-gatari hassei kō." *Kokugakuin zasshi* 70, no. 6 (June 1969): 15–25.
———. "'Bungakushi' o enshutsu shita otoko." *Kokubungaku kaishaku to kanshō* 44, no. 2 (February 1979): 15–23.
———. "Hyōgen, sono senryaku-teki na *Tosa nikki*." In *Ronshū nikki bungaku*, edited by Kimura Masanori, 127–39. Tokyo: Kasama Shoin, 1991.
———. *Ki no Tsurayuki ron*. Tokyo: Yūseidō, 1984.
———. "'Toku yaritemu' no shisō: *Tosa nikki* o yomu." *Kokubungaku kaishaku to kanshō* 75, no. 3 (March 2010): 84–91.
———. "*Tosa nikki* no hōhō: kikō bungaku no hassei to kiryoka no dentō." *Tōyoko kokubungaku* 14 (March 1982): 5–18.
Hashimoto Satoshi. "*Tosa nikki* 'funa uta' chūshaku." *Kyoto Daigaku kokubungaku ronsō* 29 (March 2013): 1–14.
Hayashi Rokurō. "Shōsōin komonjo-chū no guchūreki." In *Kokiroku to nikki*, edited by Yamanaka Yutaka, 49–67. Kyoto: Shibunkaku, 1993.

Heichū monogatari. Edited by Shimizu Yoshiko. In SNKBZ 12. Tokyo: Shōgakukan, 1994.

Heldt, Gustav. "Between Followers and Friends: Male Homosocial Desire in Heian Court Poetry." *U.S.-Japan Women's Journal* 33 (2007): 3–32.

———. *The Pursuit of Harmony: Poetry and Power in Early Heian Japan*. Ithaca, NY: East Asia Program, Cornell University, 2008.

Henitiuk, Valerie. "Going to Bed with Arthur Waley: How Murasaki Shikibu Does and Does Not Become World Literature." *Comparative Literature Studies* 45, no. 1 (2008): 40–61.

Hérail, Francine. "The Position and Role of Provincial Governors at the Height of the Heian Period." *Cipango: French Journal of Japanese Studies* 3 (2014). https://doi.org/10.4000/cipango.607.

Hibbett, Howard. *The Chrysanthemum and the Fish: Japanese Humor since the Age of the Shoguns*. Tokyo: Kodansha International, 2002.

———. "Saikaku and Burlesque Fiction." *Harvard Journal of Asiatic Studies* 20, no. 1/2 (1957): 53–73.

Higashihara Nobuaki. "'Nami no soko naru hisakata no sora' Tsurayuki-teki kyōzō uchū to suihei takai kan." *Kōchi joshi daigaku kiyō bunka gakubu-hen* 58 (March 2009): 1–14.

———. *Tosa nikki kyokō ron: Shoki sanbun bungaku no seisei to kokufū bunka*. Tokyo: Musashino Shoin, 2015.

Higo Ryūkai. "*Tosa nikki* ni mirareru chimei sakuzatsu ni tsuite." *Meiji daigaku bungei kenkyū* 59 (February 1988): 58–86.

Higuchi Hiroshi. "*Tosa nikki* ni okeru Tsurayuki no tachiba." In *Heianchō nikki* I, edited by Nihon bungaku kenkyū shiryō kankō-kai, 36–53. Tokyo: Yūseidō, 1971.

Higuchi Yoshimaro. "Shinsen waka no seiritsu." *Kokugo to kokubungaku* 44, no. 10 (October 1967): 22–43.

Hijikata Yōichi. *Nikki no seiiki: Heianchō no ichininshō gensetsu*. Tokyo: Yūbun Shoin, 2007.

Hirasawa Ryūsuke. *Ōchō bungaku no shihatsu*. Tokyo: Kasama Shoin, 2009.

———. "*Tosa nikki* ni okeru kundokugo: Tsurayuki no shiyō ito." *Shirayuri joshi daigaku kenkyū kiyō* 26 (December 1990): 29–48.

Hirota Osamu. *Murasaki Shikibu shū uta no ba to hyōgen*. Tokyo: Kasama Shoin, 2012.

Holcombe, Charles. "Trade-Buddhism: Maritime Trade, Immigration and the Buddhist Landfall in Early Japan." *Journal of the American Oriental Society* 119, no. 2 (1999): 280–92.

Honchō monzui. Compiled by Fujiwara no Akihira (989–1066). Edited by Ōsone Shōsuke, Kinpira Tadashi, and Gotō Akio. SNKBT 27. Tokyo: Iwanami Shoten, 1992.

Honma Ken'ichi. "*Tosa nikki* to *Nittō guhō junrai kōki*." In *Nihon bungaku sōkō: Nishio Sensei kanreki kinen ronshū*, edited by Nishio Mitsuo Sensei kanreki kinen-kai, 44–58. Tokyo: Tōyō Hōki Shuppan, 1968.

Horikawa Noboru. "*Tosa nikki* no bōtō no ichibun o megutte no shōron." *Shōwa gakuin tandai kiyō*, 13 (March 1977): 1–16.

———. "*Tosa nikki* no hōhō keisei shiron: byōbu uta no hyōgen kōzō to no kanren o chūshin ni shite." *Gengo to bungei* 79 (November 1974): 61–80.

Horiuchi Hideaki. "Nikki kara nikki bungaku e." *Kokubungaku kaishaku to kanshō* 50, no. 8 (July 1985): 6–12.

Horton, Mack H. "Literary Diplomacy in Early Nara: Prince Nagaya and the Verses for Envoys from Silla in *Kaifūsō*." In *China and Beyond in the Mediaeval Period: Cultural Crossings and Inter-Regional Connections*, edited by Dorothy C. Wong and Gustav Heldt, 261–78. Amherst, NY: Cambria Press, 2014.

———. "Portrait of a Medieval Japanese Marriage: The Domestic Life of Sanjōnishi Sanetaka and His Wife." *Japanese Language and Literature* 37, no. 2 (October 2003): 130–54.

———. *Traversing the Frontier: The* Man'yōshū *Account of a Japanese Mission to Silla in 736–737*. Cambridge, MA: Harvard University Asia Center, 2012.

Hughes, David W. *Traditional Folk Song in Modern Japan: Sources, Sentiment and Society*. Folkestone, UK: Global Oriental, 2008.

Hutcheon, Linda. *A Theory of Parody: The Teachings of Twentieth-Century Art Forms*. New York: Methuen, 1985.

Ichihara Sunao. "*Tosa nikki* nigatsu kunichi no jō no imi suru mono." *Bungaku gogaku* 130 (June 1991): 64–73.

Ichinoe Wataru. "Akinari to *Tosa nikki*: 'Kaizoku' ron no tame ni." *Kokugo to kokubungaku* 86, no. 12 (December 2009): 41–53.

———. *Ueda Akinari no jidai: Kamigata wagaku kenkyū*. Tokyo: Perikansha, 2012.

Ide Yukio and Hashimoto Tatsuhiro, eds. *Tosa nikki o aruku: Tosa nikki chiri ben zenyakuchū*. Kōchi-shi: Kōchi Shinbunsha, 2003.

Ii Haruki. "Tameie-bon *Tosa nikki* ni tsuite." *Chūko bungaku* 71 (2003): 1–11.

Iizuka Hiroshi. "*Tosa nikki* no waka: byōbu uta to no kanren ni tsuite." *Bungaku kenkyū* 47 (July 1978): 12–21.

Ikeda Kikan. *Koten no hihyō-teki shochi ni kansuru kenkyū*. Tokyo: Iwanami Shoten, 1941.

———. "Nikki bungaku to kikō bungaku." In *Heianchō nikki* I, edited by Nihon bungaku kenkyū shiryō kankō-kai, 1–6. Tokyo: Yūseidō, 1971.

Ikeda Naotaka. "*Tosa nikki* no tabi: kai uta to tabi zengo no kiji kara." *Kokubungaku kaishaku to kanshō* 71, no. 3 (March 2006): 56–63.

Ikeda Tsutomu. "*Tosa nikki* wa hatashite Tsurayuki no saku ka." *Seijō bungei* 6 (January 1956): 1–15.

Imai Takuji. *Heianchō nikki no kenkyū*. Tokyo: Keibunshu, 1935.

Imanishi Yūichirō. "The Formation of the *Ise monogatari* and Its Background." In *An Ise monogatari Reader: Contexts and Receptions*, edited by Joshua Mostow, Tokurō Yamamoto, and Kurtis Hanlon, 15–27. Leiden: Brill, 2021.

Imazeki Toshiko. "*Tosa nikki* kō: josei kataku no imi." In *Heian bungaku ronshū*, edited by Sekine Keiko Kyōju taikan kinen-kai, 344–65. Tokyo: Kazama Shobō, 1992.

Ing, Michael David Kaulana. *The Dysfunction of Ritual in Early Confucianism*. Oxford: Oxford University Press, 2012.

Io nushi. Edited by Hanawa Hokiichi. In GR 18. Tokyo: Zoku Gunsho Ruijū Kanseikai, 1934. 1983 reprint.

Ise monogatari. Edited by Fukui Teisuke. In SNKBZ 12. Tokyo: Shōgakukan, 1994.

Ishihara Shōhei. *Heian nikki bungaku no kenkyū*. Tokyo: Benseisha, 1997.

———. "Nikki bungaku no hassō: shukaku no settei to 'katari' no hōhō." In *Ronshū nikki bungaku*, edited by Kimura Masanori, 38–58. Tokyo: Kasama Shoin, 1991.
———. "Setsuwa, denpan, imi." *Kokubungaku kaishaku to kanshō* 44, no. 2 (February 1979): 146–60.
———. "*Tosa nikki* no sōzō." *Teikyō kokubungaku* 9 (September 2002): 1–22.
Ishizaka Taeko. *Heianki nikki bungei no kenkyū*. Tokyo: Shintensha, 1997.
Itō Haku. *Man'yōshū no hyōgen to hōhō. Kodai wakashi kenkyū* 5. Tokyo: Hanawa Shobō, 1975.

Jackman, Barry, trans. *Tales of the Spring Rain: Harusame Monogatari by Ueda Akinari*. Tokyo: University of Tokyo Press, 1975.
Jackson, Reginald. *A Proximate Remove: Queering Intimacy and Loss in* The Tale of Genji. Berkeley, CA: University of California Press, 2021.
Jin, Ha. *The Banished Immortal: A Life of Li Bai (Li Po)*. New York: Pantheon Books, 2019.
Johnson, Jeffrey. "Saikaku and the Narrative Turnabout." *Journal of Japanese Studies* 27, no. 2 (Summer 2001): 323–45.
Jun, Teng. *The History of Sino-Japanese Cultural Exchange*. London: Routledge, 2019.

Kakehi Kumiko. *Ri Haku*. Tokyo: Kadokawa Shoten, 1988.
Kamitani Kaoru. *Kana bungaku no bunshōshi-teki kenkyū*. Ōsaka: Izumi Shoin.
———. "'Yomu' uta kara 'iu' uta 'kaku' uta e." In *Kōza Heian bungaku ronkyū*, edited by Heian bungaku ronkyū-kai, 153–73. Tokyo: Kasama Shobō, 1984.
Kamiyasu Kōji. "Abe no Nakamaro no zaitōka o megutte: jissaku-setsu no kanōsei." *Nihon bungaku bunka* 1 (2001): 33–44.
Kanai Toshihiro. "'Omuna' no tame ni: *Tosa nikki* no hyōshō to ronri." *Chūō daigaku kokubun* 50 (March 2007): 26–34.
Kanda Tatsumi. *Ki no Tsurayuki: aru ka naki ka no yo ni koso arikere*. Kyoto: Mineruva Shobō, 2009.
———. "*Tosa nikki* ron no tame no nōto: shinifian to shite no kaimen." *Heianchō bungaku kenkyū* 6 (December 1997): 114–17.
Kanechiku Nobuyuki. "Waka and Media: Kohitsu-gire, Kaishi, Tanzaku." In *Waka Opening Up to the World: Language, Community, and Gender*, edited by Haruo Shirane, Kanechiku Nobuyuki, Tabuchi Kumiko, and Jinno Hidenori, 378–89. Tokyo: Benseisha, 2012.
Kanesuke shū. Edited by Shinpen kokka taikan henshū iin-kai. In KT 3:1. Tokyo: Kadokawa Shoten, 1983.
Kang, Etsuko Hae-jin. *Diplomacy and Ideology in Japanese-Korean Relations: From the Fifteenth to the Eighteenth Century*. London: Macmillan Press, 1997.
Kanpyō gyoki. By Emperor Uda. Edited by Ichishima Kenkichi. In ZZGR 5. Tokyo: Kokusho Kankō-kai, 1909.
Kashima Tōru. "Fune no naka no 'mienai' hitobito." In *Tosa nikki no Koperunikusu-teki tenkai*, edited by Higashihara Nobuaki and Joel Joos, 163–82. Tokyo: Musashino Shoin, 2016.
Katagiri Yōichi. *Ise monogatari no kenkyū*. 2 vols. Meiji Shoin, 1975.
———. *Kokin wakashū no kenkyū*. Tokyo: Meiji Shoin, 1991.

Katō Kōji. "Ki to keri ga shimesu jishō no seiki to ninshiki to hatsuwaji to no jikan-teki kyori ni tsuite: *Tosa nikki* o shiryō toshite." *Tezukayama gakuin daigaku kenkyū ronshū* 32 (1997): 24–41.

Kawaguchi Hisao. *Heianchō Nihon kanbungaku shi no kenkyū* (jō). Tokyo: Meiji Shoin, 1982.

———. "*Tosa nikki* no seiritsu to sono kanbungaku-teki chiban." In *Heianchō nikki* I, edited by Nihon bungaku kenkyū shiryō kankō-kai, 97–102. Tokyo: Yūseidō, 1971.

Kawajiri Akio. "'Kike shū' to kokushi hensan: 'Kisoigariki' o chūshin toshite." *Shikan* 150 (March 2004): 1–13.

Kawanaka Tatsuo. "Waga kuni no kodai bungaku ni arawareta shikisai ni kansuru kenkyū: *Tosa nikki* no 'kurenai kōku yoki koromo kizu' no kōsatsu." *Matsuyama Shōdai ronshū* 12, no. 3 (October 1961): 113–21.

Kawashima, Terry. *Itineraries of Power: Texts and Traversals in Heian and Medieval Japan*. Cambridge, MA: Harvard University Asia Center, 2016.

———. *Writing Margins: The Textual Construction of Gender in Heian and Kamakura Japan*. Cambridge, MA: Harvard University Asia Center, 2001.

Keene, Donald. "The Comic Tradition in Renga." In *Japan in the Muromachi Age*, edited by John Whitney Hall and Toyoda Takeshi, 241–78. Berkeley: University of California Press, 1977.

———, trans. "The Tale of the Bamboo Cutter." In *Modern Japanese Fiction and its Traditions: An Introduction*, edited by J. Thomas Rimer, 275–305. Princeton, NJ: Princeton University Press, 1978.

———. *Travelers of a Hundred Ages: The Japanese as Revealed through 1,000 Years of Diaries*. New York: H. Holt, 1989.

Kikuchi Yasuhiko. "Ki no Tsurayuki kenkyūshi." *Kokubungaku* 37, no. 12 (October 1990): 123–27.

———. *Kokinshū igo ni okeru Tsurayuki*. Tokyo: Ōfūsha, 1980.

———. "*Tosa nikki* ni okeru uta no eisha to shite no yōdō no imi ni tsuite." *Kokugo to kokubungaku* 46, no. 12 (December 1969): 23–35.

———. "*Tosa nikki* ron: *Kokinshū* kenkyū kiryobu to no kanren ni oite." *Bungei kenkyū* 59 (June 1968): 18–26.

Kikuta Shigeo. "*Tosa nikki* no bungei-teki kōzō: chokushin suru jikan to taikō suru jikan no kōzu." In *Ōchō nikki no shinkenkyū*, edited by Uemura Etsuko, 47–68. Tokyo: Kasama Shoin, 1995.

———. "*Tosa nikki* no jikan-teki kōzō: kuronosu to aiōn no kōzu." *Jinbun shakai kagaku ronsō* 11 (2002): 1–17.

Kiley, Cornelius. "Estate and Property in the Late Heian Period." In *Medieval Japan: Essays in Institutional History*, edited by John W. Hall and Jeffrey P. Mass, 109–26. Stanford: Stanford University Press, 1988.

———. "Provincial Administration and Land Tenure." In *The Cambridge History of Japan 2, Heian Japan*, edited by Donald S. Shively and William H. McCullough, 236–340. Cambridge: Cambridge University Press, 1999.

Kim, Eun Gug. "The Fall of Parhae: A Temporal and Spatial Approach." In *A New History of Parhae*, edited by Northeast Asian History Foundation, 53–61. Leiden: Brill, 2012.

Kim, Yung-Hee. *Songs to Make the Dust Dance: The Ryojin Hisho of Twelfth-Century Japan*. Berkeley: University of California Press, 1994.

Kimu Soyon. *Heian jidai no warai to Nihon bunka: Tosa nikki, Taketori monogatari, Genji monogatari o chūshin ni*. Tokyo: Waseda Daigaku Shuppanbu, 2019.

Kimura Masanori. "Nikki bungaku no hōhō to tenkai." In *Ronshū nikki bungaku*, edited by Kimura Masanori, 7–38. Tokyo: Kasama Shoin, 1991.

———. "Nikki bungaku no honshitsu to sōsaku shinri." In *Nihon bungaku no sōten* 2, edited by Hisamatsu Sen'ichi, et al., 99–126. Tokyo: Meiji Shoin, 1968.

———. "*Tosa nikki* no kōzō." *Meiji daigaku bungei kenkyū* 10 (March 1963): 56–74.

———. "*Tosa nikki* no shudai wa nani ka." *Kokubungaku kaishaku to kanshō* 44, no. 2 (February 1979): 98–106.

Kimura Shigemitsu, ed. *Rekishi kara yomu* Tosa nikki. Tokyo: Tōkyōdō Shuppan, 2010.

King, Ross. "Ditching 'Diglossia': Describing Ecologies of the Spoken and Inscribed in Pre-modern Korea." *Sungkyun Journal of East Asian Studies* 15, no. 1 (April 2015): 1–19.

Kisoigariki. By Ki no Haseo. In *Heian Kamakura mikan shishū*, ed. Kunaichō Shoryōbu, 38–43. Tokyo: Meiji Shoin, 1972.

Kitayama Mitsumasa. "*Tosa nikki* no shōgatsu gyōji." *Shinjodai kokubun* 4 (March 1993): 10–18.

Kitazumi Toshio. "Abe no Nakamaro 'Ama no hara' no uta shikō." *Bungaku bunka* 88 (October 1980): 74–83.

Klein, Susan Blakely. *Allegories of Desire: Esoteric Literary Commentaries of Medieval Japan*. Cambridge, MA: Harvard University Asia Center, 2002.

Knechtges, David R. "Wit, Humor, and Satire in Early Chinese Literature (to A.D. 220)." *Monumenta Serica* 79 (1970–71): 79–98.

Kobayashi Masaaki. "Seisa to shutai o hakai suru mono: *Tosa nikki* shōkō." *Aoyama gakuin joshi tanki daigaku kiyō* 48 (December 1994): 79–102.

Kobayashi Shōji. "Fujiwara Sumitomo no ran sairon." *Nihon rekishi* 499 (December 1989): 1–19.

Kobayashi Taichirō and Harada Ken'yū. *Ō I*. Tokyo: Shūeisha, 1964.

Kohon setsuwa-shū. Edited by Miki Sumito, Asami Kazuhiko, Nakamura Yoshio, and Kouchi Kazuaki. In SNKBT 42. Tokyo: Iwanami Shoten, 1990.

Kojima Noriyuki. *Kokufū ankoku jidai no bungaku* 1. Tokyo: Hanawa Shobō, 1968.

Kok, D. P. "Visualizing the Classics: Reading *Surimono* and *Kyōka* Books as Social and Cultural History." PhD diss., Leiden University, 2017.

Kokin wakashū. Edited by Ozawa Masao and Matsuda Shigeho. SNKBZ 11. Tokyo: Shōgakukan, 1994.

Kokin wakashū mokuroku. Edited by Hanawa Hokiichi. In GR 16. Tokyo: Zoku Gunsho Ruijū Kansei-kai, 1934. 1983 reprint.

Komachiya Teruhiko. "Hyōgen ron no oku kara." *Kokubungaku kaishaku to kanshō* 44, no. 2 (February 1979): 81–88.

———. "*Tosa nikki* to *Takamitsu nikki*." *Kokubungaku kaishaku to kanshō* 37, no. 4 (April 1972): 58–65.

Komatsu Hideo. *Koten sainyūmon: "Tosa nikki" o iriguchi toshite*. Tokyo: Kasama Shoin, 2006.

———. *Nihongo shokishi genron*. Tokyo: Kasama Shoin, 1998.

Kondō Kazuichi. "*Tosa nikki* ni okeru shizen: sono shūkan-sei ni tsuite." *Kokugo kokubungaku hō* 9 (January 1959): 26–32.
Konishi Jin'ichi. *A History of Japanese Literature*, vol. 2: *The Early Middle Ages*. Princeton, NJ: Princeton University Press, 1986.
———. *Tosa nikki hyōkai*. Tokyo: Yūseidō, 1951.
———. "Tsurayuki bannen no kafū." *Bungaku* 43: 8 (August 1975): 976–87.
Konjaku monogatari shū. Edited by Mabuchi Kazuo, Kunisaki Fumimaro, and Inagaki Taiichi. SNKBZ 35–38. Tokyo: Shōgakukan, 1999–2002.
Kornicki, Peter. *The Book in Japan: A Cultural History from the Beginnings to the Nineteenth Century*. Honolulu: University of Hawai'i Press, 2000.
———. "Ikeda Kikan and the Textual Tradition of *The Tosa Nikki*: European Influences on Japanese Textual Scholarship," *Revue d'histoire des textes* 3 (January 2008): 263–82.
Kristeva, Tsevatana. "Ichininshō no bungaku keishiki: Nihon no nikki bungaku to Yōroppa ni okeru jidenbungaku no dentō." *Kokusai Nihon bunka kenkyū sentaa kiyō Nihon kenkyū* 9 (September 1993): 27–53.
Ku, Nan Hee. "Exchanges between Parhae and Japan." In *A New History of Parhae*, edited by Northeast Asia History Foundation, 97–108. Leiden: Global Oriental, 2012.
Kubota Takao. "*Tosa nikki* ni miru 'Yodo-gawa.'" In *Yodo-gawa no bunka to bungaku*, edited by Osaka Seikei joshi tanki daigaku kokubungaku-ka kenkyūshitsu, 54–73. Osaka: Izumi Shoin, 2001.
Kubukihara Rei. "Haikaika: wakashi no kōsō josetsu." In *Waka to wa nani ka*, edited by Kubukihara Rei, 99–125. Tokyo: Yūseidō, 1996.
Kudai waka. Edited by Hanawa Hokiichi. In GR 8. Tokyo: Zoku Gunsho Ruijū Kanseikai, 1932.
Kujōdono goyuikai. Edited by Hanawa Hokiichi. In GR 27. Tokyo: Gunsho Ruijū Kanseikai, 1931. 1983 reprint.
Kurokawa Yōichi. "Abe no Nakamaro no uta ni tsuite: Aasaa Weirii no setsu ni kanren shite." *Bungaku* 43, no. 8 (August 1975): 988–99.

Lane, Richard. "Saikaku and Boccaccio: The Novella in Japan and Italy." *Monumenta Nipponica* 15, no. 1/2 (1959): 87–118.
Lardinois, André. "New Philology and the Classics: Accounting for Variation in the Textual Transmission of Greek Lyric and Elegaic Poetry." In *The Reception of Greek Lyric Poetry in the Ancient World: Transmission, Canonization and Paratext*, edited by Bruno Currie and Ian Rutherford, 39–71. Leiden: Brill, 2020.
Lazarus, Ashton. "Folk Performance as Transgression: The Great Dengaku of 1096." *Journal of Japanese Studies* 44, no. 1 (February 2018): 1–23.
Leggieri, Antonio. "Magistrates, Doctors, and Monks: Satire in the Chinese Jestbook *Xiaolin Guangji*." In *The Rhetoric of Topics and Forms*, edited by Gianna Zocco, 369–80. Berlin: De Gruyter, 2021.
Lejeune, Philippe. *On Autobiography*. Translated by Paul John Eakin and Katherine Leary. Minneapolis: University of Minnesota Press, 1989.
Lévi-Strauss, Claude. *Introduction to the Work of Marcell Mauss*. New York: Routledge, 1987.

Levy, Indra. *Sirens of the Western Shore: The Westernesque Femme Fatale, Translation, and Vernacular Style in Modern Japanese Literature.* New York: Columbia University Press, 2006.
Liji. Edited by Takeuchi Teruo. SKT 27–29. Tokyo: Meiji Shoin, 1977.
Lim, Sang-sun. "The Movement to Restore Parhae." In *A New History of Parhae*, edited by Northeast Asian History Foundation, 62–69. Leiden: Brill, 2012.
Lin, Shuen-fu. "The Nature of the Quatrain from the Late Han to the High T'ang." In *The Vitality of the Lyric Voice: Shih Poetry from the Late Han to the T'ang*, edited by Shuen-fu Lin and Stephen Owen, 296–331. Princeton, NJ: Princeton University Press, 1986.
Lowe, Bryan D. *Ritualized Writing: Buddhist Practice and Scriptural Cultures in Ancient Japan.* Honolulu: University of Hawai'i Press, 2017.
Lukács, György. *Solzhenitsyn.* Cambridge, MA: MIT Press, 1971.
Lunyu. Edited by Yoshida Kenkō. SKT 1. Tokyo: Meiji Shoin, 1961.
Lurie, David. *Realms of Literacy: Early Japan and the History of Writing.* Cambridge, MA: Harvard University Asia Center, 2012.

Mack, John. *The Sea: A Cultural History.* London: Reaktion Books, 2010.
Macmillan, Peter, trans. *Tales of Ise.* New York: Penguin, 2016.
Mair, Victor. "Buddhism and the Rise of the Written Vernacular in East Asia: The Making of National Languages." *Journal of Asian Studies* 53, no. 3 (August 1994): 707–51.
Makura no sōshi. Edited by Matsuo Satoshi and Nagai Kazuko. SNKBZ 18. Tokyo: Shōgakukan, 1997.
Man'yōshū. Edited by Kojima Noriyuki, Kinoshita Masatoshi, and Tōno Haruyuki. SNKBZ 6–9. Tokyo: Shōgakukan, 1994–96.
Markham, Elizabeth. *Saibara: Japanese Court Songs of the Heian Period.* Cambridge: Cambridge University Press, 1983.
Marra, Michele. *The Aesthetics of Discontent: Politics and Reclusion in Medieval Japanese Literature.* Honolulu: University of Hawai'i Press, 1991.
Masuda Katsumi. "Uta-gatari no sekai." *Kikan kokubun* 4 (March 1953): 15–22.
Matsuda Takeo. *Kokinshū no kōzō ni kansuru kenkyū.* Tokyo: Kazama Shobō, 1965.
Matsumoto Yasushi. "*Tosa nikki* no kaigyaku: ichigatsu jūsannichi no jō 'to iite' wa junsetsu de aru." *Nihon bungaku* 29, no. 9 (September 1980): 81–85.
Mauss, Marcel. *The Gift: Forms and Functions of Exchange in Archaic Societies.* New York: W. W. Norton, 1967.
McCullough, Helen Craig, *Brocade by Night: 'Kokin Wakashū' and the Court Style in Classical Japanese Poetry.* Stanford, CA: Stanford University Press, 1985.
———, trans. *Kokin Wakashū: The First Imperial Anthology of Japanese Poetry, with Tosa Nikki and Shinsen Waka.* Stanford, CA: Stanford University Press, 1985.
———, trans. *Ōkagami, The Great Mirror: Fujiwara Michinaga (966–1027) and His Times.* Princeton, NJ: Princeton University Press, 1980.
———, trans. *Tales of Ise: Lyrical Episodes from Tenth-Century Japan.* Stanford, CA: Stanford University Press, 1968.
McCullough, William H. "The Capital and Its Society." In *The Cambridge History of Japan 2, Heian Japan*, edited by Donald S. Shively and William H. McCullough, 97–182. Cambridge: Cambridge University Press, 1999.

McCullough, William H., and Helen Craig, trans. *A Tale of Flowering Fortunes: Annals of Japanese Aristocratic Life in the Heian Period*, 2 vols. Stanford, CA: Stanford University Press, 1980.
McKinney, Meredith, trans. *The Pillow Book*. London: Penguin Books, 2006.
Mekada Sakuo. "Kyūseiki totōzō nikki kō." *Bungei to shisō* 22 (February 1962): 16–46.
Mezaki Tokue. *Ki no Tsurayuki*. Tokyo: Yoshikawa Kōbunkan, 1981.
Mills, D. E. *A Collection of Tales from Uji: A Study and Translation of* Uji Shūi Monogatari. Cambridge: Cambridge University Press, 1970.
Miner, Earl. *Japanese Poetic Diaries*. Berkeley: University of California Press, 1969.
Mitamura Masako. *Makura no sōshi hyōgen no ronri*. Tokyo: Yūseidō, 1995.
Mitani Eiichi. *Tosa nikki*. Tokyo: Kadokawa Bunko, 1960.
Miyake, Lynne K. "*The Tosa Diary*: In the Interstices of Gender and Criticism." In *The Woman's Hand: Gender and Theory in Japanese Women's Writing*, edited by Paul Schalow and Janet Walker, 41–73. Stanford, CA: Stanford University Press, 1996.
Miyazaki Shōhei. *Nyōbō nikki no ronri to kōzō*. Tokyo: Kasama Shoin, 1996.
———. "*Tosa nikki* no genzai." *Kokubungaku kaishaku to kanshō* 44, no. 2 (February 1979): 161–66.
Miyoshi, Masao. "Translation as Interpretation." *Journal of Asian Studies* 38, no. 2 (February 1979): 299–302.
Mori Akira. "*Rainanroku: Tosa nikki* no senkō bungaku to shite." *Seijō bungei* 78 (October 1976): 21–28.
———. "*Tosa nikki* no jishōsei: 'tomare koumare, toku yaritemu' no imi." *Nishō gakusha daigaku ronshū* (1976): 37–58.
Morimoto Motoko. "Shikashū to wa nani ka." In *Ōchō shikashū no seiritsu to tenkai*, edited by Waka bungaku ronshū henshū iin-kai, 1–28. Tokyo: Kazama Shobō, 1992.
Morishita Sumiaki. "*Tosa nikki* ichigatsu nanuka jō shikai: 'koi' • 'mitsu' no kakekotoba nado." *Sanuki daigaku kokugo kokubungaku* 23 (March 1996): 40–48.
Morita Kenkichi. "*Tosa nikki* ron: nikki bungaku-shi ron no tame ni." *Nihon bungaku kenkyū* 28 (November 1992): 27–38.
Morita Yasushi. "Tenjō nikki." In *Kokiroku to nikki*, edited by Yamanaka Yutaka, 107–15. Kyoto: Shibunkaku, 1993.
Morley, Brendan Arkell. "Poetry and Diplomacy in Early Heian Japan: The Embassy of Wang Hyoryŏm from Parhae to the Kōnin Court." *Journal of the American Oriental Society*, 136, no. 2 (April-June 2016): 343–69.
Mostow, Joshua S. *Courtly Visions:* The Ise Stories *and the Politics of Cultural Appropriation*. Leiden: Brill, 2014.
———. "Mother Tongue and Father Script: The Relationship of Sei Shōnagon and Murasaki Shikibu to Their Fathers and Chinese Letters." In *The Father-Daughter Plot: Japanese Literary Women and the Law of the Father*, edited by Rebecca L. Copeland and Esperanza Ramirez-Christensen, 115–42. Honolulu: University of Hawai'i Press, 2001.
———. *Pictures of the Heart: The Hyakunin Isshu in Word and Image*. Honolulu: University of Hawai'i Press, 1996.
———. "*The Tale of Light Snow:* Pastiche, Epistolary Fiction and Narrativity Visual and Verbal." *Japan Forum* 21, no. 3 (2010): 363–87.

Mostow, Joshua S., and Royall Tyler, trans. *The Ise Stories: Ise monogatari*. Honolulu: University of Hawai'i Press, 2010.
Murai Yasuhiko. "Watakushi nikki no tōjō." In *Kokiroku to nikki*, edited by Yamanaka Yutaka, 71–76. Kyoto: Shibunkaku, 1993.
Murasaki Shikibu nikki. Edited by Yamamoto Ritatsu. In SNKS 35. Tokyo: Shinchōsha, 1980.
Murasaki Shikibu shū. Edited by Yamamoto Ritatsu. In SNKS 35. Tokyo: Shinchōsha, 1980.
Murase Toshio. *Ki no Tsurayuki den no kenkyū*. Tokyo: Ōfūsha, 1981.
———. *Kyūtei kajin Ki no Tsurayuki*. Tokyo: Shintensha, 1987.
Murofushi Shinsuke. "*Tosa nikki* to Tsurayuki." *Atomi gakuen kokugoka kiyō* 15 (March 1967): 37–48.
Nakajima Riichirō. "*Tosa nikki* no chosha wa josei de aru." *Dokusho shunjū* 7, no. 8 (July 1956): 8–10.
Nakakoji Shun'itsu. "Ō I ga Abe no Nakamaro ni okutta shi ni arawareru 'Kyūshū,' 'Fusō' oyobi 'kotō' no imi ni tsuite." *Ōtemon gakuin bungakubu kiyō* 39 (December 2003): 17–33.
———. "Tōshi no Nihon kodai shizō, hosoku: Abe no Nakamaro, Kūkai, Tachibana no Hayanari, Ennin, Ensai-ra no san'yo." *Ajia bunka gakua nenpō* 1 (November 1998): 86–98.

Nakamura, Kyoko. *Miraculous Stories from the Japanese Buddhist Tradition: The Nihon ryōiki of the Monk Kyōkai*. Cambridge, MA: Harvard University Press, 1973.
Nakanishi Susumu. "Tsurayuki no hōhō." *Bungaku* 54, no. 2 (February 1986): 114–27.
Nakazato Shigekichi. "Kikō bungaku toshite mita *Tosa nikki*." *Chūō gakuin daigaku ronsō* 3, no. 2 (November 1968): 29–53.
Nanba Hiroshi. "*Tosa nikki* no honshitsu: nikki bungaku no rekishi-teki igi." In *Heianchō nikki* I, edited by Nihon bungaku kenkyū shiryō kankō-kai, 64–72. Tokyo: Yūseidō, 1971.
Nanshoku ōkagami. Edited by Teruoka Yasutaka. In SNKBZ 67. Tokyo: Shōgakukan, 2000.
Nelson, Steven G. "Court and Religious Music: Music of *Gagaku* and *Shōmyō*." In *The Ashgate Research Companion to Japanese Music*, edited by David Hughes, 35–76. London: Routledge, 2008.
Nenzi, Laura. *Excursions in Identity: Travel and the Intersection of Place, Gender and Status in Edo Japan*. Honolulu: University of Hawai'i Press, 2008.
Newhard, Jamie. *Knowing the Amorous Man: A History of Scholarship on* Tales of Ise. Cambridge, MA: Harvard University Asia Center, 2013.
Nickerson, Peter. "The Meaning of Matrilocality: Kinship, Property, and Politics in Mid-Heian." *Monumenta Nipponica* 48, no. 4 (Winter 1993): 429–67.
Nihei Michiaki. "*Tosa nikki* zenshi: tabi no nikki no shihatsu." *Kokubungaku kaishaku to kyōzai no kenkyū* 51, no. 8 (July 2006): 24–31.
Nihon kiryaku. Edited by Kuroita Katsumi. KST 10–11. Tokyo: Yoshikawa Kōbunkan, 1929.

Nihon ryōiki. By Kyōkai. Edited by Nakada Norio. SNKBZ 10. Tokyo: Shōgakukan, 1995.
Nihon sandai jitsuroku. Edited by Kuroita Katsumi. KST 4. Tokyo: Yoshikawa Kōbunkan, 1934.
Nihon shoki. Edited by Kojima Noriyuki, Naoki Kōjirō, Nishimiya Kazutami, Kuranaka Susumu, and Mori Masamori. SKNBZ 2–4. Tokyo: Shōgakukan, 1994–1998.
Niimanabi. By Kamo no Mabuchi. Edited by Sasaki Nobutsuna. In NKT 7. Tokyo: Kazama Shobō, 1926. 1991 reprint.
Nishimura, Sey. "Retrospective Comprehension: Japanese Foretelling Songs." *Asian Folklore Studies* 45, no. 1 (1986): 45–66.
Nishinoiri Atsuo. "*Tosa nikki* no umi: Miyako shikō to no kakawari ni tsuite." *Bunka keishōgaku ronshū* 2 (2005): 110–21.
Nitta Ichirō. "*Tosa nikki* ni tsuite: bōji, shiranami no kyakujin, Tosa no tomari nado no gikyokusei." *Shikoku joshi daigaku kiyō* 1, no. 1 (December 1981): 1–10.
Noguchi Takeshi. "*Sandai jitsuroku* no kōsotsu kiji." *Shinshū Hōnan joshi tanki daigaku kiyō* 4 (1986): 131–204.
Nomura Seiichi. "Kyūtei bungaku toshite no *Makura no sōshi*." In *Makura no sōshi hyōgen to kōzō*, edited by Mitamura Masako, 8–17. Tokyo: Yūseidō, 1994.
Nugent, Christopher M. B. *Manifest in Words, Written on Paper: Producing and Circulating Poetry in Tang Dynasty China*. Cambridge, MA: Harvard University Asia Center, 2010.

Ogawa Kōzō. "'Funa-yakata no chiri mo chiri, sora yuku kumo mo tadayoinu' kō: *Tosa nikki* jūnigatsu nijūshichinichi jō no imi." *Kinki daigaku bungaku geijutsu bunka* 5, no. 2 (December 1993): 13–27.
———. "'Hito' no kaze nami / 'nami' no hito: *Tosa 'nikki'* no hōhō toshite no 'i.'" *Kinki daigaku bungaku geijutsu bunka* 9, no. 2 (March 1998): 1–24.
———. "'Ima' ni hitoku sareta 'mukashi': *Tosa nikki* ichigatsu nijūichi nichi jō no enkei." *Kinki daigaku bungaku geijutsu bunka* 5, no. 3 (February 1994): 1–12.
———. "*Tosa nikki* ni okeru 'nanuka' no tokuisei." *Kumamoto tandai ronshū* 37, no. 2 (October 1986): 91–116.
———. "*Tosa nikki* ni okeru waka no seishō: waka zen-gojūkyūshu no hairetsu kōzō." *Kumamoto tandai ronshū* 35, no. 3 (May 1985): 243–74.
———. "*Tosa nikki* no bunshō zōkei e no yōken, joshō." *Kokugo kokubun kenkyū to kyōiku* 10 (January 1982): 94–103.
———. "Zōtō o kyohi suru uta no sekai: *Tosa nikki* ni okeru shōwasei." *Kumamoto tandai ronshū* 39, no. 3 (March 1989): 97–120.
Ogawa Tamaki. "Mikasa no yama ni ideshi tsuki ka mo." *Bungaku* 36, no. 11 (November 1968): 37–39.
Oi no kobumi. By Matsuo Bashō. Edited by Imoto Nōichi and Hori Nobuo. In SNKBZ 71. Tokyo: Shōgakukan, 1995.
Okada, Richard H. *Figures of Resistance: Language, Poetry, and Narrating in* The Tale of Genji *and Other Mid-Heian Texts*. Durham, NC: Duke University Press, 1991.
Ōoka Makoto. *Ki no Tsurayuki*. Tokyo: Chikuma Shobō, 1971.

Orikuchi Shinobu. "Haikaika no kenkyū." In *Orikuchi Shinobu zenshū* vol. 10, edited by Orikuchi Shinobu zenshū kankōkai, 262–83. Tokyo: Chūō Kōronsha, 1975.
Ōsugi Mitsuo. "*Tosa nikki* ni okeru eikai no gihō." *Kōgakuan ronsō* 25, no. 1 (February 1992): 1–16.
Owen, Stephen. *The Great Age of Chinese Poetry: The High T'ang*. New Haven, CT: Yale University Press, 1981.
———. *Readings in Chinese Literary Thought*. Cambridge, MA: Harvard University Asia Center, 1992.

Palmer, Edwina. "A Poem to Carp About?: Poem 16–3828 of the *Man'yōshū* Collection." *Bulletin of the School of Oriental and African Studies* 74, no. 3 (2011): 417–36.
Park, Jin Suk. "Perceptions of Parhae in North Korea, Japan, and Russia." In *A New History of Parhae*, edited by Northeast Asian History Foundation, 180–88. Leiden: Brill, 2012.
Persiani, Gian Piero. "China as Self, China as Other: On Ki no Tsurayuki's Use of the *wa-kan* Dichotomy." *Sino-Japanese Studies* 23 (2016): 31–58.
Piggott, Joan R. "Court and Provinces Under Regent Fujiwara no Tadahira." In *Heian Japan, Centers and Peripheries*, edited by Mikael Adolphson, Edward Kamens, and Stacie Matsumoto, 35–65. Honolulu: University of Hawai'i Press, 2007.
Piggott, Joan R., and Yoshida Sanae, eds. *Teishinkōki: The Year 939 in the Journal of Regent Fujiwara no Tadahira*. Ithaca, NY: Cornell East Asia Series, 2008.
Plutschow, Herbert. *Japan's Name Culture: The Significance of Names in a Religious, Political and Social Context*. Surrey, UK: Curzon, 1995.
Pollock, Sheldon. "The Cosmopolitan Vernacular." *Journal of Asian Studies* 57, no. 1 (February 1998): 6–37.
Porter, William N., trans. *The Tosa Diary*. Rutland, VT: Tuttle Publishing, 1981. Reprint from London: H. Frowde, 1912.

Rabinovitch, Judith N. "Wasp Waists and Monkey Tails: A Study and Translation of Hamanari's *Uta no Shiki* (*The Code of Poetry*, 772), Also Known as *Kakyō Hyōshiki* (*A Formulary for Verse Based on The Canons of Poetry*)." *Harvard Journal of Asiatic Studies* 51, no. 2 (December 1991): 471–560.
Rambelli, Fabio. "Buddhist Sacred Commodities and the General Economy." In *Buddhist Materiality: A Cultural History of Objects in Japanese Buddhism*, edited by Fabio Rambelli, 259–323. Stanford, CA: Stanford University Press, 2007.
———. "Sea Theologies: Elements for a Conceptualization of Maritime Religiosity in Japan." In *The Sea and the Sacred in Japan*, edited by Fabio Rambelli, 181–99. London: Bloomsbury Academic, 2018.
Reischauer, Edwin O., trans. *Ennin's Diary: The Record of a Pilgrimage to China in Search of the Law*. New York: Ronald Press, 1955.
———. *Ennin's Travels in T'ang China*. New York: Ronald Press, 1955.
Ritsu-ryō. Edited by Ienaga Saburō et al. *Nihon shisō taikei* 3. Tokyo: Iwanami Shoten, 1976.
Rose, Margaret A. *Parody: Ancient, Modern, and Post-modern*. Cambridge: Cambridge University Press, 1993.

Ruijū kokushi. Edited by Kuroita Katsumi. KST 5–6. Tokyo: Yoshikawa Kōbunkan, 1933–34.
Rüttermann, Markus. "'So That We Can Study Letter-Writing': The Concept of Epistolary Etiquette in Premodern Japan." *Japan Review* 18 (2006): 57–128.
Ryōjin hishō. Edited by Shinma Shin'ichi and Tonomura Natsuko. In SNKBZ 42. Tokyo: Shōgakukan, 2000.
Ryō no gige. Edited by Kuroita Katsumi. KST 22. Tokyo: Yoshikawa Kōbunkan, 1939.

Saga no kayoi. By Asukai Masaari. Edited by Mizukawa Yoshio. In *Asukai Masaari no nikki zenshaku*. Tokyo: Kazama Shobō, 1985.
Saibara. Edited by Usuda Jingorō. In SNKBZ 42. Tokyo: Shōgakukan, 2000.
Saito, Mareshi. *Kanbunmyaku: The Literary Sinitic Context and the Birth of Modern Japanese Language and Literature*. Leiden: Brill, 2021.
Sakaki, Atsuko. *Obsessions with the Sino-Japanese Polarity in Japanese Literature*. Honolulu: University of Hawai'i Press, 2006.
Sakakura Atsuyoshi. "*Taketori* ni okeru 'buntai' no mondai." *Kokugo kokubun* 25 (November 1956): 683–93.
———. "*Tosa nikki* no uta to ji no bun." *Kokugo kokubun* 22, no. 5 (May 1953): 400–401.
Sakamoto, Tarō. *The Six National Histories of Japan*. Vancouver: University of British Columbia Press, 1991.
Sanetaka kōki. By Sanjōnishi Sanetaka. Edited by Takahashi Ryūzō. 13 vols. Tokyo: Zoku Gunsho Ruijū Kansei-kai, 1957–67. 2000–02 reprint.
Sarashina nikki. By Sugawara no Takasue no Musume. Edited by Yoshioka Hiroshi. SNKBT 24. Tokyo: Iwanami Shoten, 1989.
Sarra, Edith. *Fictions of Femininity: Literary Inventions of Gender in Japanese Court Women's Memoirs*. Stanford, CA: Stanford University Press, 1999.
Sasaki Kōji. *Uta-gatari no keifu*. Tokyo: Ōfūsha, 1982.
Sasanuma Satoshi. "*Tosa nikki* no waka kan: josei kataku o hajō saseta mono." *Saitama daigaku kokugo kyōiku ronsō* 8 (2005): 11–18.
Satō Kazuyoshi. *Heian waka bungaku hyōgen ron*. Tokyo: Yūseidō, 1993.
Satō Miyako. "*Tosa nikki* ni okeru 'parodi.'" *Monogatari kenkyū* 1 (March 2001): 22–32.
———. "*Tosa nikki* ni okeru shin-janru sōzō no hōhō: kōro shinin no uta no parodi." *Denki tsūshin daigaku kiyō*, 20, nos. 1–2 (2007): 111–123.
Satō Shigemi and Ikezoe Hirohiko. "Heianchō no shokubunka kō: *Tosa nikki* no shoku ni tsuite." *Obihiro-dai tanki daikiyō* 37 (2000): 37–49.
Satō Shin'ichi. "Ki no Tsurayuki *Tosa nikki* to Sugawara no Michizane *Kanke bunsō* mimaki 'Kansō jisshu' no hyōgen ni tsuite: kajitori o jiku to shite." In *Tosa nikki no Koperunikusu-teki tenkai*, edited by Higashihara Nobuaki and Joel Joos, 245–314. Tokyo: Musashino Shoin, 2016.
Schafer, Edward H. "Fusang and Beyond: The Haunted Seas of Japan." *Journal of the American Oriental Society* 109, no. 3 (1989): 379–400.
———. *The Golden Peaches of Samarkand: A Study of T'ang Exotics*. Berkeley: University of California Press, 1963.
———. *The Vermilion Bird: T'ang Images of the South*. Berkeley: University of California Press, 1967.

Schalow, Paul Gordon, trans. *The Great Mirror of Male Love*. Stanford, CA: Stanford University Press, 1990.

———. *A Poetics of Courtly Male Friendship in Heian Japan*. Honolulu: University of Hawai'i Press, 2007.

Segal, Ethan Isaac. *Coins, Trade, and the State: Economic Growth in Early Medieval Japan*. Cambridge, MA: Harvard University Asia Center, 2011.

Seto Hirota. "Hōhō toshite no nikki: *Tosa nikki* no uta to jikan." *Tokowa kokubun* 25 (December 2000): 1–14.

Shibuya Takashi. "Bunshō kara mita *Tosa nikki* no seikaku." *Bungei kenkyū* 37 (April 1961): 14–24.

———. "*Tosa nikki* ni okeru waka: sono igi to kinō." In *Heianchō nikki* I, edited by Nihon bungaku kenkyū shiryō kankō-kai, 86–96. Tokyo: Yūseidō, 1971.

Shida Nobuyoshi. "Kai uta zakkō." *Yamanashi daigaku gakugei gakubu kenkyū hōkoku* 13 (1962): 1–6.

Shields, Anna. "Remembering When: The Uses of Nostalgia in the Poetry of Bai Juyi and Yuan Zhen." *Harvard Journal of Asiatic Studies* 66, no. 2 (December 2006): 321–61.

Shigeta Shin'ichi. *Shomintachi no Heiankyō*. Tokyo: Kadokawa Shoten, 2008.

Shijing. Edited by Ishikawa Tadahisa. SKT 110–12. Tokyo: Meiji Shoin, 1997–2000.

Shimizu Takayuki. *Tosa nikki no fūdo*. Kōchi-shi: Kōchi Shimin Toshokan, 1987.

Shimura Midori. "Heian jidai josei no mana kanseki no gakushū: jūisseiki goro wo chūshin ni." *Nihon rekishi* 457 (June 1986): 22–38.

Shinsen waka. Compiled by Ki no Tsurayuki. In Kikuchi Yasuhiko, *Kokinshū igo ni okeru Tsurayuki*. Tokyo: Ōfūsha, 1980.

Shirane, Haruo. "Shiika, shokubunka, sakana." In *Bungaku ni egakareta Nihon no shoku no sugata*, edited by Haruo Shirane, Komine Kazuaki and Watanabe Kenji, 30–39. Tokyo: Shibundō, 2008.

———. *Traces of Dreams: Landscape, Cultural Memory and the Poetry of Bashō*. Stanford, CA: Stanford University Press, 1998.

Shoku Nihongi. Edited by Kuroita Katsumi. KST 2. Tokyo: Yoshikawa Kōbunkan, 1933.

Shoku Nihon kōki. Edited by Kuroita Katsumi. KST 3. Tokyo: Yoshikawa Kōbunkan, 1934.

Shūi wakashū. Edited by Komachiya Teruhiko. SNKBT 7. Tokyo: Iwanami Shoten, 1990.

Simpson, Emily B. "An Empress at Sea: Sea Deities and Divine Union in the Legends of Empress Jingū." In *The Sea and the Sacred in Japan*, edited by Fabio Rambelli, 65–78. London: Bloomsbury Academic, 2018.

Sloane, Jesse D. "Parhae in Historiography and Archaeology: International Debate and Prospects for Resolution." *Seoul Journal of Korean Studies* 27, no. 1 (June 2014): 1–35.

Smith, Robert F. W., and Gemma L. Watson, eds. *Writing the Lives of People and Things, AD 500–1700: A Multi-disciplinary Future for Biography*. New York: Routledge, 2016.

Soda Fumio. "*Tosa nikki* no hyōgen ishiki: jojutsu kanten no tenkan ni miru." *Heian bungaku kenkyū* 24 (March 1960): 65–72.

Steininger, Brian. *Chinese Literary Forms in Heian Japan: Poetics and Practice*. Cambridge, MA: Harvard University Asia Center, 2017.

Stinchecum, Amanda Mayer. "Who Tells the Tale?: 'Ukifune': A Study in Narrative Voice." *Monumenta Nipponica* 35, no. 4 (Winter 1980): 375–403.
Stockdale, Jonathan. *Imagining Exile in Heian Japan: Banishment in Law, Literature, and Cult*. Honolulu: University of Hawai'i Press, 2015.
Sugimoto Naojirō. *Abe no Nakamaro den kenkyū (shutaku hotei-bon)*. Tokyo: Ikuhōsha, 1940. 2008 reprint.
———. "Abe no Nakamaro no shi no shūhen: 'shitsudai' no shi no baai." *Tōhōgaku* 39 (March 1970): 58–73.
Sumpter, Sara L. "From the Monstrous to the God-Like: The Pacification of Vengeful Spirits in Early Medieval Japanese Handscrolls." In *Twisted Mirrors: Reflections of Monstrous Humanity*, edited by Seth Alcorn and Steven Nardi, 103–11. Leiden: Brill, 2020.
Suzuki Hideo. "*Tosa nikki*: nakiko o shinobu uta." *Kokubungaku kaishaku to kanshō* 62, no. 5 (May 1997): 24–29.
Suzuki Kazuhiko. "*Tosa nikki fune no tadaji* ni tsuite: Tachibana Moribe no kokugo ishiki." *Yamanashi daigaku geigakubun kenkyū hōkoku* 12 (1961): 23–32.
Suzuki, Tomi. "Gender and Genre: Modern Literary Histories and Women's Diary Literature." In *Inventing the Classics: Modernity, National Identity, and Japanese Literature*, edited by Haruo Shirane and Tomi Suzuki, 71–95. Stanford, CA: Stanford University Press, 2001.
Suzuki Tomotarō. *Tosa nikki*. In *Nihon koten bungaku taikei* 20. Tokyo: Iwanami Shoten, 1957.
———. "*Tosa nikki* no kōsei: toku ni taishō-teki shuhō ni tsuite." In *Heianchō nikki* I, edited by Nihon bungaku kenkyū shiryō kankō-kai, 73–85. Tokyo: Yūseidō, 1971.

Tahara, Mildred, trans. *Tales of Yamato: A Tenth-Century Poem-Tale*. Honolulu: University Press of Hawai'i, 1980.
Tahmoresi, Kevin W. "The *Wenyuan yinghua*: Selecting Refined Literature." PhD diss., George Washington University, 2020.
Takahashi Bunji. "Heianchō bungaku 'fūkei' ron (ichi): 'fūkei' to sōnen, *Tosa nikki*, *Kagerō nikki* no koto nado." *Komazawa kokubun* 21 (February 1984): 13–23.
———. "*Tosa nikki*: uta no jikansei to kūkansei o megutte." *Kokubungaku kaishaku to kyōzai no kenkyū* 37, no. 12 (October 1992): 110–16.
Takahashi Tōru. "Allusion to and Transformation of the *Ise monogatari* by 'Murasaki Shikibu.'" In *An Ise monogatari Reader: Contexts and Receptions*, edited by Joshua Mostow, Tokurō Yamamoto, and Kurtis Hanlon, 42–63. Leiden: Brill, 2021.
Takahashi Yasunari. *Dōke no bungaku: renesansu no eikō*. Tokyo: Chūō Kōronsha, 1977.
Takano Yasuyo. "*Tosa nikki* ni okeru kajitori no zōkei ni tsuite." *Kokubungaku kaishaku to kanshō* 29, no. 11 (November 1983): 31–37.
———. "*Tosa nikki* o yomu: 'kokoro' o shiten toshite." *Kaishi* 2 (September 1980): 18–25.
Takano Yoshio, ed. *Tosa nikki kochūshaku taisei*. Tokyo: Nihon Tosho Sentaa, 1979.
Takata Chika. "*Tosa nikki* no kyokō hōhō: 'Uda no matsubara' chiri hitei kō." *Kōchi joshi daigaku bunka ronsō* 8 (2006): 26–32.
Takei Mutsuo. "*Tosa nikki* no katarite: keigo shiyō, bōji no haha to no kanren ni oite." *Seitoku daigaku kenkyū kiyō* 32 (December 1999): 178–84.

Takemura Giichi. *Tosa nikki no chiri-teki kenkyū: Tosa kuni hen.* Tokyo: Kasama Shoin, 1977.
Takeoka Masao. *Ise monogatari zenhyōshaku: kochū jūichishu shūsei.* Tokyo: Yūbun Shoin, 1987.
———. *Kokin wakashū zenhyōshaku: kochū shichishu shūsei.* 2 vols. Tokyo: Yūbun Shoin, 1976.
Taketori monogatari. Edited by Katagiri Yōichi. In SNKBZ 12. Tokyo: Shōgakukan, 1994.
Takeuchi Michiko. "*Tosa nikki* no tensu, asupekuto." *Kokubungaku kaishaku to kanshō* 58, no. 7 (July 1993): 62–68.
Tamagami Takuya. *Genji monogatari hyōshaku.* 12 vols. Tokyo: Kadokawa Shoten, 1965.
Tamai Kōsuke. *Nikki bungaku gaisetsu.* Tokyo: Meguro Shoten, 1945.
———. *Nikki bungaku no kenkyū.* Tokyo: Hanawa Shobō, 1965.
Tanaka Jūtarō. *Makura no sōshi zenchūshaku.* 5 vols. Tokyo: Kadokawa Shoten, 2010.
Tanaka Kimiharu and Tanaka Kyōko. *Ki no Tsurayuki shū zenshaku.* Tokyo: Kazama Shobō, 1997.
Tanaka Noboru. *Kōtei Tsurayuki shū.* Osaka: Izumi Shoin, 1987.
Tanaka Shin'ichi. "Ki no Tsurayuki ni miru kana sanbun no kokoromi." *Kinjō Gakuin daigaku ronbunshū, kokubungaku-hen* 42 (March 2000): 45–63.
Teiji'in uta-awase. Edited by Ozawa Masao and Matsuda Shigeho. In SNKBZ 11. Tokyo: Shōgakukan, 1994.
Teishin kōki. Edited by Ichishima Kenkichi. In ZZGR 5. Tokyo: Kokusho Kankō-kai, 1909.
Tesaki Masao. "*Shinsen waka* no henshū ni okeru Tsurayuki no ito: 'kajitsu sōken' to iu koto no imi suru mono." *Tomiyama daigaku bunrigakubu daigaku kiyō* 12 (1962): 1–14.
Testart, Alain. "Uncertainties of the 'Obligation to Reciprocate': A Critique of Mauss." In *Marcel Mauss: A Centenary Tribute. Methodology and History in Anthropology,* vol. 1, edited by Wendy James and N. J. Allen, 97–110. New York: Berhahn Books, 1998.
Tōda Akiyoshi. "Aounabara furisake mireba: *Tosa nikki* no Abe no Nakamaro no uta." *Hikaku bunka ronsō* 18 (2006) 27–49.
Tōkai Ryōzō. "Oko no hōhō: *Tosa nikki* no baai." *Geibun kenkyū* 76 (October 1999): 1–24.
Tokuhara Shigemi. *Murasaki Shikibu shū no shinkaishaku.* Tokyo: Izumi Shoin, 2008.
Torii Fumiko. "Tosa jōruri no kyakushoku-hō: migawari-mono no *Tosa nikki* no isō." *Tōkyō joshi daigaku kiyō ronshū* 37, no. 1 (September 1986): 1–26.
Torizuka Keiko. "Edo jidai ni okeru *Tosa nikki* no chūshakusho ron (*Tosa nikki shō* to *Tosa nikki kōshō* to no hikaku)." *Koten ronsō* 2 (September 1951): 18–50.
Tosa nikki. By Ki no Tsurayuki. Edited by Kikuchi Yasuhiko. In SNKBZ 13. Tokyo: Shōgakukan, 1995.
Tosa nikki shō. By Kitamura Kigin. Edited by Kitamura Kigin kochūshaku shūsei. Tokyo: Shintensha, 1978.
Tsukishima Hiroshi. "*Tosa nikki* to kanbun kundoku." In *Heianchō nikki* I, edited by Nihon bungaku kenkyū shiryō kankō-kai, 113–19. Tokyo: Yūseidō, 1971.
Tsumoto Nobuhiro. "*Tosa nikki, Sarashina nikki* ni miru Teika no shosha ishiki: honbun kaishaku ni kanren shite." *Waseda daigaku kyōiku-gakubu gakujutsu kenkyū (kokugo kokubungaku hen)* 26 (1977): 27–40.

———. "*Tosa nikki* wa naze, nan no tame ni kakareta ka." *Kokubungaku kaishaku to kyōzai no kenkyū* 38, no. 2 (February 1993): 34–37.
Tsurayuki shū. Edited by Kimura Masanori. In SNKS 80. Tokyo: Shinchōsha, 1988.
Tsutsumi Kazuhiro. "*Ichijō sesshō gyoshū* kara setsuwa e: uta-gatari, uta monogatari kara setsuwa e no josetsu." *Gengo bunka kenkyū* 15 (December 2007): 1–13.
Tyler, Royall, trans. *The Tale of Genji.* London: Penguin Books, 2002.

Uchida Miyuki. "*Tosa nikki* 'Wada no tomari no akare no tokoro.'" *Chūko bungaku* 74 (2004): 12–22.
Ueno Makoto. *Kentōshi Abe no Nakamaro no yume.* Tokyo: Kadokawa Shoten, 2013.
Uji shūi monogatari. Edited by Kobayashi Yasuharo and Masuko Kazuko. SNKBZ 50. Tokyo: Shōgakukan, 1996.
Utsuho monogatari. Edited by Nakano Kōichi. SNKBZ 14–16. Tokyo: Shōgakukan, 2001.

Venuti, Lawrence. *The Translator's Invisibility.* London: Routledge, 1995.
Videen, Susan Downing, trans. *Tales of Heichū.* Cambridge, MA: Harvard University Council on East Asian Studies, 1989.
Viswanathan, Meera S. "Poetry, Play, and the Court in the *Tosa Nikki*." *Comparative Literature Studies* 28, no. 4 (1991): 416–32.
von Verschuer, Charlotte. *Across the Perilous Sea: Japanese Trade with China and Korea from the Seventh to the Sixteenth Centuries.* Translated by Kristen Lee Hunter. Ithaca, NY: East Asia Program, Cornell University, 2006.
Vos, Frits. *A Study of the Ise-Monogatari with the Text According to the Den-Teika-Hippon and an Annotated Translation.* 2 vols. Hague: Mouton, 1957.

Wakatai jisshu. Edited by Sasaki Nobutsuna. In NKT 1. Tokyo: Kazama Shobō, 1926. 1991 reprint.
Wakayama Shigeru. *Bungaku no naka no toshi to kenchiku: Man'yōshū kara Genji monogatari made.* Tokyo: Maruzen, 1991.
Waley, Arthur. *The Life and Times of Po Chü-i, 772–846 A.D.* London: George Allen & Unwin, 1949.
———. *The Poetry and Career of Li Po.* London: George Allen & Unwin, 1950.
Wallace, John R. *Objects of Discourse: Memoirs by Women of Heian Japan.* Ann Arbor, MI: Center for Japanese Studies, 2005.
Wang, Ao. *Spatial Imaginaries in Mid-Tang China: Geography, Cartography, and Literature.* Amherst, NY: Cambria Press, 2018.
Wang, Richard. *Ming Erotic Novellas: Genre, Consumption, and Religiosity in Cultural Practice.* Hong Kong: Chinese University Press, 2011.
Wang, Zhenping. *Ambassadors from the Islands of Immortals: China-Japan Relations in the Han-Tang Period.* Honolulu: Association for Asian Studies and University of Hawai'i Press, 2005.
———. *Tang China in Multi-Polar Asia: A History of Diplomacy and War.* Honolulu: University of Hawai'i Press, 2013.
Watanabe Hideo. *Heianchō bungaku to kanbun sekai.* Tokyo: Benseisha, 1991.

———. "Ki no Tsurayuki: utakotoba no sōzō." In *Kokinshū*, edited by Ueno Osamu, 256–75. Tokyo: Benseisha, 1993.
———. "Narihira denki kai hoketsu: kokushi kōsotsu denki no kijutsu." *Nihon bungaku* 24, no. 5 (1975): 94–107.
Watanabe Kyūji. "Ko o nakushita oya no 'kokoro': *Tosa nikki*." *Kokubungaku kaishaku to kanshō* 73, no. 3 (March 2008): 53–60.
———. "*Tosa nikki* no kaigyaku hyōgen: sono naizai-teki igi ni tsuite." *Nihon bungei ronshū* 23–24 (December 1991): 53–68.
———. "*Tosa nikki* no naimen-teki keisei ni kansuru oboegaki: *Kokinshū* ribetsuka no eikyō to Ki no Natsui no kage." *Yamanashi Eiwa tanki daigaku kiyō* 14 (December 1980): 14A–36A.
———. "*Tosa nikki* shiron: Tsurayuki bungaku no kōzō-teki tokushitsu o tōshite." *Nihon bungei ronshū* 12 (March 1985): 62–82.
Watanabe Minoru. "Imi no fuyo: *Tosa nikki*." In his *Heianchō bunshō shi*, 55–69. Tokyo: Tokyo Daigaku Shuppankai, 1981.
Watanabe, Takeshi. *Flowering Tales: Women Exorcising History in Heian Japan*. Cambridge, MA: Harvard University Asia Center, 2020.
———. "Gifting Melons to the Shining Prince: Food in the Late Heian Court Imagination." In *Devouring Japan: Global Perspectives on Japanese Culinary Identity*, edited by Nancy K. Stalker, 48–64. Oxford: University of Oxford Press, 2018.
Watanabe Yasuaki. "Waka ni okeru 'sakusha.'" In *'Sakusha' to wa nani ka: keishō, sen'yū, kyōdōsei*, edited by Haruo Shirane, Tomi Suzuki, Komine Kazuaki, and Toeda Hirokazu, 113–27. Tokyo: Iwanami Shoten, 2021.
Watase Shigeru. "*Tosa nikki* no 'aru hito' ni tsuite." *Heian bungaku kenkyū* 68 (1982): 74–85.
Watson, Burton, trans. *The Tso Chuan: Selections from China's Oldest Narrative History*. New York: Columbia University Press, 1989.
Wu, Yenna. *Ameliorative Satire and the Seventeenth-Century Chinese Novel*, Xingshi yinyuan zhuan, *Marriage as Retribution, Awakening the World*. Lewiston, NY: Edwin Mellen, 1999.

Yamada Seiichi. *Ise monogatari seiritsu-ron josetsu*. Tokyo: Ōfūsha, 1991.
Yamada Teruaki. "*Tosa nikki* ni okeru 'omoshiroshi' 'kurushi' sunkan." *Gobun* 37 (March 1972): 1–9.
Yamada Yoshio. "*Tosa nikki* ni chiri no ayamari aru ka." *Bungaku* (January 1935): 1–15.
Yamaguchi Hiroshi. *Ōchō kadan no kenkyū: Uda Daigo Suzaku chōhen*. Tokyo: Ōfūsha, 1967.
Yamaguchi Masao. "*Tosa nikki* no bungei kōzō: iyōnaru tabidachi, aijō e no chinkon." *Kassui ronbunshū* 26 (March 1983): 147–78.
Yamamoto Kenkichi. *Chiisa na shōzōga*. Tokyo: Chikuma Shobō, 1984.
Yamanaka Yutaka. "Kojin no nikki." In *Kokiroku to nikki*, edited by Yamanaka Yutaka, 8–28. Kyoto: Shibunkaku, 1993.
Yamashita Katsuaki. *Heian kizoku shakai to guchūreki*. Kyoto: Rinsen Shoten, 2017.
Yamashita Tarō. "*Tosa nikki* no ninshō kōzō: 'onna' to 'watashi' to 'watashitachi.'" *Kodai bungaku kenkyū dainiji* 10 (October 2001): 123–36.

Yamato monogatari. Edited by Takahashi Shōji. In SNKBZ 12. Tokyo: Shōgakukan, 1994.
Yano Senzai. "'*Tosa nikki*' Teika-bon to Tameie-bon to Ki no Tsurayuki no sho ni tsuite." *Hikaku bunka kenkyū nenpō* 16 (February 2006): 74–85.
Yasuda Mariko. "*Tosa nikki* ni mochiirareta 'ofu' no imi." *Hiroshima jogakuin daigaku kokugo kokubungakushi* 36 (December 2006): 45–59.
———. "*Tosa nikki* no kajitori zō: kanbun kundokugo ni chūmoku shite." *Hiroshima jogakuin daigakuin gengo bunka ronsō* 12 (March 2009): 25–46.
Yato Mihoko. "Heianchō no Sumiyoshi shinkō: *Tosa nikki* kara *Genji monogatari* e." *Gakugei kokugo kokubungaku* 32 (March 2000): 109–17.
Yoda, Tomiko. *Gender and National Literature: Heian Texts in the Constructions of Japanese Modernity*. Durham, NC: Duke University Press, 2004.
Yoneda Yūsuke. "Rekidai tennō no hongi to itsubun." In *Kokiroku to nikki*, edited by Yamanaka Yutaka, 77–90. Kyoto: Shibunkaku, 1993.
Yoshie, Akiko. "Gender in Early Classical Japan: Marriage, Leadership, and Political Status in Village and Palace." *Monumenta Nipponica* 60, no. 4 (Winter 2005): 437–79.
Yoshihara Yoshinori, ed. *Waka no utamakura chimei daijiten*. Tokyo: Ōfūsha, 2008.
Yoshiyama Hiroki. "'Koretaka shinnō monogatari' no tenkai to *Tosa nikki*: *Ise monogatari* Ki no Tsurayuki fudesaku shiron." *Hijiyama joshi tanki daigaku kiyō* 16 (March 1982): 35–44.
Yotsugi monogatari. Edited by Inoue Kōji. In ZGR 32:2. Tokyo: Gunsho Ruijū Kanseikai, 1926.
Yun, Jae-Woon. "Chinese Perceptions of Parhae." In *A New History of Parhae*, edited by Northeast Asian History Foundation, 171–79. Leiden: Brill, 2012.
———. "Parhae as an East Asian Maritime Power." In *A New History of Parhae*, edited by Northeast Asian History Foundation, 109–18. Leiden: Brill, 2012.

Zhang, Cong Ellen. *Transformative Journeys: Travel and Culture in Song China*. Honolulu: University of Hawai'i Press, 2011.

Index

abalones, 118–19, 124, 322
Abe no Mushimaro 阿部虫麻呂 (d. 752), 267–68
Abe no Nakamaro 阿倍仲麻呂 (or 阿部仲麿 698–770): anecdote in *Tosa nikki*, 254, 273–74, 289–90, 291–94, 296–97, 298, 327; farewell banquet, 257–61, 266, 269, 273, 279, 327; legacy, 255–56, 257, 265–67; poems, 255–56, 265–70, 297–98; *setsuwa* on, 298–99; *shi* about, 256, 259–65, 272, 279, 288; *shi* by, 256–59, 266, 268, 279, 288, 297–98; in Tang China, 254–55, 269, 274, 283, 290, 297; voyage and return to Chang'an, 264, 265
Abe no Nakamaro, *waka*: in anthologies, 169, 298–99; in *Kokinshū*, 266–69, 272, 298; parodies, 55; poems inspired by, 21; in *Tosa nikki*, 272–75, 279–80, 288, 290, 294, 296, 298, 327–28
Abo 阿保, Prince (792–842), 220–21
Abutsu 阿仏 (1222–1283), 162
aishō 哀傷 (Lamentations), 273–74
Akinari. *See* Ueda Akinari
Akiyama Ken 秋山虔 (1924–2015), 39
almanacs. *See guchūreki*

ama no hara 天の原 (the high plains of Heaven), 267
Ama no Kawa 天の川 (Heaven's River), 233, 244–45
Ama no Kawara 天の河原 (Heaven's Riverbed), 125, 244
Amaterasu 天照, 259
An Lushan 安禄山 Rebellion (755–763), 265, 274–75, 283
Analects (*Lunyu* 論語), 154
anecdotes. *See setsuwa; uta-gatari*
Angles, Jeffrey, 123
Ankan 安閑, Emperor (466–535, r. 531–535), 88
Annam 安南, 255, 265, 283
anonymous poems: in *Tosa nikki*, 169, 176–77, 179, 180, 184–85, 188–90, 243, 282, 294–95; as *waka*, 121–22, 156, 189–90, 228–29, 239–40, 287, 294–95
ao 鰲 (Leviathan), 262–63, 266
aomuma no sechie 青馬節会 (Presentation of White Steeds), 82–83, 316
aounabara 青海原 (cyan sea plains), 273, 274–75, 278–80, 288, 327
Aoyama Gakuin 青山学院, 38
Arabic language, 255
Aristotle, *Poetics* (ca. 355 BCE), 67, 304, 306

Ariwara no Narihira 在原業平 (825–880): anecdotes about, 209, 220, 222, 249; family members, 220–21, 350; life of, 218, 220, 231–32, 233; poem from mother, 217–20; poems inspired by *waka* of, 21, 55; poetry, 169, 170–71, 225, 226, 228, 243–44, 252, 318; *Sandai jitsuroku* biography, 220–22, 226; and Tsurayuki, 225; *uta-gatari*, 219, 225, 233; *waka* anthology, 219–20, 226
aruji 主 (hosts), 77, 90–91, 285–86, 311, 344
Ashikaga Yoshihisa 足利義尚 (1465–1489), 30
Ashikaga Yoshimasa 足利義正 (1435–1490), 30
asomi or *ason* 朝臣 (lords), 221, 226
Aston, William G. (1841–1911), 163–64
Asukai Masaari 飛鳥井雅有 (1241–1301), 29, 59, 159, 302–3
Atsuyoshi 敦慶, Prince (888–930), 350
attribution, 153–54, 156–58, 161, 229. *See also* authorship
authorship: of anthologies, 248; collective, 156; as commercial and legal concept, 37; differentiation from narrator, 1, 5, 7; gender and, 29–30, 158–59, 302–3; medieval views on, 26–30; ownership and, 158; print culture and, 31, 65–66; of *Tosa nikki*, 3, 4, 5, 19–20, 40, 65–66, 109, 301–2; of vernacular fiction, 20, 25–27
autobiographical readings, 21–25, 40–41
Awaji no tōme 淡路専女 (dame of Awaji), 60–61, 331, 340
Awata 粟田, 239, 351
azuki 小豆, 85, 323
azuma uta 東歌 (Eastland songs), 138, 142. See also *kai uta*
Azuma-ya 東屋 ("Eastland Cottage"), 121

Bai Juyi 白居易 (772–846), 32, 270–71, 282–83, 285, 287, 298
Bakhtin, Mikhail (1895–1975), 10, 67, 68n124, 123, 126, 305–6
Bal, Mieke, 10

banquets, 50, 83, 90–91. *See also* farewell banquets; food
Bao Ji 包佶 (d. 792), 260–61, 263, 279
Bashō. *See* Matsuo Bashō
beggar nun, 121–22, 123, 143
bekki 別記 (separate records), 53
bereaved mother character: grief of, 100–104, 321, 343; identity of, 61, 64; mourning rituals, 100–101; *waka* by, 40, 101, 102, 106, 189–90, 242–43, 338. *See also* dead girl character
bettō 別当 (stewards), 46–47, 48, 352
Bialock, David, 68
Bicchū 備中 province, 71
birthday celebrations, 46, 54, 192, 230, 273–74, 350–51, 352
Bizen 備前 province, 75–76
Bokuyū. *See* Hitomi Bokuyū
boor character, 83–85, 157, 186–88, 316–17
Botan kuroku 牡丹句録 (Peony Verse Record, 1899), 40
Brodzki, Bella, 290
Buddhism: almsgiving, 88–89, 342; censuses and temples, 47; copying scriptures, 157–58; karmic merit, 89–90, 157–58; and landscapes, 272; pilgrimage accounts, 50; poetry by priests, 271–72; prayers to gods and buddhas, 92, 200, 330, 334, 335; and translation, 296; vegetarian fasts, 86–87, 341. *See also* incantations; lector character
bungaku 文学 (literature), 38–39
Butler, Judith, 42

caesura, 281–82
calendars: inauspicious dates, 57, 74; information in almanacs, 57–58; taboos, 57, 58. See also *guchūreki*
calligraphy, 21, 25, 27–29, 31, 65, 157, 174, 202, 302
Cambodia, immigrants from, 254
Cangwu 蒼梧, Mount, 264, 292
capital: arrival of *Tosa nikki* travelers, 105, 346; floods and disease, 173; journeys

to and from, 22, 91, 181–82, 268–69; terms used for, 183. *See also* Chang'an
Cavanaugh, Carole, 158–59
Chang'an 長安, 255, 256, 257, 260, 263–64, 265, 266, 279
Chao Heng 晁衡, 255. *See also* Abe no Nakamaro
Chen, Jack, 149
children: in *funa uta*, 148–49; poems by, 100, 170, 183, 187–89; of Tsurayuki, 23–25, 34, 35, 40, 97, 188. *See also* dead girl
chin 朕 (royal "We"), 62. *See also* subjects, grammatical
China, 57, 149, 255, 269–70, 275, 280, 290. *See also* Tang dynasty
Chisato. *See* Ōe no Chisato
Chōya gunsai 朝野群載 (Records of Court and Country, ca. 1116), 45
Chūjō no shū 中将の集 (The Middle Captain's Anthology), 249
ciyi 辞儀 (etiquette manuals), 184
coins (*zeni* 銭), 148–49
Confucianism, 35, 36, 76, 84, 154, 262
Confucius (Kongzi 孔子) (ca. 551–479 BCE), 154, 259
Cormorant Hall (Udono 鵜殿), 343
cosmopolis, 255–56, 290–91, 296
cosmopolitanism: circulation of texts and, 255–56, 270–71, 297; linguistic, 290–91, 293–96; of Nakamaro, 254; poetic, 280, 284; in Tang China, 261–62, 265, 270; in *Tosa nikki*, 293–94, 295, 297, 298, 299
couplets. *See shi*
court: banquets, 50, 80; entertainment, 117, 138, 152; and *naiki no nikki*, 50, 51, 53, 54–56, 80–81, 166–67, 168; official histories, 4, 7, 51, 120, 166, 220–24, 265–66; rituals, 51, 54, 82–83; women, 301–3. *See also* capital; diplomacy
cranes (*tsuru* 鶴), 191–93, 319
Cronin, Michael, 293
cyan sea plains. *See aounabara*

Daigo 醍醐, Emperor (885–930, r. 897–930), 44–45, 52, 53, 54, 98, 173, 292, 349, 350, 351
daikenmotsu 大総監物 (warden of the palace storehouse), 173n35, 350
daily entry format, 50, 57, 165, 198–99, 248, 250
daisai 大歳 (Jupiter), 57
Dajōkan 太政官 (Office of the Council of State), 51
dancing, 33, 54, 128–29, 134, 141, 152, 155, 190, 259, 278. *See also* music; songs
Danzhou 亶州 island, 271
Day of the Rat. *See ne no hi*
Dazaifu 太宰府, 169, 271, 277
dead girl character: as ghost, 97–98, 101–4, 108–9; grief for, 79, 99–103, 107–9, 132, 312, 321, 343; poems on, 23–25, 98–104, 106–9, 132; possible inspiration for, 42–43; relationship to ex-governor, 61; Sinographs related to, 305. *See also* bereaved mother character
death: and pine trees, 191; and pollution, 100–101. *See also* bereaved mother character; ghosts; grief; mortuary practices
Decameron (ca. 1353), 307–8
De Certeau, Michel, 10
Denecke, Wiebke, 110n79, 281
Derrida, Jacques (1930–2004), 113
desi (local place), 295–96
diacritics, 30
Diamond Pure Land (Kongō Jōdo 金剛浄土), 178
diaries: daily entry format, 50, 57, 165, 198–99, 248, 250; of emperors, 50, 52, 53, 62; and facticity, 8, 62, 63, 66, 68, 197; in Heian period, 50–55; *kanbun nikki*, 39, 50, 53, 247; by men, 19–20, 50; parodies of, 7–8, 20, 57–65, 68, 251–52; perspective in, 59–65, 68; references to uneventful days, 33, 197–98; types, 50. *See also geki no nikki*; *naiki no nikki*; women's diaries

diaries, aristocratic: conventions, 235; details included, 56, 57, 63; evolution of, 51–55; gifts recorded in, 65, 70; parody in *Tosa nikki*, 56, 57, 58–59, 62, 70; recorded in morning, 56, 57, 235; references to uneventful days, 197–98; types, 50; by women, 49, 53–55
diplomacy, 257–58, 261, 263–64, 269–70, 274–76, 278–80, 284, 288, 290, 291, 293–94, 296–98
divination, 92–93
dokuei 独詠 (poetic monologue), 127
Dong Qidan 東契丹 (East Kitan), 275
Duthie, Torquil, 63, 291n73

Eastern Sea 東海, 260, 262, 279–80
Eawase 絵合 chapter (*Genji monogatari*), 28, 202–3
Echizen 越前 province, 172, 349
economies: discursive, 70, 73, 81, 89, 110, 196, 204, 264; religious, 12, 86, 90, 158
Edo 江戸 period (1603–1867), 31–38, 40, 42, 66–67, 70, 110, 118, 162–63, 164, 165, 181, 286
Egaku 恵萼, 271
Egyō 恵慶 (fl. 962–986), 20–21, 26, 49, 203, 247, 250
Egyō hōshi shū 恵慶法師集 (The Reverend Egyō Anthology), 20–21, 202, 203
Eiga monogatari 栄華物語 (Tale of Flowering Fortunes, ca. 1092), 28, 143, 208
elderly man character (*okina* 翁), 64, 151, 320, 326
elegies, 100, 102, 108, 191, 239. *See also* Li Bai
emaki 絵巻 (picture scrolls): *Kitano Tenjin engi*, 9; *Tosa nikki*'s origins as, 203–4
Emmerich, Michael, 303–4
Enchin 円珍 (814–891), 166
Enchō 延長 era (923–931), 350–51
Engi 延喜 era (901–923), 349–50
Engi gyoki 延喜御記 (Diary of the Engi Sovereign, ca. 897–930), 52

Engi shiki 延喜式 (Procedures of the Engi Era, 927), 83n23, 88n33, 94, 119n4, 174, 179, 197
Ennin 円仁 (794–864), 165–66, 271
Ensai 円載 (d. 877), 271
epilogue, *Tosa nikki*, 109–10, 202
eto 干支 (zodiac animals), 57
exchanges: anthropological view, 112–13; disappointment with, 106; of food, 85–90; of material things, 72–73. *See also* gifts; reciprocity; transactions
ex-governor character: discharge process, 71; farewell banquets, 73–75, 76–80, 310–12; household members, 9, 60, 61; illness of, 151, 305, 340–41; journey of, 1, 64–65, 197, 198–201; mansion of, 105–7; poems by, 77, 78, 185; relationship to narrator, 61, 64; replacement, 64–65, 77–78, 197, 311–12; representation of, 9, 63–64
exile, 9, 98, 108, 172, 174–75, 202, 221, 283, 286, 299

facticity: in diaries, 8, 60, 62, 63, 66, 68, 197, 247, 253
farewell banquets: drunkenness at, 74, 75, 76, 79, 128; duration, 65; for governors, 74–80; for Nakamaro, 257–61, 266, 269, 273, 279, 327; poems, 77–78, 132–33; in *Tosa nikki*, 73–75, 76–80, 310–12
feixie 誹諧 (J. *haikai*, humor), 110. *See also haikaika*
fengci 諷刺 (J. *fūshi*, poetic criticism of superiors), 110
Fifth Rank, 47, 155, 173, 176, 277, 350, 352
fish: carp, 83, 316; mullet, 89, 125, 126, 314; purchases, 86–90, 323, 341; sea bream, 87, 88, 323. *See also* shellfish; sweetfish
fishermen, 87–89, 143–44, 341
folk songs. *See min'yō*
food: gifts of, 64, 75–76, 82–85, 315, 316; literary references, 80; as medium of exchange, 85–90; for sovereigns, 80–81;

in *Taketori monogatari*, 96–97; and Tosa province, 72, 82; travelers' lack of, 80–85; vegetarian fasts, 86–87, 88, 341. *See also* banquets; farewell banquets; fish; rice; shellfish; sweetfish

Foucault, Michel (1926–1984), 8–9, 158

fudoki 風土記 gazetteers, 211

Fujioka Sakutarō 藤岡作太郎 (1870–1910), 208

Fujitani Mitsue 富士谷御杖 (1768–1823), 35–36, 40, 71, 85, 109, 169

Fujiwara no Atsutada 藤原敦忠 (906–943), 352

Fujiwara no Atsutoshi 藤原敦敏 (918–947), 49

Fujiwara no Hōshi 藤原褒子 (or Yoshiko), 351

Fujiwara no Kanesuke 藤原兼輔 (877–933), 40, 44, 46, 124–25, 239, 350, 351

Fujiwara no Kazuko 藤原佳珠子, 350, 351

Fujiwara no Kishi 藤原貴子 (or Takako, 904–962), 352

Fujiwara no Kiyokawa 藤原清河 (d. 778), 257, 264, 265

Fujiwara no Kiyosuke 藤原清輔 (1104–1177), 155

Fujiwara no Kiyotsura 藤原清貫 (867–930), 351

Fujiwara no Kōshi 藤原高子 (or Takaiko, 842–910), 231

Fujiwara no Masatada 藤原雅正 (d. 961), 46

Fujiwara no Meishi 藤原明子 (or Akirakeiko, 829–900), 226–27

Fujiwara no Michiakira 藤原道明 (856–920), 350

Fujiwara no Michikane 藤原道兼 (961–995), 208

Fujiwara no Mitsuko 藤原満子 (874–937), 349, 350, 351

Fujiwara no Morosuke 藤原師輔 (908–960), 45, 48–49, 53, 56–59, 351, 352

Fujiwara no Morotada 藤原師尹 (920–969), 351

Fujiwara no Mototsune 藤原基経 (836–891), 52

Fujiwara no Nakazane 藤原仲実 (1064–1122). See *Kokin wakashū mokuroku*

Fujiwara no Onshi 藤原穏子 (or Yasuko, 885–954), 49, 53–55, 65, 350, 351

Fujiwara no Otomuro 藤原乙牟漏 (760–790), 350

Fujiwara no Sadakata 藤原定方 (873–932), 44, 350, 351

Fujiwara no Sadakuni 藤原定国 (866–906), 349

Fujiwara no Sanesuke 藤原実資 (957–1046), 54

Fujiwara no Saneyori 藤原実頼 (900–970): family members, 46, 49, 54, 351; patronage, 46, 47–48, 49, 156–57, 351, 352; regency, 45; texts authored, 45, 53

Fujiwara no Shōshi 藤原彰子 (or Akiko, 988–1074), 210–11

Fujiwara no Shunzei 藤原俊成 (1114–1204), 25

Fujiwara no Sumitomo 藤原純友 (d. 941), 277–78

Fujiwara no Tadafusa 藤原忠房 (d. 929), 152

Fujiwara no Tadahira 藤原忠平 (880–949): diary, 46–47, 52–53, 72, 197–98; and government activities, 45, 52–53, 72, 98, 276; patronage, 46–47, 49, 350–51, 352; relatives, 45, 46, 48, 49, 53, 54, 351

Fujiwara no Tameie 藤原為家 (1198–1275), 28–29, 38, 302

Fujiwara no Teika 藤原定家 (or Sadaie, 1162–1241), 26–28, 29, 30, 38, 49, 250

Fujiwara no Tokihira 藤原時平 (871–909), 192, 224, 228, 352

Fujiwara no Tsunesuke 藤原恒佐 (879–978), 351

Fujiwara no Yasunori 藤原保則 (825–895), 75–76, 351

Fujiwara no Yasunori den 藤原保則伝 (Biography of Fujiwara no Yasunori, 907), 75–76, 92

Fujiwara no Yasutada 藤原保忠 (890–936), 350

Fujiwara no Yoritada 藤原頼忠 (924–989), 49

Fujiwara no Yoshifusa 藤原良房 (804–872), 52, 222–24, 226–28, 230, 242–43

Fujiwara Seika 藤原惺窩 (1561–1619), 31

Fukui Teisuke 福井貞助, 244

Fukumori, Naomi, 215

Fukuro-zōshi 袋草子 (Pocket Book, ca. 1156–1159), 168

Funadama Jinja 船玉神社 (Ship Soul Shrine), 94

funagimi 船君 (the lord on board), 64, 277. See also ex-governor character

funa uta 舟歌 (ship songs): authenticity of, 153–54, 160–61; compared to *waka*, 144; and mobility, 160; as popular songs, 144–45; refrains, 140–41, 145, 146; sung by youth, 144, 328; transcriptions, 118, 122, 146–52, 158–59, 320; *uta-gatari* and, 207

Furuhashi Nobuyoshi 古橋信吉, 123

furu uta 古歌 (old songs), 170–71

Fusang 扶桑 (J. Fusō, The Sunrise Tree, or Japan), 262–63, 279

fūshi. See *fengci*; satire

Fusō ryakki 扶桑略記 (Abbreviated Chronicles of Japan, ca. 1094), 168

fuyo geyujō 不与解由状 (non-deliverance of the discharge letter), 71

fuzoku uta 風俗歌 (songs of regional airs), 117, 127

ga 賀 (Blessings), 273–74

Gagakuryō 雅楽寮 (Bureau of Court Music), 141

ganmon 願文 (prayer dedications), 157–58

gazoku 雅俗 (noble and base), 31

Geki bunin 外記補任 (Record of Court Appointments, ca. 1500), 276

geki no nikki 外記日記 (outer palace diaries), 50, 51, 53

Gen no Naishi 源典侍 (character in *Genji monogatari*), 120–21, 123

genba no kami 玄蕃頭 (head of the department of Buddhist and foreign affairs), 47–48, 278, 352

gender: differences between author and narrator, 60; and emotions, 42–43, 52; inversions, 68; literacy and, 161; men and writing, 28, 29, 42–43, 52; in metaphors, 83; performativity, 42; writing and, 28, 29–30, 43, 128, 161. See also pansexuality; sexuality; women; women's diaries

Gen'ei-bon 元永本 manuscript, 237n66

Genji 源氏 (character in *Genji monogatari*), 119, 120–21, 123, 202–3, 213, 221–22, 289

Genji monogatari 源氏物語 (The Tale of Genji, ca. 1008), 25, 28, 30, 54, 60, 119, 120–21, 123, 136, 145, 153, 202–3, 213–14, 303–5, 306

genpuku 元服 (cap-donning) ceremonies, 351

genre fluidity, 246–49

Genroku 元禄 era (1688–1704), 31–33

gentry, 47, 63, 70, 73, 75, 76, 79, 186

geyu 解由 (official discharges), 71

ghosts, 24, 89, 97–98, 101–4, 108–9. See also bereaved mother character; death; grief

gifts: exchanges of, 65, 70, 73, 86; to ex-governors, 75–76; of food, 64, 75–76, 82–85, 315, 316; Mauss on, 112–13; to retainers, 77, 78. See also exchanges; farewell banquets; reciprocity

gigaku 伎楽 (masked dances), 128

gijo 伎女 (professional female dancers), 155

gishiki-sho 儀式書 (ritual formularies), 53

gishōka 戯笑歌 (jesting songs), 120

Go-Fukakusa 後深草, Emperor (1243–1304, r. 1246–1260), 29

gon-shōjō 権少掾 (assistant lesser secretaries), 172–73, 349

Gosenshū seigi 後撰集正義 (Correct Meaning of the *Gosenshū*, ca. 1304), 168

Gosen wakashū 後撰和歌集 (or *Gosenshū* 後撰集, Anthology of Later Selections of Poems, ca. 951), 21–23, 155–57, 169, 295

goshiki 五色 (the five primary colors), 193, 334

Go-Shirakawa 後白河, Emperor (1127–1192, r. 1155–1158), 27

gosho-dokoro no azukari 御書所預 (palace library custodians), 55, 166, 349

Go-Tsuchimikado 後土御門, Emperor (1442–1500, r. 1464–1500), 30

government posts, 7, 40, 45, 52n87, 72, 81, 165, 171–73, 220, 233, 243, 259, 266, 283, 303, 309, 316, 351. *See also* ex-governor character; governors; officials; ranks

governors (*kami* 守): discharge process and documents, 71–72; farewell banquets, 74–80; financial responsibilities, 71–72, 85–86; gift exchanges, 73, 86; of Kii, 119; provincial gentry and, 73, 75, 76, 79; retainers of, 77, 78; Tsurayuki as, 1, 22, 23–24, 35–36, 72, 172, 173–74, 276–77; wealth, 85–86, 91. *See also* ex-governor character

Goyō wakashū 後葉和歌集 (Waka Anthology of Later Leaves, 1156–1157), 136–37

Greek language, 141n57, 255. *See also* Aristotle; *Medea*

grief (*kanashi* 悲し): as authorial motive, 23–24, 34, 40, 97–98; for dead girl, 79, 99–103, 107–9, 132, 312, 321, 343. *See also* bereaved mother character

Guangzhou 廣州, 165

guchūreki 具注暦 (almanacs), 50–51, 55, 56, 57–58

Gulliver's Travels (1726), 111

Gunsho ruijū 群書類従 (Writings by Topic, 1819), 163

gyoki 御記 (royal diaries), 50, 52–55

Gyōkō Hōin 堯孝法院 (1391–1455), 30

Gyōrekishō 行歴抄 (Notes from a Pilgrimage, ca. 851–858), 166

gyoyū 御遊 (royal entertainments), 152

Haga Yaichi 芳賀矢一 (1867–1927), 208

hagatame 歯固め (teeth-firming) rite, 81–82, 314

Hagitani Boku 萩谷朴 (1917–2009), 41, 49, 62, 65, 70, 97, 105, 111, 126, 140, 144, 147, 183, 195, 237, 285, 309

Hahakigi 帚 chapter (*Genji monogatari*), 119

hahaso 柞 (mother oak), 155–56

haikai 俳諧 poetry, 32, 68n24, 120. *See also* Matsuo Bashō

haikaika 誹諧歌 (absurd verse), 110–11, 120, 125. See also *feixie*

Hakata 博多, 270

Hako no Ura 箱の浦 (Box Bay), 184–85, 334

Hanawa Hokiichi 塙保己一 (1746–1821), 162–63

Han 漢 dynasty (202 BCE–220 CE), 51, 141–42, 262

Hane 羽根 (Wings), 100, 170, 321

hanreki 頒暦 (distributed calendars), 50

Hanshi 班子, Princess (833–900), 349

Harris, Florence Best (1850–1909), 38, 148n69, 163

Harusame monogatari 春雨物語 (Tales of Spring Rain, 1808), 34–35

Hasegawa Masaharu 長谷川政春, 40, 55, 268

Haseo. *See* Ki no Haseo

hayashi kotoba 囃子詞 (refrains), 140–41, 145, 146, 151–52

Heian 平安 period (794–1185): diaries, 50–55; literary canon, 26, 27, 28, 30, 31; popular culture, 161; relations with continent, 270, 274–76, 278–80, 298; song culture, 117, 135, 140, 141, 146, 151–53, 159–60; travelogues, 162, 163, 166; use of money, 148–49

Heichū 平中, 136, 140. *See also* Taira no Sadabumi

Heichū monogatari 平中物語 (Tales of Heichū, 10th c.), 136, 140, 207–9, 219

Heizei 平城, Emperor (774–824, r. 806–809), 220

Henitiuk, Valerie, 304
Henjō 遍照 (816–890), 230
hentaigana 変体仮名 (variant *kana*), 295
Herdboy (Hikoboshi 彦星) star, 125. See also Tanabata
Herder, Johann Gottfried (1744–1803), 141
heterotopia, 9, 96, 104
Hida 飛騨 province, 37
Higo 肥後 province, 174
Higuchi Hiroshi 樋口寛, 41
Himiko 卑弥呼 (ca. 170–248), 261n12
Hiroi 広井, Princess (d. 859), 120
Hitachi 常陸 province, 121
Hitomaro. See Kakinomoto no Hitomaro
Hitomi Bokuyū 人見卜幽 (1599–1670), 31, 286
hizuke 日付 (calendrical dates), 57
Holcombe, Charles, 272
holograph, 25, 26–28, 30, 49
Honchō monzui 本朝文粋 (Literary Essence of Our Court, ca. 1058), 194
Honchō seiki 本朝世紀 (Record of Our Court's Reigns, 12th c.), 51
honka-dori 本歌取り (allusive variation), 68
honorific language, 54, 60, 64–65, 76–77, 87, 100, 233, 245
hosts. See *aruji*
hototogisu birds, 143, 151
Hotsu 最, 178
huaji 滑稽 (jesters), 110
Huangdi 黄帝, Emperor (2711–2599 BCE), 45n66
humor, 43, 66, 68, 70, 110, 112, 120, 126. See also parody; satire; wordplay
Hutcheon, Linda, 67–68, 111

Ichijō Kanera 一条兼良 (or Kaneyoshi, 1402–1481), 141
ie no shū 家の集 (household anthology), 248
Ihara Saikaku 井原西鶴 (1642–1693), 32–33, 66, 308
Ihibo 飯粒 (character in *Nihon shoki*), 88, 89
Ikeda Kikan 池田亀鑑 (1896–1956), 28, 38, 39, 40, 42, 50

Iken jūnikajō 意見十二箇条 (Twelve Opinions Submitted to the Throne, 914), 71
Iki no Hakatoko no fumi 伊吉博徳書 (Chronicle of Iki no Hakatoko, ca. 659–661), 166
Ikuta-gawa 生田川, 203, 212–13
imayō 今様 (current tunes), 117, 127, 178, 182
imibi 忌日 (death anniversaries), 100
in 院 (villas), 226, 237. See also Nagisa no In
incantations, 75, 89, 92, 93, 112
Inland Sea, 277–78
Inner Palace Secretariat. See Naiki
I-novels (*shishōsetsu* 私小説 or *watakushi shōsetsu*), 39
interpreters, 289, 290, 291–94, 298. See also translation
Io nushi いほぬし (Hut Master, ca. 995–1004), 163
Iran, immigrants from, 254
Ise monogatari 伊勢物語 (10th c.), 29, 32, 33, 63, 170, 172, 207–9, 219, 220, 222, 224, 230–35, 237, 240–46, 249–50, 253. See also Ariwara no Narihira
Ise no Go 伊勢の御 (Lady Ise), 33
Ise no umi 伊勢の海 ("The Sea at Ise"), 136
Ise Shrine priestesses, 53, 231, 249
Ishikawa no Asomi Iroko 石川朝臣色子, 155n79
Ishizu 石津 (Stone Port), 182, 338
Isle of Immortals. See Penglai
Isonokami no Otomaro 石上乙麻呂 (d. 750), 174, 175
Itō Haku 伊藤博 (1925–2003), 207
Ito 伊都, Princess (d. 861), 157, 220–21
iu 言ふ (to speak, speech), 128, 129, 131, 132, 140
Iwanami Shoten 岩波書店, 39
Iwashimizu Hachimangū 石清水八幡宮, 176, 278, 352
Iyo 伊予 province, 178, 276, 277
izana-tori 鯨取 or 勇魚取 (whale-hunted), 266

Izayoi nikki 十六夜日記 (Diary of the Sixteenth Night, 1283), 162
Izumi 泉 province, 73, 175, 182, 246, 310, 334
Izumi no Nada 泉灘 (Onward Stretch of Izumi), 180–81, 334, 337

Jackson, Reginald, 306
Japan Mail, The, 38
jesters, 110, 126
Ji Zha 李札, Prince (576–484 BCE), 259, 260, 261
Jia Dao 賈島 (779–843), 271–72, 279, 283–85, 298
Jian'an 建安 era (196–220), 262, 287
Jiangzhou 江州, 283
jibo 字母 (phonographs), 27
jikitai 直体 (direct style), 23
Jin 晉 dynasty (266–420), 51
Jing Zhencheng 井真成 (699–734), 255
Jingū 神功, Empress (169–269, r. 201–269), 94–95, 176
jintishi 近体詩 (J. *kintaishi*, new style *shi*), 256
jishō 自照 (self-reflections), 39. *See also* women's diaries
jō 掾 (secretaries), 172. *See also gon-shōjō*
jogaku 女楽 (women's entertainment), 155
Jōgan 貞観 era (859–877), 120n7, 174n37, 222n39, 349
jokotoba 序詞 (prefatory words), 121, 193
jōruri 浄瑠璃 (puppet theater) plays, 33
joryū nikki bungaku 女流日記文学 (women's diary literature), 3, 29, 38–44. *See also* women's diaries
Jōwa 承和 era (834–848), 34, 266n20
jubaku 呪縛 (incantations), 89
jueju 絶句 (J. *zekku*, quatrains), 281, 286–88, 296. *See also* Li Bai; quatrains; *shi*
jūnichoku 十二直 (twelve signs for auspicious dates), 57
jun'yūki 巡遊記 (accounts of pilgrimages), 50
jusha 儒者 (scholar-officials), 35, 71

Kaga 加賀 province, 172, 173, 350
kagami 鏡 (mirrors), 95, 338
Kagawa Kageki 香川景樹 (1768–1843), 35, 38, 103, 118
Kagerō nikki 蜻蛉日記 (Kagerō Diary, ca. 974), 19, 302, 303
kagura uta 神楽歌 (songs to entertain gods), 117, 127, 267
kai fuzoku 甲斐風俗 (airs of Kai), 137–38
Kainuma no ike かひ沼の池 (Shell-Marsh Pond), 210–13, 218, 226, 236, 249
Kai 甲斐 province, 137–38, 139, 313
Kaisen 戒仙, 350
kai uta 甲斐歌 (Kai songs), 118, 135–39, 141–42, 160, 313
"Kaizoku" 海賊 ("The Pirate"), 34–35
Kakaishō 河海抄 commentary (14th c.), 54
kakekotoba 掛詞 (pivot-words), 111, 186, 194, 195, 211, 287
Kakinomoto no Hitomaro 柿本人麻呂 (fl. ca. 690), 215, 217
Kako no Saki 鹿児崎 (Fawn Cape), 181, 312
kaku 書く (to write), 128
Kakyō hyōshiki 歌経標式 (A Formulary for Verse Based on the Canons of Poetry, 772), 229
kami 神 (gods), 93–96, 224; and buddhas, 92, 200, 330, 334, 335. *See also* Sumiyoshi
Kamo no Chōmei 鴨長明 (1155–1216), 162
Kamo no Mabuchi 賀茂真淵 (1697–1769), 33–34, 192
Kamochi Masazumi 鹿持雅澄 (1791–1858), 36–37
Kamo priestesses (*sai'in* 斎院), 350
kana 仮名 prose, 21, 29, 36, 38, 42–43, 54, 168
kanbun nikki 漢文日記 (diaries in Literary Sinitic), 39, 50, 53, 247
Kanesuke. *See* Fujiwara no Kanesuke
kanmon no nikki 勘問日記 (records of criminal investigations), 50

Kanmu 桓武, Emperor (737–806, r. 781–806), 157, 220, 232–33, 350
Kannada language, 295–96
kannushi 神主 (head priests), 176
Kanpyō 寛平 era (889–898), 349
Kanpyō gyoki 寛平御記 (Diary of the Kanpyō Sovereign, ca. 887–897), 52, 62
kanshi 官史 (office scribes), 154
Kanshi 勧子, Princess (or Yukiko, b. 899), 350
kanzō 萱草. See *wasure-gusa*
Kaoru 薫 (character in *Genji monogatari*), 213
kara uta 唐歌 (continental verses), 135, 281–82, 285, 290
Kasenkeshū-bon 歌仙家集本 manuscript, 49
Kasuga 春日, 267, 273, 292, 293, 327
Kasuga 春日, Mount, 189, 190
Katano 交野, 167, 232–33
Katō Bansai 加藤磐斎 (1625–1674), 32
Katō Umaki 加藤宇万伎 (1721–1777), 34
Katsura-gawa 桂川 (Laurel River), 105, 345–46
Kawachi 川内 province, 194
Kawashima, Terry, 249n98
kayō 歌謡 (songs), 127. See also songs
Keichū 契沖 (1640–1701), 33
Keien 桂園 school, 35
Kenshō 顕昭 (ca. 1130–1210), 208
keri (auxiliary verb), 5, 22, 62, 157, 163, 211, 240–41, 246–47, 251, 254, 267
ki (auxiliary verb), 246, 293
ki 記 (records), 50. See also diaries
Ki no Aritsune 紀有常 (815–877), 242
Ki no Fumisada 紀文定, 155n80
Ki no Funamori 紀船守 (731–792), 172, 277
Ki no Haseo 紀長谷雄 (845–912), 154, 167, 277
Ki no Kajinaga 紀梶長 (754–806), 277
Ki no Mochiyuki 紀望行, 154–55, 161, 230, 329
Ki no Motomichi 紀本道 (fl. mid-9th c.), 154, 176

Ki no Munesada 紀宗定, 155n80
Ki no Natsui 紀夏井 (fl. 858–866), 174
Ki no Okimichi 紀興道 (d. 834), 154
Ki no Shizuko 紀静子 (d. 866), 176
Ki no Tokifumi 紀時文 (ca. 922–996), 21, 22, 157, 277n45
Ki no Tomonori 紀友則 (ca. 850–904), 154, 172
Ki no Tsurayuki 紀貫之 (ca. 871–946): biographical information, 4–6, 7, 46–49, 154–55, 188; chronology, 349–52; daughter, 188; death date, 48; death of child, 23–25, 34, 35, 40, 97; father, 154, 155, 161, 230; and *Ise monogatari*, 241–44, 253; journey to capital, 181–82; literary career and reputation, 3, 4–5, 21, 25, 28; mother, 155–57, 159, 161; social identity, 35; son, 21, 22, 157, 277n45. See also *Tosa nikki*; *waka*, by Tsurayuki
Ki no Tsurayuki, official career: diplomacy, 278, 291, 298; familiarity with diaries, 55–56, 80–81; as governor of Tosa, 1, 22, 23–24, 35–36, 72, 172, 173–74, 276–77; and palace kitchen, 80–81; positions held, 7, 55, 80–81, 166, 168, 172–73, 349–52; promotions, 47–48; Tadahira and, 46–47
Ki no Yoshihito 紀淑人 (fl. early 10th c.), 277
Kibi no Makibi 吉備真備 (695–775), 166
kichiji 吉事 (auspicious events), 57
kidendō 紀伝道 (history and letters), 154
Kigin. See Kitamura Kigin
Kii 紀伊 province, 119, 175, 277
Kike shū 紀家集 (Ki House Collection), 167
kikō-bu 紀行部 (travel section in *Gunsho ruijū*), 163
kikōbun 紀行文 (travel writing), 162–63
Kikuchi Yasuhiko 菊池靖彦 (1936–2001), 183
kinai 機内 (home provinces), 175
King, Ross, 290–91

Ki no shōsaku kashū 紀将作歌集 (The Ki Head Carpenter's Anthology of Verse), 48. See also *Tsurayuki shū*

Kinshi 勤子, Princess (or Isoko, 904–938), 49, 350, 351

Kintada. See Minamoto no Kintada

kiryo-bu 羈旅部 (Travel section in *Kokinshū*), 169–71, 268–69, 273–74

Kishi keizu 紀氏系図 (Ki Clan Genealogy, 19th c.), 155n80, 188n71

Kishimoto Yuzuru 岸本由豆流 (1788–1846), 36, 88, 165

Kishi sanmyaku 紀氏山脈 (Ki Clan mountain range), 230

Kisoigariki 競狩記 (Account of a Hunt for Wild Herbs, 898), 167

Kitamura Kigin 北村季吟 (1624–1705), 32, 34, 35, 36, 188, 286

Kitano Tenjin engi 北野天神縁起 (Legendary Origins of the Kitano Shrine, early 13th c.), 9

Kiyohara no Motosuke 清原元輔 (908–990), 21

Kiyosuke-bon 清輔本 manuscript, 237n66

Kiyoyuki. See Miyoshi no Kiyoyuki

Klein, Susan, 227–28

kō 候 (seventy-two calendrical climates), 57

Koguryŏ 高句麗 kingdom (37 BCE–668 CE), 166

Kohon setsuwa shū 古本説話集 (A Collection of Anecdotes from Old Books, 12th c.), 23–24, 299

koi 恋ひ (longing), 98, 132

Kokinshū dōmōshō 古今集童蒙抄 (A *Kokinshū* Primer, 1476), 141

Kokin waka rokujō 古今和歌六帖 (A Compendium of Old and New Waka in Six Scrolls, late 10th c.), 21, 121, 287, 295

Kokin wakashū 古今和歌集 (or *Kokinshū* 古今集, Anthology of Old and New Poems, ca. 905), 3, 23, 34, 40, 55, 70–71, 120–22, 124–25, 129, 138, 139, 140, 142, 143, 154, 156, 169–71, 172, 176, 183, 185, 189–90, 191, 193, 219, 225–29, 236–37, 240, 266–69, 272, 273–74, 287, 298, 349

Kokin wakashū mokuroku 古今和歌集目録 (*Kokin wakashū* Annotated and Indexed, ca. 1113), 6, 48, 154, 172, 257

Kōkō 光孝, Emperor (830–887, r. 884–887), 167, 231n60

kokoro 心 (heart or mind), 70–71

kokubunji 国分寺 (provincial head temples), 64

kokugaku 国学 (nativism), 33–36

Konjaku monogatari shū 今昔物語集 (Collection of Tales of Times Now Past, ca. mid-12th c.), 23–24, 89, 298–99

Korean peninsula, 270, 278–80, 291. See also Koguryŏ; Koryŏ; Parhae; Silla

Koresada 是貞, Prince (d. 903), 349

Koretaka 惟喬, Prince (844–897), 176, 222–25, 227, 230–34, 236, 238, 242, 342

Kornicki, Peter, 37n42, 42

kōro shinin no uta 行路死人歌 (travel verses for the dead), 108, 169

Koryŏ 高麗 kingdom (918–1392), 275, 283. See also Later Koryŏ

Kōshi 康子, Princess (or Yasuko, 919–957), 54, 351

koshōgatsu 小正月 (lesser New Year's Day), 85n29

Koyōshū 古謡集 (Collection of Old Songs, 1099), 137, 138

kuchi-oshi 口惜し (bitter regrets), 12, 85, 95, 97, 110

Kudai waka 句題和歌 (Poetic Lines as Waka Topics, 894), 280–81, 282

kuenichi 凶会日 (days of ill omen), 57, 74

Kujōdono goyuikai 九条殿御遺誡 (Testament of the Ninth Avenue Lord, ca. 947–960), 56–57, 58, 124n20

Kūkai 空海 (774–835), 271

Kumano 熊野, 163

kundoku 訓読 (vernacularized readings of Literary Sinitic), 43, 193, 290

kurōdo 蔵人 (chamberlains), 51

Kurosaki 黒崎 (Dark Peninsula), 182, 193, 334
kurushi 苦し (frustrating), 191
kusushi 医師 (provincial head doctors), 81, 97, 174, 314
kuten 句点 (phrase markers), 30
kuyō no ki 供養記 (records of memorial rites), 50
kyō 京 (*The Capital*), 183, 200, 312, 321, 332, 337, 343, 344, 345–46. See also capital
Kyōshi 恭子, Princess (or Yasuko, 902–915), 350
kyū 急 (rapid climax), 105
Kyūreki 九暦 (ca. 930–960), 53
Kyushu 九州, 145, 221, 262, 263, 270–71, 287

Lady Ise. See Ise no Go
Lainan lu 来南録 (A Record of Coming South, 809), 165
landscapes: and Buddhism, 272; imaginary, 192–93; liquid, 10, 165, 177, 178–80, 187–88, 204, 297; poetic descriptions, 164, 176–77, 183, 184–93; prose descriptions, 193–96; in travel poetry, 184–85. See also place names
Lane, Richard, 308
Later Koryŏ 後高麗 (935–1392), 276
Later Liang 後梁 (907–923), 275
Later Paekche 後百済 (900–936), 276
Latin language, 255
laurel tree (*katsura* 桂), 284, 324. See also Katsura-gawa
lector character (*kōji* 講師), 64–65, 76–77, 81, 92, 128, 199, 310, 315
Lejeune, Philippe, 5
Lévi-Strauss, Claude (1908–2009), 113
Li Ao 李翱 (774–836), 165
Li Bai 李白 (701–762), 255, 264–65, 286–87, 288, 290, 292–93, 295, 298
lianju 連句 (J. *renku*, linked verse compositions), 281, 283–84
Liao 遼 dynasty (907–1125), 275, 278

librarians, 27, 255, 259. See also *goshodokoro no azukari*
libraries, 7, 26, 55, 166, 274
life-writings, 4, 226, 249
Liji 礼記 (Book of Rites, ca. early 1st c. BCE), 84–85
liminality, 73, 160, 179, 204, 226, 256, 258–59, 297, 307
literacy, 42n58, 128, 131–34, 156, 161
Literary Sinitic (*kanbun* 漢文), 4, 34, 42, 43, 50, 53, 112, 128, 130, 135, 154, 165–66, 168, 193–94, 222, 247, 255, 268, 280, 292, 294. See also *kanbun nikki*; *shi*
Lowe, Brian, 157–58
Loyang 洛陽, 165
Lu 魯, 259, 260
Lucian (ca. 125–180), 111–12
Lukács, György, 306
Lurie, David, 42, 290
lushi 律詩 (regulated verses), 258, 271, 284. See also *shi*

ma-aki 間明き (blank lines), 50
Mabuchi. See Kamo no Mabuchi
Mair, Victor, 296
Makibashira 真木柱 chapter (*Genji monogatari*), 25
makurakotoba 枕詞 (poetic epithet), 193
Makura no sōshi 枕草子 (The Pillow Book, ca. 1000), 57–58, 74, 86, 87, 117, 121–22, 123, 127, 133–34, 139, 142–43, 151, 178, 186, 214–20, 236, 285, 303. See also Sei Shōnagon
manajo 真名序 (*mana* preface to the *Kokinshū*), 129, 225n46
Man'yōshū 万葉集 (ca. 759), 54, 63, 66, 102, 121, 130, 141, 142, 144, 169, 171, 172, 175, 178, 182, 189, 191, 207, 213, 266–67, 274
Masaari. See Asukai Masaari
Masaoka Shiki 正岡子規 (1867–1902), 40
Masatsura character, 82, 199, 315
masugata-bon 枡形本 (square-shaped texts), 247

Index

material things (*mono*), 71, 72–73, 80, 90, 97, 109. *See also* food; gifts; *mono* (spectral)
Matsunaga Teitoku 松永貞徳 (1571–1654), 32
Matsunoki Munetsuna 松木宗綱 (1445–1525), 30
Matsuo Bashō 松尾芭蕉 (1644–1694), 32, 162, 164
Mauss, Marcel (1872–1950), 112–13
McCullough, Helen (1918–1988), 40–41, 118, 195
Medea (431 BCE), 68
Meiji 明治 period (1868–1912), 37–38, 141
Menippean satire, 111–12
metafictional commentary, 67–68, 180, 182, 209, 246, 251–52, 305
metalinguistic commentary, 8, 11, 111, 113–14, 287, 289, 295, 297
metaphors: floral, 227–29, 238, 239; gendered, 83; for genitalia, 86, 118–19, 120–21, 124, 322; for landscapes, 185; in Nagisa poem, 227; in *waka*, 225, 287
metonyms: in Nagisa poem, 226, 227; in *Tosa nikki*, 176–77, 185, 186, 188, 194, 196
Mezaki Tokue 目崎徳衛 (1921–2000), 230
Mibu no Tadamine 壬生忠岑 (d. 920), 23
Michinoku 陸奥 province, 173, 210, 216
michi no nikki 道の日記 (road journals), 162
michiyuki 道行 (travel passages), 33
Michizane. *See* Sugawara no Michizane
Mighty Peninsula (Misaki 御崎), 324
Mikasa 三笠, Mount, 267, 273, 292, 296, 327
miko 親王 (princes), 233
mikuji-age 御髪上げ (hair-binding) ceremonies, 350
mimicry, 1, 7, 20, 43, 69
Minamoto no Ienaga 源家長 (1170–1234), 208
Minamoto no Junshi 源順子 (or Nobuko, 875–925), 350

Minamoto no Kintada 源公忠 (899–928), 47, 48, 201, 352
Minamoto no Kiyokage 源清蔭 (884–950), 352
Minamoto no Takaakira 源高明 (914–982), 54
Minamoto no Washi 源和子 (d. 947), 350
Minase 水瀬, 231, 232
Miner, Earl (1927–2004), 40, 41
Mingzhou 明州, 269–70
Mino 美濃 province, 172–73, 350
min'yō 民謡 (folk songs), 140–43, 149, 152
mitate 見立て (visual allusions), 66
Mitsue. *See* Fujitani Mitsue
Miyake, Lynne, 42
miyako 都 (capital city), 24, 77, 99, 125, 170, 183, 282, 294, 311, 314, 321, 328, 340, 341, 343. *See also* capital
miyako-dori 都鳥 (capital birds), 170
Miyataki 宮滝, 133, 167–68
Miyoshi, Masao (1928–2009), 304
Miyoshi no Kiyoyuki 三善清行 (847–919), 71, 75–76
Mizu-nashi no Ike 水なしの池 (Waterless Pond), 186
mogi 裳着 (skirt-donning) ceremonies, 350, 351
moji 文字 (letters or syllables), 28, 133–34
mokugon no kami 木工権頭 (acting head of the carpenters office), 48, 352
monogatari 物語 (tales), 4, 8, 10, 61–62, 77, 83, 96, 128n28, 163, 184, 210, 213, 216, 247–48, 251–52, 253, 307
mono no aware 物の哀れ (poignancy of the moment), 80, 106
mono (spectral), 97, 105, 109. *See also* ghosts; material things
Montoku 文徳, Emperor (827–858, r. 850–858), 176, 222–24, 227, 231n60
moon, 22, 124, 215, 243, 244–45, 264, 267, 293, 296–97, 324–25, 327–28
Moribe. *See* Tachibana no Moribe
Morimoto Motoko 森本元子, 248
Morley, Brendan, 274
Morokoshi, 269–70, 274, 291

Morosuke. *See* Fujiwara no Morosuke
mortuary practices, 108–9. *See also* death
mosha 模写 (facsimiles), 28
Mostow, Joshua, 42, 66, 208
moto-kata 本方 (left-hand chorus), 137
Motomichi. *See* Ki no Motomichi
Motoori Norinaga 本居宣長 (1730–1801), 33
Mototsune. *See* Fujiwara no Mototsune
Motoyasu 本康, Prince (d. 901), 52, 349
Motoyasu shinnō nikki 本康親王日記, 52
Motoyoshi 元良, Prince (890–943), 351
muma no hanamuke 馬の餞 (steed nose-turning rite), 74
Murakami 村上, Emperor (926–967, r. 946–967), 53
Murasaki Shikibu 紫式部 (fl. ca. 1000), 54–55, 60, 128, 209–14, 219, 289, 302. *See also Genji monogatari*
Murasaki Shikibu nikki 紫式部日記 (Diary of Murasaki Shikibu, ca. 1008–1010), 54–55, 303
Murasaki Shikibu shū 紫式部集 (Murasaki Shikibu Anthology, mid-11th c.), 209–13
Muromachi 室町 period (1336–1573), 30–31
Murotsu 室津 (Cave Harbor), 178, 182, 198, 199, 321–22
Musashi 武蔵 province, 173
music: as entertainment, 76, 128; instrumental, 81, 134, 141, 155, 239, 259; scores, 152. *See also* dancing; songs
mussels, 118–19, 124, 322
myōjin 明神 (deities), 94

Nabeshima-bon 鍋島本 manuscript, 140
nachin 納音 (determinants of individual fates), 57
nagabitsu 長櫃 (long chests), 83
Nagaya 長屋, Prince (684–729), 108, 174, 272
Nagisa no In 渚院 (Villa by the Strand), 176, 225–26, 236–38, 342

Nagisa poem: in anthologies, 209, 220, 225–30, 236–37, 240, 252; in *Ise monogatari*, 220, 230–35, 237, 240; in *Tosa nikki*, 209, 235–41, 252, 342
Naiki 内記 (Inner Palace Secretariat), 51, 55–56, 80–81, 166–67, 174. *See also shōnaiki*; *tainaiki*
naiki no nikki 内記日記 (inner palace diaries), 50, 51, 53, 55–56, 80–81, 166–67, 168
Naikyōbō 内教房 (Female Performers Office), 141, 155
naishi 内侍 (palace handmaids), 188n71
naishi no kami 尚侍 (principal palace handmaids), 350, 352
Naishi no Tsukasa 内侍司 (Palace Handmaids Office), 53
naizenshi no tenzen 内膳司典膳 (palace kitchen chefs), 80–81, 349
Nakamaro. *See* Abe no Nakamaro
Nakatsukasa-shō 中務省 (Central Affairs Ministry), 51
Nakazora no niki 中空の日記 (Empty Sky Diary, 1819), 35
namu (particle), 210, 247
Naniwa 難波, 185n65, 340
Naniwa no Kishi Obito no fumi 難波吉士男人書 (Record of the Naniwa Noble Scholar, ca. 659–661), 166
Nankaidō 南海道 (South Sea Circuit), 277
Nanshoku ōkagami 男色大鏡 (Great Mirror of Male Love, 1687), 32–33
Nara 奈良, 50n81, 265
Narashizu 奈良志津 (Level Port), 182, 198, 322
Narihira. *See* Ariwara no Narihira
Narihira shū 業平集 (Narihira Anthology), 219–20
narrator, in *Tosa nikki*: ambiguity of perspective, 3, 4, 7–8, 59–65, 305; choice of female voice, 19–20, 32, 34, 35–36, 38, 40, 41, 42, 161; comments on poems, 184–93, 317–18, 326; differentiation from author, 1, 5, 7; language

used, 43, 60, 64–65, 87, 100, 246–47; mimicry of men, 1, 7–8, 19–20, 43; self-reflexivity, 12, 19, 109, 235, 299, 303; social position of, 9, 42, 43, 59, 60–62, 64, 68–69, 285; unfamiliarity with *shi*, 285–86
nativists. See *kokugaku* scholars
Natsui. See Ki no Natsui
navigation, 10, 92. *See also* steersman
Nawa no Tomari 縄の泊り (Net Anchorage), 182, 318, 320
Nawa no Ura 縄乃浦 (Net Bay), 182
ne no hi 子日 (Day of the Rat), 46, 58, 188, 190, 305, 332–33, 351
Neo-Confucianism, 31
new year rituals, 54, 81–83, 188–89, 316
New Year's Day, 47–48, 64, 81, 125–26, 314–15
NHK Radio, 41
nichiyūshin 日遊神 (directional taboos), 57
Nihon kiryaku 日本紀略 (Abbreviated Chronicles of Japan, 11th c.), 51, 278–79
Nihon koku genzaisho mokuroku 日本国見在書目録 (Catalog of Writings Currently in Japan, 891), 287
Nihon ryōiki 日本霊異記 (or *Nihon koku genpō zen'aku ryōiki* 日本国現報善悪霊異記, Record of Miraculous Events in Japan, ca. 822), 12, 89, 108
Nihon sandai jitsuroku 日本三代実録 (or *Sandai jitsuroku* 三代実録, True Record of Three Reigns, 901), 51, 120, 126, 174, 220–25, 226, 228
Nihon shoki 日本書紀 (Chronicles of Japan, 720), 51, 88, 89, 166, 223–24
Niimanabi 邇飛麻那微 (An Introduction to Learning, ca. 1765), 33–34. *See also* Kamo no Mabuchi
Niita 新田 district, 210n11
nikki. See diaries
nikki-bu 日記部 (diary section in *Gunsho ruijū*), 163
Ninmyō 仁明, Emperor (810–850, r. 833–850), 52

Nishi-Honganji-bon 西本願寺本 manuscript, 48
Nishinoiri Atsuo 西野入篤男, 283
Nittō guhō junrai kōki 入唐求法巡礼行記 (Account of a Pilgrimage Overseas in Search of the Law, ca. 838–847), 95, 165–66
Northeast Asia, multipolarity, 14, 290, 291, 265, 274–76, 293–94, 298. *See also* Korean peninsula; trade
novellas, 14, 301, 306–8
novels, 65, 67, 123, 303–7. *See also* I-novels
nu (auxiliary verb), 246
Nurigome-bon 塗籠本 manuscript, 237n66
nusa 幣 (prayer slips), 92–93, 94, 95, 175, 330–31, 339
nushi 主 (master), 254

Ōaraki 大荒木, 120–21, 122
Ōe no Asatsuna 大江朝綱 (886–958), 167
Ōe no Chisato 大江千里 (fl. 890s), 280–81, 282. See also *Kudai waka*
Ōe no Mochitoki 大兄以言 (955–1010), 194
officials, 33, 51, 154, 169, 176, 268, 270–71, 277; scholar-officials, 35; Tang, 255, 260. *See also* government posts; governors; Ki no Tsurayuki, official career; ranks
Ogawa Kōzō 小川幸三, 84, 171
Ōhide. See Tanaka Ōhide
Ōi-gawa 大井川, 167
Ōi-gawa gyōkō waka no jo 大井川御幸和歌序 (Preface to Waka for the Royal Procession to the Ōi River, 907), 168, 193, 349
Oi no kobumi 笈の小文 (Knapsack Notebook, 1688), 162
Okada, Richard H., 225, 240n74
Ōkagami 大鏡 (The Great Mirror, ca. 1119), 188
okobito 烏滸人 (jesters), 126
Ōmi no Kimi 近江君 (character in *Genji monogatari*), 214

Ōminato 大湊 (Great Harbor), 181, 199, 314–18
Ōmi 近江 province, 352
omoshiroshi (enthralling), 190–91, 240
omote 面 (exterior), 35
Ōnakatomi no Yoshinobu 大中臣能宣 (921–991), 21
Ōnin 応仁 War (1467–1477), 30
Onmyō-ryō 陰陽寮 (Bureau of Divination), 50
onnade 女手 (women's hand), 28
"Onnagata mo su naru Tosa nikki" 女方もすなる土佐日記 ("A *Tosa Diary* Such as Female Impersonators Are Said to Do"), 32–33
Ono 小野, 231, 233
Ono no Komachi 小野小町 (fl. 9th c.), 230
Ono no Tamori 小野田守 (fl. ca. 750), 274–75
onru 遠流 (distant banishment), 174
Onshi. See Fujiwara no Onshi
oral narrative: relationship to texts, 217, 252; in *Tosa nikki*, 8, 207. See also *uta-gatari*
Orikuchi Shinobu 折口信夫 (1887–1953), 120n9
orthography, 14, 30, 97, 181, 186, 309
Ōtenmon 応天門 Disturbance (866), 174
otoko moji 男文字 (men's letters), 28
Otoko-yama 男山 (Mount Man), 122, 176
Ōtomo no Koshibi 大伴古慈悲 (695–777), 174
Ōtomo no Miyuki 大伴御行 (character in *Taketori monogatari*), 96–97
Ōtomo no Tabito 大伴旅人 (665–731), 100n57, 169
Ōtsu 大津 (Great Port), 182, 312
ou 追ふ (pursue), 174–75
Ōuta-dokoro 大歌所 (Bureau of Song), 141
Ozu 小津 (Little Port), 181
Ozu no Tomari 緒津の泊り (Thread Anchorage), 181n54, 337

Pacific Ocean, travel on, 178–79
paddies, 142–43, 223, 224
pailu 排律 (extended regulated verses), 258
palace, 45, 48, 50–53, 55, 152, 155, 166, 168, 173n35, 255–59, 264, 349–52. See also Rear Palace
palace kitchen, 7, 72, 80, 82
pansexuality, 121–22, 159–60, 222. See also gender; sexuality
parallelisms: in *shi*, 257, 259; in *Tosa nikki*, 79, 80, 130, 193–94, 195
Parhae 渤海 kingdom (C. Bohai, J. Bokkai, 698–926), 222, 265, 274–75, 278, 279–80
parody: of banquets, 75; of diaries, 20, 251–52; of diaristic conventions, 7–8, 57–65, 68, 112; in literary history, 66–68, 111, 123, 305; in *monogatari*, 96; of poetic conventions, 108, 123–24; in prologue, 8, 63, 66, 305; in *Tosa nikki*, 55, 56, 57, 58–59, 62, 69, 70, 305–6; of *Tosa nikki* by Saikaku, 32–33; of travelogues, 8, 164–65; of *uta-gatari*, 246, 250–52. See also satire
patrons: of *ganmon*, 157–58; as readership of diary, 6–7, 20, 44, 49, 56, 151, 183; royal, 44–45, 349–50; screen *waka* composed for, 192, 349–51; Tadahira and family as, 46–47, 49; Tsurayuki's dependence on, 44–45, 49, 159
Penglai 蓬莱 or Penghu 蓬壺 (Isle of Immortals), 258, 264
Persiani, Gian Piero, 271
Persian language, 255
personal diaries. See *watakushi no nikki*
picture scrolls. See *emaki*
Piggott, Joan, 278
Pillow Book, The. See *Makura no sōshi*
pine saplings (*komatsu* 小松), 107, 188, 191, 332, 347
pine trees, 107, 108, 190, 191–93, 319, 334, 337, 338
pirates: in Akinari's short story, 34–35; euphemism for, 187; fear of, 92–93, 181,

197, 200, 330–31, 334; raids, 277–78; rumors of, 92, 200, 276–77, 329. *See also* Taira no Masakado

pivot-words. See *kakekotoba*

place names: absence from diary entries, 181; allusions to Ki clan history, 172, 175–77; fictional, 177, 180–83, 184–85, 204, 250; in *monogatari*, 8, 249, 250; origin myths, 96, 211; in poetry, 150, 178, 292; in songs, 136–37, 139, 142, 150; as temporal markers, 181; in title of texts, 249–52. *See also* landscapes

poems, in *Tosa nikki*: anonymous, 169, 176–77, 179, 184–85, 188–90, 243, 294–95; in anthologies, 21–23, 99–100; attributed to Tsurayuki in anthologies, 21, 22; autobiographical readings of, 21–25, 40–41; by children, 21, 100, 170, 183, 187–89; on dead girl, 23–25, 98–104, 106–9, 132; distinctions from song, 127–31; emotions expressed in, 98–104, 107–9; at ending, 105; by ex-governor, 77, 78, 185; at farewell banquets, 77–78, 132–33; fictional authorship of, 5, 21–22, 23; by food donors, 83–85; guidelines for, 41, 78, 183–84, 285; landscape depictions in, 183–93; maritime *waka*, 279, 280, 283–85, 286–87, 288, 294–95; by Nakamaro, 272–75, 279–80, 288, 290, 294, 296, 298; by Narihira, 209, 235–41, 243–44, 252, 318, 342; and narrator, 124, 184–93, 317–18, 326; perspectives in, 62–63; scholarship on, 35, 68, 171, 192; sequencing of, 171; in *setsuwa*, 23–25; from *shi*, 132, 280, 281–88, 292–93; social distinctions and, 183–84; spoken vs. composed, 132–34; by women, 21, 282

poem tales. See *uta monogatari*

poem-tellings. See *uta-gatari*

poetry matches (*uta-awase* 歌合), 43, 45, 46, 47, 50, 132, 185, 349, 350, 352

Pollock, Sheldon, 295–96

ponds, 106, 186, 210–11, 212–13, 286, 316, 346

popular culture, 151, 161, 304

Porter, William N. (1849–1929), 38, 192n79, 195

postal route, diplomatic, 265, 274

prayer slips. See *nusa*

Presentation of White Steeds. See *aomuma no sechie*

print culture, 31, 65–66

prologue, *Tosa nikki*, 1, 2, 8, 12, 19–20, 58, 63–64, 66, 69, 71, 109, 112, 162, 202, 305

provincial head doctors. See *kusushi*

puns, 73–74, 85, 88, 89–90, 95, 97, 111, 112, 124, 127. *See also* wordplay

qijuzhu 起居注 (records from rising to repose), 51

Qing Qing 秦青, 139–40

Quan Tangshi 全唐詩 (Complete Tang Poems, ca. 1705), 258

quatrains, 221, 257, 263–65, 281, 283–84, 286–88. See also *jueju*

Rabelais, François (1483–1553), 123, 126

Rambelli, Fabio, 90

ramu (auxiliary verb), 147

ranks, 24, 42, 43, 46–48, 53, 56, 61, 63, 68, 77, 82, 154–55, 158, 161, 172–73, 220, 223, 228. *See also* Fifth Rank; government posts; officials

readers, 1, 6–7, 20–21, 29, 43, 44, 49, 66, 69, 98, 151, 182, 183–84, 204, 248

Rear Palace (Kōkyū 後宮), 349

reception history, *Tosa nikki*: in early modern period, 20, 31–38, 162–64, 165; and early scholarship, 30–31, 32; and modern scholarship, 2–3, 19, 37–43, 59, 65–66; questions surrounding authorship, 26–30, 65–66; radio dramatization, 41; as travelogue, 162–64

reciprocity, 82–83, 90–91, 106, 113, 315. *See also* gifts

regencies, 45–49, 52–53, 222–23, 228. *See also* Fujiwara no Tadahira

renga 連歌 (linked verse), 66
Rengeō-in 蓮華王院 library, 26, 27
Renshi 廉子, Princess (or Kiyoko, d. 935), 192, 350, 351
rentaikei 連体形 conjugation, 62
ribetsu 離別 (Partings), 273–74
rice, 143, 223, 224. See also food; saké
Rihō ōki 吏部王記 (ca. 920–953), 52n88
ritsuryō 律令, 22, 51
rituals: court, 51, 54, 82–83; formularies, 53; mourning, 100–101; steed nose-turning, 74. See also new year rituals
rōdō 郎等 (men-at-arms), 77, 78
rōdōka 労働歌 (work songs), 140–41
rōei 朗詠 (style of chant), 135. See also *kara uta*
rokkasen 六歌仙 (six poetic immortals), 230
Ruijū fusenshō 類聚符宣抄 (Government Proclamations by Topic, 1121), 51
Ruijū kokushi 類聚国史 (A History of the Realm by Topic, ca. 892), 155n79
Ryōjin hishō 梁塵秘抄 (Secret Notes to Singing Dust Off the Rafters, ca. 1180), 119. See also *imayō*
Ryō no shūge 令集解 (Collected Commentaries to the Legal Codes, ca. 868), 53

sachū 左注 (after-commentary), 211, 269
Sadakata. See Fujiwara no Sadakata
Sadatoki 貞辰, Prince (874–929), 351
Sadayasu 貞保, Prince (870–924), 152
Sagami 相模 (b. ca. 1000), 208
Sagami shū 相模集 (Sagami Anthology, 11th c.), 208
Saga no kayoi 嵯峨の通ひ (Trek to Saga, 1269), 29
saibara 催馬楽 (drover's music), 117–18, 119–21, 134, 136, 142, 152, 159
saiji no nikki 祭事日記 (records of Shinto rites), 50
Saikaku. See Ihara Saikaku
Sakaki, Atsuko, 42, 290
Sakaki 榊 chapter (*Genji monogatari*), 153, 213

sakan 主典 (clerks), 51
saké 酒 (rice wine), 64, 74, 75, 79, 80, 81, 82, 87, 199, 232, 310, 312–13, 314, 315, 323
Saki 佐喜, 178, 182
sakimori 防人 (border guards), 144
sama 様 (gist, style, outline), 282, 288, 290, 292, 296
Sanbō ekotoba 三宝絵詞 (Illustrations and Explanations for the Three Treasures, 984), 174
Sandai jitsuroku. See *Nihon sandai jitsuroku*
Sanesuke. See Fujiwara no Sanesuke
Sanetaka. See Sanjōnishi Sanetaka
Sanetaka kōki 実隆公記 (ca. 1474–1536), 30
Saneyori. See Fujiwara no Saneyori
sangi 参議 (consultant), 350
Sanjōnishi Sanetaka 三条西実隆 (1455–1537), 30–31, 125
Sanjū rokunin kasen den 三十六人歌仙伝 (Biographies of the Thirty-Six Poetic Immortals, ca. 1094), 6, 48, 154
Sanskrit language, 255, 295–96
Sanuki 讃岐 province, 72
Sarashina nikki 更級日記 (Sarashina Diary, ca. 1060), 29, 182n57, 213, 302–3
Sarra, Edith, 218
Sasaki Nobutsuna 佐々木信綱 (1872–1963), 37–38
satire: and *haikaika*, 110–11; social criticism, 113–14; in *Taketori monogatari*, 96; in *Tosa nikki*, 70, 104, 111, 112–14; in Western literature, 111–12. See also parody
Saya no Nakayama 小夜の中山 (Mount Midst Short Nights), 137–38
Schafer, Edward (1913–1991), 265
screen *waka* (*byōbu uta* 屏風歌), 45n68, 46, 75n11, 132, 192, 201–2, 349–52
seasons, 13, 103, 130, 179, 190, 191, 213, 231
sea squirts, 118, 119n4, 124, 322
sechie no nikki 節会日記 (records of annual palace banquets), 50
sechimi 節忌. See vegetarian fasts

sedōka 旋頭歌 (repeated head verse), 134
Sei Shōnagon 清少納言 (fl. ca. 1000), 87, 133, 142–43, 151, 153, 159, 186, 214–19, 241, 302, 303. See also *Makura no sōshi*
Seikeisho'oku-bon 青谿書屋本 manuscript, 14–15, 28, 309
Seikyūki 西宮記 (ca. 969), 54
Seishin kōki 清慎公記, 53
Seiwa 清和, Emperor (850–878, r. 858–876), 222–23, 226, 231
sekki 節気 (twenty-four solar terms), 57
Senshi 宣子, Princess (902–920), 350
Seri-kawa 芹川, 167
setsuwa 説話 (anecdotes), 23–25, 35, 89, 100, 208, 298–99
Settsu 摂津 province, 194
sexuality: erotic language, 118–21, 123–27, 147–48, 159–60; social subversion and, 123, 126–27. See also gender; pansexuality
Shandong 山東 peninsula, 270
shellfish: forgetting-shells, 101, 103, 336; as genitalia, 86, 118–19, 124, 322; oysters, 89.
shi 詩 (poems in literary Sinitic): about Nakamaro, 256, 259–65, 272, 279, 288; by Michizane, 72; by Nakamaro, 256–59, 266, 268, 279, 288, 297–98; pine trees in, 191; recited at farewell banquets, 77; Tsurayuki's familiarity with, 280, 283, 285, 287–88; *waka* generated from, 132, 280–88, 292–93. See also *jueju*; *kara uta*; *lushi*; *pailu*
Shigeakira 重明, Prince (906–954), 52n88
Shiji 史記 (Records of the Historian, ca. 91 BCE), 259
Shijing 詩経 (Classic of Poetry, ca. 600 BCE), 110, 129
shikashū 私歌集 (personal *waka* anthologies), 248
Shikoku 四国, 173, 277
Shimada no Kimiaki 島田公鑒, 276
Shimasaka 島坂, 91, 105, 106, 345
Shinchōsha 新潮社, 39
Shin'in gyohon 新院御本 manuscript, 268

Shin sarugaku ki 新猿楽記 (Record of New Monkey Music, ca. 1061–1065), 77
Shinsen man'yōshū 新撰万葉集 (Newly Selected *Man'yōshū*, 893), 229, 349
Shinsen ōjōfu 新撰横笛譜 (New Selections of Flute Scores, 920), 152
Shinsen shōjiroku 新撰姓氏録 (Newly Selected Record of Clan Names and Hereditary Titles, 815), 268
Shinsen waka 新撰和歌 (New Selections of Waka, ca. 945): Nagisa poem, 229–30, 237; preface, 44–45, 46, 48, 154, 180, 229, 292, 352; scholarship on, 40–41; structure, 171, 229–30
ship songs. See *funa uta*
Shirakawa 白河, Emperor (1053–1129, r. 1073–1087), 167
Shirakawa-dono 白河殿 (Shirakawa Mansion), 46, 351
Shōgakukan 小学館, 39
Shōhei 昌平 era (931–938), 276, 351
shōjo 唱女 (professional female singers), 155
shokubun 食分 (predicted eclipses), 57
Shoku Nihongi 続日本紀 (Continued Chronicles of Japan, 797), 265
Shoku Nihon kōki 続日本後紀 (Continued Later Chronicles of Japan, 869), 266, 268
Shōmei 章明, Prince (924–990), 351
shōnaiki 小内記 (junior inner palace secretaries), 168, 350. See also *Naiki*; *tainaiki*
Shōsōin 正倉院 storehouse, 254
Shōtai 昌泰 era (898–901), 349
shōten 声点 (voice markers), 30
Shōtoku-bon 承徳本 manuscript, 137
shōwa 唱和 (choral compositions), 127
Shōyūki 小右記 (Record of the Minister of the Right, ca. 978–1032), 54
shrines (Shinto), 33, 94, 142, 167, 176, 249, 268, 278, 292, 343
Shūchūshō 袖中抄 (Sleeve Notes, ca. 1185–1190), 208

shuin 手印 (palm prints), 157

Shūi wakashū 拾遺和歌集 (Anthology of Later Gleanings, 1007), 188, 215n27, 278n48

Shun 舜, Emperor (ca. 2294–2184 BCE, r. 2255–2205 BCE), 261, 292

Shunzei. *See* Fujiwara no Shunzei

Shunzei-bon 俊成本 manuscript, 237n66

Shūshi 修子, Princess (d. 933), 351

shūshikei 終止形 conjugation, 62

shuyi 書儀 (writing models), 184

Silla 新羅 kingdom (57 BCE–935 CE), 144, 169, 265, 274, 275

Sinitic culture, 31, 42, 110, 135, 224n42, 260, 262, 263, 281, 290, 291. *See also* Literary Sinitic

Sinographs (*kanji* 漢字), 27, 28, 37, 64, 77, 94, 128, 183, 189, 221, 237, 250, 269, 290–91, 292–93, 295, 296, 297, 305, 309

snipe (*shigi* 鴫), 223, 224

social positions: blurred distinctions between, 126, 127, 160; of early *Tosa nikki* readers, 6–7, 43, 49; of governors, 77; inversions of, 9, 68; of narrator, 9, 42, 43, 59, 60–62, 64, 68–69, 285; in poems, 183–84; sexuality and, 123, 126–27; on ship, 9–10. *See also* ranks

sociolects, 67, 112, 306

Somedono 染殿, 227

Song 宋 dynasty (960–1279), 165, 258

"Song of Everlasting Sorrow" 長恨歌 (C. *Changhenge*, J. *Chōgonka*, 806), 32

songs: authenticity of, 153–54; boundaries with poetry, 118, 127–31, 134–35, 136, 140, 141, 144, 155–56, 160, 218; composing and singing, 128, 129, 140, 160; erotic language in, 118–21, 147–48, 159–60; in Heian culture, 117, 135, 140, 141, 146, 151–53, 159–60; mobility of, 159–60; and narrative context, 139–40, 150–51; performances, 117, 134–35, 136, 137, 138, 141, 144–45, 161; as popular genre, 8, 9, 141, 145, 149, 152, 161, 178; refrains, 140–41, 144, 145, 146, 151–52; transcriptions, 118, 140, 146, 153–54, 156, 158–59; Tsurayuki's interest in, 155–57, 161. *See also funa uta; furu uta; gishōka; imayō; kagura uta; kai uta; rōdōka; saibara; ta-ue uta; waza-uta*

Sonpi bunmyaku 尊卑分脈 (Lineages of Nobility and Commoners, late 14th c.), 6, 188n71

Sōō-ji 相応寺 temple, 177, 344

South Korea, 280

steersman character (*kajitori* 楫取), 9, 43, 79–80, 87, 90, 92–94, 96, 129–32, 146–52, 170, 200, 277, 313, 320, 323, 325, 328–31, 336, 337

Steininger, Brian, 73, 135n44

Stinchecum, Amanda Mayer, 304

subjects, grammatical, 62, 78, 143, 171, 187, 248, 287

sue-kata 末方 (right-hand chorus), 137

Sugawara no Michizane 菅原道真 (845–903), 9, 71–72, 98, 133, 167, 168

Sugawara no Takasue no Musume 菅原孝標女 (ca. 1008–1059), 302, 303

Sugimoto Naojirō 杉本直次郎 (1890–1973), 255

suhama 州浜 display, 351

suke 介 (deputy governors), 172–73, 350

Suma 須磨, 202–3

Sumida-gawa 隅田川, 170–71

Suminoe 住之江 (Clear Cove), 102, 103, 189–90, 338, 339

Sumiyoshi 住吉: deity, 93–95, 103, 278, 339; poems on, 189–90, 338; shores of, 175–76, 189–90, 338–39; shrine, 33, 167

Sumiyoshi taisha jindaiki 住吉大社神代記 (Account of the Divine Origins of the Grand Shrine of Sumiyoshi, ca. 8th-10th c.), 94–95

Sunrise Tree. *See* Fusang

Suō 周防 province, 47, 352

surimono 摺物 (deluxe woodblock prints), 37

Suzaku 朱雀 (character in *Genji monogatari*), 213, 222

Suzaku 朱雀, Emperor (923–952, r. 930–946), 45–47, 48, 53, 276

Suzaku'in 朱雀院 (Suzaku Villa), 46–47, 48, 352
Suzaku Avenue (Suzaku Ōji 朱雀大路), 47, 136
sweetfish (*ayu* 鮎), 81, 82, 125–26, 127, 304, 314

Tachibana no Hayanari 橘逸勢 (d. 842), 157, 271
Tachibana no Moribe 橘守部 (1781–1849), 36, 118, 188
tadagoto (plain-worded), 185
Tadahira. See Fujiwara no Tadahira
Taikō gyoki 大后御記 (Diary of the Queen Mother, ca. 929–935), 53–55, 65
tainaiki 大内記 (senior inner palace secretaries), 168, 350. See also Naiki; *shōnaiki*
Taira no Masakado 平将門 (d. 940), 98
Taira no Sadabumi 平貞文 (or 平定文, d. 923), 349. See also Heichū
taishu 大守 (grand governors), 277
Takechi no Sukune 武内宿禰 (b. 84), 176
Takeoka Masao 竹岡正夫 (1919–1985), 233, 240
Taketori monogatari 竹取物語 (Tale of the Bamboo Cutter, ca. late 9th c.), 12, 28, 63, 96–97, 110, 178, 247
Tale of Genji, The. See *Genji monogatari*
Tamai Kōsuke 玉井幸助 (1882–1969), 39, 50
Tamakazura 玉鬘 (character in *Genji monogatari*), 119, 145
Tameie. See Fujiwara no Tameie
Tameuji-bon 為氏本 manuscript, 239
Tan 鄭, 259, 260
Tanabata 七夕, 124, 231, 244n83
Tanaka Ōhide 田中大秀 (1777–1847), 37, 79, 118
Tana River (Tana-gawa 多奈川), 181, 334
Tang 唐 dynasty (618–907): capital, 255, 256, 261, 263, 269; cosmopolitanism of, 261–62, 265, 270; etiquette manuals and writing models, 184; Nakamaro's stay, 254–55, 269, 274, 283, 290, 297; officials, 255, 260; perspective on Japan, 260–65, 272; poetry, 135, 256–61, 280, 281–88; poets, 255, 259–65, 280, 282–85, 286–87, 290, 297, 298; political decline, 265, 270, 275; travelogues, 165, 166
Taohua-tan 桃花潭 (Peach Blossom Lake), 286
ta-ue uta 田植歌 (paddy planting songs), 143, 151
teihon 底本 (base texts), 32
Teiji'in 亭子院, 349, 352
Teiji'in no Miyataki gokō ki 亭子院宮滝御幸記 (Account of His Majesty Uda's Excursion to Miyataki, 898), 167, 168
Teiji'in uta-awase 亭子院歌合 (Teiji'in Poetry Match, 913), 43, 185n65, 350
Teika. See Fujiwara no Teika
Teimon 貞門 school of *haikai* poetry, 32
Teishin kōki 貞信公記 (ca. 907–948), 47n72, 52–53, 197–98
Tengyō 天慶 era (938–947), 47n72, 53n91, 53n93, 278n49, 351–52
Tenji-bon 天治本 manuscript, 140
tenjō nikki 殿上日記 (hall courtier diaries), 50, 51, 80–81
Tenshi 恬子, Princess (or Yasuko, d. 913), 231
time: grammatical tense, 59, 248, 293; in *Tosa nikki*, 58–59, 201–2, 235, 246–47, 248; in travel narratives, 201. See also seasons
Tō no Chūjō 頭中将 (character in *Genji monogatari*), 214
Tōdaiji yōroku 東大寺要録 (Essential Records of Tōdaiji, 1106), 258n5
Tōdaiwajō tōseiden 東大和尚東征伝 (Record of the Great Tang Priest's Eastward Expedition, 779), 272
tōka 踏歌 (foot stamping songs), 54, 286
Tōkai Ryōzō 東海亮造, 126
Tokifumi. See Ki no Tokifumi
Tokihira. See Fujiwara no Tokihira
Tokonatsu 常夏 chapter (*Genji monogatari*), 119, 214, 215, 217
Tokoyo 常世 (Everworld), 179
Ton'a 頓阿 (1289–1372), 30
tongyao. See *waza-uta*

toponyms. *See* place names
Torikai no Mimaki 鳥飼の御牧 (Royal Birdkeepers' Pasturage), 87–88, 89, 341
torikake 取り掛け (bestowal), 87
Tosa Diary, The. See Tosa nikki
Tosa *jōruri* 土佐浄瑠璃 troupe, 33
Tosa nikki 土佐日記 (The Tosa Diary, ca. 935–945): authorship, 3, 4, 5, 19–20, 40, 65–66, 301–2; contents, 1–3; copies, 25–29, 30–31, 38; emotions expressed, 1, 40, 198–201; ending (final entry), 36, 105–7; entries for uneventful days, 33, 197–201, 204; epilogue, 109–10, 202; fictional characteristics, 10–11, 247; historical context, 1–2, 3–4, 6; historical significance, 2, 3, 20; holograph, 21, 25, 26–27, 30, 49; hybridity, 13, 209, 246, 249–50; illustrated version, 20–21, 202–4, 247; influence, 31–32, 163, 301–8; *jōruri* play, 33; links to *Ise monogatari*, 170, 242–46, 253; maritime setting, 8–11, 73, 179–80; motive for writing, 24, 34, 35, 40, 44, 46; as novella, 301, 306–8; poetic prose, 168, 171–72, 193–96; prologue, 1, 8, 19, 63, 66, 202, 305; prose characteristics, 1, 2, 10, 30, 37, 67, 162, 164, 201–4, 295; references to characters, 63–65; survival of text, 25–28; temporal structure, 58–59, 201–2, 235, 246–47, 248; title, 182, 246, 249–50, 251–53; translations, 37–38, 40–41, 195, 309–47; writing of, 1, 5, 27, 49, 126, 291. *See also* narrator; poems; reception history
Tosa nikki chiri ben 土佐日記地理弁 (Geographical Observations on *The Tosa Diary*, 1857), 36–37, 181, 182n55
Tosa nikki fuchū 土佐日記附註 (An Appended Commentary to *The Tosa Diary*, 1661), 31
Tosa nikki fune no tadaji 土佐日記舟の直路 (A Direct Route to *The Tosa Diary*, 1842), 36, 181

Tosa nikki kai 土佐日記解 (A Commentary on *The Tosa Diary*, by Akinari in 1801), 34
Tosa nikki kai 土佐日記解 (A Commentary on *The Tosa Diary*, by Ōhide in 1832), 37
Tosa nikki kenmonshō 土佐日記見聞抄 (Notes on Impressions of *The Tosa Diary*, 1655), 32
Tosa nikki kōshō 土佐日記考證 (A Philological Analysis of *The Tosa Diary*, 1818), 36
Tosa nikki shō 土佐日記抄 (Notes on *The Tosa Diary*, 1661), 32
Tosa nikki sōken 土佐日記創見 (Personal Observations on *The Tosa Diary*, 1823), 35
Tosa nikki tomoshibi 土佐日記燈 (A Lantern Illuminating *The Tosa Diary*, 1817), 35–36
Tosa nikki zenchūshaku 土佐日記全注釈 (1965), 41, 309
Tosa no otodo 土佐のおとど (The Lord of Tosa), 174
Tosa no Tomari 土佐の泊り (Tosa Anchorage), 182, 250–51, 333
Tosa 土佐 province, 1, 22, 23–24, 35–36, 72, 172, 173–75, 179, 182, 197, 276–78
Toshikage 俊蔭 (character in *Utsuho monogatari*), 247
tōso 屠蘇 tonic, 81–82
trade: deity protecting, 94–95; in eighth century, 254, 261, 269–70, 275; with Korean peninsula, 275, 276; in ninth century, 270; poetry and, 270–71, 284, 297; in tenth century, 276
transactions, 70, 85–90, 93–96, 151. *See also* reciprocity
translation, 8, 14, 37, 38, 40, 66, 125, 163, 183n58, 195, 256, 263, 289–98. *See also* interpreters
travel: to and from capital, 22, 181–82, 268–69; homesickness, 145, 160; inauspicious dates, 74; maritime, 8–11, 139,

152, 160, 178, 179–80; as narrative, 10; translation and, 293–94
travelogues, 8, 162–69, 182–83, 201
travel poetry, 150, 163, 169–71, 184–85, 268–69, 273–74
tsu (auxiliary verb), 246
tsuibushi 追捕使 (envoys for pursuit and capture), 276, 277
Tsurayuki. *See* Ki no Tsurayuki
Tsurayuki ie no uta-awase 貫之家歌合 (Tsurayuki Household Poetry Match, 939), 47, 352
Tsurayuki shū 貫之集 (Tsurayuki Anthology, ca. mid- or late-10th c.), 4–5, 21, 27, 39, 48, 172, 173, 239
Tu 塗, Mount, 261

uchigiki 打聞き (notations), 216, 218, 236
Uda 宇多, Emperor (866–931, r. 887–897), 44–45, 52–53, 54, 62, 133, 167–68, 292, 295, 349, 350, 351
Uda Pine-Tree Plains (Uda no matsubara 宇多の松原), 191–93, 295, 319
Ueda Akinari 上田秋成 (1734–1809), 34–35, 40, 110, 169
Uji Kaga no Jō 宇治加賀掾 (1635–1711), 33
Uji shūi monogatari 宇治拾遺物語 (Tales Gleaned from Uji, ca. 1212–1221), 23
Ukifune 浮舟 (character in *Genji monogatari*), 213
ukyō no suke 右京の亮 (assistant magistrates for the western half of the city), 173, 351
uma no kami 馬の頭 (chief equerries), 232, 233
umi-matsu 海松 (also *miru* or *mirubusa*, sea pines), 189, 333
Unai Otome 菟原処女 (Maiden of Unai), 213
unipolarity, Tang empire and, 275, 298
ura 裏 (interior), 35–36
Urado 浦戸 (Bay Entry), 182, 312, 314
Urashimako 浦嶋子, 179

uta 歌, 127, 295. *See also* songs; *waka*
uta-awase no nikki 歌合日記 (records of poetry matches), 50
uta-gatari 歌語り (poem-tellings): audience involvement in, 238–40, 252; history of term, 207–9; and Murasaki Shikibu, 209–11, 213; and Nagisa poem, 209, 220, 222, 230–35, 241–42; and Narihira, 219, 225, 233; parodies of, 246, 250–52; performative features, 214, 233, 252; and Sei Shōnagon, 214–20, 236, 241; in *Tosa nikki*, 207, 209, 235–41, 246, 252–53
uta monogatari 歌物語 (poem tales), 207–9, 216, 218, 224, 249, 251
uta no hijiri 歌の聖 (poetic sages), 25
utau 歌ふ (to sing), 128, 129, 135. *See also* *iu*; *kayō*; songs; *yomu*
Utsuho monogatari 宇津保物語 (or *Utsubo monogatari*, Tale of the Hollow Tree, 10th c.), 73, 81, 136, 178, 247

vegetarian fasts, 86–87, 88, 341
Venuti, Lawrence, 293
Vera Historia (A True Story, 2nd c.), 111–12
vernacular linguistic identity, 14, 256, 263, 295–98. *See also* cosmopolis; cosmopolitanism
vernacular poetry, 135, 207, 280, 282, 283, 285. *See also* *waka*
vernacular prose, 2–5, 11–13, 15, 20, 25, 27, 33, 37–39, 41, 42, 54–55, 64–65, 67, 70, 73, 80, 130, 162, 165, 177, 191, 193, 197, 201, 209, 246–49, 301, 303, 306. *See also* *kana* prose
villas. *See* *in*; Nagisa no In
Viswanathan, Meera, 41
vocal music. *See* songs

wabun 和文 (Japanese prose), 33. *See also* *kana* prose; vernacular prose
Wada no Tomari 和田の泊り (Wada Anchorage), 342
Wa-ie 我家 ("My Household"), 119

waka 和歌 (vernacular Japanese poetry): anonymous, 121–22, 156, 189–90, 228–29, 239–40, 287, 294–95; and authorship, 23; as elite practice, 132–34; emotions expressed in, 35, 42–43, 104; fluid boundaries with songs, 118, 136–37, 140, 144, 155–56, 160, 218; food references, 80; generated from *shi*, 132, 280–88, 292–93; modern categories of, 127; parodies, 55; partial identification, 214, 217; prosody, 131, 133–34; reciting and writing, 128, 129–31, 132, 133, 160; and ritual or social propriety, 77–78, 183–84, 186–90; screen poetry, 45n68, 46, 132, 192, 201–2, 349–52; structures used in prose, 192, 193; *Tosa nikki* as primer, 41, 78, 183–84, 285; and *uta monogatari*, 207–9, 218, 224, 252. See also Abe no Nakamaro; Ariwara no Narihira; poems, in *Tosa nikki*; *uta-gatari*; vernacular poetry

waka, by Tsurayuki: in anthologies, 48, 49, 349; autobiographical readings of, 21–25, 40–41; in *Ise monogatari*, 241; last, 48; pleas for promotion, 46–48, 350, 351; reference to mother, 155–56; screen poems, 45n68, 46, 192, 201–2, 349–52. See also *Tsurayuki shū*

waka anthologies: headnotes in, 4, 20–21, 22, 48, 156–57, 209–10, 225–29, 248; as literary patrimonies, 45; and Narihira, 219–20, 226; and poems from *Tosa nikki*, 21–23, 99–100; song lyrics in, 121, 138–39. See also *Gosen wakashū*; *ie no shū*; *Kokin wakashū*; *shikashū*; *Tsurayuki shū*

wakame 若芽 seaweed, 80

wakana 若菜 (young herbs), 80, 83, 186, 316, 333

Wakana-jō 若菜上 chapter (*Genji monogatari*), 119

Wakatai jisshu 和歌体十種 (Ten Styles of Waka, ca. 1000), 23, 99–100

Waley, Arthur (1889–1966), 288, 293

Wang Lun 汪倫, 286

Wang Wei 王維 (699–759), 255, 258, 261–66, 271, 272, 279, 287–88, 297

Wang Zhenping, 274–75

warigo 破子 (cypress-wood boxes), 83

wasure-gai 忘れ貝 (forgetting-shells), 101, 102, 103, 336

wasure-gusa 忘れ草 (forgetting-herbs), 103, 190, 338, 339

watakushi no nikki 私日記 (or *shiki* 私記, personal diaries), 12, 50, 51–53, 56, 62, 63, 65

Watanabe Hideo 渡辺秀夫, 55, 111n80

Watanabe, Takeshi, 80, 240n74

waza-uta 童謡 (C. *tongyao*, song of foretelling), 110, 223–25, 228

weather: descriptions in *Tosa nikki*, 198, 200–201; forecasts, 131–32; storms, 93–94, 96, 98, 103, 131–32, 139–40

Weavermaid (Orihime 織姫) star, 125. See also Tanabata

Weizhi 魏志 (Chronicles of Wei, 297), 261n12

Wenxuan 文選 (J. *Monzen*, Selections of Refined Literature, 6th c.), 180

Wenyuan yinghua 文苑英華 (Literary Garden of Splendid Blossoms, 1204), 257–58

Western literature: novellas, 306–7; parody in, 67–68, 123, 305; satire in, 111–12

widow character, 82–83, 85, 186, 187, 316

women: authorship and ownership, 158–59; bathing and genitalia, 86, 118–20, 123–24, 322; at Heian court, 301–3; as intended readership of diary, 49; literacy, 128, 161; menstrual taboos, 59; poetry by, 183–84; professional performers, 120, 141, 155–57; stories about drowning, 212, 213; style of calligraphy (*onnade*), 28; voices adopted by male poets, 32; writers, 301–3, 304. See also bereaved mother character; gender; Ise Shrine priestesses; narrator; widow character

women's diaries, 3, 4, 19, 29, 38–40, 42–43, 53–55, 65, 109, 302–3. See also *joryū nikki bungaku*

Woolf, Virginia (1882–1941), 304
wordplay, 37, 70, 85, 88, 95, 104, 112, 120, 128, 224, 263, 277n45, 287. *See also* puns
Wu 呉 kingdom, 259
Wuyue 呉越 kingdom (907–978), 275, 276

Xia 夏 dynasty (ca. 2070–1600 BCE), 262
Xian 西安 (present-day Chang'an), 254–55
Xiang 湘 River, 44, 45n66, 292
Xuanzong 玄宗, Emperor (658–762, r. 712–56), 255, 257, 258n5, 259, 261, 265

yado 宿 (grounds), 106
Yadorigi 宿木 chapter (*Genji monogatari*), 213
Yamada Yoshio 山田孝雄 (1873–1958), 180–81
Yamanoue no Okura 山上憶良 (ca. 660–733), 102, 267
Yamashiro 山代 province, 194, 201
Yamato monogatari 大和物語 (Tales of Yamato, 10th c.), 63, 203, 207–9, 212, 249, 250
yamato uta 倭歌 (Yamato verses), 221, 232, 242, 285, 311
Yamazaki 山崎, 90, 91, 194–95, 106, 200, 201, 232, 278, 343–45
Yanagita Kunio 柳田国男 (1875–1962), 141, 143
Yao 堯, Emperor (2324–2206 BCE, r. 2333–2234 BCE), 261, 292
Yasuakira 保明, Prince (903–923), 350
Yawata 八幡 shrine, 176–77, 343
Yoda, Tomiko, 42, 289, 290
Yodo-gawa 淀川, 90, 103–4, 171, 176, 182, 226, 278, 340

yomisue 詠み据ゑ (properly-arranged compositions), 133
yomu 詠む (to compose or recite poetry), 128, 129, 131–33
Yōrō ritsuryō 養老律令 (Legal Codes of the Yōrō Era, or Yōrō Code, 718), 51
Yoshifusa. *See* Fujiwara no Yoshifusa
Yotsugi monogatari 世継物語 (Tales of Successive Reigns, 14th c.), 299
Yōzei 陽成, Emperor (869–949, r. 876–884), 167, 352
Yu Gong 虞公, 139–40
Yuan Zhen 元稹 (779–831), 282
Yue 越 kingdom, 259, 260
yuefu 楽府 (ballads), 110, 142
Yuefu 楽府 (Bureau of Music), 141–42
Yuzuru. *See* Kishimoto Yuzuru

zaigo 在五 (the fifth Ariwara son), 221
Zaigo chūjō no nikki 在五中将の日記 (Diary of the Fifth Ariwara Middle Captain), 21n5, 249
Zaigo ga monogatari 在五が物語 (Tales of the Fifth Ariwara), 249
Zaitō nikki 在唐日記 (Diary of A Sojourn Overseas, ca. 717–18), 166
Zhao Hua 趙驊 (d. 783), 259–60, 263, 264
Zhongshusheng 中書省 (Bureau of Central Writings), 260
Zhou 周 dynasty (ca. 1046–256 BCE), 259, 260
Zōki 増基 (ca. 925–56), 163
zōtō 贈答 (poetic correspondence), 127
Zuo zhuan 左伝 (The Zuo Tradition, ca. late 4th c. BCE), 259
zuryō 受領 (custodians), 71
Zuzhou 祖州 island, 271

Harvard East Asian Monographs
(most recent titles)

421. James McMullen, *The Worship of Confucius in Japan*
422. Nobuko Toyosawa, *Imaginative Mapping: Landscape and Japanese Identity in the Tokugawa and Meiji Eras*
423. Pierre Fuller, *Famine Relief in Warlord China*
424. Diane Wei Lewis, *Powers of the Real: Cinema, Gender, and Emotion in Interwar Japan*
425. Maram Epstein, *Orthodox Passions: Narrating Filial Love during the High Qing*
426. Margaret Wan, *Regional Literature and the Transmission of Culture: Chinese Drum Ballads, 1800–1937*
427. Takeshi Watanabe, *Flowering Tales: Women Exorcising History in Heian Japan*
428. Jürgen P. Melzer, *Wings for the Rising Sun: A Transnational History of Japanese Aviation*
429. Edith Sarra, *Unreal Houses: Character, Gender, and Genealogy in the* Tale of Genji
430. Yi Gu, *Chinese Ways of Seeing and Open-Air Painting*
431. Robert Cliver, *Red Silk: Class, Gender, and Revolution in China's Yangzi Delta Silk Industry*
432. Kenneth J. Ruoff, *Japan's Imperial House in the Postwar Era, 1945–2019*
433. Erin L. Brightwell, *Reflecting the Past: Place, Language, and Principle in Japan's Medieval Mirror Genre*
434. Janet Borland, *Earthquake Children: Building Resilience from the Ruins of Tokyo*
435. Susan Blakely Klein, *Dancing the Dharma: Religious and Political Allegory in Japanese Noh Theater*
436. Yukyung Yeo, *Varieties of State Regulation: How China Regulates Its Socialist Market Economy*
437. Robert Goree, *Printing Landmarks: Popular Geography and* Meisho Zue *in Late Tokugawa Japan*
438. Lawrence C. Reardon, *A Third Way: The Origins of China's Current Economic Development Strategy*
439. Eyck Freymann, *One Belt One Road: Chinese Power Meets the World*
440. Yung Chul Park, Joon Kyung Kim, and Hail Park, *Financial Liberalization and Economic Development in Korea, 1980–2020*
441. Steven B. Miles, *Opportunity in Crisis: Cantonese Migrants and the State in Late Qing China*
442. Grace C. Huang, *Chiang Kai-shek's Politics of Shame: Leadership, Legacy, and National Identity in China*

443. Adam J. Lyons, *Karma and Punishment: Prison Chaplaincy in Japan*
444. Craig A. Smith, *Chinese Asianism, 1894–1945*
445. Sachiko Kawai, *Uncertain Powers: Sen'yōmon-in and Landownership by Royal Women in Early Medieval Japan*
446. Juliane Noth, *Transmedial Landscapes and Modern Chinese Painting*
447. Susan Westhafer Furukawa, *The Afterlife of Toyotomi Hideyoshi: Historical Fiction and Popular Culture in Japan*
448. Nongji Zhang, *Legal Scholars and Scholarship in the People's Republic of China: The First Generation (1949–1992)*
449. Han Sang Kim, *Cine-Mobility: Twentieth-Century Transformations in Korea's Film and Transportation*
450. Brian Hurley, *Confluence and Conflict: Reading Transwar Japanese Literature and Thought*
451. Simon Avenell, *Asia and Postwar Japan: Deimperialization, Civic Activism, and National Identity*
452. Maura Dykstra, *Uncertainty in the Empire of Routine: The Administrative Revolution of the Eighteenth-Century Qing State*
453. Marnie S. Anderson, *In Close Association: Local Activist Networks in the Making of Japanese Modernity, 1868–1920*
454. John D. Wong, *Hong Kong Takes Flight: Commercial Aviation and the Making of a Global Hub, 1930s–1998*
455. Martin K. Whyte and Mary C. Brinton, compilers, *Remembering Ezra Vogel*
456. Lawrence Zhang, *Power for a Price: The Purchase of Appointments in Qing China*
457. J. Megan Greene, *Building a Nation at War: Transnational Knowledge Networks and the Development of China during and after World War II*
458. Miya Qiong Xie, *Territorializing Manchuria: The Transnational Frontier and Literatures of East Asia*
459. Dal Yong Jin, *Understanding Korean Webtoon Culture: Transmedia Storytelling, Digital Platforms, and Genres*
460. Takahiro Yamamoto, *Demarcating Japan: Imperialism, Islanders, and Mobility, 1855–1884*
461. Elad Alyagon, *Inked: Tattooed Soldiers and the Song Empire's Penal-Military Complex*
462. Börje Ljunggren and Dwight H. Perkins, eds., *Vietnam: Navigating a Rapidly Changing Economy, Society, and Political Order*
463. En Li, *Betting on the Civil Service Examinations: The Lottery in Late Qing China*
464. Matthieu Felt, *Meanings of Antiquity: Myth Interpretation in Premodern Japan*
465. William D. Fleming, *Strange Tales from Edo: Rewriting Chinese Fiction in Early Modern China*
466. Mark Baker, *Pivot of China: Spatial Politics and Inequality in Modern Zhengzhou*
467. Peter Banseok Kwon, *Cornerstone of the Nation: The Defense Industry and the Building of Modern Korea under Park Chung Hee*
468. Weipin Tsai, *The Making of China's Post Office: Sovereignty, Modernization, and the Connection of a Nation*
469. Michael A. Fuller, *An Introduction to Literary Chinese (Second Edition)*
470. Gustav Heldt, *Navigating Narratives: Tsurayuki's* Tosa Diary *as History and Fiction*